"Vienna Is Different"

AUSTRIAN AND HABSBURG STUDIES
General Editor: Gary B. Cohen, Center for Austrian Studies,
University of Minnesota

Volume 1
Austrian Women in the Nineteenth and Twentieth Centuries: Cross-Disciplinary Perspectives
Edited by David F. Good, Margarete Grandner and Mary Jo Maynes

Volume 2
From World War to Waldheim: Culture and Politics in Austria and the United States
Edited by David F. Good and Ruth Wodak

Volume 3
Rethinking Vienna 1900
Edited by Steven Beller

Volume 4
The Great Tradition and Its Legacy: The Evolution of Dramatic and Musical Theater in Austria and Central Europe
Edited by Michael Cherlin, Halina Filipowicz and Richard L. Rudolph

Volume 5
Creating the Other: Ethnic Conflict and Nationalism in Habsburg Central Europe
Edited by Nancy M. Wingfield

Volume 6
Constructing Nationalities in East Central Europe
Edited by Pieter M. Judson and Marsha L. Rozenblit

Volume 7
The Environment and Sustainable Development in the New Central Europe
Edited by Zbigniew Bochniarz and Gary B. Cohen

Volume 8
Crime, Jews and News: Vienna 1890–1914
Edited by Daniel Mark Vyleta

Volume 9
The Limits of Loyalty: Imperial Symbolism, Popular Allegiances, and State Patriotism in the Late Habsburg Monarchy
Edited by Laurence Cole and Daniel L. Unowsky

Volume 10
Embodiments of Power: Building Baroque Cities in Europe
Edited by Gary B. Cohen and Franz A. J. Szabo

Volume 11
Diversity and Dissent: Negotiating Religious Difference in Central Europe, 1500–1800
Edited by Howard Louthan, Gary B. Cohen and Franz A. J. Szabo

Volume 12
"Vienna is Different": Jewish Writers in Austria from the Fin de Siècle to the Present
Hillary Hope Herzog

Volume 13
Sexual Knowledge: Feeling, Fact, and Social Reform in Vienna, 1900–1934
Britta McEwen

Volume 14
Journeys into Madness: Mapping Mental Illness in the Austro-Hungarian Empire
Edited by Gemma Blackshaw and Sabine Wieber

Volume 15
Territorial Revisionism and the Allies of Germany in the Second World War: Goals, Expectations, Practices
Edited by Marina Cattaruzza, Stefan Dryoff and Dieter Langewiesche

Volume 16
The Viennese Café and Fin-de-siècle Culture
Edited by Charlotte Ashby, Tag Gronberg and Simon Shaw-Miller

Volume 17
Understanding Multiculturalism: Central Europe and the Habsburg Experience
Edited by Johannes Feichtinger and Gary B. Cohen

"VIENNA IS DIFFERENT"

Jewish Writers in Austria from the Fin de Siècle to the Present

Hillary Hope Herzog

berghahn
NEW YORK · OXFORD
www.berghahnbooks.com

First published in 2011 by
Berghahn Books

www.berghahnbooks.com

©2011, 2013 Hillary Hope Herzog
First paperback edition published in 2013

All rights reserved. Except for the quotation of short passages for the purposes of criticism and review, no part of this book may be reproduced in any form or by any means, electronic or mechanical, including photocopying, recording, or any information storage and retrieval system now known or to be invented, without written permission of the publisher.

Library of Congress Cataloging-in-Publication Data

Herzog, Hillary Hope.
Vienna is different : Jewish writers in Austria from the fin de siècle to the present / Hillary Hope Herzog.
   p. cm. - (Austrian and Habsburg studies ; v. 12)
   Includes bibliographical references and index.
   ISBN 978-0-85745-181-1 (hardback) -- ISBN 978-0-85745-182-8 (institutional ebook)
ISBN 978-1-78238-049-8 (paperback) -- ISBN 978-1-78238-050-4 (retail ebook)
   1. Austrian literature-Jewish authors—History and criticism. 2. Austrian literature—20th century—History and criticism. 3. Jews in literature. 4. Judaism and literature—Austria—History. 5. Jews—Austria—Intellectual life. I. Title.
   PT3822.H48 2011
   830.9'89240436—dc22

2010051789

British Library Cataloguing in Publication Data

A catalogue record for this book is available from the British Library

Printed in the United States on acid-free paper

ISBN: 978-1-78238-049-8 paperback   ISBN: 978-1-78238-050-4 retail ebook

Contents

Acknowledgments	vii
Introduction	1
The Historical Continuity of the Viennese Jewish Experience 6	
Chapter 1. The *Fin de Siècle*	10
The Jewish Immigrant Experience in Vienna 10	
The Jewish Confrontation with a New Political Climate 15	
Jewish Cultural Responses 22	
Arthur Schnitzler 25	
Adolf Dessauer 38	
Felix Salten 42	
Stefan Zweig 50	
Hugo von Hofmannsthal 54	
Karl Kraus 57	
Theodor Herzl 63	
Richard Beer-Hofmann 77	
Conclusion 82	
Chapter 2. Jewish Vienna Between the World Wars	93
Jewish Identity and World War I 93	
A New Jewish Identity Crisis 99	
Rising Anti-Semitism 102	
The Beginning of the End 103	
Jews and the *Anschluss* 105	

    Jewish Cultural Responses During the Interwar Years   106
    Arthur Schnitzler   109
    Felix Salten   114
    Stefan Zweig   121
    Joseph Roth   128
    Karl Kraus   139
    Hugo Bettauer   142
    Elias Canetti   147
    Veza Canetti   156
    Conclusion   164

Chapter 3. Jews and the Second Republic   174
    The Immediate Postwar Situation   175
    The Second Republic   177
    Austrian Jews and the Second Republic   181
    Jewish Identity after 1945   184
    Ilse Aichinger   185
    Friedrich Torberg   195
    Hilde Spiel   203
    Conclusion   214

Chapter 4. Viennese Jews from Waldheim to Haider and Beyond   220
    The Waldheim Affair   221
    Jewish Writers and Vienna after Waldheim   225
    Contemporary Viennese Jewish Writing   227
    Ruth Beckermann   229
    Robert Schindel   237
    Doron Rabinovici   243
    Robert Menasse   250
    Eva Menasse   255
    Elfriede Jelinek   261
    Conclusion   265

Conclusion   271

Bibliography   274

Index   285

Acknowledgements

I remember precisely where I was sitting when my fascination with Vienna began over two decades ago. Not in one of that city's great cafés while sipping a Mélange, nor in one of the stately courtyards of the Hofburg, but rather 4,000 miles removed from all of that in a small classroom Northampton, Massachusetts. There, as a student at Smith College, I had the great fortune to be introduced to Vienna by Professor Klemens von Klemperer, who had studied there until he was forced to flee during the Anschluß half a century earlier. He introduced me to the texts that would form my vision of and foment my curiosity about Vienna for years to come: Schorske and Zweig, Schnitzler and Freud, Klimt and Strauß.

I would have to wait another decade before I got my first chance to visit Vienna under a generous grant from the Austrian-American Fulbright Association and began work on a project that would eventually lead to this book. Sander Gilman guided me through the first phase of this project—a dissertation on Arthur Schnitzler—and taught me how to do cultural history. I am proud to be his student.

In the years that followed, many people would enrich my project. I am especially grateful to Steven Beller (anybody who reads just a few pages of this book will be well aware of how influential he has been on my work), Dagmar Lorenz (whose fingerprints are all over this project and who has been extremely generous in guiding my career), Robert von Dassanowsky (a great mentor and a great friend), Maria-Regina Kecht and Helga Schreckenberger and my fellow participants in the NEH-sponsored institute they directed on "Melting Pot Vienna" five years ago where this project began to take its full shape, and my colleagues at the University of Kentucky (which as an institution has also been generous in supporting my research) and at the Modern Austrian Literature and Culture Association.

Many have contributed to this project, but only one person has been there from the first tentative thoughts about potential dissertation topics to the final stages of reading the page proofs of this manuscript. And it is to that person, my husband Todd Herzog, that I dedicate this book.

INTRODUCTION

"*Wien ist anders*" (Vienna is different). This bold proclamation formed the centerpiece of an advertising campaign that emerged in the 1990s to promote tourism in the city of Vienna. The motto appeared on posters throughout the city, juxtaposed with familiar images of the city traditionally marketed to tourists: the golden Strauss statue, the Hofburg, St. Stephen's Cathedral, the Lippizaners, and the Vienna Boys' Choir. The effect of the images was to transport the viewer back to the days of Habsburg rule, to conjure up images of the city that were the most familiar and cherished—Vienna at the turn of the twentieth century. Yet the images were clearly incongruous with the slogan, invoking the question: if Vienna has changed so little, from what, exactly, was it different? The very same images were employed in a second, more successful advertising campaign by the city, anchored by the motto: "*Wien bleibt Wien*" (Vienna remains Vienna). *Wien ist anders—Wien bleibt Wien*. The tourism bureau, it seems, wanted to have it both ways, to market Vienna as a modern, cosmopolitan city while at the same time promising to deliver the Habsburg capital of a hundred years ago. In complicated ways, however, both slogans ring true. This apparent contradiction, which lies at the heart of the city's self-image, is indicative of the very complexity that defines Vienna as a cultural space.

For the Viennese Jewish writers examined in this study Viennese cultural identity has always been marked by contradictions, and the writers' own relationships to the city have similarly been fraught with contradictions and ambiguity. While Arthur Schnitzler and Sigmund Freud may readily come to mind alongside Johann Strauss and the Emperor Franz Joseph when the images of the Viennese *fin de siècle* are evoked, their presence among the cultural elite hardly afforded them a secure and self-evident position in Viennese society. The Jewish experience in Vienna across the twentieth century reflected a century-long pattern of living in tension with the city and its culture.

In a 1995 essay that referred to the advertising campaign mentioned above, Doron Rabinovici wrote, "'*Wien bleibt Wien*,' that is the most dangerous threat any city ever uttered."[1] And in Robert Menasse's 1991 novel *Selige Zeiten, brüchige Welt* (*Wings of Stone*), the central character bitterly characterizes Vienna as a city "that appears so frozen in its essence, that the phrase '*Wien bleibt Wien*' is only perceived as a lie because it sounds too euphemistic; the verb '*bleiben*' [to remain] was way too dynamic."[2] Even as these writers deftly skewer the city in which they live and write, they contribute to a rich tradition of cultural criticism produced by Viennese Jewish writers, stemming from their unique insider-outsider position in Viennese society. And yet, certainly the relationship of Jewish writers to Vienna and Viennese culture has been marked as much by affection as by distance. The filmmaker Ruth Beckermann acknowledges both feelings: "The pleasant thing, when one doesn't live here, is that one can take along what one likes, its literature, its music. ... I love Vienna, and I will never in my life understand another literature in the way I understand Schnitzler. That is very clear."[3] Beckermann lives in Vienna much of the time, and, more important, Vienna is the focal point of her artistic and intellectual engagement, as is also true of the many writers considered in this study. This study focuses on the complex and special relationship between Jewish writers and Vienna, on the simultaneous experiences of belonging and exclusion that Beckermann has characterized as feeling "*unheimlich heimisch*" (uncannily at home).

This study investigates over a century of Jewish writing in Vienna, beginning with the turn of the twentieth century and continuing into the early twenty-first century. Beginning this study at the *fin de siècle* draws my work into two major, long-standing scholarly conversations in Austrian cultural studies: the decades-long examination of Vienna 1900 launched by Carl Schorske's work and, stemming from that body of work, an assessment of the case of Jewish Vienna 1900. As it did for many scholars, Schorske's work ignited the first spark of interest I experienced for this era and established the framework that long shaped my understanding of the extraordinary cultural production of the Viennese *fin de siècle*. Schorske's essays, collected in *Fin de Siècle Vienna: Politics and Culture,* brought to light the characteristics of Viennese modernism and provided a paradigm for understanding its distinct features. The Schorskean view of Vienna 1900 depicts the city's ahistorical modernist culture as a product of the political demise of the Liberal bourgeoisie, and it presents the cultural explosion of the era as a retreat from politics into art by the disenfranchised children of the bourgeoisie. This explanatory model of an alienated cultural elite proved enticing to many scholars and came to dominate the understanding of the era and its culture. Schorske's work generated a great deal of academic interest in Viennese modernism and gave rise to a substantial body of scholarly research. Excitement over the topic spilled out from academic circles into popular culture, as a version of Vienna 1900 was transformed into highly successful cultural exhibitions and an array of marketable cultural products that caught the popular imagination.

By the 1990s, a reexamination of Schorske's thesis was under way. Projects such as *Rethinking Vienna 1900,* edited by Steven Beller, are part of a second wave of scholarship that has reinvigorated the study of *fin de siècle* Vienna and both shifted and expanded the scope of inquiry. One early debate that challenged the Schorskean model was the issue of Jewish participation in the cultural explosion at the turn of the twentieth century. Schorske's analysis does not account for the prevalence of Jews within the cultural elite of the period, and in his class-based approach the Jewishness of many turn-of-the-century artists is largely viewed as irrelevant. While some have taken a wholesale approach of downplaying the role of Jews in the production of culture around that time, a larger pool of scholars, following Schorske, have acknowledged a high degree of Jewish participation in Viennese culture while denying any distinctly Jewish element in that culture.

During the 1980s important research on the Jewish experience in Vienna emerged in the work of scholars such as Marsha Rozenblit, Josef Fraenkel, Robert Wistrich, Ivar Oxaal, Gerhard Botz, Michael Pollak, George Berkley, and Steven Beller. The work of these historians and political scientists has been crucial in presenting a detailed and nuanced account of the Jewish experience in Vienna, shedding light on such issues as migration and Jewish settlement; occupational distribution; education; social mobility; political involvement; marriage, intermarriage, and conversion; religious practice; and social organizations. More broadly, this work has been concerned with issues of Jewish identity, exploring the processes of assimilation and acculturation, as well as forces of exclusion.

An important outcome of this research was to demonstrate that the Jewish experience in Vienna was markedly different from that of other immigrant groups. Focus on ordinary people has also demonstrated that the experience of cultural elites such as Schnitzler or Zweig is not representative of the Jewish population as a whole. A third outcome of this scholarship is a clear sense that within the cultural elite to which Schnitzler and Zweig belonged, Jewish intellectuals experienced the world differently from their non-Jewish counterparts, in spite of assimilation, and thus cannot be subsumed into the bourgeoisie. In other words, these scholars have laid bare the limits of assimilation, and it thus becomes clear that the far-reaching assimilation of Jews into middle-class culture at the turn of the twentieth century did not make their Jewishness irrelevant. In drawing attention to the specificity of the Jewish experience, this body of work has changed the way we think about Vienna 1900 in important ways and reopened questions of Jewish influence on this culture.

Steven Beller's work undertakes to answer a number of questions not addressed by Schorske. In his 1989 volume *Vienna and the Jews,* as well as in subsequent work, he assesses the extent of Jewish participation in *fin de siècle* culture, examining the reasons for this high degree of Jewish participation, and finally seeks to analyze the nature of Jewish influence on this culture. Beller takes measure of the Jewish cultural elite and of the Jewish proportion of the educated, Liberal bourgeoisie, making a clear and compelling case for the predominance of Jews as producers and consumers of Viennese culture around the turn of the twentieth century. He then seeks to explain the reasons for this predominance with a close examination of the social conditions that encouraged Jewish participation in Viennese culture.

To understand the high concentration of Jews in the cultural elite, Beller zeroes in on Jewish educational patterns. While Jews were a minority within the bourgeoisie, Beller concludes that the educated segment of that population was heavily Jewish. Beller found that while Jews made up only between 9 and 12 percent of the general population, they accounted for roughly 30 percent of the students attending the city's elite *Gymnasien*.[4] Attendance at a *Gymnasium* was a basis for membership in Vienna's educated elite.

This work by Beller, along with the statistical research by Marsha Rozenblit, makes a clear case for the disproportionate involvement by Jews in *fin de siècle* culture. The next natural step is to address the nature of this Jewish influence. Beller rejects any generalized attempt to plumb the depths of "the Jewish mind" and instead adopts a more concrete approach, assessing the experiences of a number of prominent Jews within the cultural elite in the context of the historical processes of assimilation in Vienna 1900. He asks, what did their Jewishness mean to them, and, more specifically, were they more open to certain ideas as a result of their Jewish heritage? "Individuals will always appear in the history of cultural movements from the most diverse backgrounds," he writes, "but when a great many individuals appear from the same group, then the natural thing is to see if that group's history and experience provides traditions and ways of looking at the world which make individuals from that group more receptive to types of already existing thought, and inspire them to new ideas and insights."[5]

Beller places the experiences of Jewish intellectuals of the cultural elite within the broader context of the historical processes of assimilation at work at the end of the nineteenth century in Vienna, and attempts to identify certain common attitudes stemming from that unique experience. His analysis centers around identifying two traditions specific to the Jewish experience: the special emphasis by Jews on education, and the effects of Judaism as a religion of ethics and individualism. These two traditions left a clear imprint on Viennese modernist culture, he claims: the former in terms of the intellectuality of that culture, and the latter as an intense preoccupation with ethics within the realm of aesthetics.

In the introduction to his volume, Beller suggests that he does not seek to provide the last word on Jewish influence, but rather to reopen the debate on this subject and perhaps redirect it by putting forward a possible framework for assessing that influence. My study eagerly steps into this reopened conversation and offers a contribution to the debate over the Jewish influence on Viennese culture. While my work follows Beller methodologically in approaching the question by evaluating the specific experiences of Jewish individuals involved in Viennese culture, I focus specifically on literary works and explore what they reveal about the nexus of Jewishness and Viennese culture. This study is devoted to Jewish writers of the past century who have placed at the very center of their work the question of what it meant to be Jewish at the particular time and place in which they lived. Following Beller's work, I examine the ways in which these Jewish writers reflect on their heritage, their experiences of anti-Semitism, and on the limits of assimilation. One important aspect of Viennese Jewish culture—from the turn of the twentieth century to the present—is the continued attempt to translate these experiences into literary fiction and use this medium as a space in which to explore the meanings of these experiences and the nature of their identity. At the center of my work is an exploration of the particularly acute experiences of these Jewish writers concerning the crisis of the individual, widely considered to be central to Viennese modernism, seeking again the distinct traces of Jewish influence within modernist culture.

This investigation of Viennese Jewish literature seeks not only to assess the experience of these writers as Jews, but specifically as Jews in Vienna, whose relationship to the city and its culture was distinct from that of the mainstream Gentile population or from other minority groups. The second half of the nineteenth century was marked by the waves of immigration into the city from the Crown lands of the empire, yet Jews assimilated into a fundamentally different Vienna than other immigrant groups. Even as extensive assimilation processes created a significant gulf separating the lives of urban, cosmopolitan, middle-class Jews from Jews in the Austrian provinces, their experience remained markedly different from that of the non-Jewish Viennese population. This work focuses on the special relationship between Austrian Jewish writers and the city that stood at the center of Jewish life in the Austro-Hungarian Monarchy and later the Austrian nation. I consider the varied ways in which these writers map the city in their writing and how they characterize their relationships to it. Beller describes Viennese Jewish artists and intellectuals as simultaneously occupying the margins of society and the center of culture. This study is an examination of this insider-outsider position across the twentieth century, considering the effects of this unique vantage point on the work they created. Jewish literature was continually produced against the grain of mainstream culture. I identify a century-long pattern of living in tension with the city and its non-Jewish populace. From Arthur Schnitzler to Doron Rabinovici and Ruth Beckermann, numerous Jewish intellectuals have expressed the feeling that life in Vienna is untenable, while acknowledging that for them, life anywhere else is unimaginable.

The Historical Continuity of the Viennese Jewish Experience

Vienna 1900 was the inspiration and point of departure for this study, but, importantly, it is not its sole focus. As I examine the literature of later eras, I attempt to assess the impact of the legacy of the Jewish *fin de siècle* on later Jewish writers in Vienna and trace a series of continuities and changes through later decades. In the first chapter, which covers the long turn of the twentieth century through the First World War, my analysis focuses on the critical models for understanding Austrian society crafted by the writers of this period, the role of Jews in that society, and the phenomenon of Austrian anti-Semitism that are elaborated in these works; as subsequent chapters demonstrate, these are models to which later writers continually return.

The second chapter focuses on the interwar period, leading up to the *Anschluss*, and examines the voices of Jewish writers during these turbulent years. Following the collapse of the Habsburg monarchy, Austrian Jews were plunged anew into a profound identity crisis, as the modes of identification that had sustained them—albeit with considerable difficulty—were no longer viable. The Jewish writers I examine were not prepared to embrace the nationalist identifications that emerged from the war; the nations in which they lived were similarly unwilling to accept them into a national community. Caught in an untenable position, these writers diverged widely in their responses and generally found, within a deeper identification as Jews, a productive place from which to write. The chapter then examines the later works of a number of writers considered in the first chapter, alongside Joseph Roth, Elias and Veza Canetti, and Hugo Bettauer.

Chapter 3 treats the postwar period up to the 1986 election of Kurt Waldheim as president, an important turning point in Austrian national discourse. Here I consider the situation of Jewish writers who chose to return to Austria from exile and continued to write in the German language. In the conservative climate of postwar Austria, these Jewish returnees were not welcomed back but were merely tolerated on the condition that their presence remained undetectable. Nevertheless, writers such as Friedrich Torberg and Ilse Aichinger came to the fore as some of the most important literary voices of the period, helping to shape both the way the culture dealt with its Nazi past and the new directions that Austrian literature would take.

The final chapter focuses on the period since the Waldheim election, examining the works of the writers Robert Menasse, Doron Rabinovici, Ruth Beckermann, Eva Menasse, and Robert Schindel, a generation of Jewish writers who are the children of émigrés and survivors (and in Schindel's case, victims of the Shoah), as well as the Jewish-identified writer Elfriede Jelinek. I assess the crucial role played by these writers in challenging the nation to reflect critically on its past, on the alternative collective and personal histories of Jewish experience created in their works, and on the ways in which these writers relate to the cultural legacy of Jewish writers of prior generations.

Throughout the study I seek to examine the relationships between prominent Jewish writers of different eras, as well as to illuminate the various ways in which they negotiated a cultural identity as Jewish writers in Vienna. What emerges from this analysis is an extensive web of literary relationships between Jewish writers of different eras, as well as discernable continuities across the century—a rather remarkable development in a century full of radical breaks in Austrian-Jewish relations. The legacy of *fin de siècle* Jewish Vienna was vital to the generations of Jewish writing that have followed. The interwar period also yielded a number of writers who would stand as literary antecedents for Viennese Jewish writers of the present. The tradition of Viennese Jewish writing lives on in its contemporary expression in a way that differs from, say, German Jewish writing, as Jewish writers in Germany have been far less inclined to look to other German Jewish texts for referents and models. In all its rich variety, Viennese Jewish literature is remarkably cohesive, precisely because Jewish writers after the turn of the twentieth century consciously viewed themselves as the inheritors of the *fin de siècle* Viennese Jewish tradition. Referencing this tradition has helped the writers of later generations to reflect on what it means to be an Austrian Jew. The tradition informs their self-conceptions as writers and provides the discursive practices from which they draw upon in their own writing. This study seeks to uncover these vital connections between past and present, and reveal the way they can shed new light on the writers at either end of these literary relationships.

In order to keep the focus squarely on Viennese Jewish writing, I am limiting my focus in this work to writers who lived and worked for the bulk of their careers in the city of Vienna, excluding those whose ties to the city were brief or tenuous or whose work was written from and appeared primarily outside of Vienna, whether from exile, from another part of the Habsburg Empire, or from another European city. Readers may well identify a particular writer they feel should be included, but this work is set squarely at the intersection of Jews, Vienna, and literature.

With the exception of Stefan Zweig's memoirs, *Die Welt von Gestern*, which is less an autobiography than a portrayal of Vienna 1900, I have not included the works written by Viennese writers in exile. My sense of these works is that the trauma of the exile experience was singular, presenting tremendous challenges for these writers and a set of concerns specific to the exile experience. I have focused, therefore, on exiled writers who chose to return, who sought to create a new Austrian and Viennese identity for themselves and reinsert themselves into the Austrian literary scene in the postwar context.

This work focuses a great deal on the concept of identity, Jewish identity in particular, and pursues questions related to different writers' understanding of what it meant or means to have Jewish origins, to have a relationship to Jewish tradition or culture, or to frame one's self-understanding in reference to a particular historical narrative or collective experience, as well as how they experienced being perceived as Jewish by others. Given the centrality of identity to this study, it bears elaborating my understanding of this construct. First, I approach identity as a construct, not as something that is *a priori* present in us, inherent and fixed, but as a dynamic process that unfolds over a lifetime. It is of course not only Jewish writers for whom identity construction requires this kind of continual change and adaptation. For all people identity must be reconceived according to significant developments in one's life; it must be continually renegotiated in response to the social environment in which one lives and as the result of a reflected engagement with the past and present. The Jews of this study had to respond to concrete historical events that repeatedly redefined the terms of Jewish existence over the course of the twentieth century. Each chapter of this book corresponds to a dramatic change in the political, social, and cultural landscape that forced an entirely new orientation and reexamination of Jewish identity.

It is also my view that identity is constructed via social and communicative processes and that for writers, the process of writing is the central avenue to identity. It is not the case that, for example, Schnitzler, Bettauer, or Torberg was in possession of a certain identity and gave voice to that identity in his writing, but rather that the writing process itself was important in producing and giving form to an identity. While I consider the biographies of these writers as an important element in their relationships to their Jewish, as well as Viennese, identities, I do not wish to map the lives of these authors onto their texts. Instead, I attempt to examine the issues surrounding identity that the authors faced in their lives and look closely at the way they reflected on those issues in their writing. I consider their many texts in light of a continuing process of constructing and reconstructing identity.

In this study I have adopted a rather expansive approach to the question of who is considered a Jewish writer. I have consciously chosen to include a number of writers who never strongly identified as Jews but stemmed in part from a Jewish background, considering them to be products of the historical process of assimilation.[6] For these writers Jewishness may never have represented a positive, freely chosen identity, but merely a problem. My argument for the inclusion of such writers is that even where there was no positive sense of what it meant to be Jewish, there was awareness of the implications of being perceived as a Jew. Even at the turn of the century, Schnitzler's memoir *Jugend in Wien* (*My Youth in Vienna*) expresses his view of the inescapability of this perception, and this would of course only intensify with the rise of fascism. The Holocaust subsequently had the effect of forging Jews into a new collective that seemed to render any individual identification in terms of religion, history, or culture secondary, or even irrelevant. Throughout the twentieth century, writers of Jewish background have thus been wresting with the meaning of a Jewish identity. Hugo von Hofmannsthal, Karl Kraus, Hugo Bettauer, Hilde Spiel, and Elfriede Jelinek very strongly merit examination here alongside more expected choices, as they illuminate the broad range of responses to these central questions.

Notes

1. Doron Rabinovici, "Literatur und Republik oder Ganz Baden liest die Krone," in *"Was wird das Ausland dazu sagen": Literatur und Republik in Österreich nach 1945* (Vienna: Picus Verlag, 1995), 128.
2. Robert Menasse, *Selige Zeiten, brüchige Welt* (Salzburg: Residenz, 1991), 16.
3. Cited in Andrea Reiter, "Ruth Beckermann und die jüdische Nachkriegsgeneration in Österreich," in *'Other' Austrians: Post-1945 Austrian Women's Writing*, ed. Allyson Fiddler (Bern: Peter Lang, 1998), 162.
4. Steven Beller, *Vienna and the Jews: 1867–1938, A Cultural History* (Cambridge: Cambridge University Press, 1989), 52. See also Marsha Rozenblit, *The Jews of Vienna, 1867–1914: Assimilation and Identity* (Albany: SUNY Press, 1983).
5. Beller, *Vienna and the Jews,* 70.
6. Ibid., 74.

Chapter 1

THE *FIN DE SIÈCLE*

The Jewish Immigrant Experience in Vienna

This study of the rich tradition of Viennese Jewish literature must begin with an account of how Vienna became established as the center of Jewish life in the Habsburg Empire. Before taking up the literature as a reflection of Central European Jewish life, therefore, I want first to address how, when, and for what reasons the Jews came to Vienna, looking first at the history of Jewish migration to the city and then examining Viennese Jewish life and the particular nature of the city the Jewish immigrants encountered. The story of twentieth-century Jewish literature in Vienna thus begins in the nineteenth century, and 1867 presents itself as perhaps the best point of departure. This year of the Compromise Agreement, or *Ausgleich,* which created Austria-Hungary, was also the year of the long-awaited emancipation of the Jews.[1] Austria's Liberal government lifted restrictions on occupation and residence that had been in place since the Middle Ages and set Jews on equal footing with all other Austrian citizens in terms of civil, political, and religious rights. The lifting of restrictions on Jewish residence was a tremendous impetus to Jewish migration, especially to Vienna.

The Jewish experience of modernity was deeply connected to processes of migration and urbanization. The larger phenomena of urbanization and the movement of Jews from small towns and rural areas to the cities, witnessed all across Europe, were particularly striking with respect to Jewish immigration to Vienna. During the 1860s the city's Jewish population grew by a remarkable 46 percent each year.[2] In 1857, only 1 percent of Austrian Jews were living in the capital. By 1900, this number had reached 13 percent, and by 1910, with Jews making up 13 percent of the city's total population, Vienna was the third-largest Jewish community in the world.[3]

This growth of the urban Jewish population occurred at a time of tremendous general growth in cities across the Habsburg Empire. Most of the empire's major cities doubled their populations from the late 1860s through 1910. Vienna grew by 234 percent during this period, and by 1910 the population exceeded two million.[4] In this same year fewer than half of Vienna's residents had been born in the city.[5] Urbanization was thus a general trend in late nineteenth-century Austria-Hungary, and most of the urban population growth came from migration. Yet while the Jews participated in the broader progression of urbanization, the process of Jewish immigration to Vienna was fundamentally different from the migration of non-Jews in the empire. Jewish migration was prompted by circumstances distinct to the Jews—it followed its own patterns demographically and temporally—and the immigrant Jewish experience in the city differed markedly from that of other ethnic immigrant groups. These differences had a significant impact in defining the Jewish experience of Vienna.

Prior to World War I, there were three significant waves of Jewish immigration to Vienna from the Crown lands: the first wave came from Bohemia and Moravia during the 1850s and 1860s; the second, the Jews from Hungary, came through the 1880s; and the third wave, Galician Jews, came during the final decades of the Austro-Hungarian Empire. While the non-Jewish population also migrated from the provinces to the city, this migration was largely a response to agricultural crises and rural overpopulation and mainly involved people who sought new employment opportunities with the lifting of the guild restrictions and the creation of new jobs in industry. Jews of the provinces, on the other hand, were not peasants and thus were not responding to a depression in agriculture; nor were they to enter the urban proletariat in large numbers. Jews entering Vienna also sought greater economic opportunities, but of a different character. Many Jews were looking to enter professional life and increase their prestige and status through new employment, professional training, or university study. Their migration to Vienna was prompted primarily by a desire for upward mobility.

In addition to economic impulses, numerous important social and cultural factors drew Jews to Vienna. Albert Lichtblau has stressed the importance of these noneconomic factors, citing the attraction of the city itself and the vibrant cultural life that flourished in the cultural and intellectual center of the monarchy.[6] He notes the importance of an already established (albeit relatively small) Jewish community, complete with social clubs, news organs, charity organizations, synagogues, hospitals, and *cheder*s, as well as friends and relatives clustered in the Leopoldstadt, Vienna's second district and the home to the greatest concentration of Jews from all social classes and from all over the empire. Political motivations played a role as well, as many Jews in the Crown lands sought to escape from provincial anti-Semitism. The Jews of the monarchy also identified the city of

Vienna with the liberal, progressive forces that had granted them emancipation, and they certainly had hopes of encountering a more hospitable political climate than they had left behind.[7] Like other late nineteenth-century immigrants to Vienna, Jews sought opportunities unavailable to them in the provinces; however these opportunities were less about economic survival and more about political, cultural, economic, and social advancement.

Jewish migration differed from immigration patterns among non-Jews not only in motivation, but also in form, in that Jews more often moved as families, rather than as individuals seeking employment in industry or domestic service. They traveled long distances and often crossed provincial borders. They were also more likely to come to Vienna from other cities and were thus generally familiar with urban life, a factor that further distinguished them from non-Jewish immigrants.[8] Jews thus traveled to Vienna not only for the reasons that people throughout Europe were flocking to urban centers in the same period, but for the specific opportunities that this particular city offered them at this particular time. The story of nineteenth-century Austrian Jewish migration is not simply one of urbanization, but of "Viennaization."

The distinctiveness evident in the immigration patterns of Jews is part of a broader trend that encompassed not only their arrival in Vienna but their integration into the city and their experiences as they established themselves there. The work of social and cultural historians has uncovered evidence in all aspects of Jewish life—economic, professional, social, cultural, political, private, and religious—indicating that during the long turn of the century the Jews in Vienna experienced the city very differently from their non-Jewish fellow citizens.[9]

Jews who settled in Vienna are clearly to be counted among the winners in the process of economic modernization, as were Jews elsewhere in Europe at the time. Having been previously clustered in Europe's urban centers and concentrated in trade, Jews were better poised to adapt to the conditions of modernization. While Carl Schorske's influential work on the dramatic cultural developments of this period might lead us to view the occupational transformation of Viennese Jews as a wholesale withdrawal from commerce and the world of business in general to the temple of the arts, it is important to recall that this was the experience of only a small minority of the educated Jewish elite.[10] As Marsha Rozenblit has argued, "The salient change precipitated by urbanization and consequent opportunities for economic and general assimilation was the transformation of a people famous for its trading ability into a clerical and managerial group."[11] The Jews thus became predominantly white-collar employees in a city of artisans and, increasingly, part of the working class. Jews took positions as clerks, salesmen, and managers in the city's banks, insurance companies, and other large firms, raising their prestige and professional security.[12] While this transformation demonstrated their acculturation, it did not amount to economic assimilation, because, again, their employment patterns were distinct. Newly immigrated Jews did not become domestic servants or join the city's growing proletariat but, through past experience in their countries of origin, they moved in trade or, with the better education available in Vienna, into higher-paying jobs.

For many Jews, Vienna was a gateway to the liberal professions, particularly law and medicine. If we turn to the university, the Jewish presence in these fields was particularly noteworthy. In 1890, the peak of Jewish enrollment in the medical school, Jews made up a remarkable 48 percent of medical students at the University of Vienna.[13] The university was especially attractive to Jewish students; half of Austria's Jewish students chose to study in Vienna.[14] The popularity of the medical school was unparalleled. Its importance as a training ground for the physicians of the empire is exemplified by the case of Arthur Schnitzler's father, Johann, who came to Vienna from the Hungarian town of Nagy-Kanizsa nearly penniless and proceeded to put himself through medical school by tutoring students, eventually achieving prominence as a widely renowned laryngologist. Johann Schnitzler did not come to Vienna with the immediate goal of obtaining employment simply to subsist—he came to educate himself in a career in which he could advance himself professionally.

Although Johann Schnitzler is a dramatic example of upward mobility through education, Steven Beller has drawn attention to the special emphasis Jewish families generally placed on education.[15] In his work Beller identifies considerable differences in attitudes towards education among Catholics and Jews, evidenced by the fact that Jews attended the city's *Gymnasien* and university in numbers that far exceeded their proportion of the population. Beller traces this striking statistical difference to the central role that learning and study traditionally played in Judaism and to the gradual process by which secular studies came to replace religious study for many Jews, while retaining its centrality to the culture and the prestige with which it was viewed.

Clearly, in embracing the Enlightenment tradition of *Bildung*—a fusion of education, self-cultivation, and character formation—Jews were seeking to participate in a humanist tradition that resonated deeply with the German majority in Austria, and, by the nineteenth century, with the middle class in particular. George Mosse articulated the importance of *Bildung* in the *embourgeoisement* and, hence, social acceptance of the Jews. He notes, "*Bildung* was readily embraced by Jews as helping to complete the process of emancipation."[16] Education and the absorption of German culture was to be a path to acculturation into the German majority and an entrance ticket to the liberal middle class. Ironically, however, the Jews' embrace of the cultural goals and ideals of the middle class again set them apart, as the zeal with which they pursued education and self-cultivation produced a quantitative difference from their Gentile counterparts.[17] Beller argues, "The very strategy of assimilation through *Bildung* was jeopardizing the acceptance of Jews in general, by making them something special again: no longer Jewish, but not really Gentile either."[18] This serves as a reminder that the

Jewish pursuit of education and participation in culture was not solely motivated by the desire to assimilate, as this pattern of behavior was clearly not the best way to fit in.

If integration into the middle class was the aim of Jewish assimilation, the family was the arena in which these processes unfolded. The creation of a cult of domesticity, establishing the home as a haven from the pressures of the outside world, was the hallmark of the bourgeois model of the family. Jewish women were at the center of the household, and they thus played a critical role as both agents of acculturation and guardians of Jewish tradition. Women were largely excluded from university study through social pressures, and their presence at home was an important status symbol. Yet since the notion of *Bildung* brought the project of self-cultivation and education into the home, it thus brought it into the domain of women.[19] Jewish women therefore acted as the arbiters of culture and the overseers of *Bildung* within the family.

In Marion Kaplan's account of the German Jewish middle class, Jewish women's lives are seen as marked by deep conflicts. In terms of their personal ambitions, emancipation of the Jews and their acculturation, as well as the move to an urban environment, opened up new possibilities that they could now hope to realize; yet they also faced discrimination both as women and as Jews.[20] Women's roles as cultural mediators were similarly complex. As assimilatory processes unfolded and one's relationship to Jewishness increasingly became a private matter to be negotiated within the home, women had to steer their families on a careful path between Germanness and Jewishness. Kaplan writes: "Faced with contradictions and constant flux, mothers had to raise proper German children while affirming (and redefining) Jewishness, to present a family in the appropriate light to a society intolerant of differences, and to create a refuge for a minority to come home to."[21] Jewish women thus played important roles in carving out and making visible a bourgeois identity while maintaining certain ties to a Jewish heritage, if not to Judaism itself. To fulfill these dual and often conflicting roles, they employed an arsenal of skills and abilities, drawing on their education, cultural knowledge, and domestic and social networking skills.

These familial negotiations were undertaken in the company of other Jewish families, as Jews settled in Vienna largely in the company of other Jews. At the turn of the century Jews were concentrated above all in the second district, Leopoldstadt (which, due to its significant Jewish population, was often referred to as the *Mazzesinsel,* or matzo island), and also in the first district and in the bourgeois districts around the Ring—Mariahilf, Neubau, Josefstadt, and Alsersgrund. Immigrant Jews tended to cluster according to region of origin, such as in Brigittenau, the twentieth district, which housed many Jews from the eastern provinces. Jewish neighborhoods were not restricted to the poor or to the immigrant generation, however, but were occupied by Jews of different economic classes. Leopoldstadt in particular continued to be populated by Jews of all classes and origins. None of these areas, of course, were exclusively Jewish.[22] The *Mazzesinsel* moniker of Leopoldstadt had as much to do with its place in the popular imagination as with its actual demographic makeup; the majority of the residents of the second district would likely never have eaten matzo! Still, while the patterns of Jewish settlement did not mean that Jews lived among other Jews exclusively, it remained the case that Jews in Vienna were more segregated in their residential patterns than other ethnic groups.[23]

With their concentrations of Jewish businesses, synagogues, and community organizations, Jewish neighborhoods provided an important link to Jewish identity during a period in which that identity was weakening under the pressures of secularization, upward social mobility, and integration into Gentile society. At the same time, the existence of these neighborhoods slowed or limited the assimilation of Jews into Viennese Gentile society.

Jewish immigration to Vienna at the time of mass urbanization was thus markedly different from the pattern of other ethnic groups who migrated to the city at the same time. They were at once more segregated (geographically) and more economically and socially integrated (at least with other Jews). And, while other populations flocked to cities in search of employment, Jews migrated particularly to Vienna in search of the upward mobility made available to them by this specific city's educational, cultural, and social opportunities. All of these opportunities can be traced to the particular political climate of Vienna, which embraced a form of liberalism that attracted Jewish migrants in the first place. This political climate was complicated and volatile, however, and would change dramatically during the period of mass Jewish migration, as we shall see.

The Jewish Confrontation with a New Political Climate

To fully understand the position of Viennese Jewry at the end of the nineteenth century and the beginning of the twentieth, it is vital to consider the political climate, which shifted dramatically during this period. The fate of the Jews at this time was in large measure determined by the political alliance between Jews and Liberals. To a great extent it was the promises of Liberalism that had drawn Jews to the Habsburg capital; the Jews had contributed to the establishment of the Liberal Party and had benefited from its accession to power, and, as Jews increasingly became associated with this political movement, they came under fire when strong political opponents to the party emerged. Jews were featured prominently among the 1848 revolutionaries in Vienna. They had access to political power and the benefits derived from it during the period of Liberal ascendancy in Austria (from the 1860s through the early 1870s). Conversely, Jews were most keenly affected by the reordering of the ideological and political landscape that may be said to have begun with the stock market crash of 1873 and progressed through the rest of the decade, effecting the gradual exclusion of Jews from the political process.

The attraction of Jews to Liberalism can be attributed to a combination of factors, some of which were particular to the Jews and others common to the bourgeoisie. Fundamentally, Jews were drawn to Liberalism as the political expression of the values of the Enlightenment, particularly the doctrine of toleration espoused by Lessing and Moses Mendelssohn. The emancipation of the Jews was a protracted process, marked by a number of regressions and retractions. In Austria, emancipation was formally accomplished in the constitution, the *Staatsgrundgesetz* of 1867, which made all citizens equal before the law, gave all citizens equal access to public office, guaranteed freedom of religion, and made civic and political rights independent of religious belief.

In light of the form in which emancipation was granted, the Jews felt indebted not only to political Liberalism, but to the Crown as well. Lacking a territorial claim in the empire, the Jews differed sharply from national communities like the Czechs and Magyars and really had no other political allegiance open to them other than allegiance to the imperial power. The intensity of their loyalty to the emperor seems to have been a particularly Jewish phenomenon, setting them apart even in their Austrian patriotism. Manfred Dickel describes this phenomenon as "a sort of dissimilating overassimilation."[24]

In addition to the specific appeal that Liberalism had for them as Jews, Jews were also drawn to Liberalism as an expression of their class interests. Middle-class Jews saw themselves represented by the Liberal program in the same way that their Gentile bourgeois counterparts did; they supported the Liberal agenda of a centralized, constitutional government, the dismantling of aristocratic privileges, free enterprise, secularization, material progress, and a unified legal system. This political allegiance to the Liberals and to Franz Joseph was viewed as a further means of fusing Jews and Gentiles within the middle class and of identifying the Jews with the German majority in the city. The enthusiastic embrace of German culture by Jews developed a political counterpart during the 1870s in the form of German nationalism. By the end of the decade, however, German nationalism, in the form of pan-Germanism, had become the clear domain of the anti-Semites.[25]

New forms of anti-Semitism emerged in Austria during the nineteenth century. The Catholic Church reacted with hostility to Jewish involvement in the revolution of 1848, continuing to view Jews as Liberals and, therefore, as fundamentally hostile to the Church. Alongside religious and social anti-Semitism, economic anti-Semitism was also potent in Austria, as Jews were associated with economic Liberalism and "un-German" capitalism. After the stock market crash of 1873, middle-class Jews found themselves being made scapegoats for the market's collapse even as they suffered severe financial losses themselves.

The universities, which had long played a key role in drawing Jews to Vienna and aiding in their professional and social advancement, now played a central role in legitimizing and popularizing anti-Semitism in the city. Anti-Jewish hostility at the University of Vienna had been palpable for decades but became a cause célèbre that spilled from the medical school into the streets of the city in 1876. In this year, Theodor Billroth, one of the most distinguished surgeons of the era and professor of surgery in Vienna, published a study of medical education at German universities in which he vehemently declared the unsuitability of Jews for the study and practice of medicine.[26] By the 1880s Jews composed nearly 40 percent of the university's medical students, and the majority of these were young Eastern European Jewish men participating in the widespread phenomenon of educational migration from the provinces to the capital. Billroth opposed the medical school's open-admission policy, claiming that these Jews arrived in Vienna penniless, facing a struggle for survival, and ill prepared for the rigors of medical study. He called for the adoption of a *numerus clausus* specifically targeting Eastern European Jews, claiming that their continued presence in such numbers would compromise the school's reputation as one of Europe's most important centers of medical education.

Billroth's arguments went beyond this invective against poor, provincial Jewish students. Ultimately he argued that Jews were not merely ill prepared for medical study but unfit to practice medicine. He identified a fundamental difference between Germans and Jews, a "deep cleavage between pure-German and pure-Jewish blood."[27] Billroth's anti-Jewish argument shifts terrain here, in that he now asserted a divide that could no longer be bridged through education or adoption of German culture. His argument demonstrated the biological determinism that became a key component of modern anti-Semitism. Billroth later repudiated this stance and became a vocal opponent of anti-Semitism, but not before his public declarations had contributed to the legitimacy of anti-Semitism in the academic world. Freud's experience of the virulent anti-Semitism of the medical school during these years was decisive in his turning away from German nationalism toward the gradual acceptance of a positive identification as a Jew. Arthur Schnitzler describes the anti-Semitic climate at the university in his memoirs, relating frequent scuffles between individual German nationalists and Jewish students, beatings of Jewish students by members of German nationalist fraternities, and stormy debates on the status of Jewish students from the eastern provinces. Theodor Herzl also experienced his first significant encounter with anti-Semitism at the university. As a result, Herzl, like Freud, came to reject the German nationalism he had previously embraced, quitting his fraternity in 1883 in the wake of an anti-Semitic speech by Hermann Bahr. Schnitzler recalls this episode in *Jugend in Wien,* characterizing it as a powerful determinant in shaping Herzl's later political views.[28]

The university was clearly a hotbed of anti-Semitic activity, but anti-Semitism was increasingly moving into the political arena as a key element of what Schorske has referred to as "politics in a new key." In the later 1870s, Georg Ritter von

Schönerer emerged on the political stage, an apostatized Liberal who adopted anti-Semitism as an integral part of his political platform. In 1879 Schönerer formed the *Volkspartei* (People's Party) in opposition to "Jewish" free-market capitalism. In 1882 the party was reorganized as the *Deutschnationale Partei* (German National Party). That party's Linz Program of 1885 included the demand for "the removal of Jewish influence from all sections of public life."[29] As a result of the new election law of 1882, which enfranchised the lower middle classes, Schönerer found an electorate for whom his mixture of German nationalism and anti-Semitism resonated. He did not achieve large-scale electoral success, nor did the party rise to the level of a mass movement, but his infusion of nationalism and anti-Semitism into the ranks of the embattled Liberals did make a significant impact.

Before long, Schönerer was eclipsed as the force behind political anti-Semitism. In 1888 he was removed from the leadership of his party, jailed for four months, and stripped of his political rights for five years, after he and a number of his political allies stormed the editorial offices of the *Neues Wiener Tageblatt* and violently attacked its staff. By then Schönerer had a potent political rival in Karl Lueger. Lueger was a Vienna-born politician who stemmed from the lower bourgeoisie—the five-florin men who received the franchise in 1882 and who were to become the core of his followers. By the late 1880s Lueger became involved with the Catholic Reform movement, and by 1890 he was the political leader of the Christian Social Union. Lueger was a gifted orator and skillful politician who marshaled a blend of anti-Liberalism and anti-Semitism as negative forces of integration that held together an unlikely alliance of the lower middle classes, sections of the clergy, and, increasingly, teachers, civil servants, and men of low-level, white-collar positions. The two strands of Lueger's politics merged very effectively, as the association between Liberalism and Jews had come to be so prevalent that the term *Judaeoliberalismus* (Judeo-Liberalism) emerged as a term of opprobrium.[30]

Over the 1890s Lueger waged a battle for Vienna, facing down opposition from within the Church and chipping away at the strength of political opponents among the Conservatives and Liberals. By 1897 the battle had been won and Lueger was Vienna's mayor, though it took five rounds of elections by the Christian Social–controlled city council before the emperor would confirm him. Vienna thus became the first major city in the Western world to be governed by an openly anti-Semitic political party.[31]

Lueger's brand of racial anti-Semitism had been a crucial and central element of his campaign. It therefore must have come as a surprise to his constituents when, once in office, Lueger steered clear of the "Jewish Question" in favor of an ambitious campaign of municipal improvements, including an extensive building program of roads, bridges, schools, and other facilities, the takeover of privately owned utilities, and the founding of an employment agency and savings bank.[32]

These tangible achievements, as well as the mayor's political skills and powerful personality, made *"der schöne Karl"* (the handsome Karl) exceedingly popular; this era, until his death in 1910, clearly belonged to Lueger politically.

The Lueger era was a time of striking contradictions for Vienna's Jews. The Lueger administration enacted no discriminatory policies against Jews. Personally, Lueger conducted business and even socialized with Jews, famously quipping, "I determine who's a Jew." With this remark Lueger cast anti-Semitism as a political tool that could be put to good use when it proved beneficial to do so. Nevertheless, even if intended to diminish the potency of anti-Semitism as one more political tool in the arsenal of a powerful politician, the remark underscores the extent to which one's racial, religious, and cultural background had become the operative determinants of identity and social position. As Michael Pollak has suggested, "To be or not to be a Jew, as well as the religious, cultural and racial standards alleged to justify such a classification, became matters of such importance that there was little or no chance of evading classification."[33] In a series of notes at the conclusion to *Jugend in Wien,* Schnitzler comments powerfully on the extent to which the "Jewish Question" had permeated his society:

> It was not possible, especially for a Jew in the public eye, to ignore the fact that he was a Jew, since the others didn't ignore it, not the Christians and even less the Jews. One had the choice of being considered insensitive, importunate, or fresh or sensitive, shy, or suffering from a persecution complex. And even when one kept one's inner and outer composure so that one didn't show one tendency or the other, it was just as impossible to remain fully unaffected as someone could remain indifferent who let his skin be anaesthetized but had to look on with alert and open eyes as unclean knives scratched at it, cut into it until it bled.[34]

Anti-Semitism resonated in Schnitzler's Vienna. It had become an effective political force because it addressed some of the social dislocations that had resulted from urbanization and industrialization, or more specifically, the feelings of alienation produced by these developments. For the lower tradesmen and artisans threatened by economic modernization, anti-Semitism provided a sense of social belonging, espousing an organic community from which the Jews, as the group supposedly to blame for the dislocations associated with modernity, were excluded. Lueger may not have discriminated against the Jews once in office, but he did much to foment the aggressive anti-Jewish prejudices of his constituents, discernibly altering the climate for relations between Jews and non-Jews in Vienna.

Jewish responses to anti-Semitism took many forms. Jewish identity had been thoroughly destabilized through the spread and strengthening of anti-Semitism. As Schnitzler's comment suggests, whether or not an individual Jew held to any positive convictions about what it meant to be Jewish, a Viennese Jew at the turn of the twentieth century was sure to be conscious of the problem of being a Jew in that society.[35] Historical developments in the latter half of the nineteenth century had created generations of Jews in Vienna with very different experiences. For the generation who had come of age midcentury, the promise of emancipation had seemed to hold open the possibility of forging a Jewish identity for oneself. One could choose a positive identification by embracing the Jewish religion or cultural heritage, or one could also reject any identification with Judaism or Jewishness altogether; in between, there was a great range of religious, social, political, and cultural positions to be negotiated in determining a relationship to the Jewish religion and its traditions.[36] While these processes were not free from external pressures, they did appear to be a private matter, a matter of individual choice. By century's end this was no longer the case, as categories of identity had been ideologized as a result of anti-Semitism and the conflicts between the various nationalities in the empire. For the next generation, a reexamination of identity was inescapable. A number of widely divergent projects emerged in response to these intense pressures, all variously engaged in the task of restabilizing identity.

For some Jews, politics remained the appropriate arena for seeking a solution to the problems created by anti-Semitism. Austrian Social Democracy held a strong appeal for many who sought to reject the prevailing tendency to link identity to religious affiliation. In Socialism, some Jews recognized a humanistic doctrine that could replace the religious tradition from which they had increasingly distanced themselves. The movement offered a theoretical solution to the problems of anti-Semitism in that Jews and non-Jews working side by side for the revolutionary cause were integrated in a new, shared political identity. Prior to World War I, however, the involvement by Jews in the Social Democratic Party was largely limited to certain segments of the Jewish intelligentsia, who filled the ranks of the party leadership. The party adopted a highly ambivalent stance toward populist anti-Semitic politics for a variety of reasons, including the fear of being labeled a "Jewish party." For the less affluent Jews in the city, a number of obstacles to participation in the movement existed. Even the poorer immigrant Jews did not truly belong to the proletariat, nor did they live in large numbers in the working-class districts of the city. Beyond this, a significant cultural gap persisted between the Eastern European Jewish immigrants and the modern, urban Socialist movement.[37]

While the Social Democratic Jewish leaders appeared intent on dissociating themselves from their Jewishness, other political alternatives emerged for those who sought to reclaim a Jewish identity in response to the pressures of anti-Semitism. As assimilation as a path to integration was increasingly called into question by the rise of anti-Semitism, many young Jews began to assert a new form of Jewishness in late-Habsburg Vienna. Zionism was established as a political movement following the 1896 publication of *Der Judenstaat* (*The Jews' State*) by Theodor Herzl; however Zionism had appeared at the university among Jewish students more than a decade earlier. These Jewish nationalist students supported a Jewish homeland in Palestine but also concerned themselves more broadly with the struggle against assimilationism and the recognition of a Jewish national identity. This youthful participation in Zionist organizations was mirrored outside of the university as well, with the strongest participation in the movement stemming from middle-class youth.[38] While the majority of Viennese Jews were opposed or indifferent to the Zionist cause, there was a proliferation of Zionist organizations during this period, as well as enough official support for the movement to suggest that Zionism had an impact on Vienna's Jewish community.

Alongside political Zionism, there was also a non-Zionist form of Jewish nationalism, which Rozenblit refers to as Diaspora nationalism.[39] Diaspora nationalism arose in the context of the nationalities conflict in the empire, as anti-Semitism and chauvinistic nationalism effected the exclusion of the Jews from membership in any of the numerous national camps. Many young Jews, especially university students, came to believe strongly in Jewish national identity and campaigned for official recognition of their legitimacy as a nation. They viewed assimilationism as an outmoded, failed project and argued against a hyphenated identity as German, Czech, or Polish Jews. In 1907 Heinrich York-Steiner wrote, "We Jews are by nationality neither German nor Czech, not Frenchmen or Englishmen. Whoever maintains the opposite ... places us Jews is a false light and besmirches our character."[40] These nationalist activists sought to embolden other Jews to resist assimilationism and the pressures of anti-Semitism and instead proudly affirm their membership in the Jewish nation and seek its equality alongside other national communities.

Even more numerous than the adherents to these forms of Jewish nationalism were the various groups of integrationists within the Viennese Jewish community. The mainstream of the Jewish community can be said to have held to the course of assimilationism and largely attempted to ignore the virulent anti-Semitism that had taken hold. The Jewish establishment, including, for example, the best-known Liberal newspaper, the *Neue Freie Presse*, simply did not openly acknowledge the strength of anti-Semitism in the political sphere.

The core of the Viennese Jewish community was represented by the *Israelitische Kultusgemeinde* (IK), which was officially recognized in 1890 and had been charged with the responsibility of overseeing the religious life of the community with functions such as direction of the synagogues, religious education, supervision of rabbis, as well as kosher food production. The IK represented those Jews with some measure of involvement in the religious and cultural life of the community, but it excluded nonpracticing Jews who sought no involvement and the ultra-Orthodox, whose cultural differences essentially excluded them from the structured community. With the rise of political anti-Semitism, the IK was clearly put on the defensive, as anti-Semitic attacks made painfully clear to the Jews their "non-elective affinity with other Jews" and demonstrated the need for defense and protection.[41] When Joseph Bloch assumed leadership of the IK, he called for a more activist stance against anti-Semitism and sought to reform the organization. Faced with a major division within the community from the Zionists, the integrationist leaders of the Jewish community did not achieve substantial reform or launch a substantive response to anti-Semitism but limited their political engagement to occasional protests of specific instances of discrimination.

As the Jewish community became increasingly diverse and pursued a variety of responses to the anti-Semitic challenge, from minimalist to radical strategies, an increasing number of Jews chose to eschew the Jewish community and their Jewish heritage altogether. Starting in 1880 Vienna saw a substantial and steadily increasing number of Jews withdraw from the Jewish community. The city had become a veritable *"Taufmaschine"* (baptism machine), with more than half of the new converts becoming Catholic, approximately one-quarter becoming Protestants, and one-fifth declaring no affiliation.[42] Gustav Mahler, Arnold Schoenberg, Karl Kraus, Otto Weininger, and Viktor Adler were prominent Jews involved in this phenomenon in Vienna, which produced a higher rate of conversion than anywhere else in the empire. Intermarriage was a parallel phenomenon. As marriage between Jews and Christians was forbidden by Austrian law, one partner in an interdenominational couple was forced to convert to the religion of the other partner or formally declare his or her nonadherence to any faith, a requirement that inflated the conversion rate.[43] Marriage was one motivation for conversion; others were spurred by professional concerns, as Jewishness was an insurmountable obstacle in many careers. For some the withdrawal from Judaism was the natural outcome of a secularizing society, and for many the motivation was clearly the desire for integration through full assimilation.

Of course, the emergence of racial anti-Semitism placed a powerful check on the possibility of gaining acceptance through conversion. Even baptism could not wash away the Jewish blood that was thought to mark Jews as members of an inferior race. In the popular imagination of an anti-Semitic society, converted Jews remained Jews. In the face of the apparent futility of conversion as a path to integration, many Jewish converts retained some element of a Jewish identity, and some came to a full, open reaffirmation of that identity. One prominent figure who returned to Judaism was Arnold Schoenberg, in 1933.

Jewish Cultural Responses

For the Jews of the cultural elite at the center of this study, the responses to anti-Semitism outlined above were all accessible avenues of attitude and behavior. By virtue of their level of education and social position they could also turn to culture as a realm in which to wrestle with issues of identity, as well as broader social and political concerns of the era.[44] The flow of Viennese Jews into the cultural realm cannot be understood solely as a response to anti-Semitic pressures; nor should the Jewish involvement in Socialism or, for that matter, Freud's development of psychoanalysis be characterized strictly as projects concerned with the restabilization of a Jewish identity under siege. Yet clearly, a significant factor in the extraordinary level of Jewish participation in turn-of-the-century culture was the fact that the aesthetic realm remained open to educated Jews, even as the changing ideological climate foreclosed other possibilities.[45] For intellectuals like Schnitzler or Zweig, for whom the collective identities posited by Zionism or Socialism offered no solution, the modernist culture they helped to shape offered alternative, individualist solutions to the problem of Jewish identity. Whereas Johann Schnitzler could pursue medicine as a way of finding an identity in Viennese society, the liberal professions no longer provided a stable identity, and his son had to turn to literature to explore the possibilities afforded in this arena.

A number of scholars investigating the disproportionate representation of Jews in the turn-of-the-century Viennese cultural sphere have sought to identify the reasons for that concentration. Carl Schorske downplayed Jewish involvement and emphasized instead the crises of the Liberal state as the context for the cultural innovation and efflorescence we see in the period. Emil Brix and Allan Janik similarly turn their attention to broader forces at work and investigate the city of Vienna more generally, focusing not on why the Jews in particular became so active in culture, but why this specific city gave rise to such remarkable cultural activity.[46] In a 1986 article, Janik first articulated a set of factors he considered significant in having shaped a productive environment in Vienna for creative endeavors.[47] He emphasized the size of the city, with two million inhabitants, and its special role as capital of an empire with over fifty million citizens, as well its status as the empire's financial capital, largest city, imperial residence, and home to an immense bureaucracy. Janik also noted the importance of interaction with the other cities of the empire alongside local traditions that supported culture, such as the great theatrical tradition in the city. While Brix spoke in terms of "conditions of excellence," Janik also noted the darker side of the city that nonetheless contributed to Vienna development into the city that it became. Among the more negative aspects of Viennese life he highlights are the terrible living conditions of the outer districts, forced re-Catholicization, an unwieldy bureaucracy, censorship practices, and hostility to innovation. While these negative factors clearly did not directly foster the city's cultural climate, they may well have prompted oppositional critiques and the search for new solutions.[48]

Other scholars have explored the specific social conditions that encouraged Jewish participation. Albert Lichtblau follows Schorske in viewing culture as an alternative to politics: "With culture as a different type of politics, writers could fight against the prevailing anti-intellectual currents and duplicitous double standards."[49] However Lichtblau places more emphasis on the specific Jewish nature of this fight, characterizing Jewish involvement in culture as a response to the destabilizing effects of modernization, the decline of religion, and the resulting search for an arena that could still provide a form of identity as well as social prestige. Whereas a generation earlier medical school might have seemed to offer a path toward a professional identity and social prestige, by the close of the nineteenth century Jews had to turn increasingly to the arts in order to secure these opportunities.

This generational shift is crucial to the understanding of the Jewish relationship to Vienna at the end of the nineteenth century: the turn to culture that would come to define the Jewish experience of Vienna to this day was the response of a new generation to new political, social, and economic conditions. The writers who congregated at the Café Griensteidl—Hermann Bahr, Arthur Schnitzler, Hugo von Hofmannsthal, Felix Salten, Richard Beer-Hofmann, and others—consciously cast themselves as *Jung Wien* (Young Vienna) and saw themselves as representative of a new direction in Viennese literature, as well as Viennese Jewish culture. For Theodor Herzl, they represented a transitional generation, distanced from Judaism and Jewish tradition yet not fully integrated into Gentile secular society. Certainly the experiences of the previous generation no longer seemed to provide an effective compass in their own lives. The values of the fathers had been shaken, their validity undermined. After 1873, the combination of Germanization and economic utility, previously seen as a certain path to integration and one of the chief attractions that drew Jews to Vienna in the first place, had proven unsuccessful. In the wake of the nationalities conflict, the end of the Austro-Habsburg Empire seemed imminent, rendering identity an unstable construct for all subjects of the empire. For the Jews, identity questions were especially fraught, as the long-standing identification with German culture had not led to integration and acceptance. As the old roads seemed to be closing, the generation of Jews that came of age in the closing decades of the nineteenth century opened themselves to experimentation and innovation by necessity.

Even as they were pushed into the realm of cultural innovation by a climate with a specific hostility toward them, Jews found affinities with other intellectuals of this generation. They all shared a common crisis of identity and responded with a collective turn inward, a shift of attention toward individuality and subjectivity, which then took them in many different directions. The subjectivities into which individuals withdrew were understood as fundamentally unstable constructs. For Ernst Mach the self was "unsavable." For Freud, identity was illusory, and the self could be better understood in terms of successive, transitory, multiple, and even conflicting identifications. Hofmannsthal's famous *Chandos* letter, seemingly under the influence of Mach, sought to overcome the problem of a subjectivity reduced to a series of perceptions, allowing the deconstructed ego to reconstitute itself through mysticism. Throughout the works of Viennese modernism, such attempts at solving the identity crisis by reconstructing an individual identity were numerous, arduous, and frequently unsuccessful. For Jacques Le Rider, author of the excellent study *Modernity and Crises of Identity*, the indeterminacy of identity and responses to this crisis are the salient features of Viennese modernism. He writes:

What was most notable about the Viennese modernists was that before they made the crisis of identity into a theme for their works of theory, literature or art, they lived it, experienced it as a loss of identity of themselves as subject, followed by a reconstruction which was often precarious. To most of them the "modern condition" seemed the result of the fading and loss of traditions, the triumph of forces of disorganization and disintegration, putting every individual into a state of uncertainty and disorientation, which was hard to overcome.[50]

The Jewish experience of this crisis was the most acute. For Le Rider, the destabilization of Jewish identity that resulted from the failure of the assimilationist project is one of the central aspects of this broader Viennese cultural crisis. This crisis experience may have been common to the modernists—both Jews and non-Jews, as Le Rider suggests—and it may have been shared by all Jews coming of age in the closing decades of the nineteenth century, modernist and traditionalist alike. It was, however, not typically viewed as a universal crisis by those affected; rather, they experienced it on an individual level, as a personal crisis. According to Beller, "The result was now that they were no longer really Jews, but neither were they Germans or Austrians. They lacked a collective identity. The denial of the past, a precondition of assimilation, now produced not a group of people, but only a 'sum of individuals,' dependent solely on their own resources and their education, not their heritage."[51]

The literary work produced by the Jews involved with Viennese modernism may be understood in large measure as a response to these crises. Their varied responses reveal the richness of Jewish culture in Vienna at the turn of the last century. Some of the projects they undertook reveal an attempt to distance themselves from a personal struggle with the Jewish Question, as when Herzl collectivized identity problems in political and national terms or when Freud universalized problems of identity as fundamental to human development. Others adhered resolutely to an individual approach, whether or not they envisioned the possibility of reconstructing a stable identity. Richard Beer-Hofmann reaffirmed a relationship to Judaism and a Jewish identity in his work, while Arthur Schnitzler reflected critically on the relations between Jews and non-Jews and explored the detrimental effects of anti-Semitism in Viennese society. In their lives and in their work, the writers I examine in this chapter all represent different responses to what was known as "the Jewish Question." Taken together, they provide us with insights into the Jewish experience of Vienna around 1900.

Arthur Schnitzler

Of the numerous important turn-of-the-century writers, Arthur Schnitzler is widely held to be the best chronicler of Viennese society—Jewish and non-Jewish alike. In their 1977 study, Rolf-Peter Janz and Klaus Laermann identified Schnitzler as an insightful social commentator;[52] for Bruce Thompson, Schnitzler's works represent "the fullest exposition of Viennese society by any of the generation of writers living and writing in Vienna at the time."[53] More recently, Peter Gay employed Schnitzler's life as his point of entry into a broader discussion of the attitudes and behavior of the Austrian bourgeoisie.[54] Schnitzler's works are deservedly seen as vivid chronicles of bourgeois society. They are as deeply rooted in the culture of Jewish Vienna, as was the author himself, and they present this culture in all of its paradoxes and ironies. They also bring brilliantly to life the city in which he lived and worked and contain Schnitzler's pointed commentary on the social issues that dominated Viennese life during this period. In the following pages I reconstruct Schnitzler's Jewish Vienna through an examination of his literary engagements with the topic.

Schnitzler's unparalleled combination of vivid city writing and pointed social commentary come to the fore in his 1908 novel *Der Weg ins Freie* (*The Road to the Open*), a text that is both a *Großstadtroman* (novel of the metropolis) and Schnitzler's most extensive treatment of the Jewish Question. Set in Vienna, the novel is populated by Viennese characters and treats the Jewish Question in its particular Viennese manifestation. *Der Weg ins Freie* brings to light the unique character of Vienna's social and political landscape at the turn of the twentieth century. In Schnitzler's narrative anti-Semitism emerges as a potent political force with tangible effects beyond the political arena, yet hostility to Jews seems masked by the well-known Viennese charm and sociability, and social interaction between Jews and non-Jews continues uninterrupted in many circles.

The anti-Semitism portrayed in this novel is not only a political, social, or intellectual issue—it is a geographical issue, and Schnitzler's exploration of anti-Semitism therefore takes on a pronounced spatial character. He maps the city of Vienna according to the discourse of anti-Semitism. As the novel follows its protagonist, the aristocratic Georg von Wergenthin, through the city, it navigates through a number of specific locations that are more or less charged with the issue. While some streets, neighborhoods, and private spaces are frequented or inhabited by Jewish characters, bringing Georg into contact with Jews and the Jewish Question, Georg also continually seeks out other sites that provide a respite from such confrontations. As a member of the declining aristocracy, Georg von Wergenthin is both a privileged and somewhat marginal figure in Viennese society. His aristocratic title affords him access to several social worlds, that of the lower bourgeoisie, the predominantly Jewish upper bourgeoisie, and the aristocracy. His musical interests draw him to the city's cultural elite, which is also dominated by Jews. Yet Georg is adrift; he moves between these groups but belongs to none of them completely. His movements through the city are a reflection, perhaps even an unconscious expression, of his own ambivalence vis-à-vis Jews and anti-Semitism, as he alternately seeks the company of his Jewish friends and acquaintances and then withdraws from it.

At the sizeable Ehrenberg home on the Schwarzenberg Park, a prestigious address shared by the upper bourgeoisie and the nobility, Georg is a welcome guest among a crowd of predominantly wealthy, assimilated Jews. While the guests in the Ehrenberg salon are both young and old, this symbolic space belongs to the older, liberal, and assimilated generation, while the symbolic domain of its offspring, the young, post-assimilatory generation of educated-but-disoriented Jewish intellectuals, is the café.[55] Georg moves within the younger social circle in the cafés he frequents, on strolls through town and the picturesque outskirts of the city, in the cultural institutions of the first district, and at the summer retreats favored by the wealthy.[56] In the company of Jews, the subject of the treatment of Jews by Gentile society seems always close at hand. Georg has many conversations in the novel related to this issue, yielding moments of insight into the differences between his life and those of his Jewish friends. However there are other moments in which Georg exhibits impatience and even disdain for what he identifies as a Jewish preoccupation with the problems associated with being Jewish in Vienna. In the first chapter he reflects on this preoccupation:

> Georg smiled amiably. In reality, however, he was rather deflated. In his view there was absolutely no need for the old Doctor Staub to officially announce to him his affiliation to Jewry. He was well aware of it, and he didn't hold it against him. He didn't hold it against anyone; but why did they always bring it up themselves? Wherever he went, he only encountered Jews who were ashamed that they were Jews or those who were proud of it and were afraid one might think they were ashamed.[57]

In describing Georg as deflated (*enerviert*) by his acquaintance's reference to his Judaism, Schnitzler not only reveals the discrepancy between Georg's external and internal reactions to these comments, but also reflects the author's desire to explore the psychological effects of anti-Semitism on Jews and non-Jews alike. In his memoirs Schnitzler noted, "Yet it was not actually the political, not even so much the social, but primarily the psychological side of the Jewish Question that interested me according to my whole disposition."[58] In Schnitzler's fictive world, the rising power of anti-Semitism produces a widespread crisis of Jewish identity. He presents a panorama of responses to anti-Semitism, refusing a single or straightforward "road to the open." Various characters in the novel adopt distinct positions vis-à-vis the Jewish Question—Social Democracy, Zionism, exile, assimilationism, even vehement disavowal of any connection to Jewishness, suggestive of self-hatred. Each of Schnitzler's Jewish characters responds differently to the pressures of anti-Semitic hostility, and each bears the psychological effects of the struggle with discrimination and prejudice, ranging from cynicism to hypersensitivity, from aggression to resignation.

Schnitzler's crucial literary move, however, was to not limit his portrayal solely to the effects of anti-Semitism on Jewish Vienna. Rather, he traces the social and psychological effects throughout bourgeois society, detailing the effects of anti-

Semitism on non-Jews as well. The young Baron von Wergenthin, for example, may be far removed from any personal experience of discrimination or prejudice, yet he is very much affected by the tense atmosphere that has taken hold in the city as a result of the spread of anti-Semitism. While he spends most of his time in the company of Jewish intellectuals and the Jewish social elite, he often inwardly faults them for allowing the Jewish Question to poison the atmosphere, as he does above. At a later moment in the novel Georg suddenly finds this climate unbearable: "What did he have to do with these people? A kind of horror took hold of him, he turned away and resolved to finally seek out the club once again, whose rooms he hadn't entered for months."[59] Georg is horrified and feels a powerful pull to distance himself from this group and "their" problems. He briefly withdraws into his privileged class at the aristocratic social club favored by his brother, seeking the simplicity of being among his peers. For a time the club provides the respite he seems to need: "He felt more and more comfortable and resolved from now on to visit these airy and nicely appointed rooms more often, where pleasant, well-dressed young people gathered, with whom one could be well and easily entertained."[60] This respite proves short lived, however, as he is soon drawn back to the livelier and more open atmosphere of the cafés.

A similar escapist impulse follows one of Georg's most extensive discussions of anti-Semitism with his friend Heinrich Bermann. Georg is generally cautious during such exchanges, more observer than participant, but here he is alone with Bermann and they are both quite forthright in expressing their opinions. Georg sees Bermann as obsessed with his perceptions of hostility toward the Jews and suggests he is suffering from a persecution complex. Bermann's response is vehement:

> What you choose to call a persecution complex, dear Georg, is in reality nothing other than a continuously alert, very intensive awareness of a condition in which we Jews find ourselves. And much more than a persecution complex, one could speak of a security complex, of being left alone, of a safety complex which is perhaps less noticeable, but for the afflicted represents a far more dangerous form of illness[61]

Following this defense of Bermann's sensitivity on this issue, Bermann and Georg seem to reach some measure of consensus. They both reject Zionism, casting the movement as a "quite external solution to a highly internal matter."[62] Georg also seems to support Bermann's rejection of any collective solutions in favor of solitary "journeys into the open" as a better means by which to find a way out of the anger, doubt, and disgust engendered by anti-Semitism. Soon thereafter, however, Georg is again struck not by his affinity to Bermann and his circle, but by his emotional distance from them and the differences between them: "They often make one nervous, these overly clever, pitiless, Jewish connoisseurs of human nature, these Bermanns and Nürnbergers."[63] Once again, Georg longs for the simplicity of being with his brother and peers, where common race and class background obviate the need for such difficult discussions. Although Georg bristles when Bermann suggests that a racial divide separates them, in his private thoughts Georg tacitly recognizes, and at times even desires, this divide. In the midst of an escalating debate on Jews and politics at the Ehrenberg salon Georg exchanges a glance with Demeter Stanzides, a Habsburg officer and fellow aristocrat, "like two friends thrown together on an island."[64] The geographical metaphor here is important: even when he cannot physically remove himself from contact with the troubling issues that infuse the streets and houses of Vienna, he imagines himself as inhabiting a world apart.

The aristocratic social club is one of several sites in which Georg seeks to escape from the Jewish Question. When Georg seeks such a refuge he repeatedly makes a spatial retreat to localities where he is far less likely to come in contact with Jews or Jewish problems. He is drawn to Anna Rosner and her family's middle-class home in the Wieden suburb perhaps as much for the simplicity of a relationship unburdened by ethnic difference as by Anna's attractive personal qualities. From the start, Georg pursues their relationship as a private and essentially self-enclosed social unit, separate from all other aspects of his life. Anna never meets his brother and only rarely sees his friends or their common acquaintances. They meet in private rooms or withdraw into the music room of her family home, away from her parents and brother. Georg feels closest to her when they travel together outside Vienna. When Anna becomes pregnant the couple embarks on a trip to Italy and then retreats to the suburbs, not only because bourgeois social codes dictate that an unmarried pregnant woman should withdraw from society until the baby is born, but because such a withdrawal suits Georg's mood and temperament as well. Georg's visits to Anna out in the rented house at the edge of Salmansdorf are undertaken on foot or by bicycle, and Georg spends much time on solitary walks through the woods and hills near the house. The isolation of the place provides him a needed contrast to the city: "Only after he had passed beyond the lively streets did he come to feel at peace with himself."[65]

Georg and Anna often discuss music and occasionally speak in vague terms about the future; they pointedly do not speak of anti-Semitism or the relations between Jews and Gentiles. Like the company at the club, Anna offers Georg freedom from such concerns. Whereas Schnitzler frequently employs language related to illness and nervousness to describe the effects that encounters with Jews have on Georg, the relationship with Anna can for the most part be characterized as unburdened and peaceful. (The son they have together eventually dies, at which point this is less the case.) After the intense exchange with Bermann mentioned above, Georg positively flees towards Anna, trying to shake the feeling of discomfort that stemmed from the discussion. Schnitzler depicts Georg's arrival at the apartment he has rented for his rendezvous with Anna as the threshold to another world:

> And once again, as ever, when he had climbed the steps of the old palace turned rental house and entered the spacious, low-ceilinged rooms, Georg felt as though he had

escaped his familiar world, as though he had entered into other aspects of a wondrous double existence.[66]

Just as Georg seeks in Anna a foil for his own tendency toward frivolity and lack of discipline, he looks to her to provide an uncomplicated contrast to his other relationships. Not surprisingly, this attempt is ultimately unsuccessful, as Anna does not function purely as a screen for Georg's projections. He does find temporary refuge in his private world with Anna, but his wish to escape is incompatible with his nagging sense that he ought to, at long last, grow up and take a more serious course in life. The island on which he longs to live simply cannot be found in the city in which he actually resides. Georg's inability to maintain these separate spheres is a significant element of Schnitzler's commentary on the psychological effects of anti-Semitism in Viennese society, from which, in the author's view, there was no escape.

Schnitzler's spatial considerations in this novel are not limited to the different social and cultural codes he assigns to each locality within the city. The novel also reflects on the city of Vienna as a whole by having a number of characters move in and out of the city and bring to bear the perspectives gained from their travels on their own views of Vienna. Without exception, Georg's darker moods and experiences of anxiety occur within or near the city center, in the coffeehouses, the private homes of his social circle, on the street, or, for example, in a *chambre separé* (private room) of a restaurant in the first district, where he ponders the pointlessness of his existence. In the wake of such feelings Georg seems to crave distance from Vienna, as he is often far removed in his thoughts, indulging in travel fantasies or dwelling in memories of travel as a child or his thoughts about a former lover. When he and Anna are alone together in Italy for three months during her pregnancy, he relishes this time with her and enjoys being in unfamiliar surroundings: "Oh, how liberating and cleansing it is to be detached from one's familiar surroundings!"[67] Indeed, while their relationship is crumbling after their baby's death, Georg implores Anna to go away with him, certain that they can salvage their relationship if they could only go away together once again. He seems to lay blame for the end of the affair on the familiar surroundings in which it had played out and repeatedly imagines how it might have been different elsewhere. "Not in this room, not in this city; but best of all in another place, with which neither of them were familiar, in new and foreign surroundings."[68] In what has by now become a familiar pattern, Georg imagines that physical distance from the space in which he lives, works, and travels is the only way to distance himself from the problems of his everyday life. His psychological concerns are strongly linked to geography.

Georg's musical compositions have a similarly pronounced geographical component. He cherishes memories of melodies that seemingly rise out of the waves on the Italian coast, and he fantasizes about at last getting down to serious work in some exotic locale. Music, like anti-Semitism and romantic problems, seems to emanate directly out of the geography. As Anna's due date approaches, he relishes the idea of dedicating himself to his work in the peaceful setting of her suburban retreat. Georg's friends seem to share his notion that he might be capable of better work outside Vienna. Willi Eisler urges him to accept a conducting post in Detmold, claiming that the Viennese would forever consider him a mere dilettante without the authenticating stamp of approval from "the Reich." Frau Ehrenberg laments that the Viennese air seems to have a paralyzing effect on the city's artists, citing Georg, Bermann, and Nürnberger as those whose potentials so far exceed their output—exemplars of this common crisis of artistic creation. At the end of the novel Georg is poised to leave the city, and while it remains unclear whether his transition to maturity and serious work will continue to be endlessly deferred, it is clear that he seeks to bolster his resolve by equating his leave-taking from Vienna with a farewell to the way of life that has characterized his youth.

If Georg's personal identity crisis remains unresolved at the end of the novel, this is even more true of the Viennese crisis produced by anti-Semitism as portrayed here. As Jacques Le Rider has argued, "The novel has no 'message' unless it be the awareness of the contradictions and insufficiencies of all these reactions by assimilated Jews to anti-Semitism."[69] Clearly Schnitzler rejects the collective solutions that are espoused by the Zionists, the Social Democrats, and the strict assimilationists; however the novel goes beyond simply revealing the insufficiencies of these collective responses. In denying Bermann and, significantly, Georg, a clear "road to the open," Schnitzler casts doubt on even the possibility of an individual solution to the identity crises created or exacerbated by anti-Semitism. The only respite from the problems that plague Schnitzler's Vienna seems to exist on an imaginary island, removed from the characters' everyday surroundings.

A crisis of masculine values, which is identified by Jacques Le Rider as the defining characteristic of the Viennese *fin de siècle*, also occupies a significant position in both of Schnitzler's literary treatments of the Jewish Question. If in *Der Weg ins Freie* Schnitzler seeks to portray the paralyzing effects of anti-Semitism on a new generation of Jewish intellectuals and their Gentile counterparts, one could say that his drama *Professor Bernhardi* brings together the Jewish and masculine identity crises even more directly. In what Felix Salten termed Schnitzler's "*Männerstuck*" (men's play),[70] Schnitzler places Jewish masculinity under the pressure of a direct confrontation with anti-Semitism in the public sphere. In this work Schnitzler addresses a number of contemporary challenges to Jewish masculinity and, in my view, suggests a possible alternative form of Jewish masculinity in the figure of Bernhardi. Strikingly, although perhaps not surprisingly, this model of Jewish masculinity draws on the experiences of Schnitzler's father. While the characters of *Der Weg ins Freie* negotiate recognizable Viennese terrain, *Professor Bernhardi* goes a step further in making its characters deal with recognizable historical events.

A number of contemporary reviews of the play viewed it as a *Schlüsselstück*. Equations of Bernhardi with Schnitzler's father, the well-known throat specialist Johann Schnitzler, were made in a number of press reports, most famously in the review by Danish critic Georg Brandes.[71] Despite all of the controversy surrounding the censor's ban on producing *Professor Bernhardi* on any Austrian stage and the frequent anti-Semitic attacks levied against the author, it is noteworthy that Schnitzler's most vigorous defense of his work actually concerned the claim that the play was based on his father. In a letter to Brandes, Schnitzler did acknowledge certain similarities between his father's life and the central plot of the play, explaining how his father had been one of the founders of a private medical clinic, how he had guided it to a preeminent position within the Viennese medical community, and how late in his life his father had vigorously defended the clinic against attacks motivated by anti-Semitism and professional jealousy. More forcefully, however, took pains to emphasize to Brandes that his protagonist was his own creation.[72] Schnitzler later claimed that similar events in his father's life played no role in his conception of the work and even suggested that he had forgotten about them at the time of the novel's writing. Yet in *Jugend in Wien* Schnitzler devotes several pages to an account of these events and their significance in his father's life, and he appears to be quite sensitive to the extent to which the episode pained his father. By allegedly "forgetting" this period in his father's life, Arthur Schnitzler appears to have been uneasy about the role his father played in his conception of the work and perhaps with the broader themes discussed in it.

As I mentioned above, Felix Salten considered *Bernhardi* to be Schnitzler's *Männerstuck,* and, indeed, with the play's nearly exclusively male cast of characters, *Bernhardi* presents itself as a forum for Schnitzler's reflections on masculinity. Johann Schnitzler plays a crucial role in his son's conceptions of masculinity and, as we see in the figure of Bernhardi, of Jewish male identity in particular. Schnitzler's diaries and memoirs reflect his father's far-reaching influence on his development into manhood, on his personal as well as professional choices. In the Schnitzler household medicine was the locus of male professional identity, and, as we know, Schnitzler followed his well-known father (as well as his grandfather and brother) into a medical career, largely in response to his father's wishes. In both personal and professional terms Schnitzler came to a conception of masculinity largely through relating to—and reacting against—his father.

The image of the father as a figure that one simultaneously identifies with and revolts against looms large in the culture of this era. As Mark Anderson elegantly demonstrated, the young Franz Kafka arrived at his cognizance of the social world by absorbing the commercial exchanges in his father's fancy-goods shop.[73] From the *Vaterkomplexe* of Daniel Paul Schreber and Otto Gross to Freud's elaboration of the Oedipal complex and to the aesthetic revolt against tradition by writers of the *Jung Wien* circle, the father-son relationship was a central battlefield for competing models of masculinity at the turn of the twentieth century.

For many young Viennese Jewish men in 1900, the father-son relationship was particularly fraught with the particular circumstances of the immigrant generation and its children, as their fathers' lives had been shaped by a different geography, a different set of economic conditions, political beliefs, and relationship to religious tradition. Attempting to understand Freud's own apparently intense and sustained Oedipal conflicts, Yosef Yerushalmi has suggested that "the relationship seems to follow an archetype of the relations between immigrant Jewish fathers and their talented sons. All such sons have been, in a sense, father-slayers."[74] As Daniel Boyarin has deftly shown, the well-known incident related by Freud in which he laments his father's passive response to having his fur cap knocked off his head in public by an anti-Semitic thug figured for Freud not only as an illustration of his father's emasculation, but specifically as a Jewish failure on his father's part.[75] For Jewish men of Freud and Schnitzler's world, generational conflict and gender issues often intersected in these complicated ways.

Another Jewish physician, Max Nordau, well aware of the arguments being made from within the medical community about a supposed inferiority of the Jew's body, sought to literally reshape Jewish male bodies in the creation of the "new muscle Jew." Through sport Nordau aimed at the reformation of both the body and the mind to overcome the degenerative effects of years of ghetto life. Theodor Herzl's Zionist project may also be seen in this light, constructed in part as a means to reform and thus redeem Jewish masculinity. In his diaries Herzl decried the limpness of assimilated Western Jewry as well-behaved, timid ghetto creatures.[76] Zionism would address these perceived shortcomings: Herzl drew on symbols of virility in marketing the appeal of Zionism—his own image as a strong and heroic leader was featured in much of the movement's propaganda—and he envisioned a vanguard of young, muscular Jews to build up the new homeland. Notably, both Nordau's and Herzl's responses to the problems of Jewish masculinity involved distancing oneself from the debilitating effects of the city. Their "roads to freedom" differed significantly from those deliberated by Georg von Wergenthin, but they corresponded closely in the insistence that geography was both the problem and the solution, that who you are is a direct reflection of where you are.

These men sought to counter the negative images of Jewish maleness projected by bourgeois society yet refrained from rejecting outright the social norms from which they were excluded; rather, they accepted these norms of manliness and explored new ways of proving their conformity to them. At the turn of the twentieth century tremendous pressure was brought to bear on Jewish masculinity, and those variously engaged in a struggle to articulate a positive Jewish male identity came into conflict not only with negative images of the outsider, but also with accepted notions of masculinity from within the Jewish community. Thus the Jewish male's search for respectability in the new century involved both generational conflict and struggles against the dominant bourgeois characterizations of Jews.

Arthur Schnitzler was well aware of this discourse and was similarly implicated in it. In *Professor Bernhardi* he offered his most direct response to the question of Jewish masculine conduct, creating in the figure of Bernhardi a possible alternative form of Jewish masculinity, one that differs significantly from the responses of Freud, Nordau, or Herzl. Schnitzler chose the medical world, the world inhabited and (for Schnitzler) indelibly marked by his famous father, as the setting for this engagement with the theme of Jewish masculinity. Johann Schnitzler, from within the world of the Viennese medical community, embodied for his son the representative man, physician, and Jew, both as model and foil. As I mentioned above, during the years in which Schnitzler was working on his drama, the Jewish male physician was an object of intense public scrutiny. The level of success achieved by a large number of Jewish doctors in Vienna made them a notable presence to those within and beyond the medical community. Recall that it was the openness of Vienna toward Jews who sought to study and practice a profession such as medicine that originally attracted them to the city and enabled them to rise to such prominence. Once they had achieved it, however, anti-Semitism penetrated the institutions of the medical community, making the position of the Jewish doctor a contested one. Medicine thus offered Schnitzler an arena for examining the interaction of social, political, professional, and legal pressures brought to bear on the Jewish man at the turn of the century. Once again, he took a universal problem—the crisis of Jewish masculinity—and tied it to a concrete community with recognizable historical and geographical references. For Schnitzler, universal issues were always, first and foremost, local issues.

In *Professor Bernhardi* Schnitzler constructs debates similar to those experienced by his father at the peak of his career. Like Johann Schnitzler, Bernhardi undergoes a professional crisis in which anti-Semitism is mobilized as a powerful political tool that exerts pressure on his professional role as a Jewish male physician. From the opening scene, the parallels are clear. The play is set in a private clinic, much like the one founded by Schnitzler's father. After an initial struggle against considerable opposition at its founding, the clinic reaches a high level of success, both as a private practice and as a teaching institution. Schnitzler points at once to the splintering of clinic personnel into discernible factions and makes clear that these political camps diverge along confessional lines. Relations between Jews and Gentiles within the clinic form an important subtext for all issues that emerge in the clinic, from the diagnosis of individual cases to personnel decisions and financial issues. The central conflict of the play stems from a medical case in which Bernhardi blocks a priest from visiting the deathbed of a young girl who is dying from a severe infection that resulted from an illegal abortion performed elsewhere. Although close to death, the girl is euphoric as the result of her medications and believes herself to be fully recovered. Bernhardi wishes to shield her from the harsh realization of her imminent death by preventing the priest's arrival to administer the last rites.

The incident rapidly escalates, splitting the clinic's personnel, and then turns into a full-blown scandal involving the board of directors, the Ministry of Education, and ultimately the Parliament. As the situation intensifies, Bernhardi attempts to maintain an ironic detachment. When he is warned that the board of trustees is likely to resign, he remains skeptical, stating, "And all of this is supposed to have happened because I fulfilled my duties as a doctor."[77] While he continually downplays the gravity of the situation, Bernhardi is willing to take steps to defuse the situation for the good of the clinic. He explains, "I certainly have no desire at all to play the hero at any cost. I have demonstrated countless times that in the case of emergencies I am the man to take the actions I deem necessary."[78] The debate over the proper course of action is thus framed as a kind of test of virility in which heroism is equated with the demonstration of strong will and refusal to compromise. Bernhardi can imagine forsaking the role of hero only because he has already proven his virility in fighting for the establishment of the clinic.

Bernhardi's initial response to the affair that has crystallized around him is thus a moderate one. Like Johann Schnitzler, his actions are motivated by a sense of professionalism in which the interests of the clinic and his obligations to his patient are paramount. He believes he has acted correctly in barring the priest from the girl's bedside, yet he is not intractable when he determines the clinic might be harmed by his actions. As the issue becomes complicated by a number of competing hidden agendas, Bernhardi becomes less flexible in his response. When Bernhardi balks at being manipulated by his chief opponent, Ebenwald, in an internal personnel matter, an investigation into his conduct with the priest is quickly launched in Parliament. The clinic's board of trustees resigns, a move that represents an immediate political and material threat to the clinic. Under this pressure, submerged tensions and suppressed hostilities erupt, and the Bernhardi affair becomes a referendum on anti-Semitism.

Schnitzler constructs the position adopted by each of Bernhardi's colleagues as evidence as to the kind of man each of them is. The form of engagement of each man in the evolving affair also serves to further illuminate Bernhardi's conduct, as his character—which remains difficult to pin down throughout the drama—becomes more distinct in contrast with the other men around him. In the opposing camp, there is the recent convert, Dr. Schreimann, whose exaggerated Austrian dialect and prominent *Schmiss* (dueling scar) on his cheek signal his desire for total assimilation. Schreimann maneuvers against Bernhardi because he desperately wants the powerful Gentile Ebenwald's approval. Dr. Filitz is the fool of the work, for whom the most urgent aspect of the case is the fact that his wife was not received by a baroness slated to be the patroness of the clinic's ball. Ebenwald is a far more formidable opponent, well connected and politically skilled, and therefore able to exploit the situation to his own benefit. Throughout the affair his actions are aimed at consolidating his own power within the clinic. Bernhardi confronts

Ebenwald as an anti-Semite and pawn of his cousin's conservative political party, and he condemns Ebenwald's backroom political maneuvers. In so doing Bernhardi at last comes to recognize the political and personal aspects of the affair. He takes a firm stand against a politically expedient response, which he deems to be harmful to the interests of the clinic. As he tears up a letter of apology he had begun, Bernhardi appears determined to prove once again that he is a man of strong will. As the affair escalates, however, this firm refusal to be manipulated is undermined by his failure to fully grasp the political implications of the case.

Just as the character of Bernhardi is contrasted with his opponents, he is also presented as diverging sharply in character from his most avid supporters. Dr. Löwenstein is among the most partisan of the physicians, who views the opposition strictly as anti-Semites spreading a smear campaign. His bitterness obscures his view of the issue, and Bernhardi admonishes him repeatedly for his rashness. He follows none of Löwenstein's suggestions and several times does the opposite of what he proposes. With the exception of Cyprian, the other physicians do not consider the matter to be an issue of medical ethics. Instead, all focus is placed on the political ramifications of Bernhardi's actions. Bernhardi's conduct is shown to be of a different order, as he alone frames the matter in terms of professional responsibility, first to his patient and later to the clinic. Although his supporters chastise him for failing to comprehend the nature of the campaign against him, he sees himself as uniquely focused on the appropriate issue.

The drama escalates, shifting terrain from a professional to a personal realm, as Bernhardi is removed from his position, the board of directors resigns, and a parliamentary inquiry brings the immediate threat of a prison sentence. Indeed, during the parliamentary hearing Bernhardi is charged with religious obstruction and sentenced to two months in prison. He comes to see that the case has been handled purely as a political affair and believes that he has been delivered up by his opponents within the clinic and the ministry. Seeing no possibility of justice, he refuses to appeal the decision: "The trial today was a farce. I shall never again associate with these people and their like."[79] He has no interest in receiving a pardon or a reversal of the ruling, as each of these resolutions would stem from within a system he now views as corrupt. As we saw emphasized in *Der Weg ins Freie,* the only tenable response to the main problem is to remove oneself from it physically. Bernhardi is briefly interested in making his own views of the case public. While in prison he begins to draft an essay explaining the professional motivations behind his actions and exposing the base political motivations of his opponents. In the end, however, he retreats into passivity, making no statements on his own behalf and remaining silent in response to the efforts of his supporters. He does not take advantage of the political tide beginning to shift in his favor, rejecting the possibility of emerging from the affair as a political hero. Ebenwald is installed as the clinic's director, while Bernhardi serves out the prison term and suffers the suspension of his license to practice medicine.

Bernhardi's conduct is certainly less than satisfying, yet in the end he remains an autonomous, rational man of will, who defines his actions—and lack of action—by his own terms, enacting a personal code of ethics that enables him to live with himself in the absence of public validation. He seems to have found the island that Wergenthin and so many of Schnitzler's other characters perpetually search for. It comes at the expense of his professional identity and leaving the institution to which he had devoted so much of his life—and, for a period, it takes the form of a prison cell. It is not an easy choice, but it appears to be the only choice.

In many respects, Bernhardi's passivity in the face of the political battle waged against him is similar to the positions adopted by Johann Schnitzler in the controversies in which he was involved. Both Bernhardi and Johann Schnitzler avoided openly acknowledging the anti-Semitic motivations in the issues surrounding their clinics. It is with a mixture of strength and stubbornness that they rejected the political parts they were asked to play. Their behavior was chiefly driven by a commitment to their professional responsibilities as physicians. Bernhardi's conduct is based at first on his sense of the patient's best interest, later by the desire to protect the interests of his clinic, and finally, when the issue has narrowed to his own fate, he steadfastly maintains that the issue is purely professional, rather than political or personal. The public identities of both Johann Schnitzler and Bernhardi rest on their understanding of what constitutes appropriate conduct for a physician. For both, appropriate behavior did not include engaging in a political struggle that would take the focus away from their professional identifications and place it on their personal religious or ethnic identities. Clearly there was a price to be paid for this insistence on self-definition as a Jew in this climate, yet in his drama, Arthur Schnitzler holds open the possibility of that self-definition; although he must deal with the consequences, Bernhardi ultimately insists that his case is not a referendum on the Jewish Question.

In *fin de siècle* Vienna, the cultural stakes were high. Schnitzler portrays the good Jewish doctor, who chooses not to fight the good fight, in juxtaposition to the educated, successful, and assimilated Jewish physician, who is not immune to the negative stereotypes surrounding Jewish men. Schnitzler's mirroring in the play of the professional issues his father faced during his career is not only a gesture of redeeming his father's noncombative professionalism, it is a broader move toward redeeming a masculinity that does not conform to the codes of manly behavior prescribed by the non-Jewish bourgeois society. Schnitzler replaces the dominant masculine paradigm equating manliness with aggression and conquest with a different model of honor and valor based on a personal code of professional ethics. In the center of this drama of Jewish masculinity stands a passive Jew, whose conduct presents an image to the world and mirrors the anti-Semitic discourse of the nineteenth century that equated Jewish men with femininity and passivity. While the passivity of Schnitzler's Jewish doctor is undeniable, it does not bring about the prescribed feminization. Bernhardi chooses his own course of action, presenting to the world an image of his own making, and emerges with his masculinity intact. His conduct denies the public sphere any jurisdiction in determining appropriate modes of male behavior, asserting instead a private notion of manliness and honor untouched by political concerns and social prejudices. Schnitzler does not seek to obscure the professor's passivity but rather reconfigures it so that it does not represent a negative trait. *Professor Bernhardi* may thus be seen as a story of successful Jewish male self-fashioning in the face of considerable pressures from mainstream Gentile models of masculinity.

Arthur Schnitzler lived in a turbulent and conflicted time and place for Jews, and he sought to understand and work through the crises that he and others faced by producing literary works that were clearly situated in that very period. Schnitzler's works bring vividly to life the world of assimilated Viennese Jewry at a time when anti-Semitism had penetrated it and had produced visible effects across the political, social, and cultural spheres. Schnitzler's response to the identity crisis acutely experienced by Jews was to confront the "Jewish Problem" directly in two significant works, exploring the full range of responses by Jews, as well as to turn his critical gaze to the other preoccupations of the bourgeoisie, bringing into focus the inconsistencies and hypocrisies underlying the social norms and moral codes that governed the social world in which he lived. His works carefully avoid providing easy solutions to these problems and instead depict the world in all of its complexity and contradictions. What is especially noteworthy about Schnitzler's writing is that while it directly engages difficult and universal issues of identity (be it gender, class, professional, ethnic, or religious identity), he always grounds these issues in a specific time and a particular place. The paths that his characters take through their lives are always closely bound with the paths they take through the physical spaces they inhabit. The problems they confront seem to be located in that famous "*Wiener Luft*" that blows through the city Schnitzler both loved and lamented. It is the streets, cafés, and homes that make up the city just as much as the people who travel the streets, frequent the cafés, and live in the city's homes. The problems that Schnitzler confronts in his works are tied up in the very geography of the city. And for the solution to these problems, one needs only consider the similarity of the titles of so many of his works: *The Lonely Way* (1903), *The Road to the Open* (1908), *The Vast Domain* (1911), and *Flight into Darkness* (1931).

Adolf Dessauer

Two years after the publication of Schnitzler's *Der Weg ins Freie*, a novel with the title *Großstadtjuden* (*Metropolitan Jews*) appeared in the realm of popular literature.[80] Like Schnitzler's novel, this work features a panorama of Viennese Jewry, presenting more stereotypical Jewish types than highly developed characters, yet nonetheless depicting a wide array of responses to the pressures on Jewish identity at the turn of the twentieth century. The novel was written by Adolf Dessauer, an Austrian banker and a writer of Jewish descent. Unlike Schnitzler's novel, which pointedly avoided proposing any solution to the Jewish Question, Dessauer's book concludes on a note of extreme optimism, and the whole work is conceived as a programmatic endorsement of mixed marriages between Jews and Christians as a means of achieving reconciliation between the two groups.

Adolf Dessauer was born in 1849, which places him in the generation of Karl Emil Franzos and Fritz Mauthner. Accordingly, the values that shape this work are those of the bourgeois Liberal *Gründerzeit* generation. Dessauer addresses a number of the central issues facing Viennese Jews at the time, but his approach to these problems is informed by a persistent faith in the assimilationist project, even in the face of new pressures, rather than a consideration of any of the new, more radical collective solutions to the Jewish Question that emerged at the end of the nineteenth century.

The novel presents a broad spectrum of Jewish responses to anti-Semitism and the obstacles to the full integration of Jews into Viennese society. Each Jewish character is a recognizable type, reflecting a particular attitude toward their Jewish background commonly held by Jews at the time. Within just two families—the bourgeois Kastner family and the wealthy Jordan family—Dessauer presents nearly all of the typical approaches taken by Jews, with the significant exception of Zionism, the absence of which is explicable perhaps because the movement, in spite of its Viennese roots, failed to gain a foothold within Vienna's middle-class Jewish community.

When the book begins, the Kastners of Leopoldstadt, proprietors of a bookstore, have recently changed their name from Kohn, largely to appease their son, Leopold, who was deeply troubled by this unmistakable marker of Jewish identity. Leopold is the embodiment of the self-hating Jew, who over-assimilates to the point of adopting anti-Semitic views and imitating the Gentile Viennese even avoiding working too diligently, "as all that was clever, diligent, or zealous in business he stubbornly considered to be Jewish, and he wanted to avoid being Jewish at all costs."[81] Leopold is reminiscent of Schnitzler's Oskar Ehrenberg, as he goes to great lengths in his attempt at "passing" and tries everything "to be as jaunty, Christian, and Viennese as possible."[82] Having incorporated the stereotypes surrounding the Jews' relationship to language, by which *mauscheln* (speaking unclearly in Yiddish) was cast as an outward expression of the inherent negative qualities of the Jew, Leopold attempts to erase any signs from his speech that could identify him as a Jew, first taking on the Viennese dialect of the lower bourgeoisie and then, in a single day, switching to an imitation of the aristocracy as a result of an encounter with a baroness.[83] In a similar vein, two young women from Prague related to the Kastner family try to take on the particular Hernals dialect of a *Vorstadtmädchen* (woman from the Viennese suburbs) whom they know, a baker's daughter who becomes their model of the ideal young Viennese woman and whose appearance and mannerisms they immediately seek to emulate.

Leopold's sister, in contrast, is proud of her Jewish heritage and, rather than feeling embarrassed by her family as her brother does, is a devoted daughter who works enthusiastically to support the family business. Frau Kastner is the good Jewish housewife for whom family is paramount and who hopes to see her children marry within the Jewish community. Herr Kastner shares his wife's devotion to family and plays host to regular gatherings of relatives from far and wide.

Among these relatives, still other Jewish types are represented. A sister-in-law born in Vienna feels superior to her husband's family, which immigrated from Trebitsch. As an *"echte Wienerin"* (real Viennese woman)—and in spite of her Jewish background—she likes to feign ignorance of Jewish ways. The novel reflects a clear social hierarchy operating within the Viennese Jewish community, which places the *Eingeborene* (natives) at the pinnacle. Frau Kastner, for example, is enamored of the old Jewish families, *"die Tolerierten"* (the tolerated), who have lived in the city since before the emancipation, and sees them as a kind of Jewish aristocracy. She views these Jews as better educated than other Jews or Christians, as arbiters of taste and those who enjoy the best relations with Christians, and as dignified, even if their fortunes have diminished over time. She wants nothing more than for her son to marry into this milieu, to find himself "a genteel Jewish housewife in the style of bygone days!"[84] In *Die Welt von Gestern,* Stefan Zweig recalls this concern with nuances of social position with a mixture of amusement and irritation:

> We were always being told who were "fine" people and who were not "fine"; every one of our friends was researched as to whether he was from a "good" family, and the origin and fortune of every last relative was scrutinized. This constant classifying, which was the real subject of every familial and business discussion, seemed to us at the time highly ludicrous and snobbish, because in the end it could only be a matter of fifty or a hundred years difference that they emerged a little earlier out of the same Jewish ghetto.[85]

Dessauer satirizes this preoccupation with status in a scene at a large party hosted by the Jordan family, at which the guests are consumed with speculation over who among them will next be ennobled, and conversation revolves around the going rate to purchase an aristocratic title. There is a further depiction of this obsession with status, doubly coded as bourgeois and Jewish in the novel, in the figure of the father of the family from Prague, who made his fortune in timber and wants nothing more than to be seen as an aristocrat. He thus has given himself over completely to what he sees as the central pursuits of the nobility—hunting, gambling, and womanizing. Not only are his aristocratic aspirations unrealizable, as a Jew his acceptance among what Felix Salten termed the *Sport- und Automobilgrafen* (sports and automobile gentry) can only be partial.[86]

The industrialist Jordan presides over a household in which family members have become estranged from each other and in which each member is pursuing a path that sharply diverges from, and conflicts with, those of the others. The father Jordan is a self-made man whose enterprise now leaves no aspect of the Austrian economy untouched. He is proud of his Jewish heritage, and while he is distanced from Jewish tradition, he appears to be comfortable with a Jewish identity. His wife and one of his daughters, however, want the family to convert, in keeping with the daughter's ambition to marry the son of the baroness. Jordan's son has eschewed a role in the family business and instead is pursuing an unlikely career within the civil service, in which he attempts to build his reputation by making speeches against the kind of cartels his father has created. A second daughter has become a committed Socialist. These relationships highlight a central theme in the novel—the intensification of generational conflicts brought about by the increased pressures on Jewish identity at the turn of the twentieth century.

In another parallel to Schnitzler's novel, Dessauer creates a non-Jewish character to explore and comment on the Jewish society described above. Arthur Schmeidler, a salesman who also lives in Leopoldstadt, is a friend to the Kastner family and a self-avowed *Judenfreund* (friend to the Jews) in general. He differs from Schnitzler's Georg von Wergenthin in that his relationships with these Jewish acquaintances seem altogether unburdened. Schmeidler seems less personally affected by the prevailing anti-Semitic climate than Georg and more committed to combating it. In response to the suggestion that he is more kindly disposed toward the Jews than they are to themselves, he replies, "Actually that would only be natural, because I chose my role as friend to the Jews myself, but the Jews' role is handed to them by fate."[87]

Schmeidler marries the Kastner's daughter, Lotti, in a love match that is contrasted with two other marriages in the novel that are motivated wholly by self-interest—for financial gain or to boost social status. The view of marriage as a financial arrangement recalls the joke from the Viennese cabaret, "Hundert Stück Südbahn heiraten hundert Stück Nordbahn" (A Hundred Shares of the Southern Railway Marries a Hundred Shares of the Northern Railway).[88] Jewish-Gentile relations cannot be improved through such purely strategic alliances. By contrast, the novel holds up the marriage between Schmeidler and Lotti as a promising path to the future: "And what a gain as the crowning to all of this, if the whole city would fill with Christian-Jewish couples like us. That would really offer a cheery look into the future!"[89] As it approaches its conclusion, the novel gives itself over to promotion of the *Mischehe* (mixed marriages) based on love and mutual respect as a solution to the problems affecting Jewish-Gentile relations. The young couple launches an ambitious campaign to improve these relations, creating an extended salon bringing Christians and Jews together in personal contact as a means of bridging the gulf between them. These "Schmeidler evenings" enjoy a short-lived success, but attendance wanes after a time, and according to a friend of the couple, they simply fall out of fashion.

This notion of the vogue of a particular attitude of Gentile society toward the Jews is, rather oddly, Dessauer's last word on the subject within this work. Reflecting on the failed undertaking, Lotti remarks:

> I don't believe in the alleged hatred and hostility of a real Viennese. They are like butter to him, that melts at the first ray of sun. Why try to persuade and convert him? That seems to me not at all necessary. Viennese anti-Semitism, as I see it now, is a fashion, a mood, a joke. But fashions change, moods alter, and even the most successful joke loses its effect when one has heard it too often. ... Oh, you'll see, how it will happen: one morning Vienna will wake up and nobody is anti-Semitic anymore.[90]

The sweeping aside of the problem as one that will disappear of its own accord seems unmotivated for this character so committed to improving relations between Jews and Christians and surprising in a novel of nearly five hundred pages devoted to the issue. This trivializing gesture of the novel's conclusion is of course a radical miscalculation of the problem of anti-Semitism. Given the effectiveness of Dessauer's satire of prejudice and blindness on the part of both Jews and Christians, it is perhaps best understood as wishful thinking on the part of the author, a reflection of the need of those of Dessauer's generation to continue to believe in the assimilationist project and in the frivolity of Viennese anti-Semitism. Dessauer was in his sixties when he wrote this work. While the character of Schmeidler may function as his mouthpiece on the subject of mixed marriages, the author's own personal views may come closest to the aging Jordan, who laments that the younger generation of Jews has eyes only for the faults of their parents and is blind to any of their positive qualities. Dessauer, too, seems to call on his readers to turn a more forgiving eye to the faults of Jews and Gentiles alike. The liberal optimism underscoring such a view is rather poignant precisely in its quixotic frailty.

Felix Salten

Like Theodor Herzl, Felix Salten was an assimilated Viennese Jew born in Budapest. Salten was born on 6 September 1869, as Siegmund Salzmann. His father, Philipp Salzmann, was the first man in his family to abandon a three-hundred-year-old rabbinical tradition, opting instead for a career as an engineer. In many respects Salten's father's biography is representative of Jewish men of his generation, not only in his progression away from Jewish tradition and increasing orientation toward non-Jewish, secular bourgeois values, but in his westward migration to seek professional and social advancement. Philipp Salzmann's initial move was from the northeastern Hungarian town of Miskolc to the rapidly growing, middle class–oriented Jewish community in Budapest. There he married and established a large family, but Budapest was only a way station for the Salzmann family. Just two years after Jewish emancipation, and directly following the birth of Siegmund, their seventh child, the family left Budapest for Vienna. Philipp Salzmann oriented his life around the emancipatory hopes of his generation, staking his life, family, and career on a metropolitan existence in the imperial capital; unfortunately, he also experienced the vulnerability of the immigrant existence, the other side of the coin to the many stories of professional success and social advancement of Jews from the provinces in the city. In Vienna Salzmann lost his fortune through speculation in coal mines, and he died in 1905, leaving his wife with five sons and two daughters to raise alone.

Salzmann's bankruptcy resulted not only in financial difficulties for the family, but in a loss of social status as well, indicated by their change of address during these years; the family moved from the bourgeois ninth district to a tenement in Währing, a new suburb of the working class and petite bourgeoisie. This was a period during which Vienna experienced an acute housing shortage, and rents were consequently very steep. The family's sudden move into a working-class milieu was a precipitous fall, recorded in stark terms in Salten's later autobiographical sketches written for the Viennese press.[91] These feuilleton pieces describe a youth of real poverty. The large family was crowded into a small apartment, furniture was auctioned off, there was often not enough to eat, and the family could not always keep all of the seven children in shoes.

Quite suddenly, the material manifestations of a bourgeois existence all but disappeared, but that is not to say that the family ceased to define itself in bourgeois terms. While their finances mirrored their working-class neighbors, they continued to be intellectually oriented toward the middle class.[92] Felix Salten, then still called Siegmund Salzmann, was sent to *Gymnasium,* albeit the nearby school in Hernals, a suburb like Währing, dominated by the lower-middle and working classes. Salten came into conflict here and left the school for the more prestigious Wasa-Gymnasium, of the ninth district (where Stefan Zweig, for example, was also educated). Salten left this school without finishing, as well, and the circumstances of his leaving are not entirely clear. The family's economic circumstances may have played either a direct or an indirect role, but Salten was also a poor student with a high rate of absenteeism. His own brief account of the matter refers to a further conflict, this time with a Latin teacher.[93]

Salten's life then underwent a rather rash and remarkable transformation. Upon leaving the *Gymnasium,* he took a job with an insurance firm to help support the family. Within a few years, by 1890, he had begun a friendship with Arthur Schnitzler and soon joined the *Jung Wien* literary circle that met at the Café Griensteidl. During the 1890s he launched a journalistic and literary career that would lead him to influential positions, fame, and a wide international readership. He thus eventually came to the same the kind of success experienced by the most prominent members of the *Jung Wien* group, and yet it is striking how much his experience during his formative years differed from theirs. Salten had intimate knowledge of poverty, and he knew what it meant to possess and then to lose material stability, privilege, and social status. He was not the product of an elite university education but was an autodidact whose embrace of German culture seems to have been an entirely personal choice and not the result of his parents' assimilatory ambitions.[94] He was not able to pursue a university education, nor did he have the luxury afforded other young Jews of the upper bourgeoisie to develop a career path over time or try out several alternatives.

In the course of his friendship with the *Jung Wien* authors, there certainly appear to have been moments when these differences became evident. Through his association with the group he became an early target of the satire of Karl Kraus (who will be discussed later in this chapter), a dubious honor that plagued him for years. While Salten was not named in Kraus's essay "Die demolirte Literatur" ("Demolished Literature"), he was recognizable to Kraus's readers and thus he was embarrassed by Kraus's attack on his command of grammar. According to Edward Timms, Salten responded to Kraus's publication with physical violence.[95] In light of Salten's poor academic performance and failure to attain the *Matura*, this was surely a criticism that stung. Salten's friends, including his close friend Arthur Schnitzler, whose diaries contain frequent criticisms of Salten, were sometimes critical of what they viewed as his careerism and egocentrism. In letters Salten would occasionally caution them to keep in mind the instability of his material and social position.

Salten was not spared from the kind of financial troubles his family had known. His writing and work in the theater were frequently interrupted for journalistic stints that could pay the bills and help support his mother and sisters. During the 1890s he worked for many different newspapers, contributing to fifty different papers over the course of his lifetime.[96] In 1895 Salten became Herzl's successor as feuilleton editor at the *Wiener Allgemeine Zeitung*. From 1902, Salten served as *Burgtheater* critic for *Die Zeit*. During World War I he worked in the war archive in Vienna, and after the war he was the premier Sunday feuilletonist for the *Neue Freie Presse*. He became well known for his literary work in the late 1920s. He served as chairman of the Austrian PEN-Club and president of the Association of Jewish Writers and Artists.

A celebrated Austrian writer by the early 1930s, Salten was fired from the *Neue Freie Presse* after the *Anschluss*. He was able to emigrate to Switzerland because his daughter had married a Swiss actor. In exile Salten was merely tolerated, permitted to publish only animal stories, as the Swiss sought to protect the domain of their own writers. Not surprisingly, the animal stories written during this period thematize the problem of survival under difficult conditions.[97] Salten died in Zurich in 1945 in straitened circumstances, after a lengthy illness. His later writings, produced at this time, will be taken up in the next chapter.

Until very recently Salten has not received significant attention either for his literary work or his writing for the feuilleton. Apart from frequent references to Salten as the probable author of the erotic novel *Josefine Mutzenbacher*, the scholarly community has had relatively little to say about the author and his work. In the popular realm, even Salten's most famous story, *Bambi*, is more readily associated with Walt Disney than with its author. Indeed, this work has been largely absent from the canon of children's literature for decades.[98] Even less attention has been devoted to his other writing. However some excellent work in recent years has perhaps begun to reverse this trend.[99] My focus in this book is on a number of turn-of-the-century feuilletons in which Salten's relationship to Vienna comes to the fore, as well as (in Chapter 2) on those literary works in which Salten reflects on the Jewish Question and Zionism.

Salten's involvement with journalism and with the feuilleton in particular were significant not only in terms of his career and livelihood, but also seem to have had a discernible impact on his literary endeavors. Karl Kraus lambasted Salten repeatedly in *Die Fackel* for his mixing of literature and journalism, seeing in all of Salten's work the feuilleton's tendency toward trivialization. And even Schnitzler lamented the journalistic thrust of his friend's style, characterizing in his diaries what he deemed Salten's best work, *Heimfahrt* (*The Journey Home*), with the backhanded compliment of "*genialischer Feuilletonismus*" (brilliant feuilletonism).[100] Salten's relationship to language appears to have been influenced by his work in journalism. His attempt to render language in as realistic a manner as possible prompted his use of the Viennese dialect, incomplete sentences, and, at times, clichéd phrases. The sentimentality of much of his prose certainly finds echo in the feuilletons he produced and this influence should come as no surprise. Salten's journalistic career took place during a period of increased significance for the feuilleton, and Salten's involvement with journalism was long and fruitful. Stefan Zweig recalls the paradoxically exalted status of all that was written *unter dem Strich*,[101] as well as the exclusivity of the elite ranks of the feuilletonists, noting that among the young writers Hofmannsthal (who will be discussed later) alone managed to get a piece accepted by the *Neue Freie Presse*, while the rest of them had to "smuggle" their efforts into the paper's back pages. Zweig concludes, "Whoever wrote for the front page had their name forever engraved in marble in Vienna."[102] One might also recall that the mixture of journalism and literature for which Salten has been criticized is frequently viewed as the hallmark of the style of his contemporary Peter Altenberg and an expression of his uniqueness.[103]

An important collection of Salten's feuilletons is *Das österreichische Antlitz* (*The Face of Austria*), which appeared around 1909. In these essays, Salten's patriotic, though not uncritical, relationship to Austria is a recurrent theme. The title stems from one of several essays devoted to the aging emperor whom, along with the monarchy he represented, Salten treats with awe and respect. The more striking feature of the volume is its representation of the city of Vienna. The city is not merely the setting for Salten's observations, but the real focus of the work, even of pieces ostensibly devoted to narrower subjects, such as Lueger, Altenberg, or a beloved *Heuriger*.

Throughout the volume the narrative voice takes a number of different guises, while maintaining the perspective of an observer moving about the city. "Die Wiener Straße" ("The Viennese Street") describes a routine after-work stroll through the first district taken for over forty years by a sixty-year-old bachelor, who is presumably representative of Vienna's vast civil service. These evening walks are an occasion for observing his fellow Viennese, and his observations, not the least of attractive women, have been a constant source of pleasure in his life. The stroller takes obvious pride in his knowledge of the city, street by street, and in the familiarity of the scenes that unfold before him: "How much have I learned to see since I was a young man and have gone walking every day after work; and how much could I say."[104] The emphasis in this piece is on the way in which these strolls through the streets of Vienna have shaped the narrator. The speaker does not merely describe a passive enjoyment—the streets themselves have taught him to see and have given him much to discuss.

> But I would just like to note that many qualities were developed in me in those early years precisely through my evening walks. The Burgplatz, for example, Graben, the Kohlmarkt … that is where I gradually developed a sense of propriety, quite involuntarily; an affinity for better ways of life and a certain sensitivity regarding the vulgar and the tasteless.[105]

The elegant streets of the first district, its imposing institutions and its similarly elegant inhabitants, have cultivated this man and refined his sensibilities. He does not attend the *Burgtheater,* but he mingles in the foyer with the spectators after a performance and feels as though he is partaking of the city's luster. If this is merely an illusion, the narrator is unperturbed. Salten is not explicitly critical of this bourgeois idealization of the city center and the way of life for the Austrian elite embodied within it; rather, he constructs this embrace of an illusory, imagined Vienna as quintessentially Viennese.[106]

This elevating effect is ascribed to the city's inner districts in a second essay as well. En route to a charity event attended by the aristocracy, the narrator feels the effect of the event's posh address even before making any contact with the social elites: "The wagon rolls through the Augarten gate and right away one feels a bit elevated."[107]

In "Frühjahrsparade" ("Spring Parade"), Salten maintains the wide-eyed perspective of his childhood as he witnesses a military exercise in the Hofburg: "One didn't see the emperor personally, but one did sense the splendor of his presence, a hint of Imperial power."[108] As an adult witnessing a scene that had deeply impressed him as a child, the effect is undiminished—"This effect never fails."[109]

While these feuilletons reveal the appeal of Vienna's center, others collected in this volume depict the draw of the periphery. If the inner districts offer the opportunity to mingle with and observe the city's elite, the outer districts as described by Salten are places with the potential for different social encounters.

Salten visits Stahlehner, a *Heuriger* in Hernals as it is about to be demolished, and laments the loss of a special space where the mixing of social classes was uniquely possible. "The Stahlehner was the place where the courtly instincts of our fiacre drivers and the cabdrivers' impulses of our counts fell into each other's arms."[110] He evokes Bratfisch, the Crown Prince Rudolph's fiacre driver, as the last of the great romantics among the city's coach drivers. The *Wiener Gemütlichkeit* capable of bridging the gap between classes evoked in this essay is an expression of the Viennese character that is now relegated to the past. The essay is not strictly nostalgic, as Salten's position is one of the detached observer. While he lived in Hernals as a child and was intimately familiar with the area and milieu, he never perceived himself as belonging there and did not view himself as having access to the kind of easy fraternal relations he ascribed to these strands of the Viennese.

Salten returns to the world of *Alt Wien* in the essay "Beim Brady" ("At Brady's"), in which the small, suburban Brady restaurant figures as the site of the last traces of Viennese *Gemütlichkeit*. Salten's casting of the suburbs as the site of an authentic Vienna that has been lost is made explicitly: "And when one goes to Brady, then the way out there is already like a stroll into the past."[111] The inner districts of the city belong to the present, but the suburbs are constructed as relics of the past. In "Spaziergang in der Vorstadt" ("Stroll in the Suburb"), Salten returns to Währing, the neighborhood of his childhood, in a remembrance of beer and wine gardens and other places that have vanished or lost their former character. The introduction of the streetcar to this area means that the city has now encroached on what was formerly a world apart; to discover what he terms the authentic Vienna of the past requires a greater spatial distance from the center, he suggests, all the way to Pötzleinsdorf.

With personal knowledge of the Vienna of the working class and lower bourgeoisie, and having carved out a place for himself within the bourgeois center that afforded him access to the elites of Austrian society, Salten was well positioned to understand and comment on the dynamics at work between these very different experiences of life in the imperial capital. If here Salten is concerned with illustrating the ways in which the modern metropolis is chipping away at the remaining vestiges of *Alt Wien,* other feuilletons adopt a defensive posture vis-à-vis the encroachment of the suburbs on the city. This, too, seems to be bound up with Salten's biography. By escaping from the working-class suburban milieu, Salten turned to the culture of the urban center as a bulwark against the world he was looking to leave behind. He writes from the perspective of the privileged, inner-city feuilletonist.[112] One of the (usually implicit) targets of his criticism in these early feuilletons is the particular form of *Neu-Wienertum* (the new Viennese) emerging in the suburbs, namely Lueger's constituents, now a visible, self-conscious, and powerful presence throughout Vienna, including the realms Salten had considered sacrosanct.[113]

It is vital in Salten's search for authentic Vienna in the outer districts of the city that he depicts himself as a border-crosser, a *flâneur* with access to all parts of the city. He reminds the reader of the rich variety of Viennese life available to all if one would only move freely about the city and its outer reaches, as he does.

> And so we live in a great city. Living all the time within just a tiny speck, in two, three streets. Contenting ourselves with the feeling of abundance that booms around us. All the remote places we forcefully conjure up, having captured them in paper and books on our table. But it happens that we miss the most vital thing even when nothing more is required to see it than a walk from one city neighborhood to another.[114]

When Salten turns to the Prater he reveals a selective and subjective vision of the park sheltering an idyll for the marginalized of Viennese society. Salten's treatment of the Prater is far removed from the observations of the roving reporter present in his other feuilletons, as he represents the park as a world apart, divorced from any Viennese context. The Prater is encoded as *die ewige Vorstadt* (the eternal suburb), and here he seems to have found the self-enclosed world that eluded him in his ventures into the outlying districts. In his 1911 essay "Wurstelprater," with photographs by Emil Mayer, Salten presents the *Wurstelprater* as a closed world, separate from the rest of the park and sealed off from the rest of the city. He is not concerned with the Prater as a whole and eschews those parts of the park dominated by the aristocracy and the bourgeoisie.[115] Salten's *Volksprater* constructs the working classes in a nostalgic representation of *Alt Wien*. As Siegfried Mattl has argued: "In the 'Wurstelprater' of Salten and Mayer, a society entertains itself that is forged beyond modern social categories like class and profession, a group not characterized through its activities and functions, but rather through its appearance and modes of behavior: the good-for-nothing, the crook, the drinker."[116]

Salten and Mayer establish themselves as *flâneurs*, much in the model of Peter Altenberg, whom Salten admired. They are bourgeois observers of urban life, and in the gaze of the *flâneur*, they construct, assess, see beneath the surface, and reveal the secrets of the objects of their attention. Mattl sees the text as part of a broader trend of the period exoticizing the city, not articulating a new metropolitan identity but maintaining the fiction of a familiar, knowable world.[117]

Salten's *Wurstelprater* is a utopian space in which nationalism, anti-Semitism, and class struggle play little or no role. The visitors he observes are marginal figures, largely recent immigrants to the city eking out a living. In the vignette "Five-Kreuzer Dance," Salten depicts their pain, homesickness, and isolation. Yet ultimately he describes them as forging—in the *Wurstelprater* itself—a kind of hybrid identity: "All of these people here have one thing in common: that they are foreign in this enormous city, whose work mills devour them, stripped of their essence, ground up and used up."[118] The music and dancing transform the scene and unite the people. The transformative power of the dance is sexual at its core.

Salten writes, "Quite simply, like nowhere else, the simple human drives are revealed. The desire of a woman for a man. The desire of a man for a woman."[119]

In the vignette "Rendezvous," Salten casts the Prater as an unparalleled hunting ground for those seeking the company of the opposite sex. "Everyone here is on the hunt, and no one seeks in vain. No girl who wouldn't consort with some man, no man who can't manage to conquer some girl."[120] The *Wurstelprater* has its own sexual economy, and the operative social hierarchy places the young lieutenant at the top as the most desirable and successful lady killer. Strikingly, however, Salten depicts the Prater itself as the most potent seducer. "Over there another couple on a bench. Is there a more dangerous matchmaker than such a bench in a public park, above all in a *Praterallee*? They don't even have to know each other, they only have to happen to sit together on a bench. And before anyone has spoken a single word, they're already familiar and connected just by sitting together."[121]

Salten seems to adopt a variety of poses in these brief portraits, as his relationship to his subject is not uniform throughout the essay. Here he seems to be self-consciously aiming for a distanced, almost scientific objectivity, like an animal behaviorist describing the mating rituals he observes at some previously unknown breeding ground. Elsewhere his tone is more personal, suggesting an empathetic or admiring view of his subjects, though always remaining the outsider.

Salten's *Wurstelprater* is a space of sexual possibility and, more broadly, of social interaction with the power to transform the isolated, working-class immigrants of Vienna into a cohesive group, to overcome any linguistic, cultural, political, and professional differences. The park itself figures as an active agent in forging connections between strangers. It has produced its own distinct social economy, and it schools the uninitiated in its ways. In the imagined space of his *Volksprater*, Salten establishes an alternative to the social landscape afforded by the rest of the city.

Salten's *Wurstelprater* seems to exist outside of time as a hermetic cultural space. The utopian spaces of some of his other feuilletons evoke the past as a counterimage to the present, a space of possibilities no longer realizable. In his movement from past to present and from the center to the periphery, Salten is actively engaged in the construction of Vienna as an Austrian idea. No singular, cohesive image of Vienna or the Viennese emerges from these writings, yet whether they critique or celebrate a particular Viennese characteristic, Salten's writings always reflect the author's relationship to the city and its inhabitants from his insider-outsider position as a Jewish intellectual. Each privileged site in Salten's mapping of the Vienna through the feuilleton enacts its own requirements on—and creates new possibilities for—the people who move through the city, including Salten. In Salten's self-styling as a border-crosser he is uniquely positioned to move among all of these significant sites, chronicling his observations for his readers, many of whom lacked similar access to worlds that were closed off to them or that belonged to the past.

Stefan Zweig

In Stefan Zweig we have another knowledgeable chronicler of the city of Vienna. In his memoirs, *Die Welt von Gestern* (*The World of Yesterday*), Zweig crafted a beautifully written account of the Vienna of his youth, fondly remembered and vividly brought to life. The work is a retrospective account, written in New York and in Brazilian exile in 1941, a conscious remembrance of a world that had vanished. I will consider this work in the next chapter, along with a number of other texts in which he seems to reflect on his Jewish identity in important ways.[122] First, however, I will briefly examine Zweig's life and work while still in Austria, still embedded in the socio-historical context of *fin de siècle* Vienna.

Zweig was born in Vienna in 1881, the son of Moritz Zweig, a textiles industrialist. His family belonged to the upper bourgeoisie, and from the start Zweig experienced the affluence and prestige attached to an address on the Schottenring. His maternal side, the Brettauer family, had moved to Vienna in the early 1870s, shortly after the emancipation of the Jews. Zweig's maternal grandfather was a midcentury banker, and the family was involved in the financial world all across Europe. The rise to prominence and the processes of assimilation was the work of prior generations and not part of Zweig's personal experience. In this respect his biography differs sharply from Salten's far more modest beginnings and, to a lesser extent, also diverges from the experiences of Freud and Schnitzler, whose families' social and material advancement was more gradual.[123] Zweig's family was distanced from Judaism, and he received no religious training.

Zweig was educated at the Wasa-Gymnasium from 1891 to 1899, then began to study *Germanistik* and *Romanistik* at the University of Vienna. Zweig seized his first opportunity to travel abroad, which would become a lifelong pursuit; he visited France upon receiving the *Matura* and undertook a semester in Berlin in 1902. He supplemented his studies with a good deal of travel, making numerous visits during these years to France, Spain, Belgium, England, and Germany. In 1904, he received his doctorate of philosophy from the University of Vienna.

Zweig's initial literary achievements came early in his career, also coinciding with his studies. He first became known as a poet, with a volume of poems entitled *Silberne Saiten* (*Silver Strings*) that appeared in 1901. He also became known as and a translator, first of Baudelaire, then later of Emile Verhaeren, Verlaine, Keats, Yeats, and Walt Whitman. Zweig's first volume of novellas, *Die Liebe der Erika Ewald* (*The Love of Erika Ewald*), appeared in 1904, and a second, *Brennendes Geheimnis* (*Burning Secret*), appeared in 1911. In 1902 Zweig published his first feuilleton piece for the *Neue Freie Presse,* under the editorship of Theodor Herzl, whom Zweig greatly admired. In 1907 Zweig moved into his own apartment at Kochgasse 8, in Vienna's Josefstadt, which would become the home base from which he would launch further travels to India, the United States, Canada, Cuba, and various destinations within Europe, prior to the outbreak of World War I.

Zweig's relationship to his Jewish heritage evolved over the course of his lifetime. It was a relationship that was always marked by ambivalence, but also one that deepened as a result of the cataclysmic events of two world wars. Zweig's encounter with Galician Jews devastated by World War I, along with the trauma of coming to grips with post–World War One reality, is generally viewed as a decisive turning point in his life, which deepened his attachment to his Jewish identity. This will be explored in the following chapter. In this earlier period, Zweig's ambivalence is evident. He accepted his Jewish identity, commenting, "Being a Jew does not weigh me down, it does not excite me, it does not torment me and doesn't isolate me; I feel it just as I feel my heartbeat when I think of it and don't feel it when I don't think of it."[124] This statement may well be more clearly affirmative than Zweig's actual experience at the time, but nonetheless it is important to note that he never disavowed a Jewish identity nor considered conversion. Zweig opposed Zionism, in spite of his admiration for Herzl. In *Die Welt von Gestern* he recalls that he perceived a lack of sufficient respect for the Zionist leader on the part of the movement's adherents in Vienna, but his opposition was likely motivated more strongly by a rejection of a national solution for what he viewed as a supranational people.[125]

Zweig has always been regarded as a cosmopolitan European writer. His work is classified in the category of world literature, as he may be the most widely read German-language author, with more of his works translated into more languages than any other German-language writer. His ties to Austria are generally considered to be minimal, and his relationship to the city of Vienna is usually discussed only in relation to the memoirs. Yet Zweig did have a relationship to Vienna, and like his relationship to a Jewish identity, it changed over time. Vienna was the setting for much of his work, and the terrain explored in the early work certainly feels like familiar ground to readers of his *Jung Wien* contemporaries. Leon Botstein has detected a rather esoteric view of the city in Zweig's works, stemming from his privileged upbringing: "Zweig's description of his native city might well be compared to that of a New Yorker whose view of New York was based on life on the East Side of Manhattan below 96th Street."[126] Certainly Zweig's Vienna is a product of his personal experiences; in the early works Vienna is a created space—later, a remembered one. After World War I, Vienna was the site where Zweig was first confronted with the harsh reality of the destruction of the world he had known. Not surprisingly, Zweig consistently located his strongest critiques of the bankrupt postwar moral and social landscape in Vienna.

Personally and professionally Zweig needed to distance himself from the familiar, as evidenced by his extensive travels even before he went into exile; however, when the world of his youth was destroyed, he experienced this as a terrible personal loss. The space of Vienna played a complex and important role in the development of Zweig's Jewish identity, and his Jewish identity in turn played a significant role in determining his relationship to Vienna. Zweig's Jewish identity is frequently cited as the basis for his cosmopolitanism,[127] and I would suggest that his Viennese identity was similarly determinate in his European cosmopolitan outlook. Stemming from the cosmopolitan space of the multiethnic imperial capital, Zweig was more Viennese than Austrian, and this Viennese perspective was in harmony with a way of looking at the world that transcended national borders. An understanding of Zweig's relationship to the city of his birth, as well as to his Jewish origins, can thus shed light on his way of perceiving the world and contribute to a better understanding of his extensive writings.

Zweig's depictions of Vienna in his works clearly seek to capture the city's representative quality—in David Turner's words, "[its] ability to communicate human values."[128] In his analysis of Zweig Turner has identified a number of Zweig's personal values that are treated in his novellas, including personal freedom and the condemnation of those forces that would restrict it; a critique of repressive bourgeois sexual codes and the hypocrisy surrounding them; and the elevation of state authority over personal freedom.[129] In trying to get at this representative quality, Turner claims, Zweig focused on public spaces in his rendering of Vienna's urban landscape.

With the transformations wrought by urbanization and industrialization, Viennese sites of public life shifted into new terrain, moving politics and organized social activity into the streets, parks, and public halls. Public spaces carry a special function in literary treatments, as they situate the characters in places where they can observe and be observed, places where an encounter with strangers is possible and where unconventional social interaction may take place. In Zweig's works public spaces are also significant simply in that they are removed from the familiarity of the home, and this distance from the familiar makes it possible for the characters to interact with the world in a new way.

Like Felix Salten, Stefan Zweig was drawn to the Prater as a unique space that was at once quintessentially Viennese yet divorced from the rest of the city. Zweig was attracted to the Prater for its openness, its potential for social interaction that was not possible, or at least not sanctioned, in other parts of the city. In the novella *Phantastische Nacht* (*Fantastic Night*) Zweig explores the psychological effects of a young man's experiment with casting off social and moral restraints, a move that is possible only in the unrestricted social space of the Prater. The protagonist is a man of thirty-six, a member of Vienna's high society, who is freed by an inheritance from the burden of needing to support himself. He leads the carefree and comfortable existence associated with Schnitzler's bachelor characters. His view of the city is shaped by this freedom and sense of entitlement. He speaks fondly of Vienna as "the soft and voluptuous city that like no other has elevated taking a stroll, idle observation, and elegance to nothing short of artistic perfection, a way of life."[130]

The character comes to feel stifled, however, in his comfortable life and begins to succumb to a sort of emotional paralysis that is again reminiscent of Schnitzler's characters. It is the Prater that presents him the opportunity to break out of this state. Zweig's Prater is a space in which the codes governing behavior for those in the privileged classes are not wholly absent, but where there is the potential for their suspension and for the breaking down of social barriers. The Prater figures as a Wild West space within the city where these codes do not necessarily apply; the protagonist clearly could not have had the liberating experience of the "fantastic night" in any other part of the city. The park offers a necessary distance from his home and usual haunts, allowing him to deviate from prescribed behavior. Late in the evening he fears going home, lest the powerful effects of the night disappear.

Like Salten, Zweig zeroes in on those parts of the Prater that are hosts to the largest spectacles and therefore the largest masses; his protagonist first visits the racetrack and then the *Volksprater*. At the track the protagonist watches the transformation of the crowd of spectators into a frenzied mass during a race, and while he finds them laughable, he also envies their excitement as he feels incapable of experiencing such emotion. But soon he, too, is entirely consumed by the excitement of a race, after a new intensity of emotion is triggered by his powerful attraction to a woman at the racetrack. When the protagonist wagers with money that doesn't belong to him, money he has essentially stolen, he perceives his perpetration of this crime as a total break from his previous self.

Having been intoxicated by this first contact with the baser side of himself, the protagonist moves on to the *Volksprater* in order to prolong the new experience. It is the crowd that draws him there, and he experiences an emerging sense of the power of the masses and the desire to be caught up in it. He watches with envy as men and women find each other in the crowd and pair off. Zweig's description of the *Wurstelprater* as a sexual hunting ground is very similar to Salten. The protagonist becomes increasingly desperate for this kind of human contact, but he is unable to make a connection. Conscious of the elegant clothes that mark him as an outsider, he is unable to bridge the social divide separating him from the working-class people more at home in this environment. A prostitute rescues him from his agonized state of paralysis, and he willingly follows her. Although the prostitute, along with a few accomplices, attempts to blackmail him, the protagonist experiences this encounter as uplifting. For him, a vital human connection has indeed been established. He feels sympathy for his would-be assailants and warmth and gratitude toward the prostitute, as he senses that she has recognized him as a human being and, like him, has been affected by their encounter. The Prater experience jolts this man out of his moribund state, and he is now committed to a life that is not constrained in any way by societal expectations.

Hanni Mittelmann has identified a similar interest in the outsider as the protagonist in a number of Zweig's novellas and interprets these marginalized figures as reflections on the conflicted, insider-outsider status of Viennese Jews.[131] For Mittelmann the novellas are Zweig's treatment of the rift within his own consciousness between assimilationism and the realization that, as a Jew, he will never be fully accepted by mainstream society. Mittelmann sees Zweig's male Jewish characters as exhibiting the negative traits ascribed to Jews in anti-Semitic stereotypes, framed most starkly in Otto Weininger's notorious treatise *Geschlecht und Charakter (Sex and Character)*.[132] These qualities are frequently revalued in Zweig's novellas, so that traits commonly seen as deficiencies become virtues and the norms the characters fail to fulfill are called into question. These are not stories, however, of wholly successful self-fashioning and identity formation; the characters remain outsiders and are ultimately frustrated in their attempts at overcoming differences. Nonetheless Mittelmann stresses the way in which these texts posit an alternative to the ideology of assimilation, suggesting a possible model of integration that incorporates differences. This is a compelling interpretation, indicating that while explicitly Jewish themes did not appear in Zweig's writing until World War I, reflections on the complex issues surrounding Jewish identity are present, if submerged, in his early work as well.

Hugo von Hofmannsthal

The inclusion of Hugo von Hofmannsthal in this chapter is certainly not as straightforward as my choice to discuss Schnitzler, Salten, or Zweig. Hofmannsthal appears here alongside these figures unquestionably seen as Jews because I have chosen to cast a wide net in determining whom I treat as Jewish in this volume. Hofmannsthal was one-quarter Jewish, with Jewish ancestry on his paternal side of the family, alongside Italian, Austrian, and German roots. The Hofmannsthals' assimilatory social transformation began in the early nineteenth century. In this, their experience was similar to that of other Jewish families, differing only in the degree of success of their far-reaching integration into the upper echelons of society. Hofmannsthal's great-grandfather, a prominent industrialist in the silk trade, was ennobled. His grandfather converted to Catholicism in order to marry an Italian woman. Scholarship on Hofmannsthal has been loath to directly tackle the question of his relationship to a Jewish identity, brushing it aside with the observation that he was either scarcely conscious of his Jewish background or that he repressed it.[133] In recent years, however, some scholars have made the case that Hofmannsthal's engagement with the issue was more intensive than has commonly been thought, meriting a reexamination of his public and private reflections on Jews and Jewishness.[134]

Following Steven Beller, I see Hofmannsthal as a product of the processes of assimilation and his family history as part of the historical phenomenon of the integration of Jews into Western European culture and society.[135] Even if Hugo von Hofmannsthal stands at the peak of an assimilatory social ascent that occurred over generations, it is significant that the point of departure from that process was far removed from mainstream society and likely reflected a worldview distinct from it. Moreover, the Hofmannsthals' ascent did not place the young Hugo at the very peak of Viennese society or exclude him from being viewed as an outsider, as the high aristocracy kept their distance from the parvenu *Geldadel* (monied aristocracy) to which Jews could rise. To a significant degree Hofmannsthal was seen by contemporaries—friends and critics alike—as Jewish. Felix Salten held the view that Hofmannsthal felt a distance from the traditional aristocracy because of his Jewish background.[136] Hofmannsthal's friend Leopold von Andrian portrayed him as sometimes betraying a Jewish accent. He characterized Hofmannsthal's rational bent as a product of his Jewish background, calling forth a philo-Semitic trope of the Enlightenment linking Jews to reason and rationality.[137] Critics certainly viewed him in this light, not only in their broad condemnation of Jewish influence in the *Jung Wien* circle of which he was a part, but also regarding Hofmannsthal specifically. Hofmannsthal's *Oedipus* was disparaged in the anti-Semitic press as being written in a "Jewish German." Finally, and for me the most compelling reason for Hofmannsthal's inclusion here, is the fact that Hofmannsthal himself was concerned with this perception and with his own thoughts on the meaning of this Jewish background, as becomes clear in a number of striking statements he made related to the issue. The conflicting character of these statements suggests that the matter was an ongoing concern and that his views changed over time.

Jens Rieckmann has uncovered a number of revealing comments within Hofmannsthal's correspondence as a youth in unpublished materials from his literary estate. A letter from a thirteen-year-old Hofmannsthal in which he critiques for a friend a theatrical production he had just seen demonstrates an understanding of historical, as well as contemporary, anti-Semitism. Hofmannsthal's diaries as a seventeen-year-old contain material he had considered for publication, which revolves around a family with a background fairly similar to his own reacting to a son who refuses to let his Jewish background be submerged.[138] Rieckmann sees in this very early private writing an identification of Jews with strong ethical principles, as well as the characterization of a Jewish tendency towards rationalism. This view runs through much of Hofmannsthal's early correspondence and diary entries, and according to Rieckmann it comes to be negatively coded over the course of the 1890s as overly abstract, cold, and distanced from life.

At nineteen, in June of 1893, Hofmannsthal expressed the following anxiety in his diary: "What if all of my inner developments and struggles were nothing more than the disturbances of inherited blood, insurgencies of Jewish drops of blood … against the Germanic and Romanic and reactions against these rebellions."[139] Hofmannsthal's rendering of an internal conflict between his Jewish and non-Jewish components reflects an awareness of the scientific and pseudoscientific discourses on race and inheritance prevalent at the time.[140] Additionally, there are elements of another anti-Semitic trope of the period by which rationalism was cast as a Jewish trait in opposition to the Germanic spirit.[141] Hofmannsthal was clearly ill at ease over the seemingly incompatible elements of his background, fearful that his inner life might be determined not by his rigorous education or intellectual pursuits but by a few drops of inherited Jewish blood.

Hofmannsthal's reaction to the works of his friends dealing with Jewish themes have frequently been cited as further evidence of his discomfort with anything related to Jews and Judaism. As a member of the largely Jewish *Jung Wien* literary circle, Hofmannsthal as a young writer traversed a cultural and intellectual terrain he shared with the Jewish writers, who were also his friends.[142] When they steered their writing toward reflections on Jewish identity, however, Hofmannsthal appears to have taken pains to distance himself from this writing. We have first the well-known letter to Schnitzler in which he reacts with something less than enthusiasm to *Der Weg ins Freie,* admitting that he half-consciously, half-unconsciously left the book on a train.[143] Additionally, Hofmannsthal reacted very negatively to Richard Beer-Hofmann's *Jaakobs Traum* (*Jacob's Dream*), with an apparent distaste for the theme of Israel's chosenness. In both cases Rieckmann's commentary is particularly helpful in noting that it might be inaccurate to assume that the theme of Schnitzler's work was objectionable to Hofmannsthal, as he had a very positive view of *Professor Bernhardi*. Regarding Beer-Hofmann's work, Rieckmann reminds us of the historical context in which Hofmannsthal read the work, namely in 1918, when he was deeply disillusioned with nationalism. These are important qualifications, yet Hofmannsthal's ambivalence surrounding Jewish issues is evident.

Hofmannsthal also made a number of statements regarding Vienna in which his view of the city is marked by this ambivalence regarding Jews. In a letter of the late 1890s to the mother of a friend, Hofmannsthal indicated that a "*jüdische Denkungsweise*" (Jewish mode of thinking) was particularly prevalent in Vienna: "It is just that there is hardly a milieu that would be more confusing and dangerous for an adolescent without very distinctly developed aptitudes than the Austrian, let alone the Jewish-Viennese."[144] While the notion that this was a dangerous environment for a young man casts a dubious light on Jewish Vienna, other statements from the period suggest that Hofmannsthal identified with this milieu. In 1894 Hofmannsthal confided in his diary his fears that this cultural, intellectual climate might be threatened by the encroachment of Slavs and Eastern European Jews. He wrote:

> How strange it is again that we in Vienna may perhaps be the very last thinking, the last complete people with a soul, that then perhaps a great barbarism will bring in a Slavic-Jewish, sensual world. To think of destroyed Vienna: all walls fallen, the inner belly of the city laid bare, the wounds covered over with creeping vines. ... And to be a sentinel in one of Trajan's towers of the *Karlskirche* that is still standing and to have the thought that no one here understands any longer how to walk among the ruins.[145]

Vienna does not figure prominently in Hofmannsthal's poetry, and the Vienna of his own day is certainly not a favored setting for his works. Yet the above passage suggests that Hofmannsthal identified strongly with Vienna as a unique cultural space. According to Adrian Del Caro, Vienna was Hofmannsthal's spiritual home, cherished as a cultural crossroads uniquely open to influences from all directions.[146] The view that this cultural space is deeply marked by the presence of Jewish intellectuals is unmistakable in Hofmannsthal's various observations. His view of Jewish intellectuals' involvement shifts dramatically at different periods in his life, ranging from a cautious personal identification with the Viennese Jewish milieu to a caustic rant against this very same milieu in a letter of the 1920s, in which he draws on the rhetoric of the most hateful anti-Semitic writing, referring to the Jews as vermin, mollusks, and parasites.[147] For Peter Pfeiffer, this is a textbook example of Jewish self-hatred and evidence of Hofmannsthal's continued efforts to distance himself from being labeled a Jewish writer.[148] As Hofmannsthal increasingly developed a conservative reaction to the challenges of modernity, Jewishness came to stand in for modern elements he wished to reject.

Hofmannsthal's relationship to a Jewish identity stands as a limiting case for turn-of-the-century Jewry. He was the most distanced from Jewish tradition of any of the writers considered here, yet his Jewish ancestry was a source of considerable anxiety for him. Jewishness as both an external label and internal construct played a significant role in his identity crisis and his broader response to the challenges of modernity.

Karl Kraus

The case of Karl Kraus's relationship to a Jewish identity is as laden with paradoxes and contradictions as any writer considered in this study. Many scholars, as well as some of Kraus's contemporaries, have tended to set him apart, whether they view him as a textbook case of Jewish self-hatred or revere him as a modern-day Jewish prophet with unique insight into the shortcomings of modern Jewry. Indeed, Kraus's aggressive individualism, along with the utter impossibility of fitting him into any single category, seems to favor this kind of treatment of Kraus in isolation. However, Kraus very much belongs among the Viennese Jewish writers considered here, for his experience of the identity crisis common to turn-of-the-century Jews was particularly acute, and his multiple and conflicting responses to this crisis are especially revealing of the complexity and inescapability of this dilemma. Kraus's struggle with a crisis of identity persisted throughout his life, and his divergent writings are, among other things, a work of bricolage, a piece-by-piece construction of the self over a lifetime of introspection and self-improvement. In this chapter I will examine Kraus's more direct, prewar reflections on Jewishness, focusing primarily on his treatment in *Die Fackel* (the journal he founded) of assimilationism and Zionism. In Chapter 2, I return to Kraus to consider the shape of his satire during the war and his response to National Socialism.

For the Kraus scholar Edward Timms, Kraus's satire was a work of "radical self-reconstruction." Through his satire Kraus publicly rejected the various identities ascribed to him one by one. Timms notes, "He was a Jew by birth, an Austrian by nationality, a Viennese by residence, a German by language, a journalist by profession, bourgeois by social status and a rentier by economic position. Amid the ideological turmoil of Austria-Hungary, all of these ascribed identities seemed like falsifications."[149] In the pages of *Die Fackel*, Kraus cast off these identities and creatively strove after an authentic self-definition. Kraus's case is compelling because it presents nothing but thorny questions—the applicability of the concept of Jewish self-hatred, the interpretation of his vacillating conversion experience, the nature of his relationship to anti-Semitism and use of anti-Semitic discourse, his views of radical assimilationism—which defied any easy answers.

Kraus was born in Jičín, now part of the Czech Republic, one of ten children of Ernestine and Jacob Kraus, a wealthy paper manufacturer. The family moved to Vienna in 1877, when Kraus was three years old. He grew up in Vienna and went to school in the city, achieving the *Matura* in 1892. He attended the University of Vienna, taking courses in law, German literature, and philosophy, but left the university without a degree. His first critical articles appeared in the Viennese press around 1896. At this time Kraus was part of the *Jung Wien* circle, an association he abruptly ended with the 1897 publication of his first pamphlet, "Die demolirte Literatur" ("Demolished Literature"), a stinging satire of the group. The success of this work, along with the 1898 *Eine Krone für Zion* (*A Crown for Zion*), containing Kraus's critical response to Zionism, launched Kraus's career. In spite of the latter pamphlet's harsh treatment of Theodor Herzl, then a prominent writer of the *Neue Freie Presse*, Kraus was offered a position writing the "Wiener Spaziergänge" column for the paper, formerly written by the veritable Viennese institution, Daniel Spitzer. Kraus turned down the job and launched his own independent journal, *Die Fackel*, in the same year. This satirical journal would run for thirty-seven years; in its first decade, the journal included contributions by a number of prominent contributors, including Frank Wedekind, Peter Altenberg, Else Lasker-Schüler, Adolf Loos, Oskar Kokoscha, Arnold Schoenberg, and Oscar Wilde. After 1911, Kraus was the paper's sole contributor. The mission of *Die Fackel* was one of demystification, revealing the often contradictory ideologies, political agendas, corruption, and hypocrisies beneath the elaborately constructed artifice of the decaying empire. Among his major themes were a critique of the press, an attack on bourgeois attitudes towards sexuality, the role of the artist, and the abuses of language Kraus seemed to see everywhere. For Robert Wistrich, Kraus took on the mantle in the journal of "prophet, prosecutor, and judge wrapped into one."[150]

In the same year that he launched *Die Fackel*, Kraus withdrew from the *Israelitische Kultusgemeinde*, becoming "confessionless." Just over a decade later, in 1911, Kraus quietly joined the Catholic Church; he was baptized in April, with Adolf Loos as his sponsor. There was no discussion of this move in the *Fackel*, no indication of new Christian beliefs in his public writings. For Timms, this guardedness regarding his conversion was in keeping with his role as a satirist. Kraus could not publicly espouse any religious convictions without undermining the power of his satire.[151] Kraus's embrace of Catholicism can be seen in the context of a Catholic intellectual revival that occurred across Europe in the years before the outbreak of World War I. The movement drew a number of eminent converts, particularly in France and England, as a response to some of the splintering effects of modern society.[152] Ever the individualist, Kraus did not openly align himself with this revival. He was skeptical of any organized movement; in targeting Jews in his satire, for example, he not only targeted many Jewish individuals, but also took a broader swipe at "Jews of all confessions."[153] Kraus was almost certainly silent on his conversion for the additional reason that a public declaration of his conversion would open him up to criticism as an opportunist, as Vienna's high conversion rate during these years made the baptized Jews a particular target of the anti-Semitic press.

In March of 1923 Kraus left the Catholic Church, again withdrawing his allegiance from organized religion. These shifts in direction make it difficult to ascertain what religion meant to Kraus. Certainly Judaism as a set of religious beliefs did not at any time play an important role in his life. He repudiated Orthodox Judaism, claiming the Jewish religion had fulfilled its historical purpose and was now merely a relic of the past.[154] His diatribes against "*Ghettojudentum*" ("ghetto Jews") reflect a clear disdain for the unassimilated Jews of "the East." He was no more favorable toward Western Jews who continued to espouse some relationship to Jewish tradition while demonstrating no real commitment. A special target was the so-called "Kärtnerstrasse Jew," who never goes to the temple but goes to the parish church in Ischl on August 18" to commemorate the birthday of Emperor Franz Joseph.[155]

There is little in Kraus's writings to shed light on his Christian convictions, but given his later withdrawal from Catholicism, we may conclude that conversion did not provide any durable solution to Kraus's identity crisis. Because he viewed Jewry as an ethnicity, a *Stamm*, he continued to see himself as a Jew.[156] And whereas there is scant evidence as to any positive personal gains from his religious experience, there is abundant evidence of his ongoing struggle with a Jewish identity.

Kraus's 1898 pamphlet *Eine Krone für Zion* is a biting satire of Zionism in which he expresses his assimilationist opposition to the movement as a misguided undertaking that he felt would only exacerbate anti-Semitism. In this view Kraus was in line with the opposition to Zionism by the majority of Viennese Jews. In his stinging satirical style, however, he clearly forges his own path and begins the essay with the claim that in seeking his financial support, the Zionists are trying to preempt his criticism. In this essay Kraus casts the Zionists as Jewish anti-Semites and argues that the two groups share the same goal:

> If, however, one refrains from seeing any possibility of a political danger, then good taste still has a right to protest the fact that the depths of thought from which the drunken old man calls out his "Out with you Jews!" finds its simple repetition in Zionism and that the answer "Indeed, out with us Jews!" offers little by way of variety apart from a celebratory tone.[157]

Kraus was altogether skeptical of the motivations of the Western, assimilated Jews who supported the Zionist movement, whom he saw as decrying a thousand years of Jewish suffering from positions of comfort and prosperity. He singled out the *Jung Wien* poets for particular ridicule, taking up a theme he had raised in the earlier "Demolirte Literatur," and derided the group for their superficiality. Here he claims that they had turned to Zionism as the latest fashion even though they'd never addressed a serious social topic in their works or paid attention to little beyond their own nerves. In their roles as dandyish, coffeehouse *bon vivants,* they are at least in a familiar milieu; this latest turn to Zionism is a move for which they are ill-suited. Young Zionist students, more earnest perhaps but hardly less superficial in Kraus's view, did not fare much better under Kraus's scathing critique. These were the "*Um-jeden-Preis-Juden*" (Jews-at-all-costs) among whom it had become fashionable to have a crooked nose and who demanded the rest of the population assimilate to Jewish traits, Kraus claimed.[158]

Kraus's treatment of assimilation in this essay is paradoxical, as he points to a number of negative consequences of assimilation on the one hand and makes his radical call for total assimilation on the other. He pokes fun at the Jews of the social elite who he claims see themselves as thoroughly assimilated and who distinguish themselves only in their zealous attempts at passing. He mocks the adaptability of the Jews in the same sentence in which he counsels the unassimilated, "*doch endlich einmal den Anfang zu machen*" (to finally make a start).[159] Let the Zionists become civilized Europeans, Kraus entreats. Would it not be easier to improve European culture than to found a new Jewish nationalist one?[160]

The following year, in an early edition of *Die Fackel,* Kraus made explicit his call for total assimilation. In an article on pogroms in Bohemia, in which he declared that "ghetto Jewry and anti-Semitism necessarily belong together" and in which he assigned to the Jews a share of the blame for their own mistreatment, Kraus proclaimed that the solution to the so-called Jewish Problem was to be found in the dissolution of the Jewish people. He wrote:

> Only courageous cleansing of the ranks, only the abandonment of the features of a race that, through many hundreds of years of distraction, has long ceased to be a nation can

end all this torment. The gates of gold and newspaper that still enclose the ghetto today must fall. Through dissolution to salvation! [*Durch Auflösung zur Erlösung!*] Otherwise the oft-cited twentieth century will see excesses of a much worse kind.[161]

This notion of the casting off of essential Jewish qualities was not merely Kraus's prescription for Eastern Europe, but was an expression of his personal agenda as well. Kraus had internalized the negative images of Jews of his era, and he was deeply concerned with eliminating in himself those characteristics disdained as distinctly Jewish by the society in which he lived. He was very sympathetic to the views of Houston Stewart Chamberlain, whom he invited to contribute to *Die Fackel* and with whom he collaborated on an extended article for a special edition of the journal.[162] Chamberlain saw the world in terms of a great ideological clash between Aryans and Jews, casting Jerusalem as a world-historical principal at odds with European civilization. The Jews could escape this dilemma by repudiating Judaism and ridding themselves of negative Jewish traits.

Kraus's emphasis on overcoming the self, on the transcendence of negative Jewish traits, prompted a letter from a *Die Fackel* reader asking whether he had indeed overcome these traits himself. Kraus's response was the 1913 essay "Er ist doch ä Jud" ("He's a Jew After All"). While Kraus bristles at opening himself up to direct, personal questions from his readers, he nonetheless answers directly:

> To answer the first question: that I do not merely believe but feel as if by the shock of revelation that none of the qualities of the Jew adhere to me that we would want to agree upon according to the current state of affairs.[163]

He then questions whether Jewish traits really exist, underscoring that those traits generally attributed to Jews may be found among all of the peoples of the West. Kraus implicitly accepts the idea that Jews might employ a materialist language and that the use of a language of commerce and money might be typical of Jews, yet he universalizes this tendency to anyone operating in these fields: "It is the cadence that pleasantly accompanies the rolling of money."[164] Kraus here professes an Enlightenment view of negative Jewish traits, suggesting that if such negative traits do exist, they are the result of the Jewish experience of oppression and ghetto living.

In the essay Kraus puts forward his own distinct, purportedly high-minded form of anti-Semitism, taking pains to distinguish his hostility toward Jews from the base, unreflective anti-Semitism of the lower bourgeoisie. One of his chief concerns is the possibility that his anti-Semitism could be seen as motivated by opportunism. Yet while Kraus professes a "higher" form of anti-Semitism, this did not stop him from incorporating a few jabs at some of his favorite targets. He tosses off a derogatory remark about Schnitzler's writing, then makes a number of dismissive comments on the literary output of the whole *Jung Wien* group, concluding: "I don't know whether it is a Jewish trait to find an old schnapps trader in a caftan more cultured than a member of the German-Austrian Writers Association in a tuxedo."[165] Returning to the rhetorical frame of self-examination with which he opens the essay, Kraus again deals with a paradox, as he stresses his own complete assimilation yet at the same time raises the possibility that negative Jewish traits can never be overcome. As Timms has noted, "The essay shows Kraus struggling with a dilemma which he cannot resolve."[166]

We are still faced with the question as to whether Kraus's endeavor to rid himself of Jewish attributes and his adoption of anti-Semitic language qualify him as one who experienced Jewish self-hatred. The label has long been applied to Kraus; Theodor Lessing cited Kraus as a case in point in his 1930 study *Der jüdische Selbsthass* (*Jewish Self-Hatred*), and Kraus continues to be regarded in this light.[167] The case is sufficiently complex, however, that we may at the very least leave it to Otto Weininger to stand as the archetype of Jewish self-hatred. Some scholars emphasize the paradoxical nature of Kraus's statements regarding Jews and anti-Semitism and seek to draw the kind of subtle distinction Kraus himself favored. Paul Reitter, for example, has ably demonstrated how Kraus's anti-Semitic rhetoric may have been driven by different strategic concerns at different moments. He identifies some instances in which Kraus appears to express hostile views severely, earnestly, and in a fairly straightforward manner, and he points out other points where anti-Semitism might appear to have served a more strategic purpose, employed with irony in order to assert Kraus's independence.[168] In this analysis Reitter draws on Shulamith Volkov's delineation of the way anti-Semitism can be employed symbolically as a cultural code, aligning the speaker or writer with a set of values associated with anti-Semitism.[169] Certainly, at times, Kraus employed the term "*Judentum*" as a kind of shorthand, variously denoting any of his common targets such as commercialism, opportunism, hypocrisy, corruption, and Zionism. And we are well advised not to expect Kraus to be consistent in his adoption of anti-Semitic discourse.

And yet Kraus's treatments in *Die Fackel* of Jews and issues related to Jews are so often written in such vehement terms, it is difficult to cast aside the label of the self-hating Jew. I consider Ritchie Robertson to be correct in his assertion that, "[Kraus's] criticisms of Jews have an incoherent, flailing quality which suggests that they originate, not from observation and judgment, but from a personal source too intimate and deep-seated for Kraus ever to examine it."[170] If we turn to the model of self-hatred articulated by Sander Gilman, it does seem to apply. Kraus clearly internalized the negative images of the Jew prevalent in Austrian society in the late nineteenth century and, by purging himself of those negative qualities associated with Jews, attempted to distance himself from a Jewish identity and integrate himself into the dominant, non-Jewish society. He does, at times, identify with the aggressor, and not the victim, of anti-Semitic hostility. Gilman's description of the double bind experienced by those labeled the "other" is a very apt expression of Kraus's assimilationist dilemma:

[T]he more one attempts to identify with those who have labeled one as different, the more one accepts the values, social structures, and attitudes of this determining group, the farther away from true acceptability one seems to be. For as one approaches the norms set by the reference group, the approbation of the group recedes. In one's own eyes, one becomes identical with the definition of acceptability and yet one is still not accepted. For the ideal state is never to have been the Other, a state that cannot be achieved.[171]

This was the dilemma that Kraus and his Jewish contemporaries were faced with, and Kraus suffered acutely in this situation because he was forced to confront the limits of his assimilationist model. What distinguishes Kraus's case for me, however, is the fact that his identification with the "values, social structures, and attitudes" of Gentile society was only partial. As revealed in the pages of *Die Fackel*, Kraus found much to criticize in mainstream society, not all of which was associated with Jews or informed by Kraus's perspective as a Jew in that society. Kraus was not strictly seeking integration; rather, he was pursuing critical autonomy, striving for an independent, authentic self-definition that was not determined by extrinsic influences. Through his writing Kraus's personal dilemma played out in the public sphere, and it was in a public, professional identity that Kraus sought an alternative to a Jewish one. Timms writes, "First as a moral crusader, later as an artist, finally as a satirist, he sought to define a role that transcended racial (as well as social) affiliations."[172] Kraus's struggle with his views of Jews, religion, and anti-Semitism in his years of producing *Die Fackel* reveals just how difficult this task was to achieve.

Theodor Herzl

Alongside that of Kraus, the case of Theodor Herzl is particularly revealing of the challenges and complexities surrounding Jewish identity at the turn of the twentieth century. Herzl's struggle with his Jewish identity was epic, not only in its determining role in profoundly altering the course of his life, but through his vision of a new future for the Jews. While the identity crises experienced by Kraus and Weininger may have generated more heat in terms of inwardly and outwardly directed aggression, Herzl's solution to his personal identity crisis was no less radical than Weininger's self-destruction or Kraus's extreme assimilationism. Like Kraus, Herzl conducted his struggle in the public eye, and, like Kraus, his changing views of Jewish identity and the Jewish Question cannot be easily reconciled in a smooth evolutionary process but are instead underscored by ambivalence and contradictions. Indeed, in Herzl we seem to have many figures in one: he was an assimilated Jew who first had to map out an identity that combined or chose from Hungarian and Austrian elements. He seems initially to have opted for a Viennese identity, becoming a hyperacculturated Viennese playwright, with the greater aim of becoming a recognized German writer always in mind. He moved into journalism, achieving great success as feuilletonist and foreign correspondent for one of Europe's leading liberal newspapers, ultimately assuming the post of its imposing and influential feuilleton editor. And then, in a radical turn, Herzl became the visionary force behind political Zionism, an international diplomat, the creator and leader of a mass movement, and father of the Jewish State.

These divergent versions of Herzl are all manifestations of his identity crisis as a Jew in Vienna at the end of the nineteenth century. The various intermittent identities prior to the Zionist conversion were all fraught with problems. As a Jew, he was unable to fully assimilate into Viennese society. His goal of attaining recognition as a German writer was compromised by his journalistic writing, as Felix Salten also experienced. And even within journalism, where Herzl reached the pinnacle of success as a writer and editor of international stature, this success was achieved in what had come to be seen as a thoroughly Jewish profession. The turn to Zionism was very much undertaken as an attempt to resolve this personal crisis, just as much as it was an attempt to solve the Jewish Question.

Herzl's continual self-fashioning was a response to his changing views of Jewishness and the possibilities open to Europe's Jews. Herzl's writings—his journalistic and literary works and programmatic Zionist texts—are the clearest expression of these changing views and reveal a number of crucial stages in his understanding of the Jewish Question. In his works we can trace the shift from assimilationism to a model of auto-emancipation for individual Jews, to his turn to the radical, collective solution of the creation of a modern Jewish state. In his turn to Zionism, Herzl would nationalize his private identity crisis. In the way he came to understand the world in which he lived, one's Jewish identity, which he had once viewed as an individual, private matter, became ideologized, necessitating a collective approach. In certain ways Zionism did provide the solutions Herzl was seeking, but never completely. The struggle persisted, and as we shall see, Herzl's writings at every stage are deeply marked by ambivalence, both toward Jewishness and toward his home city of Vienna.

Herzl was born in Pest, in 1860, son of a successful businessman and banker and from a mother of a prominent Jewish family in Pest. Here he was educated in the spirit of the *Haskalah,* or Jewish Enlightenment, in the liberal, secular tradition. Herzl was sent to a technical secondary school after showing proclivities in this area, but he performed poorly at the school, perhaps simply because his interests were shifting toward the humanities, to literature in particular. He joined the Evangelical Gymnasium in 1876. This placed him in an acculturated, socially Jewish milieu, where he would spend most of his life.[173]

In 1878 the family moved to Vienna, shortly after the death of his sister Pauline. Herzl entered the law faculty at the University of Vienna. As a recent immigrant and Hungarian Jew, Herzl tried at this time to shape a new identity that could be more compatible with his new surroundings. His parents were both German speakers and seemed to have embraced the Germanophilism common in Budapest's bourgeois Jewish community. A relationship to German culture had certainly been cultivated in Herzl from an early age, but he might well have developed an identity as a Hungarian, particularly as he was already eighteen when the family emigrated. However, at the University of Vienna, Herzl opted for a different orientation, taking up the German nationalism then in vogue among Viennese middle-class Jewish youth. In 1881 Herzl joined the Albia fraternity and dueling society. This was a prestigious social organization to which Herzl was initially proud to belong. Albia soon began to undergo a visible shift toward anti-Semitism as the entire Pan-German movement adopted a greater stridency under the influence of Schönerer. The initial cultural anti-Semitism of the fraternity did not trouble Herzl unduly, as he could feel personally exempt from such hostility; the target at this time was the unassimilated Jews of Eastern Europe, particularly the Eastern European Jewish students (coming from farther afield than Herzl, from the rural provinces), who had become so numerous in the university's law and medical schools. As the movement adopted racial anti-Semitism, Herzl could no longer feel unaffected. He ultimately withdrew from the fraternity in 1883 in protest of a vehemently anti-Semitic speech by Hermann Bahr at an event honoring Richard Wagner.

Herzl earned a law degree and practiced law briefly, but starting in 1885 he actively pursued a career as a playwright and freelance journalist. Herzl was successful in having an early play, *Der Flüchtling* (*The Refugee*) staged at the *Burgtheater*. However, his career as a playwright yielded only limited success, and Herzl increasingly turned to journalism. In this period, from the mid-1880s through the early 1890s, Herzl made a name for himself as a feuilletonist.

Although, like Felix Salten, Herzl became a master of this form of writing (acknowledged as such in the obituary by his colleagues at the *Neue Freie Presse*), he is not widely known in this vein, nor has this aspect of his work received a great deal of attention. There is, however, an interesting collection of Herzl's Viennese feuilletons compiled and introduced by André Heller.[174] Heller praises Herzl for his alacrity with the difficult task of describing Vienna, which Heller sees as a challenging city, not easily appraised at first glance. These articles present an interesting view of Vienna in which Herzl the feuilletonist, in the vein of Salten, is an observer of the city and the different social worlds it holds. Herzl seems, however, to be an even more detached, distanced observer than Salten. He appears as an outsider, empathetic toward the Viennese he observes, but not a part of them. Notably, Herzl's observed and recorded Vienna is largely a highly subjective and selective compilation of empty and near-empty spaces. In the pieces of this collection, Herzl favors the Prater emptying out on a Sunday afternoon, the empty nursery that prompts a father to reflect on how quickly his children have grown, and an overlooked park in the middle of the city that seems to attract only the very old and very young. Beyond this, Herzl directs his observer's gaze not at the city's showplaces—while he too is attracted to the *Volksprater* and the spectacle of the horse races, he does steer clear of the more elegant city districts—but at sites that are host to the city's downtrodden. In an essay called "Frühling im Elend" ("Springtime in Misery"), Herzl visits the *Allgemeine Krankenhaus,* which he sees both as site of the modern city's residue of suffering and misery and a uniquely rich venue for learning about human nature: "One gets to know other people and their suffering."[175] This is an early encounter of the suffering masses by the man who would come to represent their hope within the Jewish community. He describes the hospital as a place for the masses:

> The masses, from whose lap it is perpetually rising, with whose suffering we must be in contact if we ourselves are to ascend to a new morality. The path to the future must lead through the wretchedness. ... How instructive this place is, and not at all terrible, once one has overcome the first shyness. ... Everything human is singularly intensified, since suffering elevates and glorifies the created.[176]

Another feuilleton takes Herzl out to the *Zinskasernen* (tenements) of the Währing suburb. Here he focuses on a small scrap of land full of trash and broken glass that serves as the children's playground. Herzl shows a good deal of sympathy for these working-class children, who make the best of what they have. The misnamed "meadow" is a paradise for them, where they throw their whole hearts into the games played with far less passion in the wealthier districts and play their own more reckless game of mumblety-peg. Herzl does not connect this scene to any of the challenges resulting from economic modernization and urban growth particular to Vienna; rather, he recognizes something universal in the scene that connects him to the plight of the working classes everywhere.

> And one needs only to have had a good look at a setting like this to learn a great deal—a great deal in this city and in other cities, in other countries. There is a universal streak in this. That place where we always are, we recognize this the least. But when we have moved about in the neighborhoods of other people and then once again stride through our old haunts, then we concede that there is nothing local in all of these aspects of human nature, but rather universal. The same phenomena emerge at the same time in places that don't associate with each other, among people who aren't aware of each other. They are simply people, and they encounter the same conditions of life, and they consequently evolve or degenerate in the same way.[177]

These feuilletons demonstrate Herzl's special attention to the struggles of the lower classes and the marginalized in Viennese society. Robert Wistrich has also recognized in Herzl a "pronounced sensitivity to human suffering and the economic inequalities of bourgeois society," predating his Zionist conversion.[178] With an ethnographer's gaze—and perhaps the eye of the social reformer—Herzl reflects, for example, on how the different social classes experience the Prater in entirely different ways and are connected only by the dust and melancholy that pervade the park on a Sunday afternoon.[179] His eye is drawn to the unemployed man on the park bench, at a loss as to what to do with himself, and the housemaid who doesn't know how to enjoy her very limited time off from work. For Herzl, all of the working people strolling through the Prater just before the beginning of the new workweek have the air of prisoners walking in the prison courtyard, unable to break out to the real freedom one could find out in nature.

In the passage above, in describing his observations of the working-class district, Herzl underscores how his view has been influenced by experiencing the unfamiliar; if one first spends time looking at how various people live and then returns to the familiar, Herzl posits, one will see things with a new perspective. This desire to experience the unfamiliar was a deep-seated need for Herzl during these years. Like the young Stefan Zweig two decades later, the young Herzl was financed by his parents for frequent trips abroad. He combined these travels with the launch of his journalistic career, writing travel pieces that were well received by Viennese audiences. In his Viennese memoirs, *Die Welt von Gestern,* Zweig quotes Herzl relating that his *Wanderlust* was not driven purely by the desire to experience the attractions to be found abroad, but also stemmed from a frustration with Vienna: "It was abroad that I learned everything I know. Only there do we become used to thinking in broad perspectives. I feel sure that here I would never have had the courage for that first idea; they would have destroyed it with their irony before it was fully developed. But thank God, it had matured before I brought it here, so that they could do nothing to harm it."[180]

For Steven Beller, this admission is an expression of the lifelong, deeply ambivalent relationship Herzl experienced with the city of Vienna. While Herzl has at times been characterized as the archetypal Viennese, with his early dandyism, theatricality, and emphasis on outer forms, Beller sees Herzl as more at odds with Viennese society than Herzl likely would have acknowledged at the time, and he views Herzl's Jewish background as the clear impediment to his thorough integration into the city, as well as the source of Herzl's frustrations with the city.[181] Herzl the playwright could not seem to strike a chord with the Viennese theatergoing public. He achieved success in a medium dominated by Jews and was seen as part of the Jewish-press establishment. Like a number of the *Jung Wien* writers, Herzl sought recognition as a German writer while operating within a cultural milieu that was predominantly Jewish. Herzl also favored a self-stylization as an aristocrat, which further set him apart. While Vienna may have had a special relationship to self-presentation, the Viennese population served in many ways as a bulwark against the outsider, whether a Jew, Slav, or other ethnic immigrant.[182] The stumbling blocks to a complete identification with and integration into Viennese life were considerable.

The other factor in Herzl's ambivalent relationship to Vienna was certainly the rise of anti-Semitism as a political force at the precise moment that Herzl's interest in politics was awakening. It was Herzl's experience as a political correspondent in Paris that not only deepened his understanding of the political world, but also provided a new perspective from which to assess developments in his home city. Herzl wrote to a friend in 1895 of his Parisian experience: "I entered the political world, and whether I liked it or not I learned to see the world quite differently. At the same time I gained a freer and higher relationship to the anti-Semitism of my homeland."[183] Herzl's view of Vienna was thus significantly changed by his time in Paris and, it would seem, this view came to be increasingly dominated by a focus on the effects of anti-Semitism. While Herzl at this point began to seek solutions to the Jewish Problem in an ever-widening international sphere, the locus of the problem for him was Vienna.

Herzl's writing of the play *Das neue Ghetto* (*The New Ghetto*) stands as a turning point—one of several—in the development of his thinking about the Jewish Problem and in the origin of Zionism. In a frenetic few weeks in Paris in 1894, Herzl drafted the entire five-act play, incorporating a number of his central views on the issue up to that point.[184] Early in the play, which is set within Vienna's bourgeois Jewish community, Herzl introduces a number of positions he had publicly supported in recent years. Herzl had written a letter to Baron von Leitenberger the previous year in which he concluded, "The Jewish question is neither a national nor a religious question, but a social one."[185] He goes on to propose a two-pronged strategy of highly visible duels between Jews and anti-Semites, and a program of conversion. Regarding duels, Herzl wrote tersely: "Combating the symptom by brute force. Half a dozen duels would do much to raise the Jews' social standing."[186] For his part, he seems to have engaged in fantasies of challenging Schönerer, Lueger, or Alois Liechtenstein.[187] This strand of Herzl's thinking was in keeping with his affinity for the aristocracy, which espoused a code of honor closely related to that of the military. As for conversion, Herzl's expressed his standpoint at this early juncture as "submergence into the people!" In the play, however, Herzl begins to question the effectiveness of such measures. In the character of Dr. Bichler, he presents the figure of the baptized Jew but quickly has the character stipulate that conversion has solved nothing.

In another dialogue within the first act between the respected Rabbi Friedheimer and the central protagonist, Jacob Samuel, the rabbi suggests a positive side to the growth of anti-Semitism. He remarks, "Anti-Semitism isn't all bad. As the movement gains force, I witness a return to religion. Anti-Semitism is a warning to us to stand together, not to abandon the God of our fathers, as many have done."[188] From the rabbi's point of view, anti-Semitism serves as an external pressure effecting a tightening of the Jewish community. Herzl's sense of what might be gained from the movement lay in conceiving of anti-Semitism as a negative but necessary stage in overcoming the Jewish Problem.[189] The Jews were doubtless having a rough time of it, but through this external pressure Herzl thought they might find solutions to the problems of their exclusion and oppression.

Jabob Samuel, Herzl's mouthpiece in the drama, responds to the rabbi by shifting the focus from the anti-Semites to the Jews themselves. Real change, he suggests, will only come when the Jewish character is reformed. Jacob is an attorney married to a woman from a prominent Jewish family; his social world contains both Jews and Christians, and he has conformed to all of the requirements of assimilation. When this character insists that in addition to the visible, external ghetto that has kept the Jews from developing freely there exists a second set of invisible, internal ghetto walls, he gives voice to Herzl's newly acquired view that assimilation is insufficient. Jacob insists that the Jews must transform themselves from within: "Rabbi, these new barriers we must break down after some other fashion than we did the old ones. Outward barriers had to be cleared away from without, but the inner barriers we must clear away ourselves. We ourselves! On our own!"[190]

Jacob has clearly internalized the negative images of Jews evoked by anti-Semitism. This is evidenced by his ambivalence regarding certain segments of the Jewish community, chiefly the circle of "*Borsenjuden*," or Jewish speculators on the stock exchange, into which he has married. He also exhibits a tendency toward overcompensation, having developed a highly rigid moral code of conduct designed to place himself above reproach; he sees this as a kind of moral armor required by Jews: "Yes, we cannot even possess the average flaws that everyone has—otherwise we are the wretched Jews!"[191] While this view clearly involves laying much of the blame for the Jews' problems at their own feet, Jacob softens this stance somewhat by explaining that the Jews' negative traits are the result of their experience of oppression: "In our case it wasn't even nature that made us what we are, but history."[192] This represents an Enlightenment view of European Jewry, a product of the Liberal ideology of emancipation in which Herzl was educated. Throughout the evolution of his thinking on the Jewish Question, Herzl would hold to this dual focus on the emancipation and improvement of the Jews.

Herzl evidently saw the greatest need for inner transformation among the Jews he knew best, those in Vienna's bourgeois Jewish community. The play takes a stinging view of this segment of Viennese society. The Jews in the drama hold social and professional positions in keeping with anti-Semitic stereotypes. They are speculators on the stock exchange, and their financial maneuverings are cast as typical Jewish behavior. Jacob's wife was raised to marry a rich man, and her lavish spending creates financial difficulties for her otherwise cautious and responsible husband. The figure of Wasserstein exhibits exaggerated Jewish characteristics, and while he is a comic figure and somewhat sympathetic, his function is to demonstrate "Jewish difference."[193] There seems to be little hope within this milieu for the kind of self-overcoming that Herzl's hero is calling for. Indeed, the drama is deeply pessimistic on the possibility of finding a solution. If Jacob represents the best hope of escaping the ghetto, his attempt at auto-emancipation is a utopian endeavor that ends tragically in his death in a duel with a Christian nobleman. Despite Jacob's deathbed exhortation to his fellow Jews to free themselves—"Jews, my brothers, you will not be allowed to live again—until you ... I want—out! Out—of—the—ghetto!"—the play offers no individual or collective path out of the ghetto, save in the death of the hero.

Contemporary critics viewed this work as a *Tendenzstück,* a polemical play, like Schnitzler's later *Professor Bernhardi.* Felix Salten wrote in his review of the play, "A play about Jews on the stage is like a burning fuse on a powder keg."[194] Certainly any work that would bring the Jewish Question before the public eye could be expected to be controversial during the Lueger era in Vienna, but Herzl wanted precisely to take his message to a broad audience, stating of this play "*Es muss ins Volk!*" (It has to get before the people!). The play, however, was not controversial because of the subject matter alone. Herzl lit fuses on both sides of the debate with a work that is deeply ambivalent. The drama puts forward a critique of anti-Semitism, which it then undercuts in its very negative depiction of Jewish society and an emphasis on the need for the Jews to overcome the adverse qualities that characterize them. Similarly, the critique of the materialism and moral decadence of Jewish society is relativized by Herzl's attribution of these negative qualities to history. Ultimately the work presents a call for the Jew to escape the inner ghetto without offering a means by which to do so. Herzl's apparent equivocations here are significant, for they reveal that his struggle with the fate of the Jews was not a clear progression toward a straightforward solution in Zionism, but rather was marked by ambivalence at each step along the way.

Having put his views on the Jewish Question before the theatergoing public, Herzl would now begin to shift from politically inspired theater to theatrically inspired politics. Having cast doubt on the effectiveness of auto-emancipation at the individual level, Herzl was poised to move into the collective realm. He began to turn his attention toward the elaboration of a practical program, outlining his solution to the afflictions of the Jews in the book *Der Judenstaat* (*The Jews' State*).[195] This new book was also written in a frenetic three weeks, a first draft completed in June 1895. In a mental state that has variously been viewed as inspired and crisis ridden, Herzl drafted the rationale and practical form of a new Jewish state. Herzl himself reflected on his state of mind at the time: "For me these notes are not work but only relief. I am writing myself free of the ideas which rise like bubbles in a retort and would finally burst the container if they find no outlet."[196] Paris again provided Herzl the psychological distance needed to keenly assess the problem in its Viennese context, still an important locus in Herzl's thinking. Vienna now represented one strand of his understanding of the problem, an example of a society in which Jews were emancipated but continued to face the paradox of emancipation, a place where Jews faced a loss of identity through distancing themselves from the common ghetto experience of the of the past without having realized full equality within the host society. Herzl now viewed the Jews (particularly in the West) as a middle-class people who had attained a measure of economic power and social status that only enflamed the hostilities of non-Jews.[197] At the same time, Herzl's attention was increasingly drawn to the drastic plight of Eastern European Jews. Emancipation had not reached most Jewish communities in the East, and pogroms were a common occurrence in czarist Russia and the eastern provinces of the Habsburg Empire. There are thus (at least) two strands to Herzl's thinking on the nature of the Jewish Problem at this juncture, one citing the Jews' success in integrating into the bourgeoisie of Western societies as a source of increased tensions, and the other continuing to draw on a model of the Jews as a people damaged by their experience of oppression, an unhealthy presence within European society.

Herzl had now come to a conception of the Jews as a *Volk*, an approach that rendered his prior view of conversion, assimilation, and auto-emancipation as unworkable. He would now not only claim that assimilation was futile, as he had in *Das neue Ghetto,* but he would shift his argument significantly, claiming that it would not be desirable for the Jews to dissolve into the broader societies of which they were a part. Here Herzl articulates something positive in a Jewish identity and a Jewish people, which was worth preserving: "The collective personality of the Jews as a people ... cannot, will not, and must not perish."[198] He sees the Jews not only as a community forged by negative, external pressure, but as a people with a shared history and common religion. In this, Herzl is in line with the dominant thinking of the late nineteenth century, in which notions of *Volk* and *Nation* stood at the center of new nationalist ideologies throughout Europe. He departs from this thinking in two ways, however, in that there was no racial component to his conception of the *Volk* and in that the state was to serve the reinvention of the Jew, to be an instrument in the creation of the new Jew, freed of the remnants of the ghetto experience and historical oppression. Moreover, as we shall see, Herzl saw the Jews at this crucial juncture as poised to fulfill a unique historical function for European society.[199]

Herzl's Zionist turn was prompted by the immediate situation of Europe's Jews and by the influence of nationalist thinking on Herzl's view of the matter, as well as by his personal reactions to the establishment in Vienna of anti-Semitism as a viable political force. In a very rational plan, Herzl first lays out the preconditions to Jewish statehood and then details a pragmatic blueprint for its construction. The first phase of the Zionist project as elaborated in *Der Judenstaat* involves preparing the Jewish people for the exodus from Europe forty years in the future. This self-improvement program was to effect the regeneration of the Jews as a people, who would then be prepared to be reorganized into a nation. Herzl imagined an ongoing transformation, with the work beginning prior to leaving Europe and ultimately realized within the new state. His emphasis on paving the way for emigration continues to rest on a view of anti-Semitism as a product of the still-incomplete emancipation of the Jews. Anti-Semitism is ubiquitous and enduring, he concludes; in those states where Jews are openly abused, as well as where they prosper, it has set the Jews apart as a people and exercised visible effects on the Jewish character, he suggests. Herzl writes, "I understand what anti-Semitism is about. We Jews have maintained ourselves, even if through no fault of our own, as a foreign body among the various nations. In the ghetto we have taken on a number of antisocial qualities. Our character has been corrupted by oppression, and it must be restored through some other kind of pressure."[200]

According to *Der Judenstaat* the Jews were to take up Herzl's model of self-overcoming, "wip[ing] our souls clean of all the old, superseded, confused, narrow-minded ideas."[201] With a better understanding of the present historical situation, which Herzl attempts to provide in an extended discussion of historical and contemporary anti-Semitism, the Jewish *Volk* could be gradually transformed into a Jewish nation and could then begin to act as a nation in the international arena and undertake the work of forging a state built on this sense of nationhood. The nation needed to be forged as a group that was able to make political claims internally (of its members) and externally (of other nations) and have the legitimacy to enforce such claims.[202]

But how was the state to take on the authority of national sovereignty? Given the tremendous work ahead, Herzl saw the need for a strong leader to act as the legitimate representative of the Jews. As he had at this point seen himself in this light for several years, he puts himself forward as this person: "I want to place myself at the service of all Jews."[203] Herzl effectively cedes to himself the power of attorney to act as the Jews' representative; drawing on Roman law, he casts this individual as a "gestor," a sort of guardian of the people. Simply and evocatively he states, "So the gestor simply puts on the hat and leads the way."[204] This agent would act on a transitional basis, yielding to a new institution in the Society of Jews as the legal persona to constitute the new state and be charged with its political and social administration.

Herzl envisions the new state as an aristocratic republic, steering clear of democracy in which he had little confidence, envisioning instead a meritocratic system in which the people have an important role to play and every member of society can rise to become a model citizen.[205] He writes, "Political activity has to be conducted from the top. Even so, nobody in the Jews' State will be oppressed, for every Jew who wants to can get to the top and will want to get to the top. Hence there will be an enormous development towards the top in our people. Every individual will think he is advancing himself, but as a result the whole society will advance."[206] The Society of Jews was to campaign for international recognition as the state-creating power. This emphasis on gaining acceptance of the new Jewish homeland within the international arena was crucial to Herzl's conception of the state and, according to Steven Beller, gave expression to the legacy of the ideology of Jewish emancipation and the central tenets of the German Enlightenment that informed it.[207]

Herzl then turned to a second key institution of the Zionist plan, the Jewish Company. This entity was to oversee Jewish migration and settlement and would be charged with the economic planning of the new state. The explanation of the Jewish Company marks the point in the tract where Herzl gives himself over to an elaboration of very detailed planning for the new state and society. He has much to say about the management of migration, the acquisition and distribution of land, the conditions of labor, urban administration, rural development, banking, and financial organization. Throughout there is significant emphasis on technology and its application in the creation of a highly modern nation. Herzl emphasizes the unique situation of making a fresh start in a new land, largely unfettered by tradition, and being able to draw on the best advances and developments in all fields:

> From the start, everything will be determined according to plan. Developing this plan, which I can only briefly indicate, will be the task of our best minds. In this context we will use all the social and technical achievements not only of the time in which we live but also of the future times which will see the difficult execution of the plan. All those fortunate discoveries which have been made, or which still await us, will be used. In this way it can become a historically exemplary form of colonization and state formation, with unprecedented chances of success.[208]

Herzl's text resonates with this optimistic vision of Palestine becoming an exemplary nation, a model state and society. The new Jewish state would not only improve the situation of the Jews, but would contribute to the betterment of mankind. This was to be achieved through the careful selection and implementation of the best of what Europe and America had to offer in technical advancements, intellectual traditions, and legal and economic systems—and also in the fulfillment of what Herzl saw as a special mission for the new Jewish nation. The Jews' State was to be an open society based on the principle of tolerance: "Everybody is as free and unfettered in practicing his belief or unbelief as he is in his nationality. And should it come to pass that persons of other faiths or nationalities live among us, then we will accord them honorable protection and equality before the law. Tolerance we have learned in Europe, and I am not even being sarcastic when I say this. Only in a few isolated instances can you equate modern anti-Semitism with the old religious intolerance. It is in most cases a movement among the civilized peoples, with which they want to ward off a ghost from their own past."[209] Both in light of the Jews' experience of oppression and their rootedness in Enlightenment tradition, the Jews had a special mission of tolerance.

Within this treatise and in his tireless efforts in the diplomatic realm during the years following the publication of *Der Judenstaat*, Herzl revealed himself to be a man with a keen understanding of the political. Even if he was ultimately frustrated in his negotiations over a Palestinian land deal with the Ottoman court and his bid to make the new state a German protectorate under Wilhelm II, Herzl's efforts launched Zionism into the realm of international politics. He had command of both the practical aspects of politics—the negotiations, compromises, logistics, a grasp of the new institutions required for establishing a state—and the less tangible. He understood well that Zionism would need to offer inspiration as well as concrete plans. He wrote, "Believe me, the politics of a whole people—especially when it is so dispersed throughout the whole world—can only be conducted through imponderables, which float in the air. Do you know how the German empire was created? From daydreams, songs, fantasies, and black-red-gold ribbons. And in short order. Bismarck only shook the tree, which the dreamers had planted."[210] Certainly there are elements of Schorske's "politics in a new key" in Herzl's attention to the symbolic aspects of the Zionist movement, for example in the use of his own image in promoting the movement, in his conception of a Jewish flag or attention to the dress of the delegates at the Zionist Congresses.[211] But while he employed some of the methods of post-Liberal politics, this was ultimately carried out, as Beller has argued, in the name of the liberal tradition in which he was steeped.[212] Herzl mobilized the masses and made forays into the newest political approaches; however, he was intent on an appeal and a plan that were rooted in the realm of the rational.

It has often been assumed that Herzl's two significant texts of the late 1890s, *Der Judenstaat* and the novel *Altneuland* (*Old-New Land*) can be neatly divided into the brass-tacks rational argument in the former, and a more emotional appeal for Zionism within the fictional text. Florian Krobb has argued convincingly, however, that the same rhetoric of rationality, planning, and order that defines Herzl's Zionist treatise dominates the novel as well.[213] Certainly the novel makes an emotional appeal in seeking the readers' identification with both the exemplary Jewish characters who settle the new land and the two visitors to Palestine who become converts to the Jewish project. The novel is really both an elaboration of the blueprint laid out in *Der Judenstaat* and an attempt to provide an emotional foundation for the Zionist movement at a time when it needed the infusion of this imaginative account of a Jewish homeland as a model of tolerance. Herzl's writing of the novel at this juncture serves as a reminder that his treatise should not be seen as his last word on the establishment of the Jewish state, but that each of his important iterations must be viewed as part of a long and arduous process of development in his thinking.

Altneuland was written between 1899 and 1902, though Herzl had a number of plot conceptions for a novel sketched out a few years prior. Beller notes that Herzl seemed to turn to fiction at those moments in the development of the movement when he was most in doubt of his success.[214] Reactions to *Der Judenstaat* were varied within the Jewish community: The Western Jewish mainstream responded primarily with indifference. Within religious communities there were objections to Herzl's nationalization of the issue, and the cultural Zionists, mainly

Eastern European, were already established as a powerful force moving in a rather different direction. Within this context, Matti Bunzl sees the novel as both *Bildungsroman* and political utopia: "It functioned both as artistic representation of the Jewish *Volk*'s search for genuine emancipation and as a platform for the cultural program that would guarantee its achievement."[215] Herzl may well have been looking to shore up both his own hopes and the Zionist movement.

Just as the novel is almost a mix of genres, the ideas expressed within it are an amalgam of Herzl's prior thinking and his new ideas and aims. It is structured around two visits to the Jewish settlements in Palestine, one to the crude fledgling developments just before the New Year of 1902, and a return in 1923, by the German-aristocrat-turned-American-millionaire Kingscourt and his companion, Friedrich Loewenberg, a young disaffected Viennese Jewish intellectual who happily turns his back on civilization at Kingscourt's request. The story tells of the introduction of the two men to the new state and society, which unfolds as their gradual conversion to the undertaking. Much in the novel is an imaginative elaboration of ideas introduced in *Der Judenstaat*. There is no less attention to detail as Herzl describes the highly organized migration of Jews from around the world in carefully orchestrated phases, the acquisition of a land lease from the Turkish government, the reclamation and distribution of land, the rapid building of great cities, a centralized welfare system, universal health care system, free educational system, a mutualistic economic order, and a progressive constitution and legal system. In his attention to the technical, Herzl even singles out hydraulic engineers as the "true creators of our Old-New Land" for having drained the swamps, irrigated the steppe, and established hydroelectric power.[216] Here, too, the emphasis is on the implementation of the most modern and progressive technical developments and institutions. The pair's principal guides explain, for example, the ease with which new railway lines were built:

> That was another of the advantages accruing from the creation of an entirely new civilization in the region. Just because up to the beginning of the twentieth century everything here had been neglected, remaining in what might almost be termed a state of nature, the latest technical achievements could be introduced without it being necessary to get rid of the older ones. It was the same in every field—in the building of cities, the railways, the canals, in agriculture as well as in industry. The accumulated experience of all the advanced nations of the world was there to be used by the settlers who streamed into the country from every corner of the globe.[217]

Herzl depicts the Jewish nation as essentially free of the burdens of the past, the ancient land and ancient people notwithstanding, uniquely positioned to draw from the best of what the world had to offer. In the novel he also turns his attention to religion, culture, and matters of the intellect, which were treated more cursorily in the treatise. Religious freedom is a matter of course in the New Society, made clear from the outset when Kingscourt tells his hosts he is not a Jew, and they let him know that such distinctions are irrelevant. A number of different faiths coexist harmoniously within the New Society, the delicate issue of the holy sites sidestepped via a compromise position of leaving things as they are, with the holy places understood as forever the common property of all believers. The novel depicts a vital Judaism as well, entirely removed from state affairs. He describes the familial atmosphere of a Passover seder and a visit to the New Temple in Jerusalem, where the whole city is under the visible sway of the "Sabbath peace" and where Loewenberg experiences another step in his spiritual awakening.

Herzl also takes care to showcase a vital Jewish cultural scene. The passengers attend the opera on their very first night ashore. They meet a talented and successful artist; admire the lavish park system of all of the larger cities; and are introduced to the Jewish Academy, an institution like the *Academie Française* but with a charge that transcends the national in the service of mankind. They are also informed about a luxury cruise organized by the New Society to which the best and brightest of all the world were invited for a six-week voyage on the ship *Fortuna*, where their informal discussions launched a new round of the Platonic Dialogues and recommendations were made on all aspects of the New Society, which were subsequently granted the highest priority by the young government.

Herzl's Jewish characters are his primary vehicles for demonstrating the transformation of the Jewish people. In the Litwak family, from Galicia, which was transplanted from a meager existence in one of Vienna's working-class districts to the new colony by virtue of an unexpected gift from Loewenberg before he left Vienna, Herzl portrays exemplary Jews revitalized by their own labor and commitment to the nation. Their beggar child, David, has made good on his promise to Loewenberg to become an educated man of principle, and the family is the very model of tolerance. In the new land they have found prosperity and a sense of purpose, and they carry with them the commitment to faith, to the Jewish people, and to family that sustained them in their difficult prior life. Their commendable qualities are brought into sharper focus by contrasting them with another segment of Viennese society, part of the upper bourgeoisie, who have relocated to the new land without shedding a trace of the pettiness, materialism, or decadence that characterized them back in Europe. In the New Society, however, their presence is merely tolerated, not respected. Presenting such a contrast sets Herzl apart from other Jewish writers of the period for whom the unassimilated Jews of Eastern Europe are either largely overlooked or portrayed as embodying negative traits. The Litwak family is virtuous before they rise out of a desperate existence; the Jewish Viennese upper bourgeoisie is despicable in the new world as well as the old. It seems that for Herzl the effects of existence in the new ghetto, with its invisible walls, were more damaging than the lingering effects of life in the old ghetto.

In his depiction of Viennese Jews Herzl is far more charitable toward the young dispossessed Jewish intellectuals of which Loewenberg is representative.

The "cultured and despairing Jewish youth" formed a vanguard to carry out the great work of settlement, and even Loewenberg learns that it is not too late to serve the new society.[218] In Vienna the futility of their lives was not only self-defeating, but was a corrupting influence within society, as Herzl cast them as a source of moral bankruptcy within the professions. As early settlers, they find an outlet for their skills and energy that rejuvenates them and drives the nation forward. *Altneuland* belongs to the industrious, but most particularly to those whose commitment to the common good transcends the Jewish community in the service of mankind. At the conclusion to the novel David Litwak is unexpectedly elected president, a gesture through which Herzl stamps the future of the young nation as a reflection of Litwak's values of tolerance and humanity.

In these texts we have witnessed Herzl engaged in a great intellectual struggle through which he sought solutions to both the Jewish Question and his own unresolved Jewish questions as an individual. There is surprising continuity in the thinking of the younger and older Herzl, chiefly in the lingering ambivalence of his views of the Jewish character. Read together, Herzl's texts exhibit a considerable measure of experimentation in his thought, as he continually reappraised his own ideas and took measure of what he believed was possible within distinct contexts for Jews and in the international arena as a whole. David Vital also views Herzl as an adaptable and developing thinker. He writes of Herzl that "[e]ach experience, each failure, impelled him marginally to revise his views and, in the end, radically to recast the form in which he presented them—and, once he had overcome his disappointment, to fortify himself for the stage that was to follow."[219] The last years of Herzl's life were deeply challenging. The Zionist movement was fractured, having split over the Uganda crisis of 1903. Herzl was able to achieve reconciliation among the Zionist factions shortly before his death, however. His life's work did not resolve the questions it undertook to answer, but his commitment as both an indefatigable champion of the cause and as a visionary was staggering and exceptionally influential in the shaping of a modern Jewish identity.

Richard Beer-Hofmann

Richard Beer-Hofmann's response to the crisis of identity experienced by the Jewish aesthetes and intellectuals considered here is markedly different from the paths chosen by his friends and contemporaries. Like them, he was positioned to experience the crisis most acutely, occupying an outsider position as both an artist and a Jew. But while Beer-Hofmann's Jewish background undoubtedly intensified the crisis of the self that was a hallmark of *fin de siècle* Vienna, he also found a solution within this part of the problem. For Beer-Hofmann, a positive commitment to a Jewish identity provided the answer to his crisis of identity.

Harry Zohn has referred to Beer-Hofmann as the only *homo judaicus* among the *Jung Wien* circle of writers.[220] As he alone chose to move away from assimilation, to make an open, sustained commitment to Judaism, one begins to wonder how to account for the difference. What did a Jewish identity come to mean to Beer-Hofmann? What role did it occupy in his life and work? As we shall see, Beer-Hofmann's relationship to Jewishness was an evolving one; as with others in his circle, his views of Jews and Judaism underwent a significant change during World War I. In this chapter I will examine the roots of Beer-Hofmann's Jewish identity. In the following chapter I will assess the shifts in his thinking, examining the treatments of biblical Judaism in his later works.

Richard Beer was born in Vienna, in 1866, to the successful attorney Hermann Beer and Rosa Steckerl Beer. His mother died just a few days after his birth, and Richard was raised by his affluent aunt and uncle Berta and Alois Hofmann, who owned a textile firm in Brno. The Hofmanns moved to Vienna in 1880 and formally adopted Richard in 1884. He attended the prestigious Akademisches Gymnasium and subsequently studied law at the University of Vienna, earning his doctorate in 1890. He grew up in an assimilated bourgeois Jewish family that did not maintain Jewish religious practices or participate actively in the Jewish community. Only Beer-Hofmann's paternal grandmother remained religiously connected. In 1890 Beer-Hofmann became acquainted with the *Jung Wien* writers, and he soon developed a close friendship with Hofmannsthal and Schnitzler. Beer-Hofmann was highly esteemed by the other members of the group as a valuable critic of their work; other contemporary accounts, including comments by Leo Perutz and Elias Canetti, reflect a similar view. Beer-Hofmann also seems to have occupied the curious position of being esteemed as a writer even before producing any texts.[221] He began to write at the urging of Schnitzler and Hofmannsthal, turning first to novellas, followed by poetry, short stories, and dramas. His output was not extensive, and each new work was celebrated as a momentous event by his friends.

There is some debate as to when Beer-Hofmann initially developed a positive Jewish identity.[222] When registering for military service in 1885, he recorded his religious affiliation as Jewish rather than "*Israelitisch*," as was the norm, which created a stir. Nonetheless, there seems to be no textual evidence for such an early identification with his Jewish background. His correspondence and literary works do not reflect a concern with the issue until after 1895. Until this point, Beer-Hofmann had been living the very Viennese life of the aesthete, styling his life as a work of art and devoting his works of art to the reflections, dreams, and preoccupations of fictional characters who could easily have been close relations of Schnitzler's Anatol. His dandyism was unmatched within his circle, and he was satirized for it in Kraus's "Die demolirte Literatur." Over the course of the 1890s, Beer-Hofmann gradually became more critical of aestheticism, as this narcissistic inward turn began to reveal its limits. This is precisely the period in which Beer-Hofmann's sense of a Jewish identity was awakening, and these two strands would increasingly come into conflict. A number of critics have described Beer-Hofmann's aestheticism and Jewish identity as creating a rift within him, but perhaps the best way to understand the effects of these divergent views is in the sense of a productive tension that played a decisive and sustained role in his life and work, as described by Guennadi Vassiliev.[223]

Beer-Hofmann's first articulation of a new commitment to a Jewish identity appears in his 1897 "Schlaflied für Mirjam," a poem dedicated to his newborn daughter. Beer-Hofmann met her mother, Paula Lissy, in 1895. She converted to Judaism, and the two married in a Jewish ceremony in 1897, with Arthur Schnitzler as a witness.[224] Falling in love with Paula and experiencing her conversion along with the birth of their child most likely played a role in Beer-Hofmann's personal turn to Jewish tradition. The poem is a father's rather melancholy rumination on life and death, isolation, and solitude, all frequent themes of the Young Viennese writers.[225] Stefan Scherer identified the central paradox of the poem within this address by the father to his baby: an adult speaks to a child of his loneliness, and while the child is incapable of understanding, the parent's loneliness is ameliorated by telling her about it.[226] The profound isolation experienced by the adult runs through the first three stanzas, expressed most powerfully in the verses, "Blind—that's how we travel, and we travel alone / Nobody can be your companion."[227] The sorrow of these lines is offset by the repetition of the comforting words, "Sleep, my child—go to sleep, my child!" The formal unity underlying the poem's structure—four stanzas of seven verses each, uniform meter, the use of alliteration—also gives the poem a soothing tone, which is in opposition to the themes of the isolated and transitory existence of the individual.[228] The solution proffered by this acceptance of Jewish heritage lies in a self-overcoming that is rooted in the shift from seeing oneself as an individual to understanding the individual as rooted in the historical community of the Jews. The self is ultimately not abrogated, but elevated.[229] Beer-Hofmann's emphasis on blood gives the concept a biological underpinning, binding the Jews across generations. Beer-Hofmann is united with his daughter, the father reassured of the future of the race—now the child can go to sleep.

The poem rehearses a number of significant themes of Beer-Hofmann's novel of 1900, *Der Tod Georgs* (*The Death of Georg*), which he had begun working on much earlier, in 1893, but returned to throughout the decade. The novel depicts a conversion experience for the protagonist, triggered by the death of a friend, in which he moves from a solipsistic existence as an aesthete to the discovery of a meaningful life through his recognition of his position within the Jewish community. The opening chapters of the novel are less an unfolding of the plot—there is scarcely any plot—than the presentation of a series of perceptions, memories, imaginings, and dreams by the protagonist, Paul. This depiction of aestheticism, understood here as a way of viewing the world in which the perceiving subject constitutes his or her own reality and is not directly bound to the reality principle,[230] becomes a critique of aestheticism as the subject goes into crisis.

During the night in which Georg dies suddenly of a heart attack in the next room, Paul has a dream that compels him to confront the implications of his self-referential way of being in the world. He dreams that his wife of seven years is dying, and by witnessing her death as a solitary experience in which he plays no part and over which he has no control, he comes to see the extent to which he has previously denied this woman an existence separate from his. He feels responsible for her death, because he has extinguished her life as an autonomous being, never having seen or sought anything in her but a reflection of himself:

> And no matter what he thought about—her gaze and her walk, the sound of her voice when she sat by him at dusk and spoke—behind it all he once again found only himself; and his own anxious, flickering thoughts stared back at him distorted, with the intimate smile of an accomplice.[231]

When Paul awakens to discover that Georg, and not an imagined wife, has died, he struggles to reconcile his perceptions with reality, aware that his grief is directed more at the loss of his imaginary wife than at Georg. Over several months Paul contemplates death, debating the merits of an early death over a long life that encompasses the challenges of aging and possible illness. Both present unbearable possibilities for him, because, as Walter Sokel has demonstrated, he is still caught up in an egocentric view of the world centered on an unchanging self.[232] Paul finally transcends this view in the novel's final chapter. His conversion constitutes an overcoming of his prior aestheticism, or as Sokel has suggested, its twin, narcissism.[233] This conversion experience is akin to the crisis and conversion of Lord Chandos, with Jewish identity filling the role played by mysticism in Hofmannsthal's text.

In a moment of insight experienced in the park at Schönbrunn, Paul comes to an understanding of the failings of a way of being by which the world is nothing but a reflection of the self, and he begins to recognize the connectedness of all of life. In an instant, his view of life changes: "No one was allowed to live his life for himself alone."[234] His understanding of his connection to the world is conceived in terms of ties of blood. It is through the awareness of these blood ties that Paul envisions a place for himself among the generations of Jews, and through this awareness comes the recognition of a just God; justice is a central aspect of Paul's insight. Here blood is intimately connected to the Jewish ethical tradition embodied in the concept of justice.

> And behind all of them a people, not begging for mercy, winning through their struggle the blessing of their God—wandering through seas, not hindered by deserts, and always sensing the just God flowing through them like blood in their veins.[235]

Beer-Hofmann's affirmation of his Jewish heritage is not strictly speaking a religious conversion, but an embrace of Jewishness as an historical, ethical, and cultural tradition. In light of Beer-Hofmann's awakened Jewish consciousness as expressed in his literary works, he has often been characterized as a spiritual or cultural Zionist. While Beer-Hofmann's embrace of a positive Jewish identity may have been unique within the *Jung Wien* literary circle, many Jews of this generation responded similarly to anti-Semitism and the problems it created for Jews by affirming their Jewish identities. In Vienna just after the turn of the century, a "Jungjüdische Bewegung" (Young Jewish Movement) was crystallizing, espousing an ideology of renewal and youth.[236] At the center of this movement was Martin Buber, who proclaimed a Jewish renaissance and oversaw the Zionist journal *Die Welt* as the movement's main outlet. The movement aimed at the creation of a modern Jewish culture infused with *Jugendstil* ideology and aesthetics.[237] Jacques Le Rider places Beer-Hofmann's *Der Tod Georgs* within this context and sees the writer as a cultural Zionist.

A different tack is taken by Stefan Scherer, who examines Beer-Hofmann's response to Herzl's *Der Judenstaat* and concludes that he was not a Zionist. Herzl sent the book to Beer-Hofmann, who replied, "More even than all that was *in* your book, I found what was behind it sympathetic. At last, someone who does not carry his Jewishness with resignation, like a burden or misfortune, but shows pride at being the legitimate heir to an ancestral culture."[238] Scherer sees in this remark an indirect criticism of Herzl and Zionism, as Beer-Hofmann declined to address the work as a political tract.[239] Seen in this light, Beer-Hofmann's interest in a Jewish identity was strictly cultural, and he opposed political Zionism. Matti Bunzl, however, has challenged this sharp distinction between political and cultural Zionism and objected to the relegation of Beer-Hofmann to the "aesthetic temple."[240] He asks, "How accurate, however, is this structural opposition, which not only denies the cultural construction of political positions, but the political implication of cultural texts and artifacts?"[241] He views Beer-Hofmann as working—along with Buber and Ahad Ha'am and others in the Young Jewish Movement—to create a cultural program with which Western Jews could identify, one that would not require withdrawing their allegiance from Europe and its culture. Bunzl assesses Beer-Hofmann's famous utterance, "I am fully Jewish in substance, fully Austrian functionally,"[242] in terms of a dual mode of national allegiance. He interprets his work as part of a cultural program in which such dual allegiances are sustainable.

While I appreciate Bunzl's argument against any attempt to firmly separate politics and culture in this arena, I do not see Beer-Hofmann demonstrating any interest in Herzl's promotion of Jewish nationhood or see his works as operating within the framework of a Jewish national culture. Nowhere in his early works does Beer-Hofmann characterize the Jews as a nation; they are for him a historical community not bound to any nation. In fact, if we return to the crucial passage in *Der Tod Georgs*, the Diaspora existence of the Jews is underscored, as he professes his admiration for this people who wandered across seas, unimpeded by deserts. In Beer-Hofmann's declaration of a dual allegiance as both Austrian and Jew, I see not a commitment to cultural Zionism but to Jewish Diasporic culture. This is the culture that provides space for both a Jewish identity and participation in the cultural life of Austria.[243] Even when he proclaims an allegiance to Austria, I understand him to be speaking less about a national identity than a cultural one. Ultimately, what Beer-Hofmann created for himself at the turn of the twentieth century was an identity that was both Jewish and Viennese.

Conclusion

How, then, can one sum up the Jewish experience of Vienna around 1900? As I have attempted to show through this long series of individual case studies of authors who sought to chronicle their age, there is no single Jewish experience of Vienna at the turn of the twentieth century. Rather, there was a rich variety of experiences. There are, however, some common features that help us to understand Jewish Vienna around 1900.

First, the Jewish experience of Viennese modernity reflected the same basic cultural crises that affected Austrian intellectuals across ethnic and religious lines. They too experienced identity crises stemming from the redistribution of gender roles, the overthrow of Liberal political values, the dissolution of belief in the concept of a stable self, and, of course, the growing gulf in relations between Jews and non-Jews. However, the ways in which they experienced and described these crises did differ from their Gentile compatriots: they experienced these crises not as universal, but as acutely personal. For Schnitzler, for example, the Jewish identity crisis represented a solitary struggle. And while Herzl espoused a collective solution to the Jewish Question, his commitment to Zionism stemmed from his personal identity crisis and a personal conviction of its insolubility at the individual level.

Second, these authors all expressed anxieties about being caught between cultures, lacking any definite collective identity. They had assimilated enough to be no longer emphatically Jewish but had assimilated into a culture that would not see them as emphatically Austrian either. Perhaps this in-between position was, in retrospect, their de facto collective identity. Herzl, Schnitzler, and Kraus might have been far apart in terms of political and aesthetic views, but they were united in their shared position in between groups and in between periods.

Third, their incredible literary productivity was a direct result of these anxieties and crises. It was through their fiction that they sought to understand a world full of contradictions, and none of their works offered easy answers to these difficult questions. Their attempts to work through issues that could not be adequately addressed in other spheres (such as politics) were also attempts to create spaces in which they could be connected to the various cultures—past, present, and future; Jewish and Austrian—between which they were trapped.

The positions these writers created varied greatly, and I hope to have presented a careful study of them that highlights their differences and does not create a collective identity that did not exist. Such analysis can help us understand this period and these writers in all of their richness, complexity, and contradictions: They asked the same questions, faced the same challenges, and turned to the same media to address these challenges and questions, and their answers reveal a vibrant and challenging debate that would never be resolved.

Notes

1. Article 14 of the Liberal constitution declared, "The enjoyment of civil and political rights is independent of religious denomination" (translation mine). Quoted in Manfred Dickel, *"Ein Dilettant des Lebens will ich nicht sein": Felix Salten zwischen Zionismus und Jungwiener Moderne* (Heidelberg: Universitätsverlag Winter, 2007), 13.
2. Rozenblit, *The Jews of Vienna*, 18.
3. Albert Lichtblau, ed., *Als hätten wir dazugehört. Österreichisch-jüdische Lebensgeschichten aus der Habsburgermonarchie* (Vienna: Böhlau, 1999), 43.
4. Much of this growth was a reflection of the incorporation of the suburbs in 1890. See Rozenblit, *The Jews of Vienna*, 15.
5. Klaus Hödl, *Wiener Juden—jüdische Wiener: Identität, Gedächtnis und Performanz im 19. Jahrhundert* (Vienna: Studienverlag, 2006), 14.
6. See Lichtblau's account of the push-and-pull factors that contributed to Jewish migration patterns, *Als hätten wir dazugehört*, 51–54.
7. Rozenblit, *The Jews of Vienna*, 34.
8. Ibid., 18–19.
9. While they have different emphases and draw on different sources in their research, Steven Beller, Ivar Oxaal, Marsha Rozenblit, Albert Lichtblau, and Michael Pollak, among others, all point to the distinctiveness of the Jewish experience in Vienna from midcentury through World War I.
10. See Carl Schorske, *Fin-de-Siècle Vienna: Politics and Culture* (New York: Vintage Books, 1980).
11. Rozenblit, *The Jews of Vienna*, 48.
12. For a detailed breakdown of Jewish employment, see Lichtblau's presentation of occupational statistics for 1910, *Als hätten wir dazugehört*, 67.
13. Rozenblit, *The Jews of Vienna*, 49.
14. Ibid., 221, note 10. In 1900, Jews comprised 22 percent of the law students, 39 percent of medical students, and 18 percent of philosophy students.
15. See Beller, *Vienna and the Jews*, 88–105.
16. George Mosse, "Jewish Emancipation: Between *Bildung* and Respectability," in *The Jewish Response to German Culture: From the Enlightenment to the Second World War,* Jehuda Reinharz and Walter Schatzberg, eds. (Hanover, NH: University Press of New England for Clark University, 1985), 3.

17. Michael John identifies the "overzealous fulfillment of norms" as a pattern of behavior common to immigrant groups. While the Jews in Vienna threw themselves into education and *Bildung*, for other groups, anti-Semitism functioned in a similar way, as a tool in their assimilation processes. See John, "We Do Not Even Possess Ourselves: On Identity and Ethnicity in Austria, 1880–1937," *Austrian History Yearbook*, Vol. 30 (1999): 36–37.
18. Beller, *Vienna and the Jews*, 34. See also Jacob Katz, "German Culture and the Jews," in Reinharz and Schatzberg, *The Jewish Response to German Culture*, 86.
19. While bourgeois social norms acted as a brake on educational and professional opportunities for bourgeois wives, these same social pressures did open some doors for their daughters, as the model of *Bildung* applied to girls as well as boys, and the education of bourgeois daughters similarly came to be seen as a status symbol.
20. See Marion A. Kaplan, *The Making of the Jewish Middle Class: Women, Family and Identity in Imperial Germany* (New York: Oxford University Press, 1991).
21. Kaplan, *The Making of the Jewish Middle Class*, 31.
22. Several scholars view Rozenblit's account of Jewish residential patterns as overstating Jewish concentration and emphasize instead the integrated character of Vienna's neighborhoods. See, for example, Klaus Hödl, *Wiener Juden—jüdische Wiener;* Ivar Oxaal, "Die Juden im Wien des jungen Hitler," in *Eine Zerstörte Kultur. Jüdisches Leben und Antisemitismus in Wien seit dem 19. Jahrhundert*, eds. Gerhard Botz, Ivan Oxaal, and Michael Pollak (Vienna: Czernin Verglag, 1990), 47–66; and John Boyer, *Political Radicalism in Late Imperial Vienna: Origins of the Christian Social Movement, 1848–1897* (Chicago: University of Chicago Press, 1981).
23. For Rozenblit, Jewish segregation acted as a "strong brake" on the integration of Jews into Gentile society. See Rozenblit, *The Jews of Vienna*, 71–98. As indicated above, others stress the opportunities within these neighborhoods for interactions between Jews and non-Jews.
24. Dickel, "*Ein Dilettant des Lebens will ich nicht sein*," 17.
25. Michael Pollak, "Cultural Innovation and Social Identity in Fin-de-Siècle Vienna," in Ivaar Oxaal, Michael Pollak, and Gerhard Botz, *Jews, Antisemitism and Culture in Vienna* (New York: Routledge, 1987), 62.
26. Theoder Billroth, *Ueber das Lehren und Lernen der medizinischen Wissenschaften an die Universitäten der deutschen Nation nebst allgemeine Bemerkungen über Universitäten: Eine culturhistorische Studie* (Vienna: Carl Gerolds Sohn, 1876).
27. Cited in John Efron, *Medicine and the German Jews: A History* (New Haven: Yale University Press, 2001), 241.
28. Arthur Schnitzler, *Jugend in Wien* (Frankfurt: Fischer Taschenbuchverlag, 1981), 152–55.
29. Cited in Peter Pulzer, *The Rise of Political Anti-Semitism in Austria and Germany*, revised ed. (Cambridge: Harvard University Press, 1988), 147.
30. Dickel, "*Ein Dilettant des Lebens will ich nicht sein*," 19.
31. For a full account, see Pulzer, *The Rise of Political Anti-Semitism in Austria and Germany*, 156–84, as well as George E. Berkley, *Vienna and Its Jews: The Tragedy of Success, 1880s–1980s* (Cambridge, MA: Abt Books, 1988), 93–99.
32. Berkley, *Vienna and Its Jews*, 105.
33. Pollak, "Cultural Innovation and Social Identity in Fin-de-Siècle Vienna," 63.
34. Schnitzler, *Jugend in Wien*, 322.
35. Beller, *Vienna and the Jews*, 74.
36. See Lichtblau, *Als hätten wir dazugehört*, 84–86.
37. For a more extensive analysis of Jewish involvement in the Social Democracy movement, see, for example, Robert Wistrich, "Social democracy, anti-Semitism and the Jews," in Oxaal, Pollak, and Botz, *Jews, Antisemitism and Culture in Vienna*, 111–20.

38. See Rozenblit, *The Jews of Vienna*, 161–64.
39. Rozenblit, *The Jews of Vienna*, 170–74.
40. Cited in Rozenblit, *The Jews of Vienna*, 171. The quote originally appeared in a piece in Joseph Bloch's weekly *Oesterreichische Wochenschrift*.
41. Walter R. Weitzmann, "The Politics of the Viennese Jewish Community, 1890–1914," in Oxaal, Pollak, and Botz, *Jews, Antisemitism and Culture in Vienna*, 135.
42. Lichtblau, *Als hätten wir dazugehört*, 59–60.
43. Rozenblit, *The Jews of Vienna*, 128.
44. See Lichtblau, *Als hätten wir dazugehört*, 85–88.
45. Ibid., 88.
46. Emil Brix and Allan Janik, eds., *Kreatives Milieu, Wien um 1900: Ergebnisse eines Forschungsgespräches der Arbeitsgemeinschaft Wien um 1900* (Vienna: Verlag für Geschichte und Politik, 1993).
47. Allan Janik, "Kreative Milieus: Der Fall Wien," in Brix and Janik, *Wien um 1900*.
48. Janik, "Kreative Milieus: Der Fall Wien," 54. Janik also cautions us here not to overlook the chilly reception the Viennese gave to many of the city's greatest artists—"*Ich moechte betonen, dass Wien tatsaechlich ein kulturelles Treibhaus war. … aber der Tendenz der Gärtner ging dahin, was blühte, verwelken zu lassen,*" ("I would like to emphasize that Vienna was in fact a cultural greenhouse….but the gardners had a tendency to allow everything that bloomed to wither."), 46.
49. Lichtblau, *Als hätten wir dazugehört*, 88.
50. Jacques Le Rider, *Modernity and Crises of Identity: Culture and Society in Fin-de-Siècle Vienna*, trans. Rosemary Morris (New York: Continuum, 1993), 294.
51. Beller, *Vienna and the Jews*, 214.
52. See Rolf-Peter Janz and Klaus Laermann, *Zur Diagnose des Wiener Bürgertums im Fin de Siècle* (Stuttgart: Metzler, 1977).
53. Bruce Thompson, *Schnitzler's Vienna: Image of a Society* (New York: Routledge, 1990), 1.
54. Peter Gay, *Schnitzler's Century: The Making of Middle-Class Culture, 1815–1914* (New York: Norton, 2001).
55. See Florian Krobb, "Gefühlszionismus und Zionsgefühle: Zum Palästina-Diskurs bei Schnitzler, Herzl, Salten und Lasker-Schüler," in *Sentiment, Gefühle, Empfindungen: Zur Geschichte und Literatur des Affektiven von 1770 bis heute*, Anne Fuchs and Sabine Strümper-Krobb, eds. (Würzburg: Königshausen und Neumann, 2003), 155.
56. For the social topography of this area, see Thompson, *Schnitzler's Vienna*, 6.
57. Arthur Schnitzler, *Der Weg ins Freie* (Berlin: S. Fischer Verlag, 1922), 45.
58. Schnitzler, *Jugend in Wien*, 93.
59. Schnitzler, *Der Weg ins Freie*, 112.
60. Ibid., 113.
61. Ibid., 283.
62. Ibid.
63. Ibid., 299–300.
64. Ibid., 95.
65. Ibid., 377.
66. Ibid., 142.
67. Ibid., 244.
68. Ibid., 447.
69. Le Rider, *Modernity and Crises of Identity*, 182.
70. Felix Salten *Berliner Tageblatt*, 15 November 1917.
71. Brandes's review appeared in *Der Merker*, in February 1913.

72. See Arthur Schnitzler, Letter to Georg Brandes, (27 February 1913).
73. See Mark Anderson, *Kafka's Clothes: Ornament and Aestheticism in the Habsburg Fin de Siècle* (New York: Oxford University Press, 1992).
74. Yosef Hayim Yerushalmi, *Freud's Moses: Judaism Terminable and Interminable* (New Haven: Yale University Press, 1991), 63.
75. See Daniel Boyarin, *Unheroic Conduct: The Rise of Heterosexuality and the Invention of the Jewish Man* (Berkeley: University of California Press, 1997), 33–38.
76. Theodor Herzl, *Zionistisches Tagebuch, 1895–1899, Briefe und Tagebücher,* vol. II, ed. Johannes Wachen, et al. (Berlin: Propyläen, 1983), 81. Diary entry of 8 June 1895.
77. Arthur Schnitzler, *Professor Bernhardi, Das Weite Land: Dramen, 1909–1912* (Frankfurt: Fischer, 1993), 188.
78. Ibid., 192.
79. Ibid., 250.
80. This work is scarcely mentioned in literary scholarship. Ritchie Robertson refers to it briefly but dismisses it rather quickly, objecting that it "reads like an unbalanced imitation of *Der Weg ins Freie.*" See Robertson, *The Jewish Question in German Literature, 1749–1939: Emancipation and Its Discontents* (Oxford: Oxford University Press, 1999), 276. One article does present a full analysis of the work: Andreas Herzog, "Die Mischehe zur Lösung der Judenfrage: Adolf Dessauers Roman Großstadtjuden im soziokulturellen Kontext der Wiener Jahrhundertwende," http://www.kakanien.ac.at/beitr/fallstudie/AHerzog3.pdf.
81. Adolf Dessauer, *Großstadtjuden* (Vienna: Braumüller, 1910), 6.
82. Ibid., 62.
83. For a discussion of *mauscheln,* see Sander L. Gilman, *Jewish Self-Hatred: Anti-Semitism and the Hidden Language of the Jews* (Baltimore: The Johns Hopkins University Press, 1986).
84. Dessauer, *Großstadtjuden,* 212.
85. Stefan Zweig, *Die Welt von Gestern* (Frankfurt: Fischer, 1970), 25.
86. Quoted in Dickel,"*Ein Dilettant des Lebens will ich nicht sein,*" 345.
87. Dessauer, *Großstadtjuden,* 116.
88. Leitisch, *Damals in Wien,* quoted in Dickel, 30.
89. Dessauer, *Großstadtjuden,* 425.
90. Ibid., 460.
91. Manfred Dickel treats a number of these later reflections by Salten in detail. See his discussion of Salten's feuilleton pieces for the *Neue Freie Presse* on his youth, in Dickel, "*Ein Dilettant des Lebens will ich nicht sein,*" 77–122, especially 90–91 for Salten's later reaction to the dramatic shift in the family's fortunes.
92. Ibid., 109.
93. Ibid., 105–8.
94. Ibid., 121.
95. Edward Timms, *Karl Kraus, Apocalyptic Satirist: Culture and Catastrophe in Habsburg Vienna* (New Haven: Yale University Press, 1986), 5.
96. Susanne Blumesberger, "Felix Salten und seine vielfältigen Beziehungen zu Wien," in *Felix Salten—der unbekannte Bekannte,* Ernst Seibert and Susanne Blumesberger, eds., (Vienna: Praesens, 2006), 16.
97. Ibid., 25.
98. For an assessment of Salten's work in this field and its reception, see Rahel Rosa Neubauer, "Felix Salten als Autor jüdischer Kinder-und Jugendliteratur," in Seibert and Blumesberger, *Felix Salten—der unbekannte Bekannte.*
99. See the catalog to the 2006–2007 Salten exhibit of Vienna's Jewish Museum, *Felix Salten, Schriftsteller—Journalist—Exilant,* Siegfried Mattl and Werner Michael Schwarz, eds., (Vienna: Holzhausen, 2006); *Felix Salten: Wurselprater. Ein Schlüsseltext zur Wiener Moderne,*

eds. Siegfried Mattl, Klaus Müller-Richter, and Werner Michael Schwarz (Vienna: Promedia, 2004); Manfred Dickel, *"Ein Dilettant des Lebens will ich nicht sein"*; Seibert and Blumesberger, *Felix Salten—der unbekannte Bekannte;* and Jürgen Ehneß, *Felix Saltens erzählerisches Werk. Beschreibung und Dichtung* (Frankfurt: Lang, 2002).

100. Arthur Schnitzler, *Tagebücher,* 24 Nov. 1911, cited in Ehneß, *Felix Saltens erzählerisches Werk,* 315.
101. *"Unter dem Strich"* refers to the line appearing near the bottom of the front page of a newspaper, separating the hard news from the more impressionistic feuilleton writing.
102. Stefan Zweig, *Die Welt von Gestern. Erinnerungen eines Europäers* (Frankfurt: Fischer Taschenbuch Verlag, 1970, 33. edition, 2002), 123.
103. On Salten's literary style, see Ehneß, *Felix Saltens erzählerisches Werk.*
104. Felix Salten, "Die Wiener Straße," *Das österreichische Antlitz* (Berlin: Fischer, nd) 18.
105. Ibid.
106. See Dickel, *"Ein Dilettant des Lebens will ich nicht sein,"* 336.
107. Salten, "Aristokratenvorstellung," *Das österreichische Antlitz,* 39.
108. Salten, "Gewehr Heraus!" *Das österreichische Antlitz,* 228.
109. Ibid., 230.
110. Salten, "Stahlehner," *Das österreichische Antlitz,* 64.
111. Salten, "Beim Brady," *Das österreichische Antlitz,* 74.
112. Dickel, *"Ein Dilettant des Lebens will ich nicht sein,"* 352.
113. Dickel, *"Ein Dilettant des Lebens will ich nicht sein,"* 352.
114. Salten, "Spaziergang in der Vorstadt," *Das österreichische Antlitz,* 126.
115. He does treat the Praterallee as the territory of the aristocracy in other essays, collected in the volume *Wiener Adel* (Leipzig, 1905). See the discussion in Dickel, *"Ein Dilettant des Lebens will ich nicht sein,"* 345 ff.
116. Mattl, Müller-Richter, and Schwartz, *Felix Salten: Wurstelprater,* 137, translation mine.
117. Ibid., 140.
118. Ibid., 76.
119. Ibid.
120. Ibid., 104–5.
121. Ibid., 109–10.
122. While I have limited my focus in this study to writers who spent most of their careers living and writing in Vienna, in Zweig's case I am making an exception, because he is so closely associated with Vienna at the beginning of the twentieth century as a result of his memoirs.
123. On the Zweig family's move from the ghetto to the city and their ascent into affluent society, see Leo Spitzer, "Into the Bourgeoisie: A Study of the family of Stefan Zweig and Jewish Social Mobility, 1750–1880," in *Stefan Zweig: The World of Yesterday's Humanist Today, Proceedings of the Stefan Zweig Symposium,* ed. Marion Sonnenfeld (Albany: SUNY Press, 1983), 64–81.
124. Quoted in Klara Carmely, "The Ideal of Eternal Homelessness: Stefan Zweig and Judaism," in *Stefan Zweig: The World of Yesterday's Humanist Today,* 66.
125. Carmely, "The Ideal of Eternal Homelessness: Stefan Zweig and Judaism," 114.
126. Leon Botstein, "Stefan Zweig and the Illusion of the Jewish European," in *Stefan Zweig: The World of Yesterday's Humanist Today,* 91.
127. See Chapter 2 for a more extensive discussion of this linkage. See also Sarah Fraiman, "Das Tragende Symbol: Ambivalenz Jüdischer Identität in Stefan Zweigs Werk," *German Life and Letters* 55:3 (July 2002): 248–65.
128. David Turner, *Moral Values and the Human Zoo: The Novellen of Stefan Zweig* (Hull, England: Hull University Press, 1988), 198.
129. Turner, *Moral Values and the Human Zoo,* 198–199.

130. Stefan Zweig, *Phantastische Nacht: Erzählungen* (Frankfurt: Fischer, 1982), 176.
131. Hanni Mittelmann, "Fragmentation and the Quest for Unity: Stefan Zweig's Novellas as Tales of the Assimilationist Jewish Predicament," in *Stefan Zweig Reconsidered: New Perspectives on his Literary and Biographical Writings,* Conditio Judaica 62, ed. Mark Gelber (Tübingen: Niemeyer, 2007) 163–74.
132. Ibid., 164–66. On Weininger's critique of Jewishness and its connection to gender and sexuality, see Sander L. Gilman, "Weininger and Freud: Race and Gender in the Shaping of Psychoanalysis," and John Hoberman, "Otto Weininger and the Critique of Jewish Masculinity," both in *Jews and Gender: Responses to Otto Weininger,* eds. Nancy A. Harrowitz and Barbara Hyam (Philadelphia: Temple University Press, 1995,) 103–20, 141–53, as well as Le Rider, *Modernity and Crises of Identity,* 88–89, 165–68, 170–72.
133. Jacques Le Rider, among others, favors the view that Hofmannsthal repressed his own Jewish identity, steering clear of commenting on the Dreyfus Affair, for example, and making only oblique references to anything related to the Jewish Question. See Le Rider, *Modernity and Crises of Identity,* 254, 286.
134. See, above all, Jens Rieckmann, "Zwischen Bewusstsein und Verdrängung: Hofmannsthals jüdisches Erbe," *Deutsche Vierteljahrsschrift für Literaturwissenschaft und Geistesgeschichte,* 67:3 (September 1993), 466–83. See also Peter C. Pfeiffer, "1893, Hugo von Hofmannsthal worries about his Jewish mixed ancestry," in *Yale Companion to Jewish Writing and Thought in German Culture, 1096–1996,* eds. Sander L. Gilman and Jack Zipes (New Haven: Yale University Press, 1997), 212–18.
135. Beller, *Vienna and the Jews,* 13.
136. Felix Salten, "Der junge Hofmannsthal: das Bild eines Dichters," *Neue Volkszeitung,* date unknown, referenced in Beller, *Vienna and the Jews,* 77.
137. Rieckmann, "Zwischen Bewusstsein und Verdrängung," 472.
138. Ibid., 474–77.
139. Hofmannsthal, unpublished material of the Houghton Library (Tage- und Notizbücher, 147.11.3), quoted in Rieckmann, "Zwischen Bewusstsein und Verdrängung," 466.
140. On the claims of racial science regarding Jewish difference, see Sander L. Gilman's extensive work, particularly *The Jew's Body* (New York: Routledge, 1991). See, too, John Efron, "The Jewish Body Degenerate?" in his *Medicine and the German Jews: A History* (New Haven: Yale University Press, 2001), 105–50.
141. Rieckmann, "Zwischen Bewusstsein und Verdrängung" 467.
142. For a very good treatment of the contours of the modernism of the *Jung Wien* circle, and in particular the reception by these writers of Freud's work, see Michael Worbs, *Nervenkunst: Literatur und Psychoanalyse im Wien der Jahrhundertwende* (Frankfurt: Europäische Verlagsanstalt, 1983).
143. *Hugo von Hofmannsthal—Arthur Schnitzler, Briefwechsel,* eds. Therese Nickl and Heinrich Schnitzler (Frankfurt: Fischer Taschenbuch, 1983), 238.
144. Hofmannsthal, Letter to Franziska Schlesinger, 13 July 1898(?), quoted in German, in Rieckmann, "Zwischen Bewusstsein und Verdrängung," 477. Translated by the author.
145. Hugo von Hofmannsthal, *Reden und Aufsätze III 1925–1929. Aufzeichnungen,* eds. Bernd Schoeller, Ingeborg Beyer Ahlert (Frankfurt, 1980), 383. Quoted in Rieckmann, "Zwischen Bewusstsein und Verdrängung: Hofmannsthals jüdisches Erbe," 478.
146. Adrian Del Caro, "Hofmannsthal's Vienna 1890–1900: The Poetics of Transition," in *Turn-of-the-Century Vienna and Its Legacy: Essays in Honor of Donald G. Daviau,* eds. Jeffrey B. Berlin, Jorun B. Johns, Richard H. Lawson (Vienna: Edition Atelier, 1993), 47–65.
147. Cited in Pfeiffer, "1893, Hugo von Hofmannsthal worries about his Jewish mixed ancestry," 218.
148. Ibid.

149. Edward Timms, *Culture and Catastrophe*, 182–83. Timms' two-volume study of Kraus is, in my view, the authoritative work on Kraus. The second volume, published in 2005, treats the satirist's postwar writings: *Karl Kraus, Apocalyptic Satirist: The Post-War Crisis and the Rise of the Swastika* (New Haven: Yale University Press, 2005).
150. Robert S. Wistrich, *Laboratory for World Destruction: German and Jews in Central Europe* (Lincoln: University of Nebraska Press for the Vidal Sassoon International Center for the Study of Antisemitism, The Hebrew University of Jerusalem, 2007), 306.
151. Timms, *Culture and Catastrophe*, 241.
152. Ibid.
153. Caroline Kohn, "Karl Kraus und das Judentum," in *Im Zeichen Hiobs: Jüdische Schriftsteller und deutsche Literaturim 20. Jahrhundert*, eds. Gunter E. Grimm and Hans-Peter Bayerdörfer (Frankfurt: Athenäum, 1986), 149.
154. See Ritchie Robertson, "The Problem of 'Jewish Self-Hatred' in Herzl, Kraus and Kafka," *Oxford German Studies* 16 (1985): 94.
155. *Die Fackel* 386 (October 1913). Facsimiles of the entire run of *Die Fackel* are available online through the Austrian Academy at http://corpus1.aac.ac.at/fackel.
156. Paul Reitter, "Karl Kraus and the Jewish Self-Hatred Question," *Jewish Social Studies* 10.1 (2003): note 14, 108–9.
157. Karl Kraus, "Eine Krone für Zion," *Fruhe Schriften II, 1897–1900* (Munich: Kösel Verlag, 1979), 312.
158. Ibid., 306.
159. Ibid., 309.
160. Ibid.
161. Kraus, *Die Fackel*, 23 Jan. 1899, 7. The original reads: "*Nur muthiges Säubern in den eigenen Reihen, nur das Ablegen der Eigenthümlichkeiten einer Rasse, die durch die vielhundertjährige Zerstreuung längst aufgehört hat, eine Nation zu sein, kann all der Qual ein Ende machen. Die goldenen und die zeitungspapiernen Gitter, die heute noch das Ghetto umschliessen, müssen fallen. Durch Auflösung zur Erlösung! Sonst sieht das vielberufene zwanzigste Jahrhundert Excesse ärgerer Art.*"
162. For more on the influence of Chamberlain and his treatise, see *Die Grundlagen des neunzehnten Jahrhunderts*, see Timms, *Culture and Catastrophe*, 238–40.
163. Kraus, *Die Fackel* 386, 15 (1913), 3.
164. Ibid. See also Sander L. Gilman, *Jewish Self-Hatred: Anti-Semitism and the Hidden Language of the Jews* (Baltimore: The Johns Hopkins University Press, 1986), 236.
165. Kraus, *Die Fackel* 386, 15 (1913), 6.
166. Timms, *Culture and Catastrophe*, 240.
167. Jacques Le Rider, Ritchie Robertson, and Robert Wistrich, for example, treat Kraus as a Jewish anti-Semite, analyzing the character of his anti-Semitic statements and assessing his relationship to Jewish identity in this vein. See also Mark Anderson's *Kafka's Clothes*, which takes a similar position.
168. See Reitter, "Karl Kraus and the Jewish Self-Hatred Question," 80 (note 29), 110.
169. Shulamith Volkov, "Antisemitism as a Cultural Code: Reflections on the History and Historiography of Antisemitism in Imperial Germany," in *The Nazi Genocide: History Articles on the Destruction of European Jews*, vol. 2, ed. Michael Marrus (Westport, CT: 1989), 307–30.
170. Robertson, "The Problem of 'Jewish Self-Hatred' in Herzl, Kraus and Kafka," 99.
171. Gilman, *Jewish Self-Hatred*, 2–3.
172. Timms, *Culture and Catastrophe*, 239.
173. Steven Beller, *Herzl* (London: Peter Halban, 1991), 3.
174. Theodor Herzl, *Ein echter Wiener: Feuilletons, kommentiert von André Heller* (Vienna: Edition Wien, 1986).

175. Ibid., 18.
176. Ibid., 19.
177. Ibid., 90.
178. Robert Wistrich, *The Jews of Vienna in the Age of Franz Joseph* (Oxford: Oxford University Press, 1989), 452.
179. Ibid., 12.
180. Zweig, *Die Welt von Gestern*, 131–32, cited and translated in Wistrich, *The Jews of Vienna in the Age of Franz Joseph*, 493.
181. Beller, *Herzl*, 9–12.
182. Michael Burri, "Theodor Herzl and Richard von Schaukal: Self-Styled Nobility and the Sources of Bourgeois Belligerence in Prewar Vienna," in *Rethinking Vienna 1900* (New York: Berghahn Books, 2001), 108–9.
183. Alex Bein, "Some Early Herzl Letters," in *Herzl Yearbook*, vol. I, 302–4, cited in Beller, *Herzl*, 15.
184. It has often been contended that Herzl wrote the play under the influence of the Dreyfus Affair in Paris, but scholars have convincingly demonstrated that the scandal was not decisive in Herzl's shaping of this work, as the trial began after the play was written. Scholars have concluded that the Dreyfus Affair was one of several factors that influenced Herzl's thinking as he made the turn to Zionism, but not the seminal event he once characterized it as. See, for example, Wolfgang Sabler, "Theodor Herzl, *Das neue Ghetto*. Antisemitismus und Dramaturgie," in *Aspekte des politischen Theaters und Dramas von Calderón bis Georg Seidel; deutsch-französische Perspektiven* (New York: Lang, 1996), 229–54.
185. Cited and translated in Jörg Thunecke, "'Dynamite' or 'Affront'? The Jewish Question in Herzl's Play *Das neue Ghetto*," in *Theodor Herzl and the Origins of Zionism*, Austrian Studies VIII, eds. Ritchie Robertson and Edward Timms (Edinburgh: Edinburgh University Press, 1997), 63.
186. Ibid.
187. Beller, *Herzl*, 22.
188. Cited and translated from Act I, Scene 8, in Thunecke, "'Dynamite' or 'Affront'?" 68.
189. Beller, *Herzl*, 24.
190. Cited and translated from Act I, Scene 8, in Thunecke, "'Dynamite' or 'Affront'?" 69.
191. Theodor Herzl, *Das neue Ghetto, Gesammelte Zionistische Werke*, V. Band (Berlin: Jüdischer Verlag, 1935), (II, 1), 46–47.
192. Cited and translated from Act II, Scene 1, in Thunecke, "'Dynamite' or 'Affront'?" 69.
193. For a fuller analysis of this character and his *Doppelgänger* Rheinberg, see Sabler, "Theodor Herzl, *Das neue Ghetto*. Antisemitismus und Dramaturgie," as well as Robertson, "The Problem of 'Jewish Self-Hatred' in Herzl, Kraus and Kafka," 86–87.
194. Felix Salten, 7 January 1898, *Wiener Allgemeine Zeitung*, cited and translated in Thunecke, "'Dynamite' or 'Affront'?" 71.
195. "The Jews' State" is the translation recommended by David Vital in his *The Origins of Zionism* (Oxford: Oxford University Press, 1975). This rendering is appropriately specific, as Herzl's vision was not to create a state of that was particularly Jewish, but rather a modern secular state for the Jewish population. See the discussion by Henk Overberg in the introduction to his translation, *The Jews' State, Theodor Herzl: A Critical English Translation* (Northvale, NJ: Jason Aronson Inc., 1997), 3–6.
196. Theodor Herzl, 12 June 1895, cited and translated by Overberg, *The Jews' State, Theodor Herzl: A Critical English Translation*, 9.
197. Herzl, *The Jews' State*, 131.
198. Ibid., 132
199. Beller identifies three layers to Herzl's view of Jewish identity, shifting at different moments; they correspond to a negative identity (imposed from without), a positive identity, and a

normative one, based on the notion of the Jews having a special role to perform. See Beller, *Herzl*, 56.
200. Herzl, *The Jews' State*, 64.
201. Ibid., 134.
202. Ibid., 96–97.
203. Herzl, 13 June 1895, cited and translated in Overberg's critical edition of Herzl's *The Jews' State*, 98.
204. Herzl, *The Jews' State*, 99.
205. For more on the Western traditions from which Herzl derived his state theory, see Beller, *Herzl*, 57–61.
206. Theodor Herzl, *The Jews' State*, 195.
207. Beller, *Herzl*, 60.
208. Herzl, *The Jews' State*, 193–94.
209. Ibid., 196–97.
210. Theodor Herzl, *Briefe und Tagebücher*, vol. 2, 332, cited and translated in Beller, *Herzl*, 67.
211. See Carl E. Schorske, *Fin-de-Siècle Vienna*, 116–8
212. Beller, *Herzl*, 72–73.
213. Krobb, "Gefühlszionismus und Zionsgefühle," 149–63.
214. Beller, *Herzl*, 85.
215. Matti Bunzl, "The Poetics of Politics and the Politics of Poetics: Richard Beer-Hofmann and Theodor Herzl Reconsidered," *The German Quarterly* 69:3 (Summer 1996): 286.
216. Theodor Herzl, *Altneuland, Old-New Land*, trans. Paula Arnold (Haifa: Haifa Publishing Company, 1961), 175.
217. Ibid., 101.
218. Ibid., 102.
219. Vital, *The Origins of Zionism*, 248.
220. Harry Zohn, "Herzl and the Young Vienna Circle," in Gilman and Zipes, *Yale Companion to Jewish Writing and Thought in German Culture*, 233.
221. Stefan Scherer, *Richard Beer-Hofmann und die Wiener Moderne*, Conditio judaica 6 (Tübingen: Max Niemeyer Verlag, 1993), 3.
222. Ibid., 385.
223. Guennadi Vassiliev, "Richard Beer-Hofmanns 'Der Tod Georgs'. Zum Problem Ästhetizismus und Judentum," *Österreich in Geschichte und Literatur*, 46:2 (2002): 120–33. He concludes, "*Die Schwankungen zwischen Ästhetizismus und Judentum setzen sich im ganzen Leben des Schriftstellers fort und werden zum entscheidenen und befruchtenden Moment für sein Schaffen.*" (p. 133).
224. Robertson, *The Jewish Question in German Literature*, 453.
225. See Le Rider, *Modernity and Crises of Identity*, 34–35.
226. Scherer, *Richard Beer-Hofmann und die Wiener Moderne*, 81.
227. The poem is reproduced in Scherer, *Richard Beer-Hofmann und die Wiener Moderne*, 78.
228. Scherer, *Richard Beer-Hofmann und die Wiener Moderne*, 80.
229. See Walter H. Sokel, "Narzissmus und Judentum: Zu Richard Beer-Hofmanns 'Der Tod Georgs,'" *Literatur und Kritik* (Feb., March 1988): 221–22.
230. See Scherer, *Richard Beer-Hofmann und die Wiener Moderne*, 201–3.
231. Richard Beer-Hofmann, *Der Tod Georgs, Gesammelte Werke* (Frankfurt: Fischer, 1963), 563.
232. Sokel, "Narzissmus und Judentum," 15.
233. Ibid., 8.
234. Beer-Hofmann, *Der Tod Georgs*, 617.
235. Ibid., 622.
236. For more on this movement around Martin Buber, see Le Rider, *Modernity and Crises of Identity*, 289–93.

237. Le Rider, *Modernity and Crises of Identity*, 290.
238. Quoted and translated in Le Rider, *Modernity and Crises of Identity*, 274.
239. Scherer, *Richard Beer-Hofmann und die Wiener Moderne*, 388. Jacques Le Rider holds a similar view. See *Modernity and Crises of Identity*, 274.
240. Bunzl, "The Poetics of Politics and the Politics of Poetics," 279.
241. Ibid., 278.
242. Quoted and translated in Zohn, "Herzl and the Young Vienna Circle," 233.
243. For a more extensive discussion of Diaspora culture, see the insightful essay by Daniel Boyarin and Jonathan Boyarin, "Diaspora: Generation and the Ground of Jewish Identity," in *Identities,* eds. Kwame Anthony Appiah and Henry Louis Gates, Jr. (Chicago: University of Chicago Press, 1995), 305–337.

Chapter 2

JEWISH VIENNA BETWEEN THE WORLD WARS

The period between the two world wars was an exceptionally tumultuous time in modern Austrian history. The world of Austrian Jews would be profoundly changed by World War I, overturned completely by its outcome, and subsequently shaken again by the rise of the Right and the new forms of anti-Semitism that developed, first by Austria's own authoritarian regime, then by Austro-fascism and the *Anschluss*. With the identity crises of the turn of the century still unsolved, Austrian Jews were plunged into still another identity crisis, which would similarly prove largely insoluble. Yet it was the very rise of anti-Semitism that prompted Austrian Jews to come to identify more deeply as Jews. This heightened sense of Jewish identity took a variety of forms and is reflected in interesting ways in the literary engagements of Viennese Jewish writers. In the chapter that follows I will give an overview of the major developments of this period, their effects on Austria's Jews, and the various forms of Jewish responses to these developments. I will then turn to a closer analysis of individual writers and the works in which their responses took shape.

Jewish Identity and World War I

The many forms of Jewish identity painstakingly constructed by Jews in the waning years of the Austro-Hungarian Empire—occasionally adopted in a single stroke but more often the result of a laborious process—would all be shaken to the core by World War I and its aftermath. The collapse of the Habsburg Empire brought an end to the world that its Jewish subjects had known and to the particular positions they had occupied within it. Without having resolved the identity crises that accompanied the turn of the century, Austrian Jews were now confronted with the dilemma of coming to terms with a new world order in which nationhood and community were defined in ways increasingly inhospitable to Jews. In the face of new political constellations and a desperate situation after a grueling war, it was imperative—yet largely impossible—for Jews to meet the challenge of forging a new sense of identity. The chaos of the interwar period marked the foreclosure of one possibility after another for Jewish belonging and, ultimately, survival.

Prior to World War I, Vienna was host to what was by far the largest Jewish urban community in Austria. In 1910, there were 175,318 Jews in the capital, comprising 9 percent of the population of approximately 2 million residents.[1] This was a large and diverse Jewish community, encompassing a full range of possibilities for identification, from adherence to Judaism and traditional Jewish culture to secularism and assimilationism. While Zionism was certainly stronger in Galicia and Bukovina and did not gain a strong foothold in Vienna, the movement did provide some Viennese Jews with an ideology and identity. Others who also possessed a strong sense of Jewish consciousness favored a form of Jewish nationalism that was Diaspora oriented and not focused on the rebuilding of a Jewish homeland.

Vienna's Jewish community was well organized. The largest organization was the *Österreichisch-israelitische Union* (Austrian Israelite Union), which was committed to Jewish solidarity and Austrian patriotism and tended to oppose forms of Jewish nationalism.[2] The *Israelitische Kultusgemeinde* was the legally mandated Jewish religious community to which all Viennese Jews belonged, though the community tax base was supported by only about one-third of Jewish households.[3] Beyond these larger institutions, many Jewish organizations were established, seeking to assert different forms of Jewish identity in the context of turn-of-the-century Vienna, to provide a social network, and to administer welfare programs for Viennese Jews. Additionally, Vienna was home to a great many Jews who did not identify strongly with the Jewish community at large, although, as we have seen, this did not preclude them from feeling a sense of Jewish identity, whether desired or not.

In the previous chapter I explored a number of different positions regarding Jewish identity adopted by the most prominent Viennese Jewish writers at the turn of the twentieth century. While these strategies on identity diverged widely, those who experimented with them shared a common position as Jews living in the multiethnic capital of the multiethnic empire. Unlike the other minorities in Austria, Jews were not perceived—and did not see themselves—as a nation. They shared neither common territory nor a common language. They were not collectively driven by political aspirations; their economic distribution was distinct from that of other minorities. According to the Austrian constitution, the Jews were not a *Volksstamm* (nationality); rather, for the government, the Jews represented a confession or religious community.[4] This did not translate into a strictly religious sense of Jewishness, however. Jews also saw themselves as an ethnic group, as a Diaspora people united by a common history.

Within the context of the supranational Habsburg Empire, it was possible for Jews to negotiate and operate separate strands of their identity. Marsha Rozenblit has posited that Austrian Jews were able to sustain a tripartite identity under the Habsburgs. They were required to be loyal Austrian subjects, and indeed the Jews were fervent in their identification with Austria. What form this Austrian patriotism took, however, was a very different matter from, for example, what was expected in Hungary. In multiethnic Austria, which contained eleven different nations, Austrian identity did not exist; what was required instead, was a political identity consisting of loyalty to the state and the dynasty. The Jews were then free to adopt the culture of the people among whom they lived. For Jews in Vienna this, of course, meant adherence to German culture. In the absence of any tangible Austrian national identity, Jews could participate in the German *Kulturnation* without subscribing to the German national community. Rozenblit argues that "Jews in Habsburg Austria could thus be Austrians by political loyalty, Germans (or Czechs or Poles) by culture, and Jews by ethnicity, all at the same time."[5] While Rozenblit emphasizes a higher degree of comfort by the Jews with this identity than I see as having existed, I agree that the very structure of the Austro-Hungarian Monarchy created the possibility for a multilayered identity that would disappear with its demise.

Within the context of Austrian Jewry, Viennese Jews represent a special case. As I have been arguing, their experience reflected the particular Viennese context in which they lived and worked, but in a manner distinct from the rest of the Viennese population. They immigrated and integrated differently from other minority groups; they distinguished themselves in their pursuit of education and concentration in the professions. Their economic distribution was thus markedly different from other immigrant communities. They tended to live and socialize together. As so many factors distinguished the Jewish experience of Vienna from the rest of the population, it may be accurate to say that Jews encountered their own particular Vienna. One can also say clearly that this Viennese Jewish experience differed profoundly from Jewish life outside of the capital. In Vienna the Jews were more modernized, more distanced from traditional Jewish culture, more secularized, and better organized within a large urban community. The high concentration of recent immigrants, along with the city's special role as imperial capital, bureaucratic headquarters, and economic and cultural center all in one also contributed to Vienna's self-image as a cosmopolitan city. Vienna was secure in its role as the center of the Habsburg universe, and thus questions of national identity did not, at least for the dominant Germans, need to occupy center stage. Rozenblit suggests that "precisely because Viennese were less worried about their 'German-ness,' Germanization in Vienna did not necessarily entail a merger with the German *Volk*."[6] The relationship of Habsburg Jews to Vienna was particularly intense, as it reflected both aspects of the problem of Jewish identity and potential solutions.

If there were ever a moment during which the identity of Austrian Jews was resolved and undisturbed, it came at the outbreak of World War I. As Europe broke out in a patriotic frenzy in August 1914, the atmosphere in Austria was similarly charged, and Jews were among the most jubilant Habsburg citizens. Even if the Habsburgs' move to war was hurried and largely unexpected, the declaration of war on July 28 was greeted with considerable enthusiasm within the empire. The majority of the population in all of the national groups of the empire supported the Habsburg military effort.[7] Vocal enthusiasm could be heard across social classes, different religions and nationalities, voiced in the many languages of the multinational state. In spite of his pacifist beliefs, for Stefan Zweig the significance of the moment lay in its unifying quality:

> In spite of all of my hatred and revulsion towards the war, I would not like in my life to do without the memory of these first days. Like never before, thousands and hundreds of thousands of people came to feel what they ought to have felt in peacetime: that they belonged together. A city of two million felt in this hour that they were experiencing world history, a moment never to be repeated, and that everyone was called to hurl his tiny self into this glowing mass in order to purify themselves of any selfishness. All differences of social standing, language, class, and religion were swept away by the streaming feeling of brotherhood. Strangers spoke to each other on the street, people who had avoided each other for years shook hands, everyone one saw enlivened faces. Every individual experienced a heightening of the self; one was no longer the isolated person of the past, one was placed into a mass, one was *Volk,* and one's self, one's otherwise overlooked self had taken on a new meaning.[8]

This kind of testimony to the excitement for war that gripped Austria in the summer of 1914 surfaces again and again in memoirs written by Austrian Jews.[9] Certainly there were more sober voices, such as that of Arthur Schnitzler when he recorded in his diary the *"ungeheure und ungeheuerliche Nachrichten"* (dreadful and monstrous news).[10] For most Austrian Jews, however, enthusiasm for and commitment to the war were wholehearted. The most common initial reaction seemed to be less an expression of mourning the slain heir to the Habsburg throne than deep sympathy for the aged Emperor Franz Joseph, who now had to bear yet another loss.

When war did break out, it galvanized Austria's Jews. The Jews found meaning in the war foremost in the opportunity to demonstrate their Austrian patriotism. The Viennese Israelitische Kultusgemeinde called on all Jews to "be ready to sacrifice *Gut und Blut* [*"property and blood"*] for Kaiser and Fatherland," and the Austrian Israelite Union cast the Jews as the most loyal and most willing to sacrifice of all subjects of the empire; the Jewish press similarly emphasized Jews' readiness to demonstrate their *Reichstreue*. Jews would fervently carry out their patriotic duty and, some argued, in distinguishing themselves in service to the Fatherland, they could give the lie to anti-Semitic stereotypes of Jewish cowardice. Austrian Jews also found a second layer of meaning—a Jewish meaning—in the war against czarist Russia. In the summer of 1914 Russian troops invaded the Austrian provinces of Galicia and Bukovina, conquering most of this territory and imposing a military occupation that set hundreds of thousands of Jews in flight out of the provinces. Under Russian occupation, those Jews who remained behind were persecuted. Reports of this persecution that came back to Habsburg territory were often greatly exaggerated. Many rabbis, Jewish spokesmen, and Jewish press organs cast the war against Russia as a Jewish holy war.[11] The Russians were cast as barbarians of the north, and the Jews as modern-day Maccabees who would battle oppression.

The Austrian campaign on the eastern front allowed this Jewish ideology of war to drive Jewish troops and Jews on the home front for the first two years of war. Over 300,000 Jews served in the Habsburg army, with approximately 25,000 educated middle-class Jews holding commissions as reserve officers.[12] Jews on the home front supported the war effort with significant support for 8 war-bond campaigns, with aid to soldiers and their families, by administering to the religious needs of Jewish soldiers, and through relief work to the Jewish refugees from the eastern provinces. In 1915, at the apex of the flood of Jewish refugees into Vienna, there were 77,090 refugees in the city; by 1917 estimates record approximately 40,000 refugees still in the city, and while many returned home after the campaign in the east concluded, others had had their towns destroyed or felt the need to stay away because pogroms persisted.[13] Much of the work to care for these refugees in Vienna was carried out by private Jewish charitable organizations. The government contributed aid, but it was not sufficient to meet the need. This relief work functioned symbolically for civilian Jews in much the same way as military service for Jews in the army did, allowing Jews to play a positive role as both Jews and Austrians, acting out their Austrian patriotism and Jewish charity simultaneously.

The campaign on the eastern front meant that the experience of Habsburg soldiers of the war was very different from the one most familiar to us through accounts from the war's western front. Austro-Hungary never sent significant numbers of troops into that conflict but rather fought against the Russians in Galicia, Bukovina, and Russian Poland, against the Serbs and Romanians in the Balkans, and against Italy in South Tyrol. The army sustained heavy casualties, with about one million dead and millions wounded, imprisoned, or sick.[14] For Jewish soldiers, the focus on the East created a compatibility of Jewish and Austrian war goals, so that the war experience intensified their identities both as Jews and as Austrians.

Rozenblit argues that the war experience of Austrian Jews was distinct among Jewish soldiers. Whereas German Jewish soldiers had to justify fighting against respected Britain and France, and British and French Jews faced some dilemma in fighting alongside Russians, whom they deplored for persecuting Jews, Austrian Jews were uninvolved in, and could thus largely ignore, the Western campaign, and faced no such conflict between national and Jewish loyalties.[15] The result was a war experience that deepened Jewish consciousness and reinforced loyalty to the Fatherland for both Jewish soldiers and civilians in Austria.

The final two years of the war, however, would put a strain on such loyalties. When Franz Joseph died in November 1916, Jewish mourning in Austria was deep and genuine. Jewish communities expressed their loyalty to the new Emperor Karl and reaffirmed their Austrian patriotism, but the death of the revered old emperor created uncertainty about the new monarchy and the Jews' place in a changing and crisis-ridden empire. As the war dragged on, problems mounted for the new emperor. The nationalities conflict intensified, as Poles, Czechs, and Southern Slavs began to agitate not only for autonomy, but for independence from Habsburg control. Nationalist agitation fueled anti-Semitism, as Jews were seen as supporting Austria or as comprising a rival national camp. Deepening food, fuel, and housing shortages were blamed on the Jews, alongside charges of Jewish war profiteering and their undermining the war effort. Pogroms against Jews broke out in Galicia, Bohemia, and Moravia in 1918. Galicia emerged as a particular concern, its status intensely debated after the creation of the Kingdom of Poland in 1916. Austrian Jews were very anxious over the physical safety of Jews under Polish control, and Jews of divergent political views pressed for the continuity of the multinational state as the best means of protecting them.

With the worsening situation in Austria, the *Burgfrieden,* a wartime prohibition against inciting religious, political, or national animosity, was rapidly unraveling. The winter of 1917–18 was particularly hard, and the ruthless suppression of massive workers' strikes in January intensified public dissatisfaction. Anti-Semitism was enflamed by war weariness, the desperate situation of much of the populace, and nationalist enthusiasms.

The response of Austrian Jews to the proliferation of anti-Semitism near the end of the war took new forms. There were numerous attempts to unify all of Austrian Jewry under a new democratic congress or umbrella organization, although these attempts faltered over which ideological faction would prevail. In the summer of 1918, the *Israelistische Kultusgemeinde* of Vienna mobilized all Austrian Jewish communities behind a resolution condemning the rising anti-Semitism and affirming a commitment to combat it vigorously.[16] Anti-Semitism had made Austrian Jews more conscious of their Jewishness. Uncertainty about the future of the empire had the same effect. By 1918, as Rozenblit suggests, the Jews may have had the sense they were the last loyal Austrians remaining in Austria, and they continued to hope for its survival.[17]

The breakup of the empire began while the war was still under way, but it did not emerge as the clear outcome until the end of the war. In his Fourteen Points, Woodrow Wilson called for the reorganization of the empire, but not for its dissolution. The Western powers did not get behind the nationalists' demands for independence until an Allied victory was imminent. In the fall of 1918, national committees that had formed in the provinces during the war began to take control of each region. On October 4, Austria and Germany asked for an armistice on the basis of the Fourteen Points. On October 16, the emperor made a last-ditch effort to salvage the situation, calling for the reorganization of Austria into a federal state. Austrian Germans also acted to form their own organizations at this time. On October 21, the provisional National Assembly of the "independent state of German-Austria" was convened in Vienna, and on October 30, a provisional government was formed, headed by Social Democrats. On November 3, the imperial authorities signed an armistice. On November 11, faced with the dissolution of the monarchy, Karl stepped down but did not abdicate the throne.

A New Jewish Identity Crisis

While other nationalities within the empire could rejoice in a newly won national sovereignty and freedom from Habsburg rule, the Jews of the empire faced an uncertain future. Anti-Semitic violence erupted in most of the successor states during 1918. Jews were seen as politically suspect by each of the national groups because of their allegiance to old Austria. More significantly, the new nation-states demanded a different form of allegiance than the old empire. The nation was now defined in ethnic terms, as an ethnocultural community of descent.[18] This form of national identity excluded the Jews and left them with an insoluble dilemma. Jews in the successor states could easily recognize that a new national configuration required them to come to terms with a changed political reality, but while it was quite straightforward for Jews in Austria, Czechoslovakia, Hungary, Poland, and Romania to declare their political allegiance to the states in which they now lived, the dominant form of national identity left them out in the cold. Jews had not seen themselves—and had certainly not been seen by others—as part of the *Volk*, whether German, Czech, or something else. Austrian Jews were adherents of German culture, but they were not Germans. Austrian identity also had to be reinvented to suit the new postwar situation, and the majority of Austrians found their answer in a turn to Germany. An *Anschluss* movement developed that became a significant, even dominant force in postwar Austrian cultural politics,[19] but it was not possible for Jews to similarly endorse a German identity defined in national and ethnic terms. In this difficult situation they held fast to the tripartite identity of the past, by which they offered their political and cultural loyalty to the Austrian state, but not an ethnic or national allegiance. It may well have been clear to many Jews that this model was not suited to the new political reality in which states demanded the political, cultural, and ethnic or national loyalty of its people, but no clear alternative emerged in an environment that was increasingly hostile to Jews. In the new postwar world, Jewish identity was in crisis anew.

At the conclusion of the World War I, Austrian Jews were concentrated in the capital even more than before. The Russian invasion of Galicia and Bukovina at the outset of the war had produced the largest flight of Jews since the seventeenth century.[20] After the Russian evacuation, many Jewish refugees returned to their homelands, but by 1918, there remained approximately 35,000 Jewish asylum seekers in Vienna. By far the vast majority of Austrian Jews in the interwar period lived in Vienna. In 1923, there were 201,513 Jews living in the city.[21] The city's Jewish population would decline through the twenties and thirties; due to a high death rate and low birth rate, the Jewish population sank by 1.5 percent per year from 1923 to 1938.[22] Significantly, however, the concentration of Jews in the capital continued, with over 90 percent of Austrian Jews living in Vienna during these years.[23] This concentration was dramatically overblown in the anti-Semitic imagination. While many refugees were driven out in the first few years after the war, those who remained were bitterly resented, and anti-Semites estimated the city's Jewish population at anywhere from 300,000 to nearly 600,000.[24]

The experience of the new Jewish identity crisis was felt acutely in Vienna, and the Jewish community carried out intense debates as they considered what form a new Jewish identity might take. For many Jews, the Social Democrats represented the only viable political choice, although Jews had a variety of motivations for lending this party their political support. Some sought to shed their Jewish identity in favor of a Socialist one, as was the case with the convert Viktor Adler. Others remained nominally Jewish while supporting Socialism. Certainly some individuals were motivated by personal interest, looking to secure a job or a new apartment from the Socialist municipal administration that ran Vienna from 1919 to 1934. Others supported the Socialists as the only party who neither put forward an anti-Semitic platform nor formed alliances with those who did. In an increasingly polarized political climate, there were few options open to Jews. Jewish supporters ranged from pragmatic in their concerns to ideological, embracing the Socialist humanitarian ideals of social justice and equality.[25]

Jews played a prominent role within the Social Democratic Party, particularly within the upper ranks of party leadership. As there were few working-class Jews in Vienna, the profile of Jewish supporters differed from that of Gentile Socialists. Poorer Jews were not drawn to the party, as they tended to be unassimilated recent immigrants. As Robert Wistrich has argued, there was a significant culture gap between Eastern European Jewish immigrants and the modern Social Democratic movement.[26] Instead, it was the Jewish intelligentsia who was drawn to Socialism.

Ironically, the Jewish leadership of the party was among those who took the greatest pains to distance themselves from being associated with Jewish interests. Leary of being viewed as *"Judenknechte,"* or lackeys of the Jews, party leadership under the assimilationists Viktor Adler and Otto Bauer maintained neutrality on all conflicts related to the Jews and took a highly ambivalent stance regarding anti-Semitism. Wistrich notes that, "In order perhaps to refute the anti-Semitic attacks on their leadership, they indulged in strategies either of avoidance, trivialization of anti-Semitism, or even sophisticated justifications which only revealed the extent of their alienation from Jewry."[27] The party itself was not above using anti-Semitism to its own advantage; the *Arbeiterzeitung* newspaper frequently targeted Jewish bankers and wealthy Jews, combining anti-Semitism with an anti-capitalist message.[28]

In 1921 Vienna was established as a separate federal state, controlled at the time by a Social Democratic administration. On the whole, Jews received few concessions during this period of "Red Vienna." While a great deal was accomplished for the general populace in terms of housing, welfare programs, and the educational system, Jews did not see significant attention to anything resembling a particular Jewish agenda. Nor did the Socialists prove to be effective partners in combating anti-Semitism. The party's anti-clericalism led it to a rigid position on the separation of church and state, by which all religious communities were to be treated as private corporations without state interference. This position translated into a policy of no public funding for any Jewish educational or social welfare activities.[29] Harriet Pass Freidenreich identifies a pattern of strong Jewish support for Social Democrats in general politics, but weak backing of Socialists within the Jewish community. She concludes that many Jewish Socialists played a significant role as individual members of the party, but not as a group within the Jewish community.[30]

Many Jews faced with the new postwar reality retreated to a Jewish ethnic or national identity. Support for Zionism and Jewish nationalism increased after World War I, and by 1932 Zionists were the majority within the IKG.[31] The Zionists urged the recognition of Jews as a nation; non-Zionists, however, resisted Zionist leadership, fearful that any pressure for Jewish national rights would fuel anti-Semitism, as the Jews would be perceived as a state within a state.[32] Many Viennese Jews did not embrace any form of Jewish nationalism, but they supported Jewish ethnic solidarity to a far greater degree than before the war. Some Jews returned to religious observance. Many came to associate largely with other Jews. Anti-Semitism was not the sole cause of a greater assertion of Jewish ethnic identity in the time between the two world wars, but it was certainly an important factor.

During the interwar period Vienna's Jewish community was a divided entity. Numerous attempts were made to unify the various factions of the community in a defense against anti-Semitism, but ideological and political divisions ran deep.

Freidenreich underscores that this was a period of survivalist politics for Jews. The interwar period was so chaotic and the challenges posed by anti-Semitism so great that in many ways the Jewish community was simply overwhelmed.

Rising Anti-Semitism

There were factors both internal and external to Austria that contributed to the rise of anti-Semitism during the interwar period. Outside Austria, the Russian Revolution of 1917 had enflamed anti-Jewish hostilities, as did the 1919 revolutions in Hungary and Bavaria. Anti-Semitism had always intensified during periods of economic crisis, and the desperate situation of Austria at the end of the war increased resentment of both poor and affluent Jews. Postwar inflation peaked in 1921–22, destroying the savings and pensions of many Austrians. Competition for jobs was fierce. The Austrian civil service was now absurdly overstaffed, no longer serving an empire of 54 million but a drastically reduced nation of 6.5 million. Gentiles increasingly sought employment in fields that had traditionally been dominated by Jews, such as private industry and the liberal professions. Discrimination against Jews persisted in the civil service, in the field of education, in academia and the courts, as well as within Gentile-owned private enterprise. Anti-Semitism declined somewhat in the relative prosperity of the late 1920s, but it swelled again as a result of the Great Depression. Bruce Pauley argues that the Depression "struck Austria perhaps more ferociously than any other country in the world," contributing to a significant rise in anti-Semitism and support for the Nazis.[33]

Historically, anti-Semitism has peaked during periods of economic hardship, political upheaval, and at times of increased Jewish immigration; in Vienna this occurred during the First World War, from 1919 to 1923, and from 1930 to1933.[34] Anti-Semitism served a variety of functions. For conservatives, it could be instrumentalized as a code by which to attack capitalism, Liberalism, Socialism, democracy, and modern culture. "Jew" was employed as a metaphor for all manner of changes accompanying modernization for those hostile to such changes. The notion of being in league with the Jews was also an easy political charge for the political parties to make against each other. Additionally, an underlying consensual anti-Semitism played a decisive role in the identity formation of segments of the population, fostering a sense of belonging among non-Jews and intensifying their collective consciousness.[35]

At this time, however, the latent form of anti-Semitism that had for decades been a presence in Viennese life increasingly gave way to active discrimination against Jews and even physical violence. Central to this shift, as Gerhard Botz has argued, was the fact that anti-Semitism served the material interests of large segments of the Viennese population.[36] Economic anti-Semitism dominated the scene in the late 1920s and early 1930s. Austrian Jews played a leading role in the economy, and Jewish affluence persisted until the *Anschluss*. Anti-Semites recognized that they could benefit materially from the economic persecution of the Jews, and the Nazis adopted the explicit aim of eradicating Jews from the Austrian economy.[37]

In the early 1920s, anti-Semitism erupted quite frequently in Vienna, in violent attacks against Jews on the streets. Jewish university students perhaps got the worst of it, as physical attacks became commonplace, and Jews were completely unprotected as the university was regarded as outside of the jurisdiction of local police. By the late 1920s the frequency of such physical assaults had diminished, giving way to de facto economic anti-Semitism. Jewish businesses were the targets of boycotts, Jews were excluded from Austria's resort areas, and new forms of economic discrimination were in evidence.[38] Municipal contracts and licenses were withheld from Jews. They were pushed out of jobs in banking and insurance in favor of non-Jewish employees. Jewish physicians were particularly hard hit, as they were dismissed from the public positions in municipal hospitals they had gained under the Socialists.[39] The Christian Social government was concerned with halting the spread of Nazism around 1930 and thus suppressed incidents of physical violence against Jews, but they intensified their own practice of economic and social discrimination against them. By 1934, an estimated 55,000 Viennese Jews were dependent on Jewish welfare institutions.[40] The situation deteriorated over the course of the decade.

The Beginning of the End

There were two significant turning points for Austrian Jewry during the late 1920s and early 1930s. The first was the burning of the Viennese Palace of Justice on 15 July 1927, "one of the first clear signs of the end of Austria's First Republic and the coming of fascism."[41] The events of this day prompted a push to the right and created support for an authoritarian government. The second was the civil war of 1934, which indeed brought parliamentary democracy to an end in Austria and introduced an authoritarian regime. The fire at the Palace of Justice occurred during a mass demonstration in the wake of the acquittal of two members of the *Frontkämpfer* (a right-wing organization of World War I veterans) of Burgenland who had been charged with shooting and killing two people (an eight-year-old child and a war veteran) at a peaceful Socialist demonstration. The protest in Vienna climaxed at the Palace of Justice, seen as a symbol of a flawed and biased justice system, where an angry mob stormed the building and the fire was set. The day ended in a bloody showdown with police in which eighty-nine demonstrators, as well as five police officers, were killed. In the wake of this event, the political climate was thoroughly poisoned; the republic and its constitution were now in jeopardy. This was an occasion for many Jews to consider leaving Austria, as the upheaval triggered an acute sense of their own vulnerability, as well as that of the republic. The writer and psychologist Manes Sperber opted to leave Vienna at this time, and Elias Canetti seriously considered leaving as well, though he ultimately stayed in Vienna until the last possible minute.

The clash at the Palace of Justice foreshadowed further violence to come. The problems of the First Republic only intensified in the years following the fire. The Depression created high unemployment and out-of-control inflation. The rise of the Nazi movement in Austria seriously threatened the stability of the republic. In March 1933, the Christian Social chancellor Engelbert Dollfuss suspended the parliament. The government now ruled by emergency decree and began to suspend civil liberties. Some Jews chose to leave Austria at this time. In mid-February1934 skirmishes broke out across Austria between the outlawed—but still existent—Socialist paramilitary organization, the *Schutzbund*, and its conservative counterpart, the *Heimwehr*. Fighting in Vienna was intense, with one major episode occurring at the Karl-Marx-Hof, where the military shelled the apartment complex with light artillery, endangering the lives of thousands of civilians. The armed conflict lasted for four days, though its effects were far more extensive. Several hundred people were killed, over a thousand wounded, *Schutzbund* leaders were tried and executed, the Social Democratic Party was outlawed, and Socialist leaders were forced into exile. By May, Austria was formed into a corporate state led by the *Vaterländische Front* (Patriotic Front), a union of the Christian Social Party and the *Heimwehr*, which was now the only political party permitted by the authoritarian regime.

This government, under Kurt von Schuschnigg, sought to minimize the appeal of Nazism by demonstrating its own anti-Semitic credentials. The regime practiced economic anti-Semitism, tempered only by some measure of caution regarding potential damage to the whole Austrian economy through the persecution of Jews. Nongovernmental anti-Semitism was widely tolerated. The situation was one in which active discrimination was still fairly limited but in which passive anti-Semitism permeated the whole system. Bruce Pauley thus describes the precarious position of Viennese Jews under Schuschnigg: "Viennese Jews, like those in Hungary at this time, found themselves in the absurd position of looking to moderate anti-Semites for protection against radical ones."[42]

The Jewish community struggled to respond. The major Jewish organizations engaged in defense efforts, but as I argued above, the community never was able to unite effectively, and political infighting clearly hampered its efforts. The IKG tried to provide for the growing numbers of those in need of relief. They continued to approach anti-Semitism as a rational phenomenon, registering official protests with the government over specific instances of discrimination against Jews. Even before the Nazis took power, anti-Semitism had become a force that outstripped the ability of the Jewish community to deal with it effectively. After the *Anschluss,* measures taken against Austrian Jews were of course far worse than any prior expressions of anti-Semitism. Within four years, Vienna would be effectively devoid of Jews.[43]

Jews and the *Anschluss*

The *Anschluss* was immediately followed by pogromlike events in Vienna that targeted affluent and poor Jews alike. There were physical assaults on Jews, and many were forced to scrub the streets and sidewalks in front of taunting crowds. Jewish property was confiscated. Jewish children were forced to defile the businesses of their parents. Orthodox Jews were forced to commit acts of sacrilege. The rounding up and either arrest or deportation of Jews began within days of German troops moving into Austria.

After the introduction of the Nuremberg Laws in Austria in May 1938, all Jews had to carry identification cards and adopt the name Israel or Sarah. This set the stage for the introduction of "legal" discrimination in the schools, professions, and economy.[44] A *numerus clausus* was introduced at the university; the lower schools were later segregated. As I have noted, economic anti-Semitism was a high priority for the Nazis. This was carried out both through official channels, with harsh punitive legislation, and through spontaneous "Aryanization" of Jewish property, carried out by the populace. Gerhard Botz has shown that Aryanization, generally the expropriation of Jewish property, stood in as a surrogate for economic and social-welfare policies the Nazis had promised their followers; in the economic persecution of Jews, many non-Jewish Austrians came to see a means of satisfying their own material needs.[45] This also involved the creation of ghettos within Vienna, when Jewish apartments were seized in response to a chronic housing shortage and Jews were forced into pockets of Leopoldstadt.

When the forced emigration of Jews began, this was a further source of revenue for the Nazis. Not only did Jews need to find funds for travel expenses as they faced the expropriation of their property, there were fees and a *Reichsfluchtsteuer* (emigration tax) to be paid. This forced emigration was overseen by Adolf Eichmann and was organized via a highly efficient and expedited process: the Central Office of Jewish Emigration gave Jews the documents they needed, stripped them of their citizenship, confiscated their belongings, and issued exit visas, all in an hour's time. At the peak of emigration, in September 1938, ten thousand Jews left Vienna.[46] After the Final Solution was approved, Eichmann was charged with organizing the deportation of Jews to the death camps in Poland, a task he carried out with similar zeal.

Vienna witnessed further unrestrained violence against Jews as well, as Nazi politics vis-à-vis the Jews radicalized. A pogrom in Vienna broke out in October 1938, with further destruction of Jewish businesses, the burning of synagogues, and physical assaults on Jews. At least twenty-seven Jews were killed and eighty-eight severely injured.[47] Arrests, deportations, and suicides also occurred at this time. The *Reichskristallnacht* of 9 November 1938 was also particularly brutal in Vienna.

The systematic deportation of Jews began in the fall of 1939 but reached its peak between the fall of 1941 and the spring of 1942, when thousands of Viennese Jews were deported to occupied Poland and to cities in the occupied Soviet Union, where they were frequently murdered in mass shootings. They were also sent to Theresienstadt. Eichmann refashioned the IKG into an instrument of the Gestapo, forcing community leaders to draw up lists for deportation.[48] The year 1942 saw the removal of 32,000 of the 43,000 Jews in Austria.[49] By October 1942 only approximately 8,000 Jews remained in Austria, the majority of whom were elderly women.[50]

The persecution of Jews in Vienna from 1938 to 1942 was particularly vigorous, with the *Judenpolitik* of Eichmann and the Nazis more extensive and ruthless in Vienna than in the *Reich*. Before the *Anschluss*, the Viennese Jewish community was among the most vital in Europe. After the *Anschluss* it scarcely existed. Yet even before the annexation, the constriction of Jewish life had been well under way. The First Republic brought new pressures to bear on Jewish identity, intensifying divisions within the Jewish community and prompting individuals to reexamine what it meant to be an Austrian Jew.

Jewish Cultural Responses During the Interwar Years

The interwar Jews of Vienna experienced a crisis of identity that operated on three levels. Austrian identity was in need of reinvention, given that what it meant to be Austrian had changed so drastically. Viennese identity was also in flux. For seven hundred years Vienna had been the imperial center of a vast empire: a political, economic, and cultural capital in one. Now the city was the too-large capital of a too-small alpine republic, largely at odds with the rural character of most of the nation. And, as we have seen, Jewish identity had to be reconfigured as well, as prior forms of identification no longer met the political reality. How did Jews respond to these identity questions? The crisis atmosphere of the years immediately following the World War I, prolonged by the Depression, made the resolution of these issues all the more difficult. How did the Viennese Jewish writers of the interwar period respond? What were the options available to them? In this section I will outline some of the general trajectories of the various Jewish cultural responses of the interwar period. In the sections that follow I will pursue some of them in greater detail by assessing the responses of individual writers.

I have already discussed the two main political paths pursued by Jews after World War I. One was an embrace of Socialism, the other Jewish nationalism, either in the form of Zionism or Diaspora nationalism. Felix Salten exemplifies the political turn toward Zionism, and later in this chapter I will explore how he shaped his Zionist stance in the interwar period. A different political and cultural response was a turn to conservatism. In the search for a new Austrian identity, many Austrian writers—mostly Gentiles, but also a few writers of Jewish background—found a new cultural identity within a Catholic cultural revival. Hugo von Hofmannsthal is exemplary of this turn, as he came to see in Austria not a political entity but, to quote Kenneth Segar, as a "repository of three thousand years of Western culture, to be worshipped as at a shrine, but also to be constantly revitalized by its artists."[51] This was to be realized in the Salzburg Festival, which would draw heavily on German folk culture. Hofmannsthal's vision for Salzburg was indeed a German Christian vision rooted in folk culture and seemed to be a rejection of the Viennese Jewish intelligentsia. Segar contends that this vision was at odds with Austrian Jews, as its character was "provincial rather than metropolitan, Catholic-conservative rather than liberal or avant-garde, 'instinctively' German as opposed to intellectually 'alien.'"[52]

Hofmannsthal's conservative turn was not an outright repudiation of his Jewish ancestry, yet it can perhaps be better understood as another step in an extended process of distancing himself from that identity. This development was a rejection of Jewishness insofar as Hofmannsthal had come to equate Jewishness with the modern, and his was an anti-modern conception of culture. I will not consider Hofmannsthal at greater length in this chapter, as he was clearly moving far afield of the kinds of concerns that occupied the other writers I examine.

An outright repudiation of a Jewish identity was another possible response to the anti-Semitism of postimperial Austria. In this chapter Karl Kraus, one of the most important Viennese Jewish intellectuals of the late Habsburg Empire, returns with a markedly new view on Jewish identity. In the previous chapter I examined Kraus's extreme assimilationism and rejection of a Jewish identity. As we shall see, this was not his sole response, and his relationship to Jewish identity continued to be highly complex and ambivalent. During the interwar years the rejection of a Jewish identity did not constitute a solution to the dilemmas of the interwar situation, as one was likely to continue to be perceived as a Jew. For the anti-Semites, a Jew who rejected Jewishness was still a Jew. Moreover, after the publication of Theodor Lessing's *Der jüdische Selbsthaß* in 1930, a Jew who rejected Jewishness was open to charges of self-hatred as well.

Other Jewish writers responded to the challenges of Jewish identity during the interwar period by avoiding a confrontation with the present altogether via a retreat to the past. Nostalgia for the vanished and vanquished Habsburg Empire was in evidence, giving rise to the "Habsburg Myth," identified by Claudio Magris in 1963.[53] For some, the myth was evoked in order to lend cohesion to a fractured state still unsettled in a vastly changed political landscape. Some Jews who experienced this nostalgia simply carried on, to a greater or lesser extent, as though nothing had changed. When, for example, Austrian Zionist newspapers continued to report extensively on developments in the former eastern provinces of the empire, this coverage was a form of denial of the changed postwar constellations. On the other hand, as Magris pointed out, there were those like Karl Kraus who opposed this myth and were bent on dismantling it.

Longing for the premodern had a distinctly different expression for Jewish writers who looked to the East. A number of Jewish writers rediscovered Eastern European Jewry in these years, seeing in this community a source of authentic Jewry in contrast with the corrupt and decadent West. Joseph Roth, originally from a shtetl in Eastern Galicia, took up a focus on Eastern European Jewry in the twenties and thirties. Roth devoted two important works to the westward emigration of Eastern European Jews and the process of assimilation: his 1930 novel *Hiob* (*Job*) and the 1927 essay *Juden auf Wanderschaft* (*Wandering Jews*). I will examine these works in this chapter, assessing the critique of Western Jewry implied in Roth's treatment of Eastern European Jews and his view of assimilation.

Other intellectuals came through the war with a deep commitment to internationalism. This cosmopolitan position is best represented among the writers considered here by Stefan Zweig. Even before the war, Zweig had transcended the confines of the Viennese or even Austrian context in his personal identification. The world after 1918, in the throes of nationalism and which, in Zweig's view, exalted the political above all else, was traumatic to Zweig, and he struggled to find in cosmopolitan humanism a purpose that could sustain and orient him.

The prevailing tendency among Viennese Jewish writers' reactions to the experience of the First World War, the undoing of prior identifications that resulted from it, and the rise of anti-Semitism was a heightened sense of Jewish identity. For a number of writers, such as Richard Beer-Hofmann, this was accompanied by a new religious commitment. A far larger group of writers may not have personally returned to the faith of the fathers, but they did reexamine it. Much of the writing by Austrian Jews in the cultural flourishing of the 1920s references important texts of the Jewish canon and draws on Jewish myths, legends, and archetypes in ways that had not been commonly seen at the turn of the century. Zweig, Roth, and Beer-Hofmann all fall into this category. In spite of, or perhaps partially because of, the hostile climate of Vienna of the 1920s, Jewish writers generally forged stronger ties to *Judentum*, however they conceived of it.

The 1930s, of course, tell a different story, that of the gradual extinguishing of this thriving Jewish culture. As the ascendant forces of the Right sought to reclaim and redefine Austrian culture during the 1930s, they also brought about the gradual constriction of Jewish life. Steven Beller has shed light on the different facets of the disappearance of Jewish intellectuals at this time. First, there were a number of deaths of prominent writers, including Bettauer (1925), Hofmannsthal (1929), Schnitzler (1931), and Kraus (1936). A far greater segment of the Jewish cultural elite disappeared from Vienna via emigration. The years 1930 and 1933–34 marked the high points of Jewish emigration from Vienna, but a few notable writers, such as Zweig and Roth, left earlier.[54]

Those who remained had to witness the disintegration of Vienna's Jewish community and of the city's vital cultural scene, in which Jews had played such a prominent role. For Jewish intellectuals who remained in Vienna, the discrimination of the corporate state meant the foreclosure of one possibility after another for participation in the city's cultural life. Both Elias and Veza Canetti launched their literary careers at this very inauspicious time, seeing their first works in print well after many Austrian Jews chose to leave. The publication history of both Canettis was abruptly interrupted after initial successes, and in professional as well as personal terms, they did not come through this terrible period unscathed. They were, however, present in Vienna for the worst of the campaigns against Jews, and they survived to write about the experience.

Many scholars have rightly drawn attention to the fact that 1938 did not occur in a vacuum but rather was the culmination of a gradual process, the general tendencies of which were already present in the previous decade. In Kenneth Segar's words, "History tells us that in March 1938 Austria was invaded by a foreign power. Yet the situation … suggests that an *Anschluss* had been taking place at a cultural level throughout the years 1933 to 1938."[55] My analysis will thus follow those writers who remained in Vienna during these exceedingly difficult years, focusing on the way they related to a Jewish identity in crisis, as well as their strategies for coping with the rise of Austro-fascism.

Arthur Schnitzler

Schnitzler of the interwar years provides an example of a writer whose Jewish identity was shaped to a very significant degree by his experience of anti-Semitism. As I follow Schnitzler into his later years and attempt to foreground the context of the 1920s, I enter territory that the majority of critics who have worked on Schnitzler have left largely unexplored. Schnitzler is so readily associated with the turn of the twentieth century in Vienna that it is often obscured that he wrote many of his significant works after World War I. *Fräulein Else* appeared in 1924, *Traumnovelle* (*Dream Story*) in 1926, *Spiel im Morgengrauen* (*Night Games*) in 1927, *Therese Chronik eines Frauenlebens* in 1928, and his daring *Flucht in die Finsternis* (*Flight into Darkness*) in 1931, the year of his death. Schnitzler has frequently been associated with the Habsburg myth, with some viewing his works as nostalgia for the world that had disappeared and others seeing him as the voice of that bygone world, carrying it over into the new Austrian republic as though it had never disappeared. Yet Schnitzler was a very active writer during the First Republic, and he did not write in the same vein throughout his career. With the exception of his memoirs, *Jugend in Wien*, his later works are firmly rooted in the contemporary scene at the time of their writing. Luigi Reitani is one scholar to recognize this, seeing Schnitzler as addressing topical issues of Austria's political, economic, and social life after 1918, such as social disorientation, economic crisis, the emancipation of women, mass culture, and mass psychology.[56] In *Fräulein Else*, for example, reference is made to the soaring inflation rate, setting Else's family's financial troubles in the broader context of the economic turbulence of the time.

In his later works Schnitzler remains the astute and critical observer of his society, but his horizons seem to have expanded. Whereas at the turn of the century he focused largely on the bourgeois milieu he knew well from personal experience, Schnitzler's Vienna of the 1920s is a city that has been transformed. His protagonist in *Therese* lives in poverty, alienated and isolated. The city in *Traumnovelle* is a surreal, labyrinthine space in which normal social interactions have been replaced by chance encounters between strangers, allowing for the possibility of sexual exchange but no real human connections. Robert, the protagonist of *Flucht in die Finsternis*, seems to find the norms that govern bourgeois masculinity so abhorrent that he takes flight into madness as a way to escape them. The fictive Vienna of Schnitzler's later works is by and large a hostile environment. Rather than nostalgically portray a bygone Vienna, Schnitzler depicts a contemporary environment fraught with challenges, where the individual is often fighting a losing battle to gain a secure footing.

Schnitzler himself faced considerable difficulties in the 1920s. While he had always been preoccupied with his health and considered his knowledge of medicine as fuel for his tendency toward hypochondria, in these years he was plagued by tinnitus—a constant ringing in the ears—in a way that at times made it difficult to function. In 1921 Schnitzler and his wife, Olga, divorced. In 1928 his daughter Lili committed suicide. Professionally, his works were not as well received as they had been earlier in his career. While he certainly experienced success with some of his works, including receiving considerable interest in adapting many of them into film, the celebrated author was increasingly treated as an outsider. Some measure of this decline in interest can certainly be attributed to anti-Semitism.

In 1921 the controversy over the alleged immorality of *Reigen* erupted in Vienna, placing the author once again at the center of a controversy involving not only the theaters, the public, and the press, but also the constitutional court, the parliament, and the leading politic "Reigenians" of the day, from the mayor of Vienna to the Christian Social chancellor and his administration.[57] The play was staged in Berlin in 1921 and created an uproar, as well as legal troubles for the director and actors in the play. In Vienna the affair reached a larger scale, pitting the Socialist Viennese municipal administration against the Christian Social federal government. There were protest rallies before city hall, heated debates within parliament, a hullabaloo in the press, and even demonstrations in the streets. Throughout the affair, as during the campaigns against Hugo Bettauer in the mid-1920s, anti-Semitism figured prominently. The right-wing press hurled invectives about Jewish lasciviousness, the machinations of Jewish finance, and the Jew Schnitzler. Ignaz Seipel even personally chimed in against the work as "a filthy piece from the pen of a Jewish author."[58] With this level of uproar, it was impossible not to be drawn into the conflict. It is clear that Schnitzler suffered from the experience. We know from his voluminous files of press clippings, as well as his vehement, almost violent red markings in the margins of these clippings, that the author closely followed and cared about his reception, especially the criticism. Even before this particular scandal, in 1917, Schnitzler had referred to himself as "the most abused writer in the German language since the invention of the printing press."[59] Other comments make clear that he attributed this to his Jewishness.

In his two literary treatments of anti-Semitism, Schnitzler demonstrated a keen understanding of the effects of anti-Semitism on Viennese society, both Jewish and Gentile. He portrayed a wide range of complex reactions by Jews to the phenomenon. In *Der Weg ins Freie*, Schnitzler captures an image of Viennese society when political anti-Semitism held sway in Viennese politics and when latent anti-Semitism had thoroughly permeated Viennese society but social interactions between Jews and non-Jews were still possible. The novel depicts a moment when Viennese Jews were insecure with their place in the city but did not yet face explicit discrimination. In his drama *Professor Bernhardi*, Schnitzler presents an early expression of discrimination against Jews in the professions and, as in the novel, exhibits his penetrating insights into the psychological effects of anti-Semitism on its vocal proponents, its targets, and on those in whom such prejudice was unconscious.

Alongside these important works, Schnitzler's diaries and memoirs are the best source to understand his relationship to Jewishness and his assessment of anti-Semitism. *Jugend in Wien* recounts Schnitzler's experiences during the years 1862 to 1899. It was written between 1915 and 1920 and published in its current form shortly thereafter. At the beginning of the work Schnitzler weaves an assessment of his relationship to his Jewish background into an account of his family history, presenting it as a story of assimilation and acculturation. As he recounts his father's move from Nagy-Kanizsa in Hungary to Vienna to study medicine and his rise to prominence within the medical profession, as well as his mother's roots in the Viennese Jewish elite, Schnitzler presents the assimilatory process in unambiguously positive terms. The family's identification was located squarely in the Viennese Jewish bourgeois elite. Egon Schwarz has recounted how a visit to Schnitzler's paternal grandparents in Hungary impressed upon Schnitzler the gulf that separated him from a Jewish life rooted in tradition. Schnitzler recounts in *Jugend in Wien*:

> One thing is certain ... had I been forced to live temporarily or for a more durable sojourn in the city where my grandparents had their home and my father was born I would have certainly felt like a stranger or perhaps even an exile. Thus I might be tempted already at this point to take issue with the questionable view according to which someone, born, raised and permanently active in a certain country, is supposed to regard another country as his true home—not where decades ago his parents had settled, but a country where his great-great-ancestors had been at home thousands of years ago—not merely for political, social, economic reasons (which might at least be debatable) but also for emotional reasons.[60]

Thus the Hungarian town where his grandparents lived is presented as an alien world to which Schnitzler felt no particular attachment. If this place, just a generation's remove from Schnitzler's own experience, represented exile for him, Zionism and Palestine—the land of his "great-great ancestors"—were out of the question.

The memoirs present a similar picture regarding the family's relationship to the Jewish faith. Here the theme is secularization, which went hand in hand with the process of assimilation. In this respect as well, Schnitzler depicts a distance from tradition on the part of his immediate family. The family's religious observance was limited to the bare minimum permissible in Vienna's secularized bourgeois Jewish community: Yom Kippur was observed at Schnitzler's grandmother's house. Schnitzler writes that this was carried out for her benefit and characterizes her as the sole family member with a real religious commitment.

For his part, Schnitzler felt no significant attachment to Judaism. It was not part of his upbringing, and he seems never to have come to it on his own. In *Jugend in Wien* he does describe a short-lived interest in religious questions during his university studies. This did not involve intensive study of the Jewish texts, however, or engagement with tradition. Rather, he cast his religious interest in terms of a broader philosophical concern with "the eternal questions." Schnitzler resolutely determined at this juncture to chart his own course through these issues rather than follow any religious prescriptions, even though he saw himself as a mere dilettante in this realm.[61] When he wrote in the memoirs that anti-Semitism chiefly interested him in its psychological effects, he added, "The religious moment had little or no effect on me."[62] He goes on to elaborate a fundamental discomfort with religious dogma:

> Everything dogmatic, from whatever pulpit and in whatever schools it was taught, was disagreeable to me, even appeared literally out of the question. And as for the so-called faith of my fathers, in terms of what within this faith was really *faith*—not memory, tradition, and atmosphere—I had as little inner connection to this as to any other.[63]

Schnitzler is thus quite clear that his religious background was quite limited and that whatever relationship he felt toward his own Jewishness was not based on the Jewish religion. Moreover, Schnitzler's primary skepticism regarding any form of dogma was a deeply rooted aspect of his *Weltanschauung,* making any rapprochement to Judaism later in life rather unlikely.

When Schnitzler turns to the portrayal of anti-Semitism during this period in Vienna, his account is far more extensive than his rather cursory references to his Jewish background. He describes the emergence of anti-Semitism at the university in detail, and, while he downplays its impact on him personally by characterizing it as a matter of psychological interest, he also refers to it as a source of personal anxiety and bitterness. His treatment of anti-Semitism in the rest of the memoirs, in any event, belies any notion that he was personally unaffected by this phenomenon. Schnitzler's discussions of anti-Semitism include the very detailed description of the prejudice and personal attacks his father experienced in his medical career, outlined in my discussion of *Professor Bernhardi* in Chapter 1. There is also the oft-quoted passage in which Schnitzler compares anti-Semitism to being under the effects of a local anesthetic and being forced to watch while unclean knives cut into one's skin and blood is drawn. Egon Schwarz thus summarizes the merits of Schnitzler's treatment of anti-Semitism: "His great contribution was that he observed the Jewish Question in all its intricacy with the diagnostic skills of the trained physician that he was and the psychological acumen that became his trademark as a writer."[64]

These are moments in his reminiscences in which Schnitzler is most critical of Viennese society. As Ariane Huml has noted, Schnitzler's critical gaze is far more apparent in his literary works than in the memoirs.[65] One can search in vain for an in-depth analysis of Viennese society in this text. As Huml notes, Schnitzler's own conception of his memoirs as a reflection of personal experiences during his early years in Vienna preclude him from generalizations and largely from critical observations on politics and society. In contrast to Stefan Zweig, Schnitzler does not attempt to give voice to an entire generation or express the spirit of the age, though he does seek to bring to light the newest impulses of the day, especially in terms of culture.

Schnitzler's relationship to Vienna also differs significantly from Zweig's. Whereas for Zweig Vienna was long a home base from which he traveled the world before leaving Vienna definitively for Salzburg (as well as exile), Schnitzler remained firmly anchored to the city. He was never uncritical of aspects of Vienna or the Viennese, yet he was deeply attached to the city and identified as a Viennese. Vienna is also more than a mere backdrop in his literary works; it is a real presence that stands alongside his characters in fullness and depth. His portrait of Vienna is detailed and inscribed with meaning. When Schnitzler's characters move about through different parts of the city, its neighborhoods, streets, coffeehouses, and cultural institutions, even a single room or a park bench in the Prater, these spaces are all coded with meaning that Schnitzler makes clear to the reader. The various locales within the city occupied by these characters reveal information about the characters' status, class, ethnicity, gender, generational attribution, politics, profession, etc. What Gershon Shaked terms the *Soziosemiotik* (*Socialsemiotics*) of a created fictive world—a series of signs that can only be understood according to the codes of a particular group[66]—are in Schnitzler thoroughly Viennese. They would have been transparent to contemporary readers, but they are equally accessible to readers who do not inhabit Schnitzler's world, I would suggest, because of the richness of his portrayal of the city.

Schnitzler was a Viennese writer who felt a strong attachment to the city and who was pained by its failings. He suffered under the cool reception he was accorded in his later years and was keenly aware of the role played by anti-Semitism in determining that reception. As Egon Schwarz reminds us, though, Schnitzler was spared the worst, as he died in 1931. This analysis of Schnitzler's literary and personal reflections on anti-Semitism and the Jewish Question have led me to conclude that Schnitzler's experience of anti-Semitism played a significant role in determining his relationship to Jewishness. Rather than coming to a positive identification with Judaism—a position at which Beer-Hofmann arrived—or identifying with the historical community of the Jews, an element in Salten's identification, for example, Schnitzler seemed to identify himself as a Jew largely because his society identified him as such, and he regarded it as futile, even cowardly, to attempt to disavow such an identification. One would be hard pressed to find positive content in Schnitzler's view of his Jewishness, one which he reflected or commented on in a substantive way. His positive identification as a Jew certainly existed, but it remained quite vague and unreflected. His views on anti-Semitism and its effects on Viennese society and on his own life are more fully elaborated in his writing, however. It is indeed one of the ironies of this tumultuous period that the rising hostility toward Austrian Jews led so many of them to a heightened sense of Jewish identity.

Felix Salten

Felix Salten certainly came to a deeper identification as a Jew during these years. This was the solution he found to the crisis of identity that he experienced after the collapse of the Habsburg monarchy, which represented a tremendous loss to him. He had been a patriotic Austrian, *kaisertreu,* and perhaps the most successful of the writers considered in Chapter 1 at maintaining what Rozenblit identified as the tripartite identity of Austrian Jews. Salten faced a number of challenges coming to grips with the new European order that emerged from the First World War. In the First Republic, Austrian identity had to be reconceptualized, and the outcome of this process, while unclear, was not favorable to Jews, as many Austrians affirmed their membership in the German *Volk*. Jewish identity also had to be accommodated to the new postwar reality of nation-states and altered conceptions of national and ethnic belonging. Salten's identity crisis was perhaps more acute than before the war, but during the challenging interwar years, Salten also found answers in a reawakened sense of Jewish national belonging and, to an extent, a return to his religious roots in Judaism.

Salten had greeted the outbreak of war with enthusiasm, writing in the *Neue Freie Presse*, "*Es muss sein!*" (It must be.) During the war he served in the Vienna war archive, where he continued his journalistic activities.[67] Privately, Salten expressed more sober reservations about the war, as when he wrote Schnitzler just over a week after the war broke out:

> Here it's so very quiet, quite secluded, and that is somewhat comforting. Otherwise, when one is clear about what is happening now and why it is happening, one could despair. Whoever believes all of this is because of Serbia is actually enviable, since he has something to feed his sense of justice.[68]

Salten did not, however, express himself publicly with a call for peace or any clear statements against the war; rather, his position in the war archive involved writing articles in support of the Habsburg war effort. Nonetheless, his initial enthusiasm dampened gradually, and his later wartime articles no longer reflected the belief in the necessity of war, in the purifying, revitalizing power of war described in his writing of 1914. By 1917, Salten characterized the war as a catastrophe.

In the 1920s Salten was at the peak of his literary and journalistic career. He became the premier Sunday feuilletonist of the *Neue Freie Presse* and later, as of 1933, the paper's *Burgtheater* critic. He contributed to many of the major German and Austrian newspapers during the 1920s. He had also achieved renown as a writer. Salten published two successful animal stories in 1923, *Der Hund von Florenz* (*The Dog of Florence*) and *Bambi. Eine Lebensgeschichte aus dem Walde* (*Bambi: A Life in the Woods*). From 1927 to 1934 Salten served as president of the Austrian PEN Club; in 1929 he organized the PEN Club Congress in Vienna.

The occasion of Salten's sixtieth birthday on 6 September 1929 was widely celebrated. The Zsolnay publishing house commissioned many essays in his honor, with contributions by Hofmannsthal, Schnitzler, Beer-Hofmann, Freud, and Thomas and Heinrich Mann.[69] In March 1930 Salten was distinguished with an honorary title as "Bürger der Stadt Wien" ("Citizen of Vienna") In this same year Salten traveled to America with a delegation of European writers and journalists; the following year he published *Fünf Minuten Amerika* (*Five Minutes of America*).

Salten's support for Zionism was well established prior to World War I. He was frequently invited for speaking engagements outside of Vienna; for example, he spoke twice in Prague at the invitation of the Prague Bar Kochba organization and gave lectures in Czernowitz, Cracow, and Lemberg. Given his position of relative prominence within the Viennese Jewish cultural elite, a group for which skepticism vis-à-vis Zionism was the norm, Salten was all the more popular with Zionist groups. He also spoke before Zionist groups in Vienna, not only with literary readings as Schnitzler and Beer-Hofmann both did on occasion, but as an engaged political speaker.[70] During the 1920s Salten also became the head of Jarauch, a Jewish writers and artists' organization. Salten saw the justification for Zionism in the existence of a persistent hostility to Jews that had outlasted and overshadowed all manner of emancipatory developments. Such hostility seemed to him to be rooted "deep in the nature of people."[71] This view of unrelenting anti-Semitism is part of the process by which Salten came to a Jewish self-consciousness. Even if Salten's Zionist sympathies span several decades, his relationship to Zionism nonetheless unfolded as an ongoing, internal process, part of which he would detail in his Zionist book *Neue Menschen auf alter Erde* (*New People on Old Land*), published in 1925.

One aspect of the evolution of Salten's attitudes toward Zionism and Jewishness is an unfolding critique of assimilationism that surfaces in a number of texts, including his best-known work, *Bambi*. *Bambi* first appeared as a serial novel in the *Neue Freie Presse* in the summer of 1922; it was subsequently published by that paper's publishing house. Heidi Lexe has attempted to explain why Salten's text has been largely forgotten within the context of children's literature—rarely appearing in anthologies or even the lexica of children's literature—and is even infrequently mentioned in discussions of animal stories.[72] Walt Disney's 1942 film adaptation of the work has dramatically overshadowed Salten's story, but beyond this, I think Lexe has correctly asserted that internal and not external factors may be the reason the text is not among the classics of children's literature. As she suggests, the text is really best understood not when dehistoricized (as presented by Disney), but rather when read within the specific context of Vienna of the 1920s, as a text that has to do with anti-Semitism and the struggle for a Jewish identity. In a similar vein, Iris Bruce has argued effectively that Salten should be regarded as making significant contributions to Zionist children's literature.[73]

The deer that take center stage in Salten's story of forest life may be seen as a cipher for the Jewish people, with a shared history of persecution. Salten's depiction of nature underscores the diversity of the forest, and the novel presents an underlying message of tolerance. The animals form a network of interdependence, and friendships are possible among animals of different species. Bruce rightly draws attention to Bambi's encounter with the elk as an important moment of coming face to face with the "other." Focusing, however, on the humor with which Salten presents the failure of the two animals to communicate, Bruce sees the moment as a utopian encounter, "suggesting the possibility of an ideal world."[74] In my view, the scene does not dismiss these cultural differences so lightly but rather underscores that misunderstandings can easily arise from such encounters and that cross-cultural communication is challenging. The task of different species living together in peaceful coexistence is not an easy one.

Salten also puts forward a critique of assimilation, and he does so in surprisingly strident terms. In the figure of Gobo, who spends a number of months with a human family, Salten presents assimilation in strictly negative terms, as the erasure of a particular identity through the taking on of another. Gobo comes to trust humans and becomes reliant on their care; when hunters return to the forest after he has been set free, Gobo expects a friendly reunion and makes himself an easy target for the hunter's gun. Assimilation is cast as bondage, and its effects are deadly. As Annegret Völpel has argued, "The novel contains a skeptical warning against a Jewish readiness to assimilate that was going too far, that would lead to the loss of Jewish identity and that was a threat to the Jews' very existence."[75]

The novel's treatment of anti-Semitism also reflects this level of urgency. The human is unmistakably dangerous. Gobo's encounter with a friendly family does not represent a utopian alternative but leads to a misreading of the threat represented by humans, which proves fatal. What, then, can the Jews, or the deer, do in the face of this dangerous threat? Bruce sees the leader of the deer as a Herzl figure—Kraus's "King of the Jews" recast as Prince of the Forest. The Prince, in Bruce's view, delivers a strong Zionist message in rejecting Gobo's path of assimilation. This is a sound reading of the Prince's intervention at this moment in the story, but if we consider the Prince as model, and as Bambi's father he certainly plays this role in this coming-of-age tale, his message to his young son does not involve any collective solution. Rather, as Bruce recognizes, Bambi must find his own way forward in increasing isolation from the other deer. There may be Zionist longing for a Herzl-Messiah figure within the novel, but this is depicted as an early stage in Bambi's development. In my view, Salten here does not so much reject a collective Zionist path but sets the foreground for the inner struggle that must take place if one is to forge a positive, personal identity as a Jew. Leaving his characters to go it alone in this way, Salten is perhaps not far removed from Schnitzler's standpoint in *Der Weg ins Freie*, although this children's tale is more optimistic.

In his next important work dealing with Zionism, Salten would move from the level of the individual to the collective. In 1924 Salten visited Palestine on a trip funded by his publishing house, the Zsolnay Verlag, with further financial and organizational support from the Central Zionist Agency, in London. Salten published an account of this visit the following year, *Neue Menschen auf alter Erde*. The book was highly anticipated within Zionist circles, and, even before it appeared, Salten was recruited for speaking engagements as propaganda for the Jewish settlements. The influential Viennese Zionist Otto Abeles envisioned "lectures ... in a very grand style first in Vienna and then larger towns of the Austrian provinces."[76] Numerous press reports attest to the popularity of this lecture tour. Salten's book is both travel narrative and a personal account of his reaction to all he saw and experienced. It is a highly literary work as well. Manfred Dickel sees this work as weaving together metaphors of modernity with biblical stories in Salten's own construction of the Jews' historical fate and transhistorical mission.[77]

The work owes a good deal to Herzl's *Altneuland*, though the novel is never explicitly mentioned. Salten's trip corresponded to the time in which Herzl set the second visit to Palestine. Not only does Salten elaborate Herzl's whole catalog of special features of the new state, paying close attention as did Herzl to technological innovations, he also follows Herzl in structuring the appeal of his text as primarily rational rather than emotional.[78] Florian Krobb sees Salten's text as emotionally richer and less technocratic than Herzl's novel, but she still views it as a work that ultimately draws on the same model of persuasion, promoting the Zionist cause through rational argumentation.[79]

Where the text does stake an emotional claim is in Salten's depiction of his personal experience of the journey. The visit to Palestine becomes a path for Salten back to his religious roots. In this, of course, he differs from Herzl. In the first sentence of the novel Salten evokes the Jews' exodus from slavery in Egypt: "One has to go through the desert to reach Palestine from Egypt, from Africa to Asia."[80] Taking Moses' route to the Promised Land, Salten sets the tone for a journey that is spiritual as well as physical. (Herzl's visitors follow this route too, though it does not carry the same meaning.) The religious dimension of the visit is underscored again when Salten leaves Jerusalem almost as soon as he arrives, as he is not yet ready for this deeply meaningful place at this stage of his journey. Part of this journey must be carried out within, as Dickel stated: "to shed one's own agitation, which, according to Salten, stems from the Jew's conflict with himself."[81] Near the end of the narrative, Salten relates that he felt the presence of his parents and all of his Jewish forefathers throughout the journey.

In spite of this inclusion of a rediscovery of his religious roots, Salten's primary attachment is to *Judentum* (*Jewishness*) and not Judaism. His heightened sense of Jewish identification is not conceived in religious terms, as in the case of Beer-Hofmann, but rather in membership in the Jewish people, bound together not only by a shared history but a special world historical mission. Salten characterizes the Jewish people as specially chosen to convey a message, "since in them the idea of the eternal God lives; in their minds and hearts the eternity of the idea beats undyingly."[82] Salten also sees the Jews as uniquely positioned to stand as a model of tolerance, describing them in terms nearly identical to Herzl's. The Jews, Salten argues, must forego any form of nationalism; they are precluded from this not only by their history of oppression, but also by the ethical character of the Jewish religion. Like the Litwak family in Herzl's novel, Salten contends that Jews must open themselves to others. When he visits a synagogue he experiences a moment of spiritual insight, yet it does not represent a connection to the Jewish people, but to all of humankind. Salten writes, "I feel very strongly that one cannot value humanity when one loves only one's own people, that, however, one may very well nourish one's own people in one's heart when this heart is open to all people without distinction."[83]

While this mission was thwarted in the Diaspora, it could now be realized in Palestine. Here, as in *Bambi,* Salten includes a critique of Jewish assimilation, referring to the "horse-trading of assimilation" and arguing that acculturated Jews had become "refugees of their own blood."[84] This critique is not as sharp as in *Bambi,* nor does Salten engage in the kind of scathing attacks on bourgeois Viennese Jewry that Herzl undertakes.

While Salten is unequivocal in this text in his support for the Zionist cause, he exhibits a discernible attachment to European traditions of thought. His form of Zionism contains no traces of nationalism but is put forward as an expression of a liberal tradition of cosmopolitan humanism. His argument for peace and reconciliation with the Arabs, for example, is not cast in political terms but on the basis of tolerance, stemming from the ideology of Jewish emancipation. Even in his most conscious reflections as a Jew, Salten's thought is anchored in Europe, whose traditions of thought clearly shaped the way he saw the world. In addition to this intellectual influence, Europe appears ever present in his mind as a point of comparison. As Dickel has noted, while Salten moved around Palestine, the cultural topography of Austria was always with him. When Salten visits a church in Jerusalem, he recalls Mariazell; the Jordan River reminds him of the Danube; other sites bring to mind the Viennese suburbs.[85] With this text, along with his public lectures, Salten is a committed Zionist, more active in his support of the movement than other prominent cultural figures who supported the Zionist idea. But he remains a cosmopolitan Viennese, a participant in and contributor to its particular culture. Salten never seriously considered emigrating to Palestine. In spite of an increasingly hostile environment, Vienna continued to remain home for him, but his support for the movement involved helping those who wished to emigrate to do so.

If this position seems to portray Salten as conflicted, there are a number of written reflections in which he indeed acknowledges the dilemmas of a divided identity. In the Palestine book he writes:

> He among us who avows his Jewishness positively and definitively provokes inner conflicts; he is so profoundly shaken in his relationship to the world in which he lives, to the culture, shaped by the landscape, to which he belongs and contributes, to the earth, to the city of his birth, bound up with childhood memories, that all of his thinking and his whole soul must be directed at bringing them back into harmony.[86]

Salten's inner conflicts would only deepen in the ensuing years as Jewish life in Vienna came under increased pressure. There are moments when Salten's political decisions seem to reflect a lack of comprehension of the threat represented by the rise of fascism, as when he persisted in expressing a unity between German and Austrian culture even after the National Socialists took power.[87] At other times he seems to be marked by resignation, as Schnitzler often appeared to be. However there are other very significant moments when, in the face of the desperate situation of Austrian Jews during the 1930s, Salten raised a Jewish voice that refused to be silenced. In April 1927 Salten wrote an open letter to a newspaper in protest of Walter Riehl, the leader of the National Socialist organization, the *Deutschsozialer Verein*, as a candidate for the national assembly on the Christian Social Party list. A few months later, Riehl, whom Salten referred to as the "*bekannten Hakenkreuzler*" (well-known Nazi), would serve as defense attorney for the *Frontkämpfer* (*frontline soldiers*) in the Schattendorf case—the spark to the July mass demonstrations in Vienna and the burning of the Palace of Justice. In Salten's letter, he emphasizes that anti-Semitism of this time had a fundamentally different—and far more dangerous—character than in the days of Habsburg rule:

> People clearly need to be reminded that condiitons are not what they were in the days of the Lueger era [*in den Tagen der K.K. Luegerei*], that today we all stand before important decisions that will fundamentally change the face of this world. People need to be reminded that the whole comedy of the Lueger era, accompanied by the jingle-jangle of popular music, was child's play compared to the tremendous upheaval that has only just begun and that we will all hardly get to see to its conclusion.[88]

With these prescient words, Salten sounded a warning that an entirely new, virulent strain of anti-Semitism must not be dismissed as harmless rhetoric. He comes forward as a Jew because the gravity of the situation compels him to. In a 1931 article in the *Neue Freie Presse* Salten addresses Jewish readers specifically, arguing that the *Kultusgemeinde* must be supported with Jewish tax contributions to maintain their crucial work in caring for Eastern European refugees. He makes a sharp appeal for Jewish solidarity, contending that old divisions were obsolete now that the Jewish situation had been reduced to a fight for survival. Two years earlier Salten had been embroiled in conflict after the publication of his novel *Fünfzehn Hasen* (*Fifteen Hares*), which addressed a Jewish theme. The novel made Salten once again the subject of an attack by Karl Kraus, who again took aim at Salten's use of language, which he saw as sullied by an unconscious slippage into Yiddish. Kraus's ridicule of Salten's language was nothing new, but it does reveal the highly charged climate in which Salten made these other public statements as a Jewish writer, in which even an animal story written by a Jew could set off a powder keg. Nevertheless Salten's *Bambi* sequel, *Bambis Kinder* (*Bambi's Children*), in 1938, was more polemical in tone than the original; now increased hunting had introduced a new level of violence that threatened the deer population and undermined the harmony between the different animals of the forest. This text is a reflection of Salten's heightened identification with a Jewish identity.

In the last decade of his life Salten's personal circumstances grew quite difficult. He was plagued by financial troubles. He received some royalties from the United States, but as he had sold the rights to *Bambi* in 1933 (reportedly for $1,000), he saw little financial gain from the Disney film. In February 1939 Salten's daughter, who was married to a Swiss actor, was able to secure a visa for her parents to Switzerland, although Salten was restricted from journalistic activity and limited to writing animals stories in his literary career. He lost his wife in 1942 and died after a long illness in 1945.

In the 1920s and 1930s, Salten, like all Austrian Jews, would come to face an intractable dilemma. The forms of identification available to Jews in Habsburg Vienna were no longer viable; nor could Jews solve the problem of forming a new Austrian identity with the turn to Germany so common among their Gentile fellow Viennese. With both Austrian and Jewish identities contested in an atmosphere of heated identity politics, there was virtually no solution to this dilemma. Salten was able to fashion a new identity for himself by moving far outside of Vienna in his writings, and even, in the case of *Bambi*, outside of human society. In these new worlds—real and imaginary—Salten found a heightened consciousness of his Jewish heritage, a vigorous support for Zionism, and a partial rediscovery of Judaism. But as anti-Semitism found new virulent forms of expression with the rise of Austro-fascism, this hardly solved the problem. As Salten continued to feel an attachment to Austria and Vienna even as the dominant forces of the Right sought ways to exclude him from both, he also continued to face conflicts both internally and externally.

Stefan Zweig

During the interwar years, Stefan Zweig was to experience an identity crisis in a form that differed somewhat from the type I have described as characteristic for Austrian Jews following World War I. This is not particularly surprising, as Zweig's prewar identity differed from the norm in that he had suppressed his Jewish identity more than most in favor of a cosmopolitan European identity. After World War I Zweig did experience the heightened Jewish consciousness we have seen in his contemporaries, but he would struggle to define what this meant and to reconcile this Jewish identity with his European humanism.

Zweig greeted the outbreak of World War I with surprising enthusiasm, given the pacifism he had already espoused prior to the war. Zweig's early euphoria—his assertion in his memoirs that he was exempt from this sudden patriotic surge notwithstanding—discussed in the introduction to this chapter, is a good indicator of just how far-reaching the fervor among the populace was at the outset of the war. Zweig's enthusiasm, however, deflated more quickly than most. Like Salten, Zweig served in the war propaganda agency in Vienna. On assignment, reporting on the eastern front, Zweig was confronted with the devastation of this war-torn region, the suffering of the civilian population, and the privations of the front for the soldiers. In *Die Welt von Gestern* (1943), he recalls, "Above all else,

I saw the terrible misery of the civilian population, upon whose eyes the horror of what they had experienced lay like a shadow."[89] He then singles out the special misery of the ghetto Jews, living in abject poverty in intolerable conditions. This contact with Galician Jews had the same effect on Zweig as it had had on many of his fellow Western, assimilated Jews, including Beer-Hofmann: their plight stirred his deep sympathy, and the whole experience raised his consciousness as a Jew. After World War I, Zweig would write several texts addressing explicitly Jewish themes, which he had not done previously.

The war represented a decisive turning point in Zweig's life in several respects. Not only did it deepen his rather ambiguous relationship to Jewishness, but in the eyes of Joseph Strelka, it led the apolitical Zweig into a confrontation with politics and forced him to undertake, rather reluctantly, some political commitments.[90] The first expression of this was the drafting of his pacifist drama *Jeremias* (*Jeremiah*), in the spring of 1915. (The play was published in 1917.) *Jeremias* relays the story of the fall of the kingdom of Judah and the city of Jerusalem, and the destruction of Solomon's Temple at the hands of Nebuchadnezzar, the Chaldean king. Zweig's protagonist, the prophet Jeremiah, is a solitary outcast whose repeated warnings of an impending terrible war are at odds with a people gripped by war fever and convinced of an easy victory, claiming God on their side. The king, Zedekiah, ignores Jeremiah's warnings and enters into an alliance with the Egyptian pharaoh in an attempt to overthrow the powerful Chaldeans, who control the region and exact tributes from their subject kingdoms. Nebuchadnezzar is angered by this maneuvering and encamps a vast army outside the gates of Jerusalem. With no help from the Egyptians forthcoming, the Jews undergo an eighteen-month siege of Jerusalem, leading to famine and the eventual storming of the city by the Chaldean army, causing the devastation of the city and its people.

Zweig's treatment of the events related in the book of Jeremiah of the Hebrew Bible not only puts forward an anti-war message, penned during the calamitous First World War, it also contains his reflections on the defining elements of the history of the Jewish people. In *Jeremias*, Zweig focuses his attention on the suffering of the Jews and the Diaspora experience as the central elements of Jewish experience that have shaped them as a people. In these choices, I suggest, we gain a sense of those elements of Jewish experience with which Zweig increasingly came to identify during an exceedingly difficult time.

Zweig's exploration of the theme of suffering is undertaken both through the trials of the prophet Jeremiah and through the collective experience of the people of Jerusalem under siege and at war. As a direct result of the prophecy he has been chosen to deliver, Jeremiah suffers both with his people and because of them. While the kingdom is still at peace, Jeremiah is plagued by terrible dreams of the war to come and the awful knowledge that the war will mean the destruction of his people. He reveals his visions first to his mother, underscoring the horrors of war: "A time is at hand like no other in Israel, and a war like none other that has come over the earth. A time when the living will envy the dead their peace in the grave and the seeing will envy the blind their darkness."[91] His mother sees these statements as a denial of God and casts him out of her house. His prophecies are no more welcome among the Jewish people, who are under the sway of their leaders, all moving steadily toward war. The crowd derides Jeremiah, the priest Pashur forbids him from speaking before the Temple, the prophet Hananiah foments the crowd to an embrace of war as an expression of God's will. Even as he is mocked and threatened with violence—even crucifixion—Jeremiah continues to warn against the folly of inviting war with the Chaldaens: "Take away God's name from war, as God does not make wars, but people! No war is holy, no death is holy, life alone is holy."[92]

Jeremiah wins only a single follower to his views, yet he refuses to be silenced. Because of his persistence, his message reaches King Zedekiah, but ultimately the king is merely unsettled by Jeremiah's disturbing message and is not moved to change his course of action. Jeremiah's suffering is considerable—he is devastated that he has been granted these visions but not the power to avert the disaster by swaying the king or the people with his words; he watches his mother die without being able to shield her from the knowledge that war has come to Jerusalem; he is threatened with imprisonment and death; he feels tested by God but left alone in his suffering and powerlessness.

As Jeremiah's prophecy is fulfilled, he suffers alongside his people. Even as he repeatedly admonishes the Jews for forgetting the Covenant in their rush to war, Jeremiah expresses the wish that he be proven wrong, willing to be considered a fool or false prophet if his people could be spared the fate of his visions. As his prophecy is fulfilled and Nebuchadnezzar lays waste to the city, Jeremiah struggles with his faith in light of what he sees as the harshness of God's judgment against the Jews; when the people cry out that God has left them, Jeremiah angrily tells them they must stop looking to lay blame and submit humbly to God's will. But when the city is destroyed, he proclaims his allegiance to the dead and the suffering, whom he feels God has forgotten, and he turns away from God: "Your harshness is too harsh for me and too heavy is your hand! I will no longer serve your furious vengeance. I will serve you no longer. I break the bond between you and me. I break it! I break it!"[93]

Jeremiah's rebellion does not last, however. He falls into a trancelike state and proclaims that Nebuchadnezzar will fall and that Israel's avenger is already rising up. He awakens and praises God for not allowing him to turn away from Him. Jeremiah begins to comfort the survivors, imbuing their suffering with meaning: "Blessed that we lost everything in order to find Him, blessed our destiny, blessed our troubles and trials! As we were chosen to endure through our suffering and toward eternity through our renewal!"[94] Jeremiah places this suffering at the center of the Jews' special relationship to God:

> Not for peace have we been chosen among the peoples: wandering the earth is our shelter, hardship our acre, and God our home through time. ... Leave the others their happiness and pride, leave them their house and home on earth, but you let yourself be tested, you people of suffering, and believe, you people of God, as suffering is your holy inheritance and you alone are chosen for it for the sake of your eternity.[95]

Jeremiah's words of comfort reach the people in a way that his prior warnings had not. The crowd of survivors is transformed from the hysterical mass they had been before the attack to a unified people, reminded precisely in their suffering of their special relationship to God. For Sarah Fraiman, this emphasis on suffering and the notion of the spiritual superiority of the vanquished over the victor is a manifestation of Zweig's Jewish identity.[96] Zweig makes the connection explicit himself in his memoirs. He wrote:

> But in choosing a Biblical theme I had unknowingly touched upon something that had remained unused in me up to that time: that community with the Jewish destiny whether in my blood or darkly founded in tradition. Was it not my people that again and again had been conquered by all other peoples, again and again, and yet outlasted them because of some secret power—that power of transforming defeat through will, of withstanding it again and again? Had they not presaged, our prophets, this perpetual hunt and persecution that today again scatters us upon the highways like chaff, and had they not affirmed this submission to power and even blessed it as a way to God? Had trial not eternally been of profit to all and to the individual?[97]

Zweig's drama of the destruction of Israel elevates the Jews' suffering to an ideal. As Robert Wistrich has noted, the powerlessness of the Jews in relation to the Chaldean conquerors is reinterpreted as a mark of moral superiority and, as Zweig remarks above, "a way to God."[98] The ennoblement of the Jews through their suffering is immediate and visible. As they leave the city as ordered by Nebuchadnezzar, the Jews are illuminated by the rising sun, and an elderly Chaldean remarks that they march like victors and not the vanquished: "This is a procession of a king and not an exodus of the subjugated ... never has the world seen a people like this!"[99] The Chaldean soldiers are forced to admit that they did not defeat the Jews' spirit or their God. Zweig's text transforms the Jews' defeat into a victory of the spirit.[100]

Alongside the revaluation of suffering enacted in the text, Zweig also celebrates the Diaspora existence as the second component of the unique historical ethical mission of the Jews. The Jews are once again forged into a community as Jeremiah reconnects them to their historical destiny as a wandering and exiled people. As they prepare to leave, Jeremiah calls to the survivors: "Wandering people, God's people, out into the world!" The people form a single chorus. "Yes, onward to our wandering ... we want to suffer like our fathers."[101] Robert Wistrich reminds us that Zweig wrote this drama when there was very little hope for his own vision of world citizenry; at this moment Zweig turns to the Diaspora experience as an alternative to the nationalism gripping Europe, seeing in the Diaspora condition the potential for spiritual freedom. The Jews' wandering, their eternal homelessness and suffering, are, as Wistrich notes, "all raised by Stefan Zweig in the midst of the First World War to the level of a prophetic ideal and destiny."[102] This interest in a special Jewish destiny continues to occupy a prominent position in Zweig's post-1918 writings as well.

While other Austrian Jews were forced by the collapse of the Habsburg Empire to redefine their identities because it was no longer viable to sustain an identity comprised of a political allegiance to Austria, an ethnic identification as a Jew, or participation in German culture, the case was somewhat different for Zweig. Zweig's identity as an Austrian had never been particularly strong, even in terms of his allegiance to the Habsburg dynasty. His self-conception was as a European, a cosmopolitan humanist. And this European identity, just as much as Austria's postwar identity, was severely strained by the war. According to Jacob Golomb, after the ravages of war Zweig felt betrayed not by Austria, but by European humanism itself.[103] During the twenties and thirties Zweig struggled mightily to sustain himself with a continued commitment to humanism, letting this universalist principle stand in as a substitute for a stable identity.[104] However the war had understandably shaken Zweig's faith in this principle, and postwar nationalism made it exceedingly difficult to live as a cosmopolitan European. Additionally, the transcendence of politics that was a clear outcome of the war was devastating to Zweig, who wanted nothing more than to devote his life to humanism and the arts.

In Chapter 1, I discussed the way in which Zweig's Jewish and Viennese identities both fostered his cosmopolitan identification, the permeability of these identities allowing a European self-conception to emerge from them. During the 1920s Zweig encountered the dilemma that his Jewish identity (which was gaining strength but was nonetheless under strain) and his European identity (similarly strained) no longer coexisted easily. Prior to the war Zweig had subordinated his Jewishness to cosmopolitanism. As Zweig became more open to a Jewish identity, the difficult process of defining what shape that might take drew his attention away from the realm of universal European culture into the particular experience of the Jews. Looking to establish a synthesis of these identities, Zweig, as he demonstrated in the drama *Jeremias,* was concerned with exploring the role Jews occupied or could occupy within a universal European humanist culture. Sarah Fraimanviews Zweig as exploring such questions in his 1929 novella *Buchmendel.*[105]

In *Buchmendel* we meet the figure of Mendel, an Eastern European Jew who has escaped from a ghetto existence and is undergoing a process of assimilation toward Western culture. He immerses himself in that culture through his devotion to books. Several critics have noted, however, that Mendel's relationship to these books and to Western culture more broadly is merely superficial.[106]

Mendel's unique capacity for memory remains at a surface level and thus contains traces of the anti-Semitic trope of Jews being purely imitative and not creative in their own right. In this way Mendel seems to have exchanged the ghetto of his past for the kind of internal ghetto walls described by Herzl's central character in *Das neue Ghetto*. Zweig's treatment of Mendel reflects a common current in depictions of Eastern European Jews by assimilated Western Jewish writers—both admiring and prejudicial.

In the late novella *Untergang eines Herzens* (*Destruction of a Heart*, 1939), Zweig constructed another ambivalent Jewish protagonist, this time within the milieu of assimilated Austrian Jewry. The aging businessman Solomonsohn looks back over a life spent principally in the workplace, geared toward the accumulation of wealth for the benefit of his wife and daughter. He is confronted with the fact that although is wealth has allowed his wife and daughter to be enveloped within a nouveau-riche elegance, they are nevertheless thoroughly ungrateful for his efforts and even mock him for failing to conform to their bourgeois ideal informed by Christian society. This kind of generational conflict is a common theme in turn-of-the-century Viennese Jewish literature; in both Adolf Dessauer's *Großstadtjuden* and Schnitzler's *Der Weg ins Freie* successful Jewish entrepreneurial fathers reflect on their own role in their children's lack of appreciation of their hard work and unwillingness to follow in their fathers' footsteps. In Schnitzler's novel, Solomon Ehrenberg's rejection of his wife and daughter's snobbery prompts him to put on a defiant display of negative Jewish stereotypes and become a supporter of Zionism. These are stories—told with greater or lesser degrees of irony—about the limits of assimilation. Zweig's protagonist is conflicted over the choices he has made, and Zweig is similarly conflicted in his portrayal of this figure.

Zweig's ambivalence is understandable in light of his difficulty in coming to terms with the world that had emerged from World War I. Throughout the twenties and thirties he persisted in trying to work through these difficulties. Zweig channeled the bulk of his efforts into the attempt to negotiate a synthesis of his Jewish and European identities, rooted in the Diaspora condition of the Jews. Zweig was deeply disturbed by the rise of nationalism that had already emerged before the war and had gained fuel during the conflict. At this time he turned to the Jewish Diaspora experience as a counter to European nationalism.[107] This process unfolded as follows: Zweig departed from a personal view of his own role within the European cultural sphere. In light of his translation work and essays on important cultural figures in European thought, he defined this role as a mediator and translator among European cultures. Zweig then came to the conclusion that as a Jew he was in a unique position to fulfill this role; particularly as a citizen of the supranational Habsburg state, he moved freely among cultures rather than being tied to a single national culture. And in the final stage of his thought process he translated this position into a special mission for the Jews. In a 1917 letter to Martin Buber, Zweig wrote the following:

> I had chosen during the ten years of a wandering life absolute freedom among the nations, everywhere feeling myself as guest, as participant and mediator. This international feeling of freedom from the madness of the fanatic world saved me inwardly at this time and I feel grateful to Judaism, which enabled me to be free from nationhood. I held the idea of nationality to be a restricting and dangerous one, and saw in the idea that Judaism should materialize itself as a nation a renunciation of its highest mission.[108]

We return here to the valorization of the Jew's outsider position already identified in *Jeremias*. It is the eternal homeless of the Jew that, in Zweig's view, enables him to be free of the strictures of nationalism and play this role as mediator between cultures. Here Zweig seems very much to articulate a form of diasporic consciousness outlined in an article by Daniel and Jonathan Boyarin, in which they seek to validate the diasporic form of community that is not rooted in a particular land but shares space with others and makes no claims to exclusivist power.[109] In Zweig's work, Diaspora is proposed as a counter to nationalism. Jewishness is thus in the first instance a form of supranationality and rejection of nationalism. Beyond this, Zweig idealized the rootlessness of the Jewish people as the condition that makes possible the Jews' historical ethical mission of spreading the values of European civilization. In the development of this conception, Zweig seems to have been attempting to theorize—in lieu of a stable identity—a meaningful role within European society for the assimilated, cultured Jew of the Diaspora. Zweig's life in the twenties and thirties was marked by the attempt to fulfill this role. After 1934 Zweig would personally experience the extent to which the decentered Diaspora existence he attempted to valorize was related to the existential homelessness of exile.

I turn now to a text born of the despair of Zweig's final years, his memoirs *Die Welt von Gestern*. Robert Wistrich sees this text as a work of preservation, a "revealing and beautifully written testament to the liberal humanist values of Central European Jewry" before their destruction by the Nazis.[110] In this work Zweig returns to Vienna, where his cosmopolitan European humanism originated, at a time when his faith in this position had been shattered. This is of course a deeply nostalgic account, portraying a Vienna that truly existed only in Zweig's memory and imagination. Zweig records no poverty, no serious class distinctions, no social unrest in this remembered Vienna. Considering the empire as a whole, Zweig does not give an account of ethnic animosities or the nationalities conflict. He is also largely dismissive of turn-of-the-century anti-Semitism, which is particularly surprising given his vantage point from 1941. Robert Wistrich has sought an explanation for this downplaying of the anti-Semitic threat and concluded that in light of Zweig's knowledge of what was to come he must have been trying to draw a sharp contrast between anti-Semitism around 1900 and the more violent form it took in the 1930s.[111] This is a very plausible view, supported by the fact that Felix Salten made a similar gesture in the 1927 letter to the editor discussed above, in which he explicitly referred to prior forms of anti-Semitism as child's play in comparison to its latest manifestations.

Zweig's Vienna in *Die Welt von Gestern* is a remembered Vienna, written from a distance in time and space. Zweig felt a special attachment to the city he portrays, but this affection was really for a Vienna of his own making. The city was the site of Zweig's first confrontation with the new reality of 1918. His retreat from Vienna into the isolation of his Salzburg mountaintop was an expression of his profound alienation from the world as it emerged from World War I. Zweig's exile experience and eventual suicide are beyond the scope of the present study. I hope, however, that this brief focus on the work and thought of the interwar years sheds some light on the dilemmas and anxieties he carried into exile.

Joseph Roth

Roth's life story is saturated with myths, largely of his own making, as many of his writings from the years of wandering and exile contain iterations of a reimagined past. These alternative biographies generally relate to his childhood and youth. Roth invented a number of possible fathers as a response to the early loss of his father, apparently to madness, and alternately offered various Galician and Russian villages as his hometown. In fact, Moses Joseph Roth was born in Brody, a Galician shtetl near Lemberg. At the outbreak of World War I, the town had 18,000 inhabitants, the vast majority of whom were Jewish. Roth grew up in the home of his grandfather, an Orthodox tradesman named Jechiel Grübel. From 1901 to 1905 he attended the Baron Hirsch Volksschule in Brody, followed by the Kronprinz Rudolph Gymnasium, where German was the language of instruction.

Roth registered for the winter semester of 1913 at the University of Lemberg, where he was to live with an uncle and guardian, Siegmund Grübel. Lemberg may have been known as "*Klein-Wien*" (Little Vienna) in Galicia, but the city seems to have held little attraction for Roth, and the university, where courses were conducted in Polish, was similarly unappealing. Vienna was where he wanted to be. He proceeded to spend part of the fall there and was enrolled at the university by the following semester. Roth's move from the province to the capital to pursue an education echoed the major thrust of nineteenth-century Jewish migration patterns, not only in the change of address from Brody to Leopoldstadt, but also in the ascension into the German middle class—and ultimately the cultural elite—through a rigorous pursuit of *Bildung*. Roth followed a path taken by many Eastern European Jews before him, however his westward journey was a belated manifestation of this tradition—"just before the closing of the gates," as Jean Paul Bier characterized it[112]—and consequently could not have been marked by the same optimism and ambitions that would have accompanied an immigrant half a century earlier.

For Roth, the outbreak of World War I ensured that his experience as a new immigrant to Vienna would be profoundly difficult. He was soon followed to the city by his mother, who joined the flood of Jewish refugees fleeing the Russian occupation of Galicia. They lived in very straitened circumstances in an apartment in the working-class twentieth district, Brigittenau, with no steady income for Roth and only a small refugee allowance for his mother. Roth volunteered for military service in the summer of 1916. He trained in Vienna, where his company took part in the funeral procession of the Emperor Franz Joseph. The death of the aged emperor was among central experiences of the war for Roth, and this historical event would figure prominently in many of his works as a cipher for the end of the Habsburg monarchy and loss of the *Vaterland.*

In the spring of 1917 Roth was sent to Galicia, where he served in and around Lemberg. According to biographer David Bronsen, Roth was assigned to the press corps and the 32nd Infantry Division, where he remained until the end of the war.[113] While this was not Roth's first encounter with Eastern European Jews, of course (as was the case for many Viennese Jews serving in the military during the war), Roth's wartime experience in Galicia was significant in shaping his views of the eastern provinces and of his homeland, reshaping and partially taking the place of childhood memories. These views would undergo another transformation as a result of his exile experience and the disappearance of the Habsburg Empire.

After the war Roth was unable to return to his studies at the university, as the exigencies of earning a living commanded his attention. After some early publications in newspapers during the war, including feuilleton pieces, reports from the front, and fictional pieces, Roth took his first steady position as editor of *Der neue Tag* in Vienna. Here he worked alongside Egon Erwin Kisch, Alfred Polgar, and Anton Kuh. Roth held this job for a year, and when the paper folded, he moved to Berlin, where he began publishing in a number of mainstream newspapers. At the same time, Roth wrote a number of pieces for the Socialist paper *Vorwärts,* under the byline *"der rote Joseph"* (*"Red Joseph"*). In spite of his clear Socialist sympathies, one would be at a loss to try to identify a single, clear ideological orientation, as Roth's journalistic writings from this period reflect a number of conflicting impulses. There were Socialist views and anti-bourgeois critiques, but also assimilationist overtures toward the dominant German culture alongside more critical views of that culture, not to mention an ambivalent treatment of Jews and the problem of anti-Semitism, to which I will return.[114]

Roth's ideological inconsistencies are hardly surprising considering the tumult of the postwar era. Roth, like most of his contemporaries, experienced a profound spiritual crisis in the aftermath of the war. The predominant manifestation of this crisis was a deep experience of loss—loss of the *Vaterland* in the collapse of the Habsburg Empire, loss of orientation in a political world turned upside down, as well as an unsettling breakdown of traditional values as a response to the horrors of war. Roth emerged from the war in a state of crisis that would persist until his death in 1939, even as this experience of crisis gave rise to a highly fruitful period of literary creativity.

Roth's troubles were not strictly spiritual but also manifested themselves in multiple aspects of his personal life. Most critics agree that Roth's period of exile began with his move to Paris in 1925 to work as a correspondent for the *Frankfurter Zeitung*. After this, Roth never really settled anywhere and served as a sort of roving reporter for that paper over the next few years, producing travel reports from the south of France, the Soviet Union (1926), Albania and Yugoslavia (1927), and Germany and Poland (1928). Roth left Germany definitively in 1933, on the day that Hitler assumed the chancellorship, and returned to Paris. He continued to travel, going back to Austria and Poland, and spent longer periods in the Netherlands and on the French Riviera. Driven by political circumstances, Roth would lead an itinerant existence for nearly two decades, a twentieth-century incarnation of the timeless image of the wandering Jew. Roth's Diaspora life can be seen as a reflection of the existential homelessness of the Jews, a significant recurring theme in his works.

Roth's relationships with women from this period were fraught with difficulties. In 1922, while still in Vienna, Roth married Friederike Reichler. Several years later, signs of mental illness emerged, and in 1928 she entered a sanitarium. This was followed by a number of other institutionalizations, including one at the sanitarium Am Steinhof, in Vienna. Friederike's illness took a toll on Roth, and he began drinking heavily after she fell ill. In 1935 Roth filed for divorce, and Friederike eventually fell victim to the Nazi's euthanasia program in 1940. After the divorce, Roth had several relationships with other women, including Irmgard Keun, with whom he had a two-year relationship. The pair traveled extensively, shortly before his death. Roth's excessive drinking had a negative effect on all of these relationships, and even after a rapid ascension to becoming one of the most high-profile and best-paid journalists in the Weimar Republic, he was never on secure ground financially.

Roth began an extensive correspondence with Stefan Zweig in 1927, which developed into a deeper epistolary friendship that proved important to both men. Faced with hotel bills he could not pay along with other expenses of a life in exile, Roth frequently turned to Zweig to draw on his connections with various presses to help him find a publisher and a source of income.[115] While he published widely, Roth's troubles with publishers actually predated the exile period. His relationships with a number of presses soured as a result of a lack of professionalism that expressed itself in various forms, from missed deadlines to the more serious issue of selling the rights of a new work to more than one publisher.[116] Roth's conflicts with publishers put Zweig in a very difficult position, made all the more difficult by Roth's persistent campaign to convince Zweig to change publishers so that their works might appear at the same press. This was but one of several sources of considerable tension in their relationship, in addition to Roth's alcoholism and money troubles, his sharp criticism of Zweig's continued ties to German presses (which Roth viewed as unacceptably conciliatory toward the Third Reich), Roth's critical view of Zweig's talents, and the discrepancy in their class backgrounds and material circumstances.

Nonetheless the correspondence of Roth and Zweig served as an important medium for the two writers to reflect on their difficult lives in exile, on their struggles to come to terms with the loss of the world they had known and the inhospitable nature of the world that remained. Roth looked to Zweig as a mentor, at times even a father figure, and saw him as having achieved a level of success and security he could hardly imagine for himself. Zweig not only admired Roth's literary talents, but may well have been attracted to the nomadic writer as an embodiment of the Diaspora condition at a time when he was deeply interested in locating something redemptive within that state. The two shared a cosmopolitan humanism, though for Zweig this philosophy had always been rooted in a broad European perspective, while Roth held up a utopian version of Habsburg Austria as the cosmopolitan ideal.

Zweig also differed from Roth in that his cosmopolitanism never easily accommodated an additional strand of identification as a Jew. As he became more conscious of and engaged with his Jewish identity, he struggled to find space for it within his commitment to European humanist ideals. For Roth, the multiethnic Habsburg Empire had made possible a supranational position encompassing the tripartite identity that Marsha Rozenblit has described for Austrian Jews. Roth created a number of memorable cosmopolitan Austrian characters who espoused this supranational perspective, exemplified by Graf Morstin in his 1934 work *Die Büste des Kaisers* (*The Bust of the Emperor*): "My old homeland, the monarchy itself was a great house with many doors and rooms for many types of people. The house has been divided, broken up, destroyed. I have no business being there anymore. I am used to living in a house, not in compartments."[117] It is important to note that this "old homeland" is not strictly a remembered Austria, but an Austria imaginatively created out of memory.[118] Roth was aware of the weaknesses of the empire as it had really existed and often reveals an awareness of his own role in the mythologizing of the lost homeland. In *Juden auf Wanderschaft*, a text written after the devastation of the First World War, Roth laments that Austria-Hungary had possessed the potential to stand as an antidote to nationalism but that this potential was never realized: "That is, it could have furnished the proof for the opposite of this theory, if it had been governed well."[119]

Roth's notion of Austria in the late 1920s and 1930s reflected this view of a great house that could accommodate many. It was the whole and not the individual parts that interested him. In this Roth differs from nearly all of the other authors in this study, for whom Austria in large measure actually meant Vienna. It is difficult to assess Roth's relationship to the Austrian capital, because his time there was fairly limited and the city did not figure heavily in his works. While Roth can be said to have been contributing to the body of Austrian literature from abroad, he was not part of the particular cultural scene of Vienna.

The idea of Austria became of vital importance to Roth only after—indeed, significantly after—its disappearance. During the 1930s, Roth devoted a number of works to the fall of the empire, notably: *Radetzkymarsch* (*The Radetzky March*, 1932), *Die Büste des Kaisers* (*The Bust of the Emperor*, 1934), and *Die Kapuzinergruft* (*The Emperor's Tomb*, 1938). In these works Roth chronicles the processes that brought about the gradual decline of the empire. The loss of the Fatherland figures more broadly as a trope through which Roth explores the lost possibilities embodied in the Habsburg idea, as well as the loss of orientation, feelings of alienation, and condition of homelessness that accompanied the end of the empire, and even the loss of the father—an experience of his early childhood—evoked by Roth's depiction of the "last Austrians."[120]

When Roth did turn his attention to one of the many "rooms" of the great house of Austria, it was to the provinces and not the capital city. In his novel *Die Kapuzinergruft*, the aristocratic Count Chojnicki expresses a viewpoint not far from Roth's own: "The essence of Austria is not the center, but the periphery."[121] As the temporal and spatial remove from his childhood home grew, Galicia came to occupy a very significant place in his writings. The eastern provinces first became a subject of his journalistic writings in the mid-1920s, as he undertook multiple trips to Eastern Europe during his intensive period of travel writing. In his fiction, the eastern provinces loom even larger, as important settings in *Radetzkymarsch, Die Kapuzinergruft, Die Büste des Kaisers, Das falsche Gewicht* (*Weights and Measures*)*, Hiob, Der Leviathan,* and *Tarabas*. The shtetls of Eastern Europe repeatedly stand in for the empire as a whole, as Sipolje in *Die Kapuzinergruft* presents an image of "the monarchy in miniature" through the presence of the Habsburg army officers, the civil servants of the train station, the café and hotel in the Viennese style.[122] Mark Gelber has noted that Lemberg, with its multiple languages and ethnic groups and well known to Roth from his youth as well as return trips during and after the war, was known as the "city of blurred borders."[123] A major current of Roth's portrayal of the East is a celebration of the cosmopolitanism of Eastern European towns and cities.

In his fiction as well as nonfiction, Roth weaves his treatment of Galicia into a sweeping East-West dialogue in which he reflects extensively on the experiences of Eastern European Jews in terms of migration, assimilation, and *Heimat*. Roth's essay *Juden auf Wanderschaft*, which first appeared with the press Die Schmiede in 1927, addresses all of these issues. Since the appearance of David Bronsen's major Roth biography in 1974, this work has largely been viewed as an extended love letter to the Jews of Eastern Europe. More recently, a number of scholars have demonstrated effectively that Roth's depiction of Eastern Europe is both more nuanced and more problematic than had previously been thought. Mark Gelber and David Horrocks have each underscored the polemical nature of the work, calling into question a view of the work as a reliable, straightforward insider's account of the East.[124] Gelber suggests the authorial voice reflects a dual identification with both East and West, one of a number of contradictions of the work, which should not surprise, for, as Horrocks reminds us, Roth is concerned with combating a number of competing stereotypes about the *Ostjude* (Eastern European Jews). Sarah Bailey has deftly revealed the complexity of Roth's relationship to Eastern Europe by analyzing his mistreatment of Yiddish, examining the moves through which Roth suppresses and ultimately disavows his personal relationship to the language in order to create distance between himself and Eastern European Jewry.[125]

The preface to the work already suggests the complexity of the author's relationship to this subject. Roth stages an elaborate series of disclaimers, first dismissing any readership that might be hostile toward Eastern European Jews. He claims to be writing only for Western Europeans who harbor no such ill will or condescending views of the East, and he similarly foregoes any readership expecting an objective account of the subject. Rather, he confesses to approaching his subject "with love" and announces that he is not attempting to create a comprehensive account of the "Jewish problem." David Horrocks examines the spirit of the preface and concludes that Roth "appears, in a strikingly modern, relativist fashion, to be casting doubt on the very validity of any claim to an objectively detached, true account of another culture."[126] The preface's positioning moves, in which Roth professes to be offering a subjective portrait of Eastern European Jews and, indeed, to be preaching to the choir, sets the work on strange footing from the start.[127]

While Roth devotes a chapter to the Eastern European shtetl, the essay is primarily devoted to the presence of Eastern European Jews in the West. Roth undertakes to explain the motivations of those who emigrate to the West, as well as of those who choose to remain in the East. He identifies three principal groups of Jews who remain—those who love the land, those taken with the "Jewish-national idea" and who will fight for their rights where they are, and assimilated Jews who have achieved a measure of success and imagine they have already gained those rights.[128]

Roth identifies multiple reasons for leaving the eastern provinces, including flight from war and revolution or the pursuit of work or a career. There are others for whom no clear explanation is at hand. As Katja Garloff has noted, Roth ascribes a drive dimension to Jewish migration, turning a social process into a psychological one.[129] Roth writes, "Many migrate as the result of a drive and without really knowing why. They follow an indeterminate call of foreign lands and the distinct one of a relative who has arrived; the desire to see the world and to escape the ostensible end of their homeland; the will to be active and to make their strengths count."[130] As an explanatory model this is closer to the *"ewige Wanderschaft"* (eternal wandering) of Ahasver than the result of particular sociopolitical conditions.

Roth also identifies another group of Jewish emigrants with a perspective not far from Roth's own. He writes:

> [These emigrants are those] who know, feel, or just suspect that other problems are coming to the fore alongside the national, and that the national conflicts in the West are a raucous echo from yesterday and today are just noise; who sense that in the West a European idea has been born that will mature into a world idea [*Weltgedanken*] very soon or very late and not without suffering. These Jews prefer to live in countries in which racial and national questions occupy only those segments of the peoples who are numerically strong and even powerful, but who are doubtlessly backward and wander about with an odor of mustiness, blood, and stupidity. These Jews prefer to live in countries in which in spite of it all a few heads are working on the problems of tomorrow.[131]

If the preface establishes that Roth is seeking a like-minded readership, here he conjures a community of Jewish émigrés inclined toward a progressive European cosmopolitanism we know to be very close to his own point of view. Given the virulent anti-Semitism and nationalism of these turbulent years of the Weimar Republic, as well as Roth's personal isolation and struggles, this reads as a utopian fantasy.

The essay puts forward a critique of assimilation, although not without some internal inconsistencies. Assimilation in the West, in this account, is generally a regrettable process that entails a deep, if undefined loss. Roth laments, "The emigrants assimilate—unfortunately!—not too slowly, as we sometimes accuse them of, but far too quickly into our sad living conditions."[132] Throughout the essay Roth emphasizes the fundamental homelessness and loss of identity of assimilating Eastern European Jews in the West. He writes, "They gave themselves up. They lost themselves. Their sad beauty fell away from them, and a dust-gray layer of grief without meaning and lowly heartache without tragedy remained on their bent backs. ... They made compromises."[133] Roth describes the way they changed their appearance, gradually let go of their traditions, and exchanged their own culture for the concerns of the petty bourgeoisie. Speaking of Jewish soldiers serving in the Habsburg army, whose service Roth views as a futile sacrifice for which they will never be appreciated, he observes that even their religious practices have lost their unique character: "They no longer pray in synagogues and prayer houses, but in dull temples in which the service is becoming as mechanical as in every one of the better Protestant churches."[134]

The essay's critique of assimilation is an important strand within a broader critique of the West. On the very first page Roth explains that the Jews' attraction to the West is based on idealization and misunderstanding: "The Eastern Jew looks to the West with a longing that it in no way deserves. For the Eastern Jew, Germany, for example, is still the land of Goethe and Schiller, of the German poets that every Jewish youth, eager to learn, knows better than our Nazi Gymnasium student [*unser hakenkreuzlerischer Gymnasiast*]."[135] Misunderstanding is at the heart of the East-West relationship; Roth satirizes the naïve Western views of the East, dismissing them as "just as laughable as the dream of an Eastern Jew of Western European humanity."[136]

In Roth's account Eastern European Jews cannot expect to be understood by the West. Newly arrived immigrants will not be welcomed by more established Jews, who will only seek to distance themselves from them and resent their presence: "Yet another has arrived. Yet another wants to earn a living. Yet another wants to live."[137] The Socialists also have no use for them, he claims, and the Zionists are powerless. The Eastern Jew in the West is plagued by a vast bureaucracy that forces him into an inescapable struggle to obtain the proper papers. Roth casts the piety of the Jews in the eastern provinces as a natural defense against anti-Semitism, in that these Jews are indifferent to the actions of man and focused solely on their relationship with God. Both the intimate relationship and singular focus on God are lost, however, to the emigrant, and Eastern Jews will be met only with prejudice, discrimination, and social injustice.

In the section devoted to "The Western Ghettos," Roth describes inhospitable climates in both Vienna and Berlin. In Vienna, Eastern Jews new to the city settle in the "voluntary ghetto" of Leopoldstadt. Roth describes the professional possibilities open to these Jews, the bureaucratic hurdles they will face in order to be able to remain in the city, and the competition for limited resources. He concludes, "There is no more difficult fate than that of a newly arrived Eastern Jew in Vienna."[138] Only the Prater offers some respite from the struggles of this difficult existence, a space where Jews from the eastern provinces can move unmolested among non-Jewish Viennese, as Felix Salten had earlier described. Roth writes: "In the Viennese Prater there are practically no anti-Semitic remarks, although not all visitors are friends to the Jews and although the Eastern Jews wander about alongside and among them. Why? Because in the Prater one is happy."[139] This zone that is free of anti-Semitism is strictly limited to the space of the park: "In the Taborstrasse, that leads to the Prater, the anti-Semite begins to be an anti-Semite. In the Taborstrasse, one is no longer happy."[140]

Eastern European Jews in Berlin hardly fared better, according to Roth's portrayal. Berlin was a mere way station for Jews en route to America and other destinations, not a place of permanent settlement. Those who remained were simply stuck, lacking the funds or necessary visas to move on. Roth notes with some irony, "No Eastern Jew goes to Berlin of his own free will? Who in the world goes to Berlin of their own free will?"[141] In Berlin assimilation is somewhat easier than in Vienna, but this is cast in dismal terms: "Berlin levels differences and stifles idiosyncrasies."[142] According to Roth, Jewish life in Berlin is staged as a battle with the city. Berlin had only a Jewish quarter and no established ghetto; a ghetto would mean that the Jews had made an impression on the city, and this was not permitted. Jews face a constant struggle with the Prussian authorities. Roth characterizes these Jews with descriptors such as "frightened" and "sad." Only the Yiddish theater appears as a bright spot for Jews in the area, and this has a temporary, improvised quality—"Who knows if one has to hit the road again in the next hour?"[143]

Roth draws a sharp contrast between life for Eastern European Jewish immigrants in these two cities and the possibilities afforded by Paris. While Vienna segregated its Jews in the Leopoldstadt and Berlin did not permit a real Jewish presence to take hold, in Paris, the Jews could live well and achieve a measure of integration. Roth writes, "Only in Paris do the Eastern Jews begin to become Western Europeans. They become Frenchmen. They even become patriots."[144] The difference comes back to Roth's interest in cosmopolitanism. "Paris is a metropolis. Vienna was once one. Berlin is just now becoming one."[145] In Paris, Roth argues, prejudice exists but is not acted on. Roth's Paris is the Prater writ large, in that the Parisians are too happy to be bothered with anti-Semitism.

Roth's positive assessment of life in Paris for Eastern European Jews even extends to the process of assimilation. While the rest of the essay is an unequivocal condemnation of assimilation, this strident tone is wholly absent with respect to Paris. The freedoms enjoyed by Jews who have settled in Paris extend to their use of language, as they may choose to speak Yiddish—openly and loudly, Roth insists—or French, even bad French. In this atmosphere of tolerance, Jews learn French and their children no longer speak Yiddish. This is not depicted as a loss, however: "It amused me in the streets of the Parisian Jewish quarter to hear the parents speaking Yiddish, the children, French. French replies follow Yiddish questions. These children are gifted. They will accomplish something in France, God willing. And God is willing, the way I see it."[146] This is not only the most positive and optimistic assessment of Jewish existence in the essay. Roth's enthusiasm for Paris also represents a shift through which the authorial voice is increasingly identified with the West.

Roth's identification with the Eastern Jews, his clear empathy with the people and their culture, does not diminish as the polemical tone of the essay subsides; rather, a dual identification gradually takes shape. For Mark Gelber, this intermediate position enhances the power of the essay's critique. He writes, "The essential component of the *Ich* [I] makes his hard-won insights known to the reader."[147] The authorial voice of the essay is ambivalent, shifting between a clear identification with the West, aligning itself with a Western "*wir*" [we], and the highly empathetic, personal connection with the Eastern European Jews implied in the preface.

Juden auf Wanderschaft is a reflection of Roth's position between the two worlds of the Eastern European Jewish communities and the urban centers of

Western Europe. By partially belonging to both worlds, Roth could be said to have possessed a dual identity; yet such a term can only be employed if the ambiguity of the position is made clear. Wolfgang Iser sees it thus: "Dual identity means first and foremost that one has none at all, as it is a contradiction in itself to have two identities at the same time. Whoever is driven to a dual identity hangs in an in-between position, and thus experiences what is unattainable."[148] This is an apt characterization of Roth: an assimilated, acculturated Eastern Jew in the West who "disdained his own assimilation."[149] Roth's awareness of the costs of assimilation is an expression of this position between cultures. In the end, however, Roth's decentered position is one that accommodated the expression of a Jewish identity. Roth reflects further on the challenges of life carried out between two cultures in his novel *Hiob*.

For Gershon Shaked, *Hiob* (*Job*) is the "most Jewish" of Roth's works.[150] The novel is Jewish in its subject matter; in focusing on the processes of assimilation that an Eastern European Jewish family undergoes before and after World War I, Roth takes on one of the central issues facing modern Jews. Roth's principal intertextual references are Jewish as well, not only in his reinterpretation of the biblical story of Job, but also in his weaving in of the story of Joseph as a counterpoint to Job's tale. Shaked emphasizes the translation work Roth builds into the novel. Roth acts as translator, as the central character, Mendel, would not have been a German speaker. At the same time, he requires what one might call translation work on the part of the reader, as he presents a largely unfamiliar fictive world of the Eastern European shtetl. Roth depicts this Jewish *Soziosemiotik* (social semiotics) with a level of detail that would not have been immediately transparent to a German reader. Shaked explains, for example, Mendel's lowly status as a teacher of the youngest children in the village—the Hebrew-Yiddish *melamed*—a position that is poorly paid and at the bottom of the social hierarchy of the shtetl. As Roth depicts Jewish religious rites, Deborah's pilgrimage to the *Wunderrabbi*, and the interaction between Jews and Cossacks, the reader is drawn deeply into this Eastern European Jewish world. Shaked concludes, "While the Book of Job already belongs to general culture, Roth's *Job* is paradoxically much more deeply rooted in the Jewish cultural community."[151]

As in *Juden auf Wanderschaft*, assimilation is depicted here in primarily negative terms. In both texts Roth equates assimilation not with integration or acceptance but with loss and disintegration. Through the various members of Mendel's family, Roth presents different forms of assimilation. Two of Mendel's children are seduced by the Cossacks, drawn away from the family and from tradition by the very embodiment of the persecution of Eastern European Jews. Mendel's son Jonas joins the Russian soldiers and readily takes part in their excessive consumption of vodka and aggressive, unrestrained sexuality. His other son, Shemariah, immigrates to America, where he transforms himself into "Sam," a successful, now thoroughly American businessman with no relationship to his

Jewish heritage. Daughter Miriam sleeps with the Cossacks and then with other non-Jewish men, expressing an uncontrolled sexuality very much in line with contemporaneous stereotypes of *la belle juive*. Katja Garloff has demonstrated how Roth employs Miriam's undifferentiated sexual desire as an eroticized form of assimilation.[152] Drawing on nineteenth-century associations of assimilation with femininity, Roth depicts Miriam, as well as her mother, Deborah, as agents of assimilation in the novel. That these assimilatory desires are transgressive and self-destructive is evident in their fates in American exile—Deborah dies and Miriam descends into mental illness. For Garloff, Roth presents these desires of Jewish women "as one of the major causes of the social and moral decline of Eastern European Jewry."[153]

For Mendel Singer, emigration is clearly a path to destruction, as he experiences loss after loss, feels adrift in his new American surroundings, is forced to witness the disintegration of his family, experiences a loss of faith, and becomes alienated from God. Mendel's suffering is clearly linked to his family's assimilation, and, indeed, one can certainly view his fate as divine punishment for the sons' nationalistic and the daughter's sexual assimilation. However Roth's modern treatment of the Job story plays out largely in an ironic register; Mendel is not the tragic hero but the decentered modern subject ill equipped to meet the challenges with which his life presents him. Moreover, the disastrous lives of these offspring are not the novel's last word on assimilation.

Set alongside—and against the grain of—the story of Job is the Joseph legend, retold in the figure of Mendel's youngest son, Menuchim. Like the biblical Joseph, Menuchim is maltreated by his brothers and abandoned in a foreign land. (The sick child Menuchim must be left behind in Russia—with Gentiles—when Sam finances the family's journey to America.) Menuchim, long given up for dead, resurfaces in New York as a world-renowned composer. His return is cast as miraculous, just as his surprise entrance to the Passover seder at which Mendel is a reluctant guest references the coming of the Messiah. As Shaked has noted, however, Menuchim's rise is human, rather than divine. His is a positive story of assimilation. His upbringing, healing, and entrance into the musical world are all carried out in a Gentile milieu. By attaining professional success and personal happiness, the artist figure achieves what the other family members could not.

In the presentation of a hopeful story of integration alongside an overwhelmingly negative depiction of assimilation, the novel exhibits a narrative ambiguity similar to *Juden auf Wanderschaft*. In that essay Roth laments the high costs to Jewish life exacted by the processes of integration to the West. In his discussion of Eastern European Jews in Paris, however, he holds open the possibility of a positive form of assimilation and acculturation being carried out across two generations. In *Hiob*, Roth again gives voice to his ambivalence vis-à-vis the project of assimilation and the challenges of modernity symbolized by Western Europe and America.

Roth's views of the world and of his own place within it contained a number of paradoxes. While *"der rote Joseph"* (*"Red Joseph"*) was in the main a phenomenon of Roth's early years working as a journalist in Berlin, certain elements of this left-leaning Roth remained even as he became the conservative and nostalgic Habsburg legitimist of his later years. Roth was indeed nostalgic for the lost empire and the possibilities it had represented, but his writings also reflect the awareness that his referent was not real or remembered—it was an imagined community. Finally, Roth's relationship to *Judentum* undoubtedly improved over the course of his lifetime in spite of a turn to Catholicism, which may have culminated in conversion. In light of Roth's troubled life of the 1930s, one could hardly expect any resolution of such contradictions. Rather, it seems that the decentered position he occupied both enabled and necessitated his continuing to struggle with multiple, fragmented, and conflicting views of both himself and the world.

Karl Kraus

The strife-ridden interwar years produced boundless material for polemics, and the critic and satirist Karl Kraus was appropriately busy and productive. Kraus's work took on a more international focus as a result of the war experience, and even as he continued a number of campaigns from the prewar period, the targets of his critique broadened in scope as he mounted an opposition to the major tendencies of the emergent postwar order. Kraus continued to develop his approach to criticism, particularly to satire, and his unresolved identity crisis is implicated in this pursuit as he continued his attempt to put forward an autonomous critique that could not be coded (nor dismissed) as Jewish.

Like the other writers considered in this chapter, Kraus continued to struggle with identity conflicts stemming from his Jewish background in the aftermath of World War I. While he had repudiated Judaism in 1899 and joined the Catholic Church in 1911, his relationships to both faiths and their respective communities were always burdened with contradictions. Kraus pilloried the Church, Catholic politics, and Catholic morality no less after his conversion than before. He was intensely critical of the Church's stance on the war, and Catholic politicians were frequent targets of his satire. Kraus formally left the Church in 1923; the immediate occasion was to protest Hugo von Hofmannsthal's staging of his drama *Das Salzburger grosse Welttheater* (*The Great World Theater of Salzburg*) in a Salzburg church, but his views of the conduct of the Catholic Church during and after the war clearly played a role in his decision. Kraus may have been drawn to conversion in his quest for autonomy, seeking to escape being seen as a Jewish critic, but the same desire seems to have eventually driven him from Catholicism as well. The fiercely independent writer had little use for confession, class, party, or any other affiliation.

While Kraus's more direct public statements on his own relationship to Jewishness largely precede the First World War, he had by no means laid the issue to rest when the war intervened. Both before and after the war, individual Jews were often the targets of his satire, above all in his campaigns against the press. Kraus frequently took aim at individual Jews or groups of Jews, but he also inveighed against *"Juden aller Konfessionen"* ("Jews of all denominations") employing the term strategically to stand in for all enthusiastic proponents of modernity. As Caroline Kohn has indicated, the war experience had a tremendous impact on Kraus's views, and there are significant differences between his approach to Jewishness in *Eine Krone für Zion* (1898) and *Die letzten Tage der Menschheit* (*The Last Days of Mankind,* 1918/1922).[154] While it is exceedingly difficult to discern an identifiable position on Jews and Jewishness in Kraus's many contradictory statements, a number of themes from his wartime writings continue to occupy him in the ensuing years and, indeed, public readings from *Die letzten Tage der Menschheit* became the primary vehicle of his public engagement during the interwar years.

Kraus gave over 150 public readings during the years between the world wars; he published 10 books and ended his wartime interruption of *Die Fackel,* publishing 140 issues in the interwar years. His satire and critique of the 1920s were directed primarily at the persistence of the war mentality in postwar Austrian and German society. He took aim at the latent aggression and militarism underlying the postwar mentality and persisted in his anti-nationalist campaign. Through public readings of *Die letzten Tage der Menschheit* he maintained his sharp satire of profiteering capitalists and what he considered an irresponsible press that had been reduced to mere propaganda. He wrote for years about the danger of "creeping fascism" in both Germany and Austria. Kraus recognized the dangers represented by Nazism early on, railing against the *"Hakenkreuzler"* (*"Swasticka-Wearers"*) and *"Troglodyten"* (*"Troglodytes"*) from the earliest days of the movement. He protested the racially motivated violence at the universities, elaborated the dangers of a pan-German agenda, and openly opposed an *Anschluss* with Germany. He objected to the rise of Nazism within Austria, to its gradual penetration not just of the political realm, but of the cultural sphere and public domain as well.

While Kraus's attention was increasingly directed abroad, he also responded to the turbulence of Austrian politics. Like Elias Canetti (who will be discussed later in this chapter), Kraus reacted sharply to the events surrounding the fire at the Palace of Justice in July 1927. He was deeply disturbed by the verdict in the Schattendorf case exculpating the members of the *Heimwehr* from the murder charges they faced. In his essay "Der Hort der Republik," ("The Bulwark of the Republic") written in October 1927, Kraus rightly identified the crisis surrounding the fire, the clashes between police and citizens, the paramilitary violence of the militias, and the authoritarian reactions of the government as signals to the beginning of the end of Austrian democracy. For Edward Timms, this piece was Kraus's most significant polemic of the decade, identifying the self-destructive potential of the entire political system.[155]

Even as he protested the authoritarianism exhibited by the state from the fire at the Palace of Justice, the dissolution of parliament, and the civil war, Kraus supported Chancellor Engelbert Dollfuss, viewing homegrown Austro-fascism as a lesser evil to imported German Nazism. By the fall of 1933, Kraus had completed the anti-Nazi polemic *Dritte Walpurgisnacht,* (*Third Walpurgis Night*) but he refrained from publishing the work out of fear of Nazi reprisals. Significant extracts from the text do appear, however, in the July 1934 issue of *Die Fackel,* which bore the title "Warum die Fackel nicht erscheint" ("Why the Fackel doesn't appear"). This mammoth bundle of several editions of *Die Fackel,* comprising over three hundred pages, did contain Kraus's reaction to National Socialism, but far more than this, the text demonstrates the limits of satire in an environment of violence and terror. This is the context for the well-known quote drawn from this text, "*Mir fällt zu Hitler nichts ein*" ("Hitler brings nothing to my mind").[156] The lengthy *Fackel* edition had been a long time in coming, as Kraus had been very reluctant to speak once the breakdown of parliamentary democracy began and the political scene became increasingly radical and violent. Satire simply no longer seemed to be the appropriate response to the volatile and deteriorating situation in both Austria and Germany. After many months, when Kraus did resume the publication of *Die Fackel,* he was of course breaking his silence, but he did so in the form of lengthy reflections on the crisis of language. "Warum die Fackel nicht erscheint" is an extension of Kraus's intense focus on language, as he scrutinizes the rhetorical strategies of Nazi propaganda as evidence of an acute crisis of communication and reflects more broadly on the limits of language in the face of the Nazi threat. In 1933, while completing *Dritte Walpurgisnacht,* Kraus wrote the poem, "Man frage nicht" ("Don't Ask"), another work in which he struggles to express the breakdown of language:

> Don't ask about the actions I've been taking.
> I'll not speak out,
> nor say what it's about.
> And there is silence when the earth's been quaking.
> No word that fits;
> you speak with drowsy wits,
> and dream of smiling suns when morning's breaking.
> It cannot last;
> later it all was past.
> The Word expired on Hitler's world's awaking.[157]

Kraus died in June 1936, having experienced "Hitler's world" long enough to be cognizant of the Nazis' corruption of language and to struggle with the limits of language as a response to fascism, but he did not live long enough to watch "the Word" expire altogether. Kraus published the final edition of *Die Fackel* just months before his death. His dedication to the journal, as well as to other writings, over nearly forty years underscores his approach to criticism and satire as a mission, the ethical pursuit of an autonomous voice that was uniquely his own.

Hugo Bettauer

Hugo Bettauer's life and death are reflective of the volatility of interwar Vienna and the intensity of anti-Semitic hostility. In his career as a writer and journalist Bettauer was a lightning rod for the right wing, angering anti-Semites with his parody *Die Stadt ohne Juden. Ein Roman von Übermorgen* (*The City Without Jews: A Novel of Our Time*) and infuriating conservatives with his campaign to liberalize Viennese sexual morality. Bettauer was at the center of a number of controversies, all of which were silenced when he was murdered by a Nazi party member in 1925. On March 25, Otto Rothstock, a twenty-year-old unemployed dental technician, followed Bettauer into his editorial offices and shot him point-blank five times. Bettauer died sixteen days later from his wounds. This was the first assassination in Austria organized by the Nazi Party. Rothstock was defended by a Nazi lawyer; he pleaded insanity, was sent to an insane asylum, and was released just a year and a half later. He was then widely celebrated in right-wing circles and their press organs. Through the murder of Bettauer, these groups were relieved of a troublesome critical voice that had appealed to a broad segment of the population.[158] As Bettauer had become more and more popular, the controversies surrounding him became more intense, and his opponents increasingly framed their criticism in anti-Semitic terms.[159] Bettauer's best-known work, *Die Stadt ohne Juden,* was both contentious and popular, and I will examine it here as a document of its time.

First, a brief sketch of Bettauer's biography: He was born in 1872, in Baden bei Wien, the son of a wealthy stockbroker. He attended the Franz-Josephs-Gymnasium in Vienna, where he befriended Karl Kraus. In 1890, at the age of eighteen, Bettauer converted to Protestantism. That same year he volunteered for the Habsburg army but deserted after five months of service. Late in this decade he made the first of two trips to New York, where he wrote for several German-language newspapers. Bettauer also lost his inheritance through speculation while in America. In 1899 he went back to Europe, working as a reporter for the *Berliner Morgenpost.* After two years the police expelled Bettauer from Berlin (as well as from Hamburg) as a result of his sharply critical writing on a number of hot topics, including corruption within the police force. Bettauer then returned to New York, where he continued as a journalist and also began writing novels, mostly detective novels dealing with German and Austrian immigrants in New

York. A number of these were published in serialized form by the *New Yorker Morgen-Journal*. Bettauer wrote quickly and, by all accounts, sloppily, completing five novels in 1907 alone.

In 1908 he returned to Vienna, where he continued to write for the journals to which he had contributed while in America, as well as for *Die Zeit*. According to Hans Eichner, Bettauer's reporting on the desperate condition of much of the Austrian population after World War I was a stimulus to American relief efforts.[160] During the First World War, Bettauer was a war correspondent for the *Neue Freie Presse*. In 1920 he returned to fiction, producing twenty-three "Wiener Romane" in less than five years. These were works of popular fiction, but they contained a significant element of social engagement and criticism. Beth Simone Noveck characterizes these novels as "incisive portrayals of the lives of ordinary people with emphasis on the exploitation of women and the poor."[161] Nine of these works were adapted as films, including G. W. Pabst's classic *Die Freudlose Gasse* (*The Joyless Street*), from 1925.

In 1924 Bettauer founded a weekly journal devoted to eroticism, *Er und Sie. Wochenschrift für Lebenskultur und Erotik* (*He and She: A Magazine for Lifestyles and Eroticism*). The paper supported sexual emancipation, with the first issue featuring an article by Bettauer entitled "Die erotische Revolution" ("The Erotic Revolution"). The journal included medical and social articles, an advice column, serialized fiction and short stories by Bettauer, advertisements, and personals—"*Menschen, die einander suchen*" ("people in search of each other").[162] The journal and its editor incurred the wrath of Catholic and conservative camps, who called Bettauer a "*Jugend-und Sittenverderber*" (a corruptor of youth and morals) and also made frequent reference to his Jewish background.[163] At this time the Viennese Social Democratic administration was campaigning to legalize abortion, thus, as Eichner notes, "Sexual mores were high on the political agenda."[164] The censorship of Schnitzler's *Der Reigen* (La Ronde) had created a cause célèbre just a few years prior, in 1921. A campaign against Bettauer's journal was carried out both in the press and in parliament; its sale was prohibited, and anti-Semitic slurs were a common component of this public discourse. Murray Hall has determined that the National Socialist Kaspar Hellering twice urged in print that Bettauer be "exterminated."[165] Bettauer's assassination occurred just a month after the second incitement to murder.

Bettauer's topicality is in evidence in *Die Stadt ohne Juden,* which likely contributed to its popularity. The depiction of anti-Semitism in the work reveals the extent to which it had permeated Viennese society in the early 1920s and portrays its many manifestations across the city's economic, cultural, social, and political life. Political anti-Semitism is depicted as an effective tool for fostering the political integration of disparate constituencies of the major parties. It also figures in the parties' rhetoric in reference to each other, as each tries to portray the other as beholden to the Jews (*Judenknechte*). Yet Bettauer portrays economic anti-Semitism as the driving force of Viennese society, evident in all social classes, in industry and commerce, in the professions, in the suburbs and the center, and in politics and the press.

Stereotypes abound, and, indeed, the narrative voice does not avoid such negative images of the Jews but rather introduces several in the second paragraph of the novel:

> Usually at similar demonstrations here and there people with a curved nose or especially black hair were accustomed to getting thoroughly beaten up; this time there was no such incident, since there was nothing Jewish to be seen far and wide, and moreover the coffeehouses and banks on the Franzensring and Schottenring, in the wise anticipation of all possibilities, had closed their gates and pulled down their shutters.[166]

Here, in one swipe, Bettauer pokes fun of stereotypical Jewish physiognomy, at the concentration of Jews in certain professions, and at Viennese Jews' predilection for the coffeehouse.

Bettauer's text not only draws on familiar stereotypes but also makes use of what were then more fashionable weapons in the anti-Semitic arsenal, namely, metaphors of parasitism and infection. At the beginning of the novel the Social Democratic Chancellor Schwertfeger refers to the Jews in a speech before parliament as "foreign bodies who overrun our body and ultimately enslave us."[167] Here Bettauer evokes the 1920s revival of the pseudoscientific anti-Semitism of the late nineteenth century, which was underscored by the notion of an essential Jewish difference. Beth Noveck describes her view of the function of employing what she terms the "perverted metaphors of Social Darwinism" in anti-Semitic rhetoric as follows: "They turn the Aryan into the victim of the small pest's lasciviousness and, therefore, justify his attempts to eradicate the nuisance."[168] While it may seem to strain credibility to employ such language in a parliamentary speech, its use is an accurate reflection of the stridency of anti-Semitism within the political realm at the time. In the 1920s, Nazi propaganda referred to the Jews as "foreign bodies" (*Fremdkörper*). Such biological metaphors served to lend the negative representations of Jews an air of scientific objectivity, enhancing the credibility of the discourse of the Jew as the "other."

The chancellor's rhetoric is effective, as the parliament quickly moves to endorse his proposed legislation to expel the Jews from Austria. There is an attempt at opposition by the Social Democratic faction, but this is quickly put down by the majority. Bettauer depicts the Socialists as powerless and ineffectual, casting them as diminutive: "Thus the small opposition left the hall in protest."[169] The chancellor makes the case that the removal of the Jews will spur a regeneration of Austria's economic, cultural, and spiritual life. His rationale for this radical program is interesting in that it points to a distinct Austrian weakness. He argues, "The point is simply that we Austrian Aryans are no match for the Jews, that we are dominated by a small minority, oppressed and raped, because this very minority possesses qualities that we lack!"[170] Other nations, he suggests, are more like the Jews and thus are better equipped to deal with them. For the Austrians, however, the Jews are entirely foreign and, with this opposition, the Austrians are simply outmatched. He contrasts a number of qualities he sees as distinctly Jewish—intelligence, ambition, internationality—with Austrian qualities: simplicity, loyalty, piousness, respectability, dreaminess, and playfulness. The Austrians are an Alpine people, he says. As long as the two groups must coexist, Jews will always dominate.

The chancellor's proposal is made law, and the removal of the Jews begins at once. There are some unforeseen complications, however. Chancellor Schwertfeger had predicted a tremendous source of revenue for the state, as the Jews were required to pay taxes on the income they took with them out of the country; he did not imagine, however, that Jews would be assisted by Gentiles, eager to make a profit, in funneling large sums of money abroad and therefore only declare insignificant holdings to the state. Nor did Schwertfeger anticipate that targeting not only Jews, but their offspring as well (the children of so-called *Mischehen*), would cause a good many parliamentary representatives to be responsible for driving away their own grandchildren.

Nonetheless, the Viennese are jubilant at the departure of the Jews. They first give themselves over to a New Year's "liberation party," at which the Philharmonic—albeit somewhat reduced in number—plays before the Rathaus, festooned with red-and-white banners. The celebratory mood lasts through *Fasching*, enhanced by the fact that the city's acute housing shortage is ended in a flash as the Jews vacate their (choice) apartments. However a more sobering reality soon sets in: The state currency begins a precipitous descent, unemployment starts to rise, and numerous businesses begin to fail. The banking system falters, as the expected support from abroad is not forthcoming.

The new situation hits hard at all levels, from the unemployed worker to the prominent businessman who made a seemingly advantageous purchase of a Jewish-owned concern that now quickly begins to fail. The fashionable department stores, for example, find themselves with no customers, as their best clients had been Jewish women and many Christian clients were often financed by Jewish husbands and lovers; moreover, with the fashionable Jewish women no longer in the picture, Gentile women now have no competition and see no need to keep up with the latest fashions. To salvage these faltering businesses, the stores soon replace Paris fashion with Loden and flannel and convert their *Konditoreien* into "*Stehbierhalle[n] mit heissen Würsteln*" (beer joints with warm sausages).[171] Another businessman is not lacking in customers but is nevertheless at the brink of bankruptcy because of the plummeting currency. In his view he could be saved if only he had a "proper Jew" to advise him on investing in foreign currencies, as in the past.

Not all of the problems are economic. Bettauer includes a humorous chapter in which a group of *süße Mädl* (the term is difficult to translate, but refers to young, lower-class women with whom older, upper-class men have romantic relationships) lament the loss of their Jewish boyfriends. Their Christian replacements are seen as poor substitutes, as they don't take them to elegant establishments (favoring the suburban *Beisl*), give them gifts, or fund their shopping. Instead, they get drunk, act rudely, and—a stinging criticism—are sexually selfish in comparison to the absent Jewish lovers. Noveck places considerable emphasis on the fear of Jewish male sexuality as an element of this Viennese anti-Semitism of the early 1920s. In the campaign against Bettauer and his erotic journal, anti-Semitism was mobilized as part of the opposition to his sexual agenda. In a coupling of sexual anxiety and hostility toward the other, anti-Semitic fears are projected onto Jewish men. As Sander Gilman contends, "The sexuality of the Other is always threatening."[172] Noveck sees these unresolved fears at work in the campaign against Bettauer, as well as thematized by Bettauer in the novel. Indeed, Bettauer is explicit in ascribing a significant role in anti-Jewish hostility to sexual jealousy:

> Possible, even likely, that anti-Semitism got so strong, so fanatical over the course of the decades among the male population of Vienna, because the youth with the swastika saw and couldn't get over how Jewish competition snatched the pretty girls away from him![173]

Bettauer introduces an exemplary Jewish young man in the story not only to take part in an obligatory Jewish-Christian love affair, but also to be the agent that will bring an end to the new law. When the young artist Leo Strakosch leaves Vienna for Paris, his loss is felt not only by his devoted fiancé, but by her parents as well, an open and tolerant bourgeois Gentile couple who prize Leo's good qualities and recognize the folly of the law. Strakosch later returns to Vienna disguised as a French aristocrat, having borrowed the passport of a good friend. As "Henry DuFresne," Leo begins to channel the dissatisfaction of the populace into opposition to the expulsion law. He discreetly fans the flames until he provokes a call for new elections, at which point new representatives are installed, who quickly vote down the law. The Viennese celebrate the return of the Jews with zeal equal to that which they showed at their departure. Leo is carried on the backs of two men to city hall, where the mayor greets him enthusiastically as the first returned Jew. The happy ending goes even further, as Leo can surely look forward to a happy life with his betrothed and her family.

Bettauer's treatment of anti-Semitism in the novel is very different from Herzl's *Das neue Ghetto* or his Zionist treatise, all of which advance an argument for tolerance based on liberal values inherited from the ideology of Jewish emancipation. Bettauer steers clear of the realm of values in favor of a narrower, pragmatic view, characterized by Noveck as the contention that anti-Semitism is harmful to the otherwise symbiotic economic relationship between Jews and Aryans.[174] While the novel does not treat economic anti-Semitism in the crisis years following World War I exclusively, Bettauer assigns it a central role in shaping the attitudes and behavior of his Viennese Gentile characters. Historical analysis of the ensuing years, in which Viennese anti-Semitism reached its horrifying climax, has revealed that where the material interests of much of the population coincided with anti-Jewish sentiments, anti-Semitism found rash, vigorous, and brutal expression. In hindsight, Bettauer's treatment of anti-Semitism was not overly narrow but disturbingly prescient.

Bettauer's life and premature death reveal the inescapability of Jewish identity in Vienna's turbulent interwar era. Decades after his conversion, Bettauer was verbally and physically attacked as a Jew. His death was an early indicator of the radicalization of anti-Semitic hostility in Vienna, in the course of which violence would become increasingly acceptable. Clearly, fascism had become a highly dangerous force in the city by the early 1920s.

Elias Canetti

Within this group of Jewish Viennese writers of the interwar period, Elias Canetti is clearly the outlier. Given the experimental nature of his writing, his bridging of literature and anthropology, and the uniqueness of his perspective on this tumultuous era, Canetti would likely be the outlier in any conceivable grouping of writers. In the present context, Canetti's biography, as well as his poetics, set him apart. Canetti's Jewish origins are Sephardic rather than Ashkenazic, and his early-childhood experiences in Bulgaria, as well as the place his birthplace came to occupy in his later consciousness, put him in a unique position on both North-South and East-West axes within Europe. As a writer, Canetti identified strongly with Austrian literary traditions, but his identity was equally determined by a pan-European perspective and a rather idiosyncratic cosmopolitanism. Over the course of his lifetime he developed a relationship to his physical place that differed from other writers forced into exile. Rooted in his early experiences in Vienna of the 1920s, and drawing on the many places he lived, Canetti developed a topography of experiences that played a significant role in his literary work. In this section I will assess Canetti's relationship to place, to *Heimat*, and to Vienna in particular, as well as to his Jewish identity, as reflected in his early works.

Canetti was born in Ruschuk, Bulgaria, in 1905. He descended from prosperous Sephardic Jews, who were leading entrepreneurs in the textile industry. Ruschuk was a significant inland port on the Danube, a cosmopolitan Eastern European city in which more than a dozen languages were heard in the streets and markets. As an important stop on the trade route to Constantinople, Ruschuk had had a multiethnic character since the Middle Ages. The city had a thriving

Jewish quarter, populated by descendants of Jews who fled the Spanish Inquisition in 1492 to various parts of the Ottoman Empire. Canetti's descendants had lived for four hundred years in Adrianople, moving to Ruschuk in the 1860s, which was an era of modernization and reform in the city. The family became influential there, with several descendants being appointed as local administrators of the Habsburg Empire.[175]

Canetti's first language was the Sephardic-Jewish language, Ladino; as a child he also was fluent in Bulgarian and learned French and English, as well, followed by German at the age of eight. In 1911 Canetti's parents moved the family to Manchester, England, both so that his father could join his brother's textile firm there and, by all accounts, to escape the oppressive atmosphere stemming from the overbearing patriarch of the family, Canetti's paternal grandfather. Canetti's father died at age thirty, just after the move to England, and his mother subsequently moved to Vienna's Leopoldstadt with her children. This was the point at which Canetti's mother, Mathilde, taught her son German in a very intense and brutal tutorial, replete with verbal abuse for any mistakes the boy made. German had been a very important language in the relationship between Elias's parents, as it was both the private language of their romance and the carrier of the German high culture they prized very highly. Anne Fuchs has argued that in the imposition of this new "mother tongue," Canetti's mother forced her son into the position of the father, into a codependent relationship in which language became a battleground in a passionate struggle for autonomy.[176]

With the outbreak of World War I, Canetti's mother became clinically depressed and entered a sanitarium. In 1916 she moved with her children to Zurich, where Elias attended *Gymnasium*. In 1921 the family moved to Frankfurt, where he completed his secondary education. He then returned to Vienna with his younger brother Georg, again to Leopoldstadt. Canetti studied chemistry at the University of Vienna and earned a doctoral degree in 1929. Two years prior his mother moved to Paris with his brothers, and Canetti took an apartment in Hacking, where he had a view of the sanitarium Am Steinhof. During these years in Vienna Canetti was very much under the sway of Karl Kraus, at whose public readings he was a devoted spectator. In 1927 Canetti took an extended stay in Berlin, where he was immersed in the leftist literary scene through the publisher Wieland Herzfelde of the Malik Verlag. Herzfelde became a mentor to Canetti, introducing him to Georg Grosz and Bertolt Brecht and encouraging him to take up a translation project of the works of Upton Sinclair, which he did.

In Vienna, Canetti also made important contacts in intellectual and literary circles, which included people such as Fritz Wotruba, Anna Mahler, Franz Werfel, Alban Berg, Abraham Sonne (a poet who published as Avraham Ben Yitzhak), Robert Musil, and Hermann Broch. Canetti never entered the field of chemistry but worked instead as a writer, already starting work on various literary projects during his studies. Canetti wrote his only novel, *Die Blendung* (*Auto-da-*

Fé), in 1930–31, and two dramas shortly thereafter: *Hochzeit* (*Wedding*) and *Die Komödie der Eitelkeit* (*The Comedy of Vanity*). He also met and courted Venetiana Taubner-Calderon, and the couple married in 1934 and moved out to Grinzing. Veza had already published a number of stories in the *Arbeiter Zeitung* when they married, but publishing opportunities were limited in the increasingly anti-Semitic climate of 1930s Vienna.

The Canettis went into exile in 1938, stopping in Paris before settling in London in January 1939. The couple would stay in England permanently, and Canetti acquired British citizenship in 1952. They remained married until Veza's death in 1963, in spite of numerous affairs by Elias, of which Veza was well aware. In 1946 Canetti's novel appeared in a very successful translation as *Auto-da-Fé*. Canetti continued to write in German in the postwar years, however. In his first collection of aphorisms, he expressed a responsibility toward the German language:

> The language of my spirit will remain German, namely because I am a Jew. Whatever remains of this land that has been ravaged in every way, I want to protect within me as a Jew. And its destiny is mine; but I also carry along a universal human inheritance. I want to give back to their language what I owe it. I want to contribute to the fact that one has something to thank them for.[177]

Canetti maintained a long relationship with the Munich publisher Hanser, which published many of his works in the mid-1960s. His study *Masse und Macht* (*Crowds and Power*), which germinated in Vienna perhaps as early as 1925[178] and was the object of decades of intensive labor, appeared in 1960. This marked the beginning of a gradual process of increased recognition of Canetti's works. In 1962 Canetti was awarded the Literatur Preis der Stadt Wien; in 1967, the Österreichischen Staatspreis für Literatur, followed by the Büchner Prize and the Österreichisches Ehrenzeichen für Wissenschaft und Kunst in 1972; and, in 1981, the Nobel Prize for Literature. Canetti married the Zurich art restorer Hera Buschor in 1971, maintaining a second residence in Zurich. He died in that city at the age of eighty-nine, in 1994. Canetti's multivolume autobiography appeared as a trilogy between the late 1970s and mid-1980s: *Die gerettete Zunge* (*The Tongue Set Free*, 1977) covers his childhood and youth through 1921; *Die Fackel im Ohr* (*The Torch in My Ear*, 1980) relates his experiences of the next ten years; and a third volume, *Das Augenspiel* (*The Play of the Eyes*, 1985), is a record of his life from 1931 to 1937. A final volume, *Party im Blitz: Die englischen Jahre* (*Party in the Blitz: The English Years*), appeared posthumously in 2003.

As a boy Canetti left Ruschuk with his family when he was just six years old, and one would likely assume that his relationship to this city would be marked by distance or vague impressions. In fact, the city seems to have made a significant imprint and affected Canetti's later experiences. In the first volume of his autobiography, he notes, "Everything that I later experienced had already happened once in Ruschuk."[179] Some sixty years later, when he wrote his childhood memoirs, Canetti viewed himself as having mastery of a rich bank of memories, preserved intact and in sharp focus: "The events of those years are present to me in all their strength and freshness," he wrote.[180] The memoirs are thus written with vivid details, presenting carefully preserved memories in sharp focus. He depicts the colorful life of the streets, his early impressions of his grandfather's *Kolonialwarenladen* (general store)—including the sensory experiences the store offered and the opportunity to observe the customers, staff, and his grandfather (reminiscent of Kafka's early memories of his father's fancy goods shop in Prague)—and familial memories of his grandparents' home. Canetti emphasizes the diversity of the city, describing the many languages of his early experiences and the daily interactions with people of different ethnic groups. He presents this immersion in a multiethnic environment as a sort of school of tolerance, drawing a sharp line between his own views and the caste pride of his mother in relation to her family's Sephardic origins.

Canetti's depictions of Ruschuk incorporate both Oriental and Occidental influences, sometimes emphasizing the distinct nature of the Eastern European city and sometimes highlighting its ties to the West and Viennese character. Scholars who have examined the space of Bulgaria in Canetti's work conclude that temporal distance neither transformed this place into an alienated homeland—as Galicia became for Joseph Roth—or into a distanced and exotic space.[181] Canetti underscores a unity of experience between these earliest developments and the occurrences of his later life. The multicultural environment of Ruschuk proved a formative experience that informed Canetti's worldview and his sense of his own place within it. Ruschuk and Bulgaria remained with Canetti in that they comprised one layer of his concept of *Heimat*. The other places of his biography added additional layers—principally Manchester, Vienna, London, and Zurich—to which he maintained a deep attachment throughout his life. While other writers forced into exile experienced their uprootedness as an existential homelessness, Canetti seems to have forged a concept of *Heimat* rooted not in a single place, but in many. For Penka Angelova, the patchwork of the many way stations in his life constitutes a spiritual landscape that Canetti internalized as part of his sense of self.[182] She cites two aphorisms of the 1940s that express his relationship to these many places:

> He was never lacking a place, but he had many places. He protected each one with the unerring sense that one has for a single home.[183]

> They want to win him back for their lost people. He will allow himself to be won back only by every people. They do not understand that his home is everywhere, everywhere where he was and where he would still like to be.[184]

This is a cosmopolitanism based not on the fundamental condition of uprootedness or the Jewish Diaspora—versions of a cosmopolitan identity we have seen in other Jewish writers—but rather on a broad conception of *Heimat* accommodating the whole of Canetti's experience.

For Irene Di Maio, spatial imagery is the key to unlocking Canetti's worldview.[185] She argues that he frames his experiences of the word in spatial terms, and she traces the way he employs different geographical locations in his autobiographical writing not just to mark the stations of his life, but also to relate his intellectual development. Canetti connects places to concepts, creating a topography of experience based on his personal narrative; Ruschuk denotes ethnic and linguistic diversity, England order and freedom; Switzerland stands in for democracy, Vienna for culture, Berlin for creativity; and Frankfurt is equated with the chaos of Weimar-era inflation.[186] Places of residence are freely chosen, and a distinct dynamic develops that gives each site its own emotional charge.

Vienna seems always to have been a place with a particularly intense emotional charge for Canetti. It is noteworthy that Canetti had firsthand experience as a resident of two very different Viennas: the thriving political, economic, and cultural center of the Habsburg era of his early childhood and the outsized city of the shrunken Austria of the First Republic—a turbulent battleground of competing ideologies during the identity crisis of the young republic, a site of poverty and unemployment, class conflict, and anti-Semitism. (Canetti knew the post–World War II Vienna as well, of course, but from a distance, as he never seriously considered a return from exile in England.)

Vienna loomed large in Canetti's imagination even before he moved there at the age of eight, because of the central role the city played in the Canetti family romance. The city stood for high culture, not only for Canetti's parents, but for all educated middle-class Jews of Eastern Europe. Richard Lawson underscores the "Vienna-centeredness" of the Canetti family. It was the city where Jacques and Mathilde Canetti were educated, met, and fell in love, and for which they developed a shared passion for its cultural offerings, particularly the *Burgtheater*. Given the significance of Vienna for his parents, Elias Canetti "derive[d] from Vienna hardly less than from Ruschuk," Lawson argues."[187] Canetti's own initial experience of the city was certainly more conflict ridden but hardly less intense. The move to Vienna in 1912 with his mother and two younger brothers followed on the heels of the early death of his father, with whom Canetti had been close.[188] Canetti's memoirs detail an intense and protracted struggle for autonomy from his mother, both during this first stay in the city and upon his return to enter the university. His fictional works frequently highlight the confinement of interior spaces, and apartments often figure as sites of struggle to preserve the boundaries of the self under pressure from another.[189]

There were more positive emotional experiences attached to Vienna as well. This was where he met and married Veza, experienced the exciting public readings of Kraus, and joined intellectual circles that helped him make the transition to becoming a writer. One of the most powerful experiences of Canetti's time in

Vienna, however, was clearly his witnessing of the burning of the Palace of Justice in July 1927. Canetti took part in the mass uprising in Vienna in response to the exoneration of the *Frontkämpfer* accused of killing Social Democratic demonstrators in Burgenland. Canetti relates his memories of this day in the second volume of his memoirs, characterizing it as the seminal experience of his early years and referring to it as "perhaps the most decisive day of my life since the death of my father."[190] The events of 15 July were significant for Canetti in terms of his encounter with the mass. Canetti's observation of the crowd, and even participation in the protest, sparked an interest that led to three decades of intense anthropological study, which culminated in his 1960 work *Masse und Macht*. Canetti had earlier witnessed public protests in the streets of Frankfurt in the wake of the assassination of the Jewish foreign minister Walther Rathenau. In Canetti's writing streets are the public spaces occupied by crowds and beset with conflict.

Not only did the behavior of the crowd and the violent repression of public protest of 15 July make a deep and lasting impression on Canetti, but he was similarly gripped by the conflagration itself. Fire would occupy a prominent position in Canetti's only novel, *Die Blendung* (1936), which he referred to as "a fruit of the fire."[191] Fire haunts the imagination of the novel's protagonist, the independent scholar Peter Kien, a bibliophile who possesses an extensive library that is considered the best in Vienna. Kien prizes these books far beyond any mere possessions, and indeed, the books of his collection and even books that don't belong to him are more meaningful to him than any human relationship. After being driven out of the sanctuary of his library by his wife, Therese, Kien makes his way through all of the bookstores of the city and ultimately gravitates toward the book collection of the state-run auction house cum pawnshop, the Theresianum, modeled on the great Habsburg institution, the Dorotheum.[192] Here he launches a quixotic mission to liberate the books that are being pawned and save them not only this ignoble fate, but also certain "death by fire" once they have been relegated to the attic spaces of the Theresianum. Kien's suicide at the end of the novel takes the form of self-immolation in the burning of his library. The destruction of Kien's world, set in motion through his disastrous relationship with Therese, is completed during this final scene, as the books he loves and believes to be master of launch an insurrection. William Donahue characterizes the burning of the library as "a grand farewell not to a collection of irreplaceably rare books, but to a system of thought pregnant with its own destruction."[193]

The title of the English translation, *Auto-da-Fé*, refers to this fire, but the original title of the German edition, *Die Blendung*, entails a voluntary and self-imposed blinding that is most acute in the protagonist but could be said to affect all of the characters in the novel. Each character limits their perception of social reality through a constriction of their vision, either physically or via the lenses produced by their intellects, through which they view the world. This blindness is most pronounced when they move through the city, encountering (or failing to encounter) others in the social world. The novel opens with one of Kien's daily walks through the city, on which he has eyes only for the books in the bookstore windows (and this only to register their inferiority vis-à-vis his own collection). When a young boy intrudes on his space in front of one of these shop windows, Kien is at first hardly aware of the boy's presence: "The boy was small, [and] Kien [was] of unusual height. He easily overlooked him."[194] When he does eventually take notice of him because of the boy's keen interest in books, Kien merely sees in the boy a projection of his own self; when he begins to process that he has had this human interaction with the boy, he is compelled to distance himself from it, at once mentally breaking his promise to show the boy his library. On the way home, Kien is so oblivious to the people moving around him that he is unaware of being asked for directions and is shocked when the speaker becomes outraged at being ignored.

The other characters take on their own forms of voluntary blindness. Therese sees the world strictly in terms of her own financial interests and frustrated sexuality. Although the middle-aged woman's appearance is strange, an impression reinforced by the fortresslike starched floor-length blue skirt she wears, she always believes that she is attracting admiring stares from the men on the street. While out shopping for furniture, she is convinced that all eyes are focused on her and is excited by the attention: "She was causing a stir. ... Therese felt the gazes of the people. Like thirty, she thought and began to sweat out of happiness."[195] Therese replaces social reality with fantasy, rendering her as incapable as Kien of understanding others or carrying out a meaningful communicative exchange. The blindness of Benedikt Pfaff, the caretaker of Kien's apartment building, is physical, but similarly self-imposed. As self-appointed watchman, Pfaff constructs a peephole in his door, about twenty inches from the floor, before which he kneels all day to observe the comings and goings of the occupants of the house and their visitors: "Here, where no one suspected him, he knelt and watched. The world consisted for him of pants and skirts."[196]

With this kind of limited vision, the characters move through an environment of their own making, blind to the reality of the social world as experienced by others. The novel is set in Vienna, but the Vienna depicted is transformed by each of the characters according to their own preoccupations. William Donahue has noted perceptively that the city "is reduced to a spectral and insubstantial presence" in the novel, with only the Theresianum representing a solid, durable presence; the massive pawnshop in the city center evokes the economic dislocations and radically altered social and cultural conditions of this turbulent period.[197] Canetti goes further by turning a spotlight on the city's underbelly in his portrayal of the seedy pub Zum idealen Himmel and the still seedier Zum Pavian.

The Vienna depicted in *Die Blendung* is clearly the Vienna of the interwar period, cast by Canetti as a space of conflict. Human interaction sows discord rather than understanding. Individuals struggle to maintain the boundaries of self in the face of aggressive encroachment by others. Violence is always close at hand: in Pfaff's past abuse of his wife and daughter, Therese's beating of Kien, Kien's self-destruction, and the murder of the novel's Jewish characters, Fischerle and *die Fischerin*. These latter characters are killed not strictly as a result of personal animosity but as an extreme expression of racial anti-Semitism. Canetti's text reveals the extent to which the frustrations of the chaotic interwar period were channeled into intense animosity toward both Jews and women.

In his characterization of these main figures of the novel Canetti is less interested in portraying them as individuals than in employing them to represent certain concepts, irreconcilable ideas that are the sources of conflict between the characters. For Irene Boose, the characters in *Die Blendung* function as "acoustic masks," an important concept in Canetti's poetics.[198] Kristie Foell defines his concept of the acoustic mask as consisting of an "immutable and limited characteristic set of words, expressions, and intonations that both reveal and mask the individual's character but do not foster communication."[199] The characters are unaware of the masks they wear, but these masks reduce their speech—to say nothing of communication, which is precluded by their various limitations—to a narrow reiteration of the supraindividual ideas they represent. In the case of Kien, Canetti is parodying an exaggerated idealism.

Canetti's satire has a less lofty aim in other principal characters. In the characters of Therese and Fischerle, Canetti employs exaggerated—but easily recognizable—stereotypes about Jews and women common to the time. Their physiognomies, psychologies, behavior, and depictions of their "essential characters" stem directly from the anti-Semitic and misogynist discourses that held wide currency in Vienna during the twenties and thirties. Canetti's stereotyping of these characters in fact created such detestable figures that the novel has often been seen as an expression of, rather than critique of, the loathing of Jews and women. A number of critics interpret the novel, and to some extent, the writer, as misogynist.[200] Canetti himself seems to have experienced some discomfort with his characterization of Fischerle, when looking back on the novel in the wake of the Holocaust. I am inclined to take the view of William Donahue, however, and insist that the presence of stereotyping in the novel cannot be equated with an endorsement of such ideas but must be assessed in light of "the matrix of ideas and literary strategies within which these stereotypes appear."[201] Donahue views the treatment of anti-Semitism and misogyny as tools of Canetti's ideological critique, assigning to them a key role within the parodic structure of the novel. For Donahue, Weininger's *Geschlecht und Charakter* is the novel's "great intertext," and indeed the characterization of Therese and Fischerle could be mapped across the whole of Weininger's extreme—but highly influential—treatise.

Fischerle is an embodiment of nearly all of the significant anti-Semitic tropes of the era, both in terms of physical characteristics and character traits. His physiognomy is an exaggeration of the caricatures of the diseased Jewish body, from the impossibly long, sharp nose that dominates his face to such an extent he appears to have no mouth, to the even more grotesque feature of the great hump on his back. Fischerle's speech similarly marks him as a Jew, as Canetti repeatedly emphasizes his croaking voice.[202] Canetti underscores the inescapability of Fischerle's "Jewish body." While Fischerle dreams of surgery (that never comes) to remove the hump and has a special suit tailored to disguise it, his new clothes—a boldly checkered suit, black hat, and yellow shoes—merely reinforce his Jewish identity, as he becomes a caricature of the *schlemiel* straight from the pages of the anti-Semitic press. He similarly exhibits negative character traits ascribed to Jews, chiefly his avarice and the obsessive ambition of his dream to become a world chess master and marry a blonde American millionaire heiress. Fischerle's awareness of these perceived negative traits has led to his complete internalization of them; he is the self-loathing Jew of Theodor Lessing's *Der jüdische Selbsthass,* which appeared while Canetti was at work on his novel.

Through Fischerle, Canetti delivers a criticism of the ideology of assimilation. In light of his chosen vehicle of a distasteful character and preferred technique of grotesque characterization, this is not a critique easily absorbed by the reader. Canetti's distortions and exaggerations, however, seem entirely appropriate to the atmosphere in which they were written. As the possibilities for Jewish assimilation were collapsing and the antagonisms that had long existed below the surface were finding violent expression in the streets, Canetti's Fischerle provided a disturbing expression to these disturbing tendencies of the era.

If we look to this novel for a reflection by the author on what it meant to be Jewish in the Vienna of 1930, the hyperbole of Canetti's violent and alienated fictive world presents a grim picture indeed. If any of his early works offer insight into his own relationship to a Jewish identity, it must be said that there is no positive content to that identity at this time. His writing makes plain that he was an astute observer of the crises of the interwar years and the rise of the Right. The extent to which he experienced these crises as a Jew, however, is less clear. It is nonetheless significant that Canetti launched such a powerful assault on the dominant tropes of anti-Semitic discourse, through which many sought to explain and assign blame for the major social, economic, and political problems of the era. The iconic anti-Semitic stereotyping of Fischerle in *Die Blendung* was a rejection of the mechanisms by which anti-Jewish animosity became an accepted defense against the most unwelcome changes accompanying modernity. Canetti's experience of anti-Semitism in Vienna did not lead to a heightened experience of his own Jewish identity, as it did for some of his Jewish contemporaries. It did, however, fuel his interest in the dynamics of power and the roots of fascism, which would occupy him, in his massive anthropological study *Masse und Macht,* for decades to come.

Veza Canetti

Veza Canetti began her writing career on the brink of the collapse of the First Republic. Her works chronicle the disastrous events of the 1930s, and they present a unique perspective on these troubled times that sets her apart from the other writers discussed here. In Veza Canetti's writing another Vienna emerges, not the representative spaces of the central districts, the privileged spaces of the upper bourgeoisie that are the focus of other Jewish writers, nor even the exaggerated, distorted Vienna imagined by her husband as an expression of the transformed, monstrous city. In Veza Canetti's works, by contrast, we gain a picture of everyday life in the Vienna of the margins. Canetti takes the reader to the peripheral spaces occupied by the city's poor—the shabby tenements and one-room apartments of the working class, the factories, subsistence-level shops, and the streets of Leopoldstadt. She views the devastating events of these years through the lens of those least equipped to withstand the instability wrought by them—women, the poor, children, and the disabled. She writes without sentimentalizing her subjects or transforming them through a utopian vision. Rather, her texts read as though written from the understanding that comes from personal experience. Canetti's works are Viennese at their core, yet a Vienna not often seen.

For decades, this vision was inaccessible to readers. Veza Canetti's early works appeared in media that did not endure the onslaught of Nazism, and while she survived the war, her writing career did not. For years Canetti was unrecognized as an author, known only as the wife of the acclaimed writer Elias Canetti. It was not until the 1990s that her works came to light. Those scholars and critics who celebrated her rediscovery typically laid the blame for her long-standing obscurity with her husband. While it was Elias Canetti who released her novel for publication, this did not occur until 1990, and he is often viewed as having suppressed her work in order to maintain the spotlight firmly on his own writing. It is possible that Elias Canetti drew the ire of feminist critics as much for the characterization of women in his own fiction as for his managing of Veza's literary estate. It is, however, not only puzzling, but disturbing, that Elias Canetti's multivolume autobiography makes no mention of his wife as a writer. In any event, a number of her works have now been published, and a thorough assessment of these works is under way. My concern here is to shed light on the way in which Veza Canetti's perspective as a Viennese Jewish writer differs from her male counterparts and on the manner in which she managed to fuse the strands of her identity as a woman, Jew, and Socialist.

Venetiana Taubner-Calderon was born into a middle-class Viennese family in 1897. Her father, Hermann, was a salesman from a Hungarian Jewish background. Her mother, Rachel Calderon, came from a family of Sephardic Jews from Serbia. Veza's father died when she was just seven years old; she thus shared the experience of an early loss of her father with her husband, Elias. The family was faced with poverty after Hermann's death, and her mother remarried when Veza was thirteen. This man, her mother's third husband, Menahem Alkaley, was physically abusive both to Veza and her mother.

Veza attended school and attained the *Matura*, but she did not study at the university. She was an autodidact after the conclusion of her secondary education, devoting herself to the study of literature. Her youth included a number of visits to relatives in England, where she perfected her English-language skills. She held a teaching post in a private *Gymnasium* for a time, while living with her mother and stepfather in an apartment in Ferdinandstrasse of Vienna's Leopoldstadt. During the 1920s she gave private English lessons and did some translation work.

Veza was a frequent spectator at Karl Kraus's public readings, and it was at one of these readings that she met Elias Canetti in 1924. Veza was twenty-seven when they met, eight years Elias's senior. Elias began to call on her at the Ferdinandstrasse apartment. As he was at this time still in the throes of a struggle for autonomy from his mother, Elias was reportedly impressed by Veza's self-assertion vis-à-vis her domineering stepfather.[203] Veza formally left the Jewish religion in May 1931, but she returned to it for the sake of her mother when the couple married in 1934. The wedding ceremony took place in the Sephardic synagogue built by Veza's maternal grandfather, located on Zirkusgasse of the Leopoldstadt. Veza's mother died in the fall of that year, at which point the couple left the city for the suburb of Grinzing. For Dagmar Lorenz, this move represented a withdrawal from Vienna's center in the face of the rise of the Right and the radicalization of the public sphere.[204] After the *Anschluss*, the couple was forced out of the haven they had found in Grinzing and spent a number of anxious months in a rented room in Döbling awaiting visas.

Like Elias Canetti, Veza first became a published writer in the early 1930s, hardly a promising moment for a Jewish writer to launch a literary career. In Veza's case, this tumultuous period was rife with contradictions, as the moment seemed to open new possibilities and closed to them all at once. During the 1920s, in Vienna as elsewhere, women were claiming space within the public sphere. The instability of the interwar period made it possible for women to gain access to professional arenas, allowing them to become active in journalism, education, and social-welfare reform; the feminist movement gained new impetus, and women writers found new outlets for publication.[205] Rosa Mayreder continued to publish on social and sexual themes related to women. Helene Deutsch and Anna Freud undertook important work that later resulted in major publications. Eugenie Schwarzwald opened the first secondary school for girls in Vienna and engaged in other social-welfare work during and after World War I. Berta Zuckerkandl, who, like Schwarzwald, was also the host of an important intellectual salon, wrote for the *Neues Wiener Journal*. Alice Schalek became the first woman in Austria to become a professional photojournalist and travel writer. And in literature, Veza

Canetti joined Mela Hartwig, Vicki Baum, Else Feldmann, and Hilde Spiel as a regular contributor to the major Viennese newspapers and as an author of novels and dramas.

Many of these prominent professional women were Jewish, like Canetti. The Social Democratic municipal administration of "Red Vienna" (1918–34), intent on achieving the economic, social, and cultural transformation of the city for the betterment of the working class, engaged in numerous ambitious social and cultural programs that provided opportunities for involvement—the construction of communal housing, school reform, the expansion of the social-welfare system, and health-care reform. Jews were overrepresented within the party leadership, and many Jewish women got involved in this municipal work. Numerous Jewish men and women turned to Socialism as a response to the crisis of identity created by the dissolution of the empire and the new world order established after the war. This was the path chosen by Veza Canetti, who managed, despite considerable challenges, to integrate her Jewish identity with her involvement in the Social Democratic movement. The challenges she faced did not involve an incongruity of ideas or priorities but related to the reluctance of the party leadership—Jewish party leaders included—to be readily associated with Jews and Jewish concerns.

In 1932 Canetti's first publications appeared in the important *Arbeiter Zeitung*, in the feuilleton section that regularly published Joseph Roth, Erich Kästner, Ernst Toller, Maxim Gorki, Jura Soyfer, and others. Canetti, however, would not gain the recognition these writers did, as her publications appeared under a number of pseudonyms—Veza Magd, Veronika Knecht, Martina Murner, and Martin Murner. This was a fairly common practice among leftist writers, generally stemming from the same motivations as Canetti's—to disguise the Jewish background of the writer. In Canetti's case, the decision was not her own but the mandate of Otto König, feuilleton editor at the *Arbeiter Zeitung*. In a letter to Canetti, he wrote, "With the [reigning] latent anti-Semitism, one cannot publish so many stories and novels by a Jewess, and yours are unfortunately the best."[206]

In spite of this obstacle, Canetti published a number of stories in the *Arbeiter Zeitung*, which she subsequently incorporated into the novel *Die gelbe Strasse* (*Yellow Street*), and the collections *Geduld bringt Rosen* (*Good Things Come to Those Who Wait*) and *Der Fund* (*The Discovery*), all of which were first published after her death. She also placed a story in Wieland Herzfelde's 1932 anthology for the Malik Verlag, *Dreißig neue Erzähler des neuen Deutschlands* (*Thirty New Writers of the New Germany*), a publication that was later subject to the Nazi book burnings. Canetti's access to the major publishing venue of the *Arbeiter Zeitung* proved to be short lived, as the paper was shut down in 1934 after the defeat of the Socialists in the February revolt. The proclamation of the corporate state by Dollfuss in May led to the banning of the Social Democratic Party, the end of their influential newspaper, and more generally, the repression of leftist intellectuals involved in both politics and culture. Canetti nonetheless managed to publish her works in the newspapers *Die Stunde* and *Wiener Tag* as late as 1935. Julian Preece reports that the archivist Eckhard Früh has located some writings from 1937, signaling that she continued to find outlets for publishing her work in spite of the inhospitable climate. For Preece, this accomplishment is "testimony to [her] stylistic subtlety."[207]

Veza and Elias Canetti left Vienna in the wake of the pogroms in the city during the "Kristallnacht" of 9 November 1938. They spent two months in Paris with Elias's brother Georges before moving on to London. During the first three or four months of exile in London, Veza Canetti wrote the novel *Die Schildkröten* (*The Tortoises*), an account of the horrific experiences of the previous year in Vienna. By summer she had secured an English publisher for this work, but its publication was prevented by the outbreak of the war. Life in exile was exceedingly difficult. Veza wrote to Elias's brother Georges that she had moved twenty-seven times by the war's end.[208] There were health problems, both mental and physical, and she spoke often of suicide during all the years in England. The couple faced acute financial problems, as neither was able to quickly regain footing as a writer or establish relationships with new publishers.

The Canettis' marriage must have been another source of anxiety for Veza, as Elias had numerous affairs during these years, quite openly and with Veza's knowledge. Theirs was an "open marriage" at Veza's insistence, and she apparently put an end to their sexual relationship after a miscarriage before the two were married. She seems to have supported his relationships with other women, provided they did not keep him from his work. At times, though, she expressed intense jealousy, seeing her own position threatened by one of his lovers. However she felt about these liaisons, she was quite isolated during the exile years, as she and her husband often lived apart and she refrained from joining the literary circles in which he circulated. Little is known about Veza Canetti's death in 1963, which may have been suicide. There is scant information about the whole of her exile years, as she kept no diary, many of her letters were destroyed, and Elias Canetti's autobiographical writings contain many gaps where it concerns his wife.

In spite of the difficult circumstances of exile, Veza Canetti continued to write, both in English and German. Numerous attempts to find a press for her prose or a theater to produce her dramas failed. We know that she wrote as late as 1956, when she reportedly destroyed many of her manuscripts after receiving yet another rejection letter from a publisher.[209] After this she ceased writing. During the years in England, Veza Canetti's own writing was relegated to a secondary status, as her chief concern became supporting her husband in his literary projects. This support involved managing his correspondence and business affairs, typing his manuscripts (in spite of the fact that she was born without a left arm!), acting as his taskmaster to ensure that he continued to write, as well as providing significant collaboration on his work. After Veza died, Elias Canetti referred to her as the coauthor of his massive study, *Masse und Macht*.[210]

As Lisa Silverman has ably demonstrated, Veza Canetti was doubly marginalized as a woman and a Jew.[211] In light of the unholy union between misogyny and anti-Semitism at work during these years—the dual objects of satire in her husband's *Die Blendung*—her position as a Jewish woman writer was particularly difficult. Threatened with deportation in 1934 because of her Socialist involvement with the *Arbeiter Zeitung*, she was also subject to discrimination from that very paper, as it sought to avoid being regarded as overly Jewish. Silverman argues effectively that although she was part of the Social Democratic movement, Veza Canetti's gender excluded her from the ideal of *Bildung* that was actively promoted by the (largely Jewish) party leaders. This exclusion, Silverman suggests, afforded Canetti a critical distance from the great emphasis within Socialist cultural and social programs on *Bildung* as the key to the betterment of the working classes.[212] If Canetti occupied an outsider status on the two counts of gender and ethnicity within the Social Democratic movement, she was certainly doubly marginalized outside of it, in a society dominated by the rise of Nazism. Dagmar Lorenz also underscores the double marginalization of Jewish women. Examining a number of twentieth-century Jewish writers in Germany and Austria, she concludes, like Silverman, that this marginalized position afforded these women a perspective of critical distance unique among their contemporaries: "As Jews they were repeatedly the targets of anti-Semitism and remained outsiders to the powerful nationalist and Fascist movements; as women they were excluded from the centers of political and social power. They were able to retain their objectivity about the development and events of their time because they had no real stake in them."[213]

Canetti's sporadic publication history makes plain that her career as a writer was negatively affected by her Jewish identity. An examination of her works reveals that her literary expression may also be viewed as a product of the leftist, secular, Jewish intellectual subculture to which she belonged. As a Jewish woman writer, Canetti is part of an extended tradition of city literature.[214] Alongside the Viennese writers mentioned above, German Jewish women writers were actively writing in other European metropolises, including Else Lasker-Schüler, Claire Goll, Fanny Lewald, and Gertrud Kolmar. Like Canetti, they focused their writing on the dangers of urban life for women and for others located at the margins. In this vein, Canetti's work depicts Vienna from the perspective of the weakest members of its society and thus reveals an experience of the city quite different from that of other writers.

Canetti's depiction of Vienna begins "directly in front of her building."[215] Her early fiction is largely set within the "*Mazzesinsel*" (Leopoldstadt) she knew so well, and she often drew on the people she encountered there in creating the characters of her stories. Her novel *Die Gelbe Strasse* is an episodic narrative revolving around the Ferdinandstrasse in which she lived at the time of the novel's writing. Canetti paints Leopoldstadt as a world apart. Rather than focusing on the relationship between this district and the larger urban landscape, Canetti presents Leopoldstadt as a microcosm for the whole of Vienna—for Andreas Erb, the street of *Die gelbe Strasse* is the metropolis in miniature.[216] While there is some ethnic diversity and a good deal of economic diversity within the district, and its inhabitants certainly move in and out of the area in their daily lives, Canetti emphasizes the divide that separates Leopoldstadt from the rest of Vienna. Along with Brigittenau, the district is located on an island set off by the Danube and the Canal. Moreover, the existence of the Prater within the district—itself often depicted as a world apart—further sharpens this divide. Lisa Silverman sees Canetti's portrayal of Leopoldstadt as a *"Zwischenort,"* or "a space in between."[217] Canetti's treatment of border spaces highlights less the permeability of these borders than the existence of border as empty space creating a divide. Silverman argues that Canetti calls attention to the gaps that separate rich from poor, the working classes from the bourgeoisie, and the mainstream from the marginalized.

Canetti was similarly interested in the borders between private and public spaces. The public space of the street offers the possibility of human interaction and relatively free circulation, and sometimes figures as a positive alternative to the private spaces of domestic life. Canetti's texts depict domestic life as the arena in which the hardships stemming from economic marginalization are most evident and the tensions stemming from a life lived in difficult circumstances often find violent expression. Far from romanticized, the nuclear family is an agent of oppression in these texts, and women and children inevitably fare the worst. The home is no respite from the pressures of the outside world but is an atmosphere that is cramped, oppressive, and wretched.

Brigitte Spreitzer has shown that the particular spaces of Canetti's texts expose the persistence of premodern institutions and elements of society alongside the modern. Canetti's stories play out in locales such as the *Trafik* (tobacconists), one-room apartments, bordellos, and the *Volksprater*.[218] Modern life hasn't fully penetrated the environs of the socially and economically disadvantaged. Canetti intensifies this sense of a limited existence by placing disabled characters at the center of her works. This choice likely stemmed in part from her own identification with the disabled, but as Brigitte Spreitzer has suggested, it also may be seen as Canetti consciously putting forward a foil to the quintessential male modernist subject, the *flâneur*.[219] Canetti's urban subjects do not occupy the privileged position of mobility and aloofness; rather, they are portrayed as shut in, immobilized, and paralyzed by the limits and barriers imposed on those in the margins.

Nearly all of Canetti's characters endure difficult lives, and her narratives frequently entail their being pushed to a breaking point by circumstances beyond their control. Working-class characters are continually exploited and mistreated by their employers, by fellow workers higher up the ladder, or even outside the workplace by more prosperous fellow Viennese. In the story "Der Sieger" ("The Victor"), the father holds the lowest position at the company where he works and is poorly treated by everyone above him: "Management, bookkeepers, typists, and clerks were all in the habit of taking their moods out on him by ordering him around."[220] His daughter Anna is promoted from the factory floor of a linen firm to the upstairs offices as the result of her hard work but loses the job because she is less attractive than the other factory girls to her boss, who has to let someone go when business slumps. Anna has a new position within her grasp but loses it, because her former boss refuses to certify the skilled secretarial work she undertook for the firm, which she had managed without any official training and solely on the strength of her own intelligence and dedication. When her former boss withholds the simple signature that would secure Anna's future (and help support her hungry siblings), she leaves the factory in despair and is soon found frozen to death in a field just beyond the factory gates. Herr Mäusle of "Geduld bringt Rosen" ("Patience brings Roses") similarly loses a position in spite of years of exemplary service. He is brought down not by the company management but through the exploitation of an unscrupulous playboy neighbor, son of wealthy Russian Jewish immigrants. The story reveals a Vienna that is not segregated economically, as the poor Mäusle family lives in a *Kabinett* in the same building as the newly renovated, five-room apartment of the well-to-do Prokops family. But this proximity merely provides the opportunity for the privileged to take advantage of the poor.

While Canetti's characters living at subsistence level are again and again shown to be a single unfortunate event away from ruin, the depiction of these pitiable existences is consistently sober and straightforward, never sentimental. There are some brighter spots in the narratives, such as a measure of solidarity among the poor. When Herr Mäusle is hospitalized, for example, the neighbors in the building take up a collection for the family. When Anna's dead body is carried into the factory, the workers turn their backs on their employer in disgust. A poignant expression of this solidarity comes from the young boy Georgie in the story "Der Verbrecher" ("The Criminal"). As the son of an animal trainer, Georgie spends all of his time in the *Volksprater*, without ever being able to afford any of the attractions. He sneaks into a movie theater with a group of schoolboys to watch *Emil und die Detektive* (*Emil and the Detectives*) but leaves in protest when the theater staff throws out a man whose shabby clothes give him away as being unable to pay for a ticket. One final scenario reveals this social cohesion among the working class most dramatically; in the story "Drei Helden und eine Frau" ("Three Heroes and a Woman"), the cleaning woman scrubbing the staircase of an apartment building gives shelter to three young men fleeing the police during the February workers' rebellion.

These depictions of the disadvantaged in Viennese society resolutely refuse either a sentimentalization of their plight or a romanticization of their means of coping with it. Veza Canetti's stories unfold without a layer of commentary or interpretation, an aesthetic trait her writing shares with her husband's. The reader is not invited into a deep identification with her characters, first because—again, like Elias Canetti—she makes use of the grotesque in her characterization, and second, because she employs multiple perspectives that complicate the reading and frustrate any identification. Canetti's works express sharp social criticism through her focus on the oppressive social structures that fostered the rise of fascism, as well as through the boldness of her depiction of the brutality, misery, and ugliness present in this society. By not shying away from these disturbing elements she forces a confrontation leading to the recognition of unpleasant truths by the reader.

Canetti does not, however, take on the intense anti-Semitism of interwar Vienna in these early works. Jewish themes are not addressed in these stories, an omission that likely stemmed from the editorial practices of her primary outlet, the *Arbeiter Zeitung*. Her confrontation with anti-Semitism would come later in the novel *Die Schildkröten,* depicting the persecution of Viennese Jews in the summer and fall of 1938. Canetti wrote the novel during the first months of exile in England and had completed it by July 1939. While I have largely excluded works written in exile from this study, this text was written with so little temporal distance from the events related, I see it less as a product of exile than of the immediate experiences of the Canettis in their final months in Vienna.

At the center of the novel are the poet Andreas Kain and his wife, Eva. The couple is living in a villa at the outskirts of the city, a place they have clearly chosen because its tranquility and natural beauty, as well as the couple's good rapport with the local people, render it a productive working environment. This tranquility is first disrupted and ultimately shattered by the penetration of the Nazi threat into the haven they had found. This new presence is signaled first by the Nazi flag forced on the villa, which, as though sensing its inappropriateness there, will never properly unfurl, and finally through the increasingly looming presence of the Nazi Baldur Pilz. The couple is cognizant of the dangers that surround them, and the novel plays out in the excruciating months in which they await the visas that will enable them to leave.

As in Veza Canetti's earlier narratives, space plays a key role in the novel as she attempts to evoke the spread of evil throughout the city and reveal the transformation of Vienna from "the most cheerful city in Europe"[221] into a dehumanized, monstrous place. By the summer of 1938 the suburbs offer no refuge (as the Canettis experienced themselves when forced out of their Grinzing home). Kain attempts to withdraw into his study while his wife confronts the new reality represented by Pilz's entrance into the area. But as we have seen in Canetti's earlier work, interior spaces do not provide a shelter from the problems of the outside world. Eva lives in constant fear of the knock at the door; the threshold between public and private spaces proves no barrier to the existential threats to the Jews, inherent in the Nazi takeover. While the Kains' relationship is not, in contrast to the earlier works, a source of conflict, their domestic peace is broken by Pilz's intrusion into their home. Pilz takes over the villa and eventually forces them out. Even as the couple had been restricted to just Kain's study, with Pilz and his possessions filling the rest of the house and he and his wife appropriating their belongings, the Kains' forced eviction and move to the city is cast in terms of a new captivity: "Much is in the works. They are being pushed out prematurely. They will be forcibly disposed. They have to move, even before they can leave. That was clear. This cup will not pass from them. To lead Kain out of his quiet room, down into the closeness, into the dangerous city where no one knew him, where he was an outlaw."[222]

In the city, the couple crowds into Kain's brother Werner's apartment along with another Jewish man forced out of his living space. While all of the occupants try to shore up each other's courage in this terrible time, the crisis has escalated. Shortly after the Kains arrive, word comes that the city's synagogues are burning. With bitter irony, Canetti lays bare the inescapability of the crisis. While Kain faces the danger of the streets that have given over to chaos and violent conflict, the danger also comes home. While he is out, the Nazis arrive at the door to arrest him for remaining in Vienna longer than permitted. They mistake his brother Werner for him and take him away in Kain's stead. The long-awaited visas finally arrive, and the couple escapes over the border, but not before learning of Werner's death.

The Kains' protracted wait for the necessary visas leave them in Vienna long enough to watch its transformation into a hellish place; they experience the loss of their beloved *Heimat* well before leaving. This experience of loss is not restricted to those forced to leave. Canetti describes a reciprocal and vital relationship between people and place: "The places that you leave behind forever, they become a thousand times more dear to you. You are interwoven with every spot, you hear secrets in the corners, you whisper back secrets; the place dies a little, because you leave, and you die a little with the place."[223] Canetti's novel imagines consequences of the catastrophic experiences of 1938 on both her protagonists and on the place from which they were driven. The Kains survive but are diminished by the persecution they experience, and Canetti imagines a similarly diminished Vienna, devoid of the humanity that had once distinguished it.

Conclusion

The fundamental reordering of Central and Eastern Europe that occurred at the end of the First World War did not easily accommodate the Jews of the former Habsburg Empire. The nationalist principle that had acted as a strong centrifugal force during the final years of the empire dominated the process of redrawing the map and left the Jews out in the cold. After World War I Jews faced an entirely new identity crisis without the luxury of having resolved the one they faced at the turn of the century. Under conditions now even less favorable for forging a new identity, Austrian Jews were confronted with the fact that the tripartite identity of the Habsburg era was no longer viable. As postwar identities were refashioned in terms of national and ethnic belonging, the Jews faced an intractable dilemma. Rising anti-Semitism increased the pressure on Jews trying to orient themselves to a new reality.

There was no unified response to the pressure-cooker situation of the interwar years. As overt anti-Semitism became increasingly evident across the political spectrum, political options for Jewish participation were essentially limited to two alternatives, Socialism or Jewish nationalism. There was a surge in Jewish support for Zionism. Felix Salten deepened his support for Zionism in these years, moving away from the assimilationism that had existed alongside his earlier Zionist sympathies. Zionism made significant gains in Vienna, but on the whole Vienna's Jewish community was fragmented into conflicting factions.

The most pronounced tendency among Jews in responding to the new challenges of the interwar period was an intensification of their personal identifications as Jews. This was both part of the Jewish experience of the First World War and a reaction to the rise of anti-Semitism. A stronger Jewish identification took a number of forms, evident in the different paths followed by Beer-Hofmann, Roth, and Zweig. Each of these writers came to a more positive relationship to their Jewishness, but they defined that relationship in different terms.

One element of the heightened experience of Jewish identity was a turn to the East. Many Jewish writers developed a new view of Eastern Europe as a source of authentic Jewry that resisted the pressures brought to bear on Western Jewish identity. Many Jewish texts of the period focus on the Eastern European Jewish shtetl or trace the westward migration of Jews and explore their attempts at integration into Western societies. These texts reflect a high degree of ambivalence underlying Western views of Eastern European Jews, simultaneously reflecting deep admiration and internalized prejudice.

In spite of, or perhaps in response to, the great pressures on Austrian Jews following the war, the 1920s witnessed a flourishing of Jewish literature. And sadly, the following decade would gradually bring an end to Jewish intellectual life in Vienna. Many who were able to leave chose to do so, and those who remained witnessed the gradual extinguishing of Jewish life in Austria. Elias and Veza Canetti left Vienna only at the last possible moment, and each of them created works that reflect powerfully on the acute crisis atmosphere leading up to the *Anschluss*. With the rise of fascism, Jewish identity was no longer a matter of individual choice, but an imposition from without, a mark of difference that dictated a fate of exclusion and persecution. The Jews who survived National Socialism would have to try to reclaim identity as a series of individual choices.

Notes

1. Marsha L. Rozenblit, *Reconstructing a National Identity: The Jews of Habsburg Austria During World War I* (Oxford: Oxford University Press, 2001), 19.
2. Ibid., 35.
3. Rozenblit, *The Jews of Vienna*, 148.
4. Rozenblit, *Reconstructing a National Identity*, 19.
5. Ibid., 24.
6. Ibid., 33.
7. Barbara Jelavich, *Modern Austria: Empire and Republic, 1800–1986* (Cambridge: Cambridge University Press, 1987), 136.
8. Stefan Zweig, *Die Welt von Gestern*, 256.
9. See Rozenblit, *Reconstructing a National Identity*, 41–43.
10. Arthur Schnitzler, cited and translated in Peter Gay, *Schnitzler's Century*, 289.
11. See Rozenblit, *Reconstructing a National Identity*, 44–47.
12. István Deák, *Beyond Nationalism: A Social and Political History of the Habsburg Officer Corps, 1848–1918* (Oxford: Oxford University Press, 1990), 197.
13. Rozenblit, *Reconstructing a National Identity*, 66–67.
14. Ibid., 84–85.
15. Ibid., 48.
16. Ibid., 118–19.
17. Ibid., 127.
18. Ibid., 7.
19. Edward Timms, *Karl Kraus, Apocalyptic Satirist: The Post-war Crisis and the Rise of the Swastika* (New Haven: Yale University Press, 2005), 34.
20. Bruce Pauley, "Political Antisemitism in Interwar Vienna," Oxaal, Pollak, and Botz, *Jews, Antisemitism and Culture in Vienna*, 153.
21. Rozenblit, *Reconstructing a National Identity*, 169.
22. Pauley, "Political Antisemitism in Interwar Vienna," 154.
23. Ibid.
24. Ibid., 155.
25. Harriet Pass Freidenreich, *Jewish Politics in Vienna, 1918–1938* (Bloomingon: Indiana University Press, 1991), 96.
26. Wistrich, "Social Democracy, Antisemitism and the Jews of Vienna," 115.
27. Ibid., 117.
28. Freidenreich, *Jewish Politics in Vienna*, 88.
29. Ibid., 96–97.
30. Ibid., 86.
31. Rozenblit, *Reconstructing a National Identity*, 169.
32. Ibid., 157.
33. Pauley, "Political Antisemitism in Interwar Vienna," 166.
34. Ibid., 172.
35. For more on the socio-psychological function of anti-Semitism in Vienna at the turn of the twentieth century, see Hödl, *Wiener Juden—jüdische Wiener*, 20–21.
36. Gerhard Botz, "The Jews of Vienna from the *Anschluss* to the Holocaust," in Oxaal, Pollak, and Botz, *Jews, Antisemitism and Culture in Vienna*, 186.
37. Ibid., 187.
38. Freidenreich, *Jewish Politics in Vienna*, 181.
39. Ibid., 189.
40. Pauley, "Political Antisemitism in Interwar Vienna," 156.

41. Kristie A. Foell, "July 15, 1927, The Vienna Palace of Justice is burned in a mass uprising of Viennese workers, a central experience in the life and work of Elias Canetti," in Gilman and Zipes, *Yale Companion to Jewish Writing and Thought in German Culture*, 465.
42. Pauley, "Political Antisemitism in Interwar Vienna," 168.
43. Freidenreich, *Jewish Politics in Vienna*, 204.
44. Botz, "The Jews of Vienna from the *Anschluss* to the Holocaust," 192.
45. Ibid., 186.
46. Ibid., 194.
47. Ibid., 195.
48. For more on the role of the IKG and the implementation of Eichman's *Judenpolitik*, see the important study by writer and historian Doron Rabinovici, *Instanzen der Ohnmacht. Wien 1938–1945. Der Weg zum Judenrat* (Frankfurt: Jüdischer Verlag, 2000).
49. Botz, "The Jews of Vienna from the *Anschluss* to the Holocaust," 201.
50. Cited in the article on Vienna at the website of the United States Holocaust Memorial Museum, http://www.ushmm.org.
51. Kenneth Segar, "Austria in the Thirties: Reality and Exemplum," in *Austria in the Thirties: Culture and Politics*, eds. Kenneth Segar and John Warren (Riverside, CA: Ariadne Press, 1991), 360.
52. Ibid., 362.
53. Claudio Magris, *Il mito absburgico nella letteratura austriaca moderna* (dissertation, University of Turin, 1963). (The Habsburg Myth in Austrian Literature).
54. Steven Beller, "The Jewish Intellectual and Vienna in the 1930s," in Segar and Warren, *Austria in the Thirties: Culture and Politics*, 317–20.
55. Segar, "Austria in the Thirties: Reality and Exemplum," 366.
56. Luigi Reitani, "Arthur Schnitzler in den 20iger Jahren: Der Dichter einer 'versunkenen' Welt?" in *Literatur und Kultur im Österreich der Zwanziger Jahre*, ed. Primus-Heinz Kucher (Bielefeld: Aisthesis Verlag, 2007), 151.
57. For a full account of the censorship affair, see *Schnitzlers Reigen*, vol. 1, *Der Skandal: Analysen und Dokumente*, vol. 2, *Die Prozesse: Analyse und Dokumente*, ed. Alfred Pfoser, Kristina Pfoser-Schweig, and Gerhard Renner (Frankfurt: Fischer Taschenbuch Verlag, 1993). See also Gert K. Schneider, "The Social and Political Context of Arthur Schnitzler's *Reigen* in Berlin, Vienna, and New York: 1900–1993," in *A Companion to the Works of Arthur Schnitzler*, ed. Dagmar C. G. Lorenz (Rochester, NY: Camden House, 2003), 27–57. For a fine, concise account, see Egon Schwarz, "1921: The staging of Arthur Schnitzler's play *Reigen* in Vienna creates a public uproar that draws involvement by the press, the police, the Viennese city administration, and Austrian parliament," in Gilman and Zipes, *Yale Companion to Jewish Writing and Thought in German Culture*, 412–19.
58. Cited in Schwarz, in "1921," 415.
59. Ibid.
60. Ibid., 413.
61. Schnitzler, *Jugend in Wien*, 93–94.
62. Ibid., 93.
63. Ibid., 93–94.
64. Schwarz, "1921," 419.
65. Ariane Huml, "'…wilde, anarchische, unwahrscheinliche Zeit.' Das Fin de Siècle in den Autobiographien von Arthur Schnitzler und Stefan Zweig," in *Fin de Siècle*, eds. Ariane Huml and Monika Fludernik (Trier: Wissenschaftlicher Verlag, 2002), 309..
66. Gershon Shaked, "Wie jüdisch ist ein deutsch-jüdischer Roman? Über Joseph Roths *Hiob, Roman eines einfachen Mannes*," in *Juden in der deutschen Literatur. Ein deutsch-israelisches Symposion*, ed. Stéphane Moses and Albrecht Schöne (Frankfurt: Suhrkamp, 1986), 283.

67. Many Austrian writers served in the military propaganda office during the war, including Hofmannsthal, Robert Musil, Egon Erwin Kisch, Alfred Polgar, Franz Theodor Csokor, and even pacifists Zweig and Franz Werfel. See Timms, *The Post-war Crisis and the Rise of the Swastika*, 229.
68. Felix Salten to Arthur Schnitzler, 10 Aug. 1914, cited in Dickel, *"Ein Dilettant des Lebens will ich nicht sein,"* 153.
69. Dickel, *Felix Salten zwischen Zionismus und Jungwiener Moderne*, 395.
70. Ibid., 185.
71. Salten, "Ein rabbinisches Gutachten über den Zionismus," *Die Welt*, 2 Dec. 1898, cited in Dickel, *"Ein Dilettant des Lebens will ich nicht sein,"* 209.
72. Heidi Lexe, "*Bambi*—Ein Klassiker der Kinderliteratur?" in *Felix Salten—der unbekannte Bekannte*, eds. Ernst Seibert und Susanne Blumesberger (Vienna: Praesens, 2006), 106.
73. Iris Bruce, "Which Way Out? Schnitzler's and Salten's Conflicting Responses to Cultural Zionism," in Lorenz, *A Companion to the Works of Arthur Schnitzler*, 103–26.
74. Bruce, "Which Way Out?," 114.
75. Annegret Völpel, "1928, The first issue of the Jewish Children's Calendar, edited by Emil Bernhard Cohn, is published in cooperation with the Commission on Literary Works for Youth of the Grand Lodge for Germany of the Independent Order of B'Nai B'rith," in Gilman and Zipes, *Yale Companion to Jewish Writing and Thought in German Culture*, 490.
76. Cited in Dickel, *"Ein Dilettant des Lebens will ich nicht sein,"* 370.
77. Ibid., 370–72.
78. Florian Krobb, "Gefühlszionismus und Zionsgefühle," 160.
79. Ibid., 160–61.
80. Felix Salten, *Neue Menschen auf alter Erde. Eine Palästinafahrt* (Königstein/Ts.: Athenäum, 1986), 1.
81. Dickel, *"Ein Dilettant des Lebens will ich nicht sein,"* 376 (translation mine).
82. Salten, *Neue Menschen auf alter Erde*, cited in Dickel, *"Ein Dilettant des Lebens will ich nicht sein,"* 373.
83. Salten, *Neue Menschen auf alter Erde*, 177.
84. Cited in Dickel, *"Ein Dilettant des Lebens will ich nicht sein,"* 375.
85. Ibid., 393. This has also been noted by Rahel Rosa Neubauer, "Felix Salten als Autor jüdischer Kinder-und Jugendliteratur," 138.
86. Salten, *Neue Menschen auf alter Erde*, cited in Dickel, *"Ein Dilettant des Lebens will ich nicht sein,"* 394.
87. See Dickel, "Von Ragusa zum Exil," for a discussion of the stance of the Austrian PEN Club, led by Salten, vis-à-vis Germany in 1933, 431ff.. At the PEN Club congress, the Austrian delegation attempted to block a resolution condemning the Nazi persecution of writers in Germany.
88. Cited in Dickel, *"Ein Dilettant des Lebens will ich nicht sein,"* 423. The term "*Luegerei*" in the original is both a reference to the Lueger era and a play on the word *Lügerei*, the telling of lies.
89. Stefan Zweig, *The World of Yesterday* (New York: The Viking Press, 1943), 248.
90. Joseph Strelka, *Stefan Zweig: Freier Geist der Menschlichkeit* (Vienna: Öesterreichischer Bundesverlag, 1981), 30ff.
91. Stefan Zweig, *Jeremias* (Leipzig: Insel Verlag, 1920), 17.
92. Ibid., 39.
93. Ibid., 175.
94. Ibid., 201–2.
95. Ibid., 202.

96. Fraiman, "Das Tragende Symbol," 252.
97. Zweig, *The World of Yesterday,* 253.
98. Robert S. Wistrich, "Stefan Zweig and the 'World of Yesterday,'" in Gelber, *Stefan Zweig Reconsidered,* 68.
99. Zweig, *Jeremias,* 215.
100. Fraiman, "Das Tragende Symbol," 252.
101. Zweig, *Jeremias,* 206.
102. Wistrich, "Stefan Zweig and the 'World of Yesterday,'" 68.
103. Jacob Golomb, "Erasmus: Stefan Zweig's Alter-Ego," in Gelber, *Stefan Zweig Reconsidered,* 16.
104. Ibid., 17–18.
105. Fraiman, "Das Tragende Symbol," 248–65, especially 254–56.
106. See Fraiman, "Das Tragende Symbol," as well as Margarita Pazi, "Stefan Zweig, Europäer und Jude," *Modern Austrian Literature* 14: 3/4 (1981): 291–311.
107. Wistrich, "Stefan Zweig and the 'World of Yesterday,'" 68.
108. Stefan Zweig, Letter to Martin Buber, 25 May 1917, in Zweig, *Brief an Freunde,* note 13, 75, cited in Golomb, "Erasmus: Stefan Zweig's Alter-Ego," 12–13.
109. Boyarin and Boyarin, "Diaspora," 323ff.
110. Wistrich, "Stefan Zweig and the 'World of Yesterday,'" 77.
111. Ibid., 60.
112. Jean Paul Bier, "Assimilatorische Schreibweise und onomastische Ironie im erzählerischen Frühwerk Roths," in *Joseph Roth: Interpretation—Kritik—Rezeption,* eds. Michael Kessler and Fritz Hackert (Tübingen: Stauffenburg Verlag, 1990), 29–40.
113. See David Bronsen, *Joseph Roth. Eine Biographie* (Cologne: Kiepenheuer & Witsch, 1974).
114. For more on Roth's journalism of the 1920s, see David Horrocks, "The Representation of Jews and of Anti-Semitism in Joseph Roth's Early Journalism," in *German Life and Letters* 58:2 (April 2005): 141–54.
115. For more on the correspondence between Roth and Zweig, see Gershon Shaked, "Die Gnade der Vernunft und die des Unglücks. Zweig und Roth—Ein Briefwechsel," in *Stefan Zweig Heute,* ed. Mark Gelber (New York: Peter Lang, 1987), and Matjaz Birk, *"Vielleicht führen wir zwei verschiedene Sprachen...": Zum Briefwechsel zwischen Joseph Roth und Stefan Zweig* (Münster: Lit Verlag, 1997).
116. Birk, *Zum Briefwechsel zwischen Joseph Roth und Stefan Zweig,* 56—63.
117. Cited in Maria Llanska, "Die Galizische Heimat im Werk Joseph Roths," in Kessler and Hackert, *Joseph Roth: Interpretation—Kritik—Rezeption,* 151.
118. Llanska, "Die Galizische Heimat im Werk Joseph Roths," 144.
119. Joseph Roth, *Juden auf Wanderschaft* (Cologne: Kiepenheuer & Witsch, 1976; dtv München, 2006), 16.
120. See John Pizer, "'Last Austrians' in 'Turn of the Century' Works by Franz Grillparzer, Joseph Roth, and Alfred Kolleritsch," *The German Quarterly* 74:1 (Winter 2001): 8–21.
121. Cited in Llanska, "Die Galizische Heimat im Werk Joseph Roths," 152.
122. Ibid., 148.
123. Mark H. Gelber, "'Juden auf Wanderschaft' und die Rhetorik des Ost-West Debatte im Werk Joseph Roths," in Kessler, *Joseph Roth: Interpretation—Kritik—Rezeption,* 132.
124. Ibid., 127–41; and David Horrocks, "The Construction of Eastern Jewry in Joseph Roth's *Juden auf Wanderschaft,*" in *Ghetto Writing: Traditional and Eastern Jewry in German-Jewish Literature from Heine to Hilsenrath,* eds. Anne Fuchs and Florian Krobb (Columbia, SC: Camden House, 1999), 126–39.
125. Sarah Bailey, "Cultural Translation and the Problem of Language: Yiddish in Joseph Roth's Juden auf Wanderschaft," in *Transit* 1:1 (2005): 1–10.

126. Horrocks, "The Construction of Eastern Jewry in Joseph Roth's *Juden auf Wanderschaft,*" 130.
127. This dismissal of objectivity in the preface is almost certainly an answer to and critique of Alfred Doeblin's *Reise in Polen* (1925), which Roth reviewed for the *Frankfurter Zeitung* in January 1926. Doeblin casts himself as a detached, objective observer, as well as a clear outsider to the Jewish culture he is reporting on. For Mark Gelber, Roth's piece is in many respects a response to Doeblin's, though not explicitly. Roth, however, seems to have written much of his essay prior to reviewing the other work. For more on the relationship between the two works, see Gelber, "'Juden auf Wanderschaft' und die Rhetorik des Ost-West Debatte im Werk Joseph Roths," 130ff. I am also grateful to Nick Block for a very interesting paper on Doeblin's *Reise in Polen* at the Kentucky Foreign Language Conference in 2009.
128. Roth, *Juden auf Wanderschaft,* 11.
129. Katja Garloff, "Femininity and Assimilatory Desire in Joseph Roth," *Modern Fiction Studies,* 51:2 (Summer 2005): 354–73.
130. Roth, *Juden auf Wanderschaft,* 12.
131. Ibid., 11–12.
132. Ibid., 13.
133. Ibid., 15.
134. Ibid., 22.
135. Ibid., 7.
136. Ibid., 15.
137. Ibid., 54.
138. Ibid.
139. Ibid., 75.
140. Ibid.
141. Ibid., 64.
142. Ibid., 66.
143. Ibid., 70.
144. Ibid., 75.
145. Ibid.
146. Ibid., 76–77.
147. Gelber, "'Juden auf Wanderschaft' und die Rhetorik des Ost-West Debatte im Werk Joseph Roths," 129.
148. Wolfgang Iser, "German Jewish Writers during the Decline of the Habsburg Monarchy: Assessing the Assessment of Gershon Shaked," in *Ideology and Jewish Identity in Israeli and American Literature,* ed. Emily Miller Budick (Albany: SUNY Press, 2001), 264.
149. Sarah Fraiman-Morris, "Naturgefühl und Religiosität in den Werken österreichisch-jüdischer Schriftsteller: Franz Werfel, Stefan Zweig, Joseph Roth, Richard Beer-Hofmann," *Modern Austrian Literature* 38:1/2 (2005): 32.
150. Shaked, "Wie jüdisch ist ein deutsch-jüdischer Roman?," 281.
151. Ibid., 288.
152. See Garloff, "Femininity and Assimilatory Desire in Joseph Roth," 354–73.
153. Ibid., 356.
154. Caroline Kohn, "Karl Kraus und das Judentum," 149–50.
155. Timms, *The Post-War Crisis and the Rise of the Swastika,* 339.
156. Karl Kraus, *Die Fackel,* 890–905, 153. Cited in Timms, *The Post-War Crisis and the Rise of the Swastika,* 494.
157. Translated by Timms, in *The Post-War Crisis and the Rise of the Swastika,* 494.
158. A few figures related to circulation will underscore on Bettauer's popularity. His weekly journal devoted to eroticism, *Er und Sie. Wochenschrift für Lebenskultur und Erotik,* achieved

a readership of 200,000 within 5 weeks of its launch in 1924. *Die Stadt ohne Juden* (1922) sold 250,000 copies, was translated into several languages, and was adapted into a play and movie. See Beth Simone Noveck, "1925, Hugo Bettauer's Assassination by Otto Rothstock in Vienna marks the first political murder by the Nazis in Austria," in Gilman and Zipes, *Yale Companion to Jewish Writing and Thought in German Culture,* 440–47.
159. Frank D. Hirschbach, "Der Roman *Die Stadt ohne Juden*—Gedanken zum 12. März 1988," in *Austrian Writers and the Anschluss: Understanding the Past—Overcoming the Past,* ed. Donald G. Daviau (Riverside, CA: Ariadne Press, 1991), 58.
160. Hans Eichner, "City Without Jews: Hugo Bettauer's Vienna," in *Hinter dem schwarzen Vorhang: Die Katastrophe und die epische Tradition. Festschrift für Anthony W. Riley,* eds. Anthony W. Riley, Friedrich Gaede, Patrick O'Neill, and Ulrich Scheck (Tübingen: Francke, 1994), 109.
161. Noveck, "1925, Hugo Bettauer's Assassination," 440.
162. Eichner, "City Without Jews: Hugo Bettauer's Vienna," 110.
163. Hirschbach, "Der Roman *Die Stadt ohne Juden*—Gedanken zum 12. März 1988," 58.
164. Eichner, "City Without Jews: Hugo Bettauer's Vienna," 110.
165. Murray Hall, *Der Fall Bettauer* (Vienna: Löcker, 1978), 79; cited in Eichner, "City Without Jews: Hugo Bettauer's Vienna," 110.
166. I worked with an online version of this text, available through Projekt Gutenberg-DE at http://gutenberg.spiegel.de. I am therefore unable to provide page numbers and will instead make reference to the two sections of the book (Teil I, II) and give the chapter title and numbers. This passage occurs in Teil I, Kapitel I, Das Antijudengesetz.
167. Ibid. The citation reads, "*Fremdkörper, die unseren Leib überwuchern und uns schliesslich versklaven.*"
168. Noveck, "1925, Hugo Bettauer's Assassination," 442.
169. Bettauer, *Die Stadt ohne Juden,* Teil I, Kapitel 1, Das Antijudengesetz.
170. Ibid.
171. Bettauer, *Die Stadt ohne Juden,* Teil II, Kapitel 2, Loden, Die Grosse Mode.
172. Sander L. Gilman, *Difference and Pathology: Stereotypes of Sexuality, Race, and Madness* (Ithaca, NY: Cornell University Press, 1985), 158.
173. Bettauer, *Die Stadt ohne Juden,* Teil II, Kapitel 8, Die lieben süßen Mädeln.
174. Noveck, "1925, Hugo Bettauer's Assassination," 443.
175. For more on the importance of Ruschuk and Bulgaria in Canetti's life and work, see Svoboda Alexandra Dimitrova and Penka Angelova, "Canetti, Roustchouk, and Bulgaria: The Impact of Origin on Canetti's Work," in *A Companion to the Works of Elias Canetti,* ed. Dagmar C. G. Lorenz (Rochester, NY: Camden House, 2004), 261–87.
176. See Anne Fuchs, "'The Deeper Nature of My German': Mother Tongue, Subjectivity, and the Voice of the Other in Elias Canetti's Autobiography," in Lorenz, *A Companion to the Works of Elias Canetti,* 45–60. Canetti's struggle for independence from his mother figures prominently in the second volume of his autobiography, *Die Fackel im Ohr. Lebensgeschichte 1921–1931* (Frankfurt: Fischer Taschenbuch Verlag, 2002).
177. Elias Canetti, *Aufzeichnungen 1942–1985. Die Provinz des Menschen. Das Geheimherz der Uhr.* (Munich: Hanser Verlag, 1993), 97.
178. Dagmar C. G. Lorenz, Introduction, *A Companion to the Works of Elias Canetti,* 12.
179. Elias Canetti, *Die gerettete Zunge. Geschichte einer Jugend* (Frankfurt: Fischer Taschenbuch Verlag, 1997), 11.
180. Ibid., 18.
181. Dimitrova and Angelova, "Canetti, Roustchouk, and Bulgaria," 270.
182. Penka Angelova, "Topoi der Heimat in den Autobiographien von Elias Canetti," in *Elias Canetti,* eds. Kurt Bartsch and Gerhard Melzer (Graz: Literaturverlag Droschl, 2005), 94–96.

183. Elias Canetti, *Aufzeichnungen 1942–1985*, cited in Angelova, "Topoi der Heimat in den Autobiographien von Elias Canetti," 95. The original reads: "*Ortlos war er nie, er hatte aber viele Orte. Jeden hat er mit der Unbeirrbarkeit behütet, die man für eine einzige Heimat hat.*"
184. Elias Canetti, *Aufzeichnungen 1954–1993. Die Fliegenpein. Nachträge aus Hampstead. Posthum veröffentlichte Aufzeichnungen* (Munich: Hanser Verlag, 2004), cited in Angelova, "Topoi der Heimat in den Autobiographien von Elias Canetti," 95. The original reads: "*Sie wollen ihn zurückgewinnen, für ihr verlorenes Volk. Er lässt sich nur von jedem Volk zurückgewinnen. sie begreifen nicht, daß seine Heimat überall ist, überall wo er war und wo er noch gern wäre.*"
185. Irene Stocksieker Di Maio, "Space in Elias Canetti's Autoboigraphical Trilogy," in Lorenz, *A Companion to the Works of Elias Canetti*, 175–97.
186. Ibid., 176.
187. Richard H. Lawson, *Understanding Elias Canetti* (Columbia: University of South Carolina Press, 1991), 3.
188. Lawson, *Understanding Elias Canetti*, 1.
189. Di Maio, "Space in Elias Canetti's Autoboigraphical Trilogy," 188.
190. Cited in Foell, "July 15, 1927, The Vienna Palace of Justice is burned," 465.
191. Ibid., 466.
192. The transformation of the name is surely intended to establish an association with Kien's wife, Therese, linking this space of commercial exchange with this woman whose only concerns are financial and who views the books of Kien's collection solely in terms of their exchange value.
193. William Collins Donahue, *The End of Modernism: Elias Canetti's Auto-da-Fé* (Chapel Hill: University of North Carolina Press, 2001), 65.
194. Elias Canetti, *Die Blendung* (Frankfurt: Fischer Taschenbuch Verlag, 1997), 10.
195. Ibid., 80.
196. Ibid., 88.
197. Donahue, *The End of Modernism*, 3.
198. Irene Boose, "Die Komik des Wissens: Elias Canettis Roman *Die Blendung*," in *Der Zukunftsfette. Neue Beiträge zum Werk Elias Canettis*, ed. Sven Hanuschek (Dresden: Neisse Verlag, 2007), 80.
199. Foell, "July 15, 1927, The Vienna Palace of Justice is burned," 466.
200. Richard Lawson, for example, refers to the novel's misogyny and raises the question as to what Canetti might be doing in depicting these characters via extreme stereotypes, but he doesn't provide an answer. See Jenna Ferrara, in "Grotesque and Voiceless: Women Characters in Elias Canetti's *Die Blendung*," in *Proceedings and Commentary: German Graduate Students Association Conference at New York University*, eds. Patricia Doykos Duquette, Matthew Griffin, and Inike Lode (New York: n.p., 1994); and Kristie Foell in *Blind Reflections: Gender in Elias Canetti's 'Die Blendung,'* (Riverside, CA: Ariadne Press, 1994), both indict the novel's treatment of gender as misogynist.
201. Donahue, *The End of Modernism*, 44.
202. For more on the anti-Semitic physical stereotypes of Jews, see Gilman, *The Jew's Body*.
203. Julian Preece, *The Rediscovered Writings of Veza Canetti: Out of the Shadows of a Husband* (Rochester, NY: Camden House, 207), 57.
204. Dagmar C. G. Lorenz, "Veza Canettis Roman *Die Schildkröten* als Beitrag zur Kritik des anthropozentrischen Weltbildes im Nationalsozialismus," in *Veza Canetti*, eds. Ingrid Spörk and Alexandra Strohmaier (Graz: Literatur Verlag Droschl, 2005), 33.
205. For more on women's professional engagement in the twenties and thirties, see Lisa Silverman, "Jewish Intellectual Women and the Public Sphere in Inter-War Vienna," in *Women*

in Europe Between the Wars: Politics, Culture and Society, eds. Angela Kershaw and Angela Kimyongür (Hampshire, England: Ashgate Publishing Ltd, 2007), 155–70.
206. Cited in Sybille Mulot, "Das Leben vor der Haustür," in Spörk and Strohmaier, *Veza Canetti*, 155.
207. Preece, *The Rediscovered Writings of Veza Canetti*, 17.
208. Ibid., 21.
209. Veza Canetti: "Lebenschronik," in *Die Schildkröten* (Munich: dtv, 1999), 287.
210. Preece, *The Rediscovered Writings of Veza Canetti*, 8.
211. Lisa Silverman, "Jenseits der Bildung: Veza Canetti als jüdische Schriftstellerin in Wien" in Spörk and Strohmaier, *Veza Canetti*, 74.
212. Silverman, "Jenseits der Bildung," 76–79.
213. Dagmar C.G. Lorenz, "Mass Culture and the City in the Works of German-Jewish Novelists: Claire Goll, Veza Canetti, Else Lasker-Schüler, and Gertrud Kolmar," in *Gender and Judaism: the Transformation of Tradition*, ed. T. M. Rudavsky (New York: New York University Press, 1995), 178.
214. Lorenz, "Mass Culture and the City," 169.
215. Mulot, "Das Leben vor der Haustür," 158.
216. Cited in Brigitte Spreitzer, "Veza Canettis Roman *Die Gelbe Strasse* im Kontext der literarischen Moderne," in Spörk and Strohmaier, *Veza Canetti*, 12–13.
217. Lisa Silverman, "Zwischenzeit und Zwischenort: Veza Canetti, Else Feldmann, and Jewish Writing in Interwar Vienna, *Prooftexts* 26 (2006): 40.
218. Spreitzer, "Veza Canettis Roman *Die Gelbe Strasse* im Kontext der literarischen Moderne," 13.
219. Ibid., 14–15.
220. Veza Canetti, *Geduld bringt Rosen* (Munich: dtv, 1992), 49.
221. Veza Canetti, *Die Schildkröten* (Munich: dtv, 1999), 27.
222. Ibid., 122.
223. Ibid., 144.

Chapter 3

JEWS AND THE SECOND REPUBLIC

Vienna's once-thriving Jewish community was decimated by the persecution that accompanied the *Anschluss,* the Second World War, and the Holocaust. When Austria began to reconstitute itself at the end of the war, it was not at all clear that a new Austria would offer any place for the reemergence of any reconstituted Jewish community. The immediate postwar situation was sufficiently desperate that conditions were hardly favorable for exiled Jews or survivors of the camps to return. After the immediate crisis subsided, the focus on rebuilding and the establishment of a national state consumed public attention, leaving little room for concern over the fate of surviving Austrian Jews.

The national self-image of Austria that emerged after the war cast Austria as the first victim of fascism, a model that rendered Jews an unwelcome rival in claiming victim status. A new national consciousness was fostered through the instrumentalization of the wartime trauma experienced by non-Jewish Austrians, a process that integrated broad segments of the population into a new national community but that also leveled Jewish suffering and excluded Jews from this nascent Austrian community. Accordingly, the Second Republic made little effort to encourage the return of Austrian Jews, and those who nonetheless chose to come back were marginalized politically and socially. In what follows I will examine in more detail the process by which Austria coalesced as a nation and society after the Second World War, as well as the ways Austria dealt with the Jews who perished and the few who survived the war, particularly the handful of Jewish writers who returned.

In cultural terms, the tremendous achievements by Jewish artists and intellectuals that punctuated the final years of the Austro-Hungarian Empire and persisted through the 1920s gave way to silence concerning the disappearance of the Jewish intelligentsia and to a hostile climate that greeted the few Jews who chose to return after World War II. Facing the many taboos that were established with regard to any discussion of Jewish suffering, loss, and the Austrians' hand in that experience, few Jewish writers were able to make themselves heard in the first decades of the Second Republic. These first Jewish writers who managed to establish a voice within Austrian culture after the war performed a vital task by giving expression to Jewish experiences of the war and by reinserting—against considerable odds—a Jewish presence into the Austrian cultural sphere, where that presence had long played so vital a role.

The Immediate Postwar Situation

The initial moves toward the reestablishment of an independent Austrian state were undertaken before the end of the war. The Social Democratic elder statesman Karl Renner, the first chancellor of the First Republic, lobbied the Soviets to support an independent Austria. As a result of Renner's astute negotiations, the Soviets were the first among the Allies to get behind this idea. The goal of an independent Austria was made the explicit aim of the Allied Powers in the Moscow Declaration, signed on 30 October 1943 by the Soviet Union, Britain, and the United States, and later by France. The document declared the annexation of Austria by the National Socialists null and void. The *Anschluss* is explained as an unwanted military occupation by Nazi Germany, and the declaration expressly cast the Austrian people as powerless victims, "the first free country to fall victim to Hitlerite aggression."[1]

In 1945 Austria was divided into four zones of occupation under the control of the Allies, and the city of Vienna was similarly divided, with the first district preserved as an international zone. A provisional government was authorized, charged with the reestablishment of the Austrian state on the basis of the constitution of the First Republic. The Declaration of Independence of 27 April 1945 echoed the Moscow Declaration by inscribing into the founding documents of the newly formed Austrian nation the exoneration of Austria for its actions during the Second World War and defining the country as the first victim of German fascism. The reauthorized political parties—the Social Democratic Party (SPÖ), the Austrian People's Party (ÖVP), and the Communist Party (KPÖ)—were wholly in step with this version of events during (and beyond) the first parliamentary elections of November 1945. In 1946 the federal government published the *Rot-Weiss-Rot-Buch* (*Red-White-Red Book*), the aim of which was to highlight the role played by the Austrian resistance movement during the war. In this way Austrian leaders sought to create a wide gulf separating Austria's wartime experience from that of Nazi Germany, an opportunistic policy played to the advantage of the

Austrians with the occupiers. While the latter half of the Moscow Declaration did contain a hypothesis of joint responsibility, expressly assigning responsibility for the war to the Austrians for fighting alongside the Germans, Austrian leaders omitted any such expression of responsibility from the official government line. The *Rot-Weiss-Rot-Buch* states the victim theory in the strongest of terms:

> The Austrian population had from the start been opposed to the "Hitlerite war" except by those for whom the end of the war was the only possibility to shake off the Nazi yoke. ... Anyone seeking to give a correct and fair appraisal of the situation Austria found itself in right from the beginning of the occupation will have to admit that the blood tribute exacted from Austria in this war was nothing but an additional burden on a country which was already suffering under the heavy burden of occupation, and thus worse than in other occupied countries.[2]

With the early authorization of a provisional Austrian government, the Allies treated Austria more as a liberated nation than a vanquished one. This focus on an independent Austria did not, however, translate into a rapid withdrawal of the occupying powers or a singular focus on the reestablishment and reconstruction of the state. Austria remained under Allied occupation for ten years, and its fate was subject to the power politics of the emerging Cold War. World War II had ravaged Austria and destroyed its economy. Under occupation, the Western zones became recipients of Marshall Plan resources, but recovery was slow. The Soviets seized and dismantled much of Austrian industry, which had been developed by the Nazis. Suspicion of Soviet influence over the new government determined the approach of the Western powers toward Austria and persisted beyond the era of occupation into the Second Republic.

The de-Nazification of Austria was carried out in accordance with the National Socialist Law of 1947, a law of which large segments were dictated by the occupiers and only grudgingly accepted by the two major parties in Austria. Unlike in Germany, however, the responsibility for de-Nazification was placed in the hands of the provisional government and was therefore vulnerable to exploitation for political ends. By the 1948 election these parties were competing for the votes of reenfranchised former members of the Nazi Party; thus the will for a rigorous purge of former Nazis from political life was never asserted.[3] Karl Renner declared that just a small percentage of former National Socialist Party members had been steadfast believers and that the majority had simply given in to social and economic pressures. In 1946 approximately 90 percent of former party members were deemed "less incriminated" along these lines and granted amnesty. These exempted former Nazis were reinstated to their previous jobs and even compensated for the losses they suffered after 1945.[4] Within the two dominant parties and among the populace there was significant support for these amnesty measures and little enthusiasm for the difficult task of separating the followers from those really responsible for Nazi activities. In popular discourse, de-Nazification was frequently equated with Nazi repression.[5] As Brigitte Bailer has argued, the consequences of the far-reaching reintegration of the *Heimkehrer*, or former Nazis, into Austrian society went well beyond the outcome of the first postwar elections. This reintegration also prevented a thorough analysis of the Austrian experience under National Socialism, resulting in a condemnation of Nazism at only the most superficial level.[6]

There were very few Jews on hand in Austria after 1945 to protest this official and societal embrace of former Nazi Party members. By the end of the war the Jewish presence was all but erased from the Austrian landscape. Estimates of the Austrian Jewish population shortly after the war's end range from 8,000 to 11,000.[7] The Jewish population had been decimated by persecution, loss of property, forced exile, and the extermination camps. Surviving Austrian Jews who considered returning to Austria faced an inhospitable climate, initially the result of the desperate conditions created by the final two years of the war and subsequently, after recovery and rebuilding had progressed, because the new independent Austrian state consciously pursued exclusionary policies, employed exclusionary rhetoric, and fostered the tabooization of any discussions related to Austrian Jews of its recent past and present. As we shall see, in the Second Republic Jewish survivors represented an unwelcome reminder of a past that the new Austria was eager to forget.

The Second Republic

A measure of myth-making accompanies the founding of any nation, as shared stories about a people—what binds them together, where they have come from, and what they aspire to—form the core of a collective identity through which individuals come together behind a national idea. The Austrian Second Republic engaged from the start in a form of myth-making based on a particular—and especially narrow—conception of the recent past. The writer and critic Robert Menasse has expressed rather tersely what has come to be known as the founding myth of the Second Republic: "This republic was founded on an historic lie that Austria was exclusively the victim of Nazi aggression."[8] Today it is plain that this claim of victim status rests on a distortion of historical reality. This has been referred to as Austria's "existential lie," which aptly conveys a sense of its centrality in Austria's self-understanding.[9] The myth of Austrian victimhood was inscribed into the State Treaty of 15 May 1955, which established Austria as a democratic sovereign nation. From this treaty one can trace a direct line back to the Moscow Declaration of 1943, with the notable exception that as in the 1945 Declaration of Independence, the provision on joint responsibility, which had been included in the Moscow Declaration, had fallen away. In an era in which it was politically damaging to be associated with the losing side of the war, Austria's postwar leaders effectively switched sides, leaving Germany to shoulder responsibility for the war alone.[10] This posture was not challenged by the Allied Powers, who at the Moscow Conference, then again at Yalta, and in their dealings as occupiers with the Austrians, repeatedly gave tacit support to this view for their own political ends.

This "founding myth" was an extremely useful tool for Austria in the international arena, but it also played a key role in domestic affairs. A new nation needed to form a new national consciousness, and the victim myth proved to be a powerful instrument of integration. Again, this version of its recent history served to disassociate Austria from Germany, and perhaps for the first time in its long history, there was a significant drive to forge a distinctly Austrian identity. As Franz Mathis has demonstrated, Austria had not been the principal object of identification for the inhabitants of the western half of the Habsburg Empire, and those who did view themselves as Austrian, including some Austrian Jews, chiefly expressed a relationship to the Crown and not a more generalized sense of commonality.[11] The proposal to name the First Austrian Republic "*Deutschösterreich*" is suggestive of the limited attention devoted at that time to a distinctly Austrian identity. The climate after World War II was more favorable to the development of a more independent Austrian self-concept, and thus an Austrian national identity began to take shape in the immediate postwar period and the early years of the Second Republic.

One factor that certainly galvanized the Austrian people in the expression of a new collective identity was the end of the Allied occupation. The signing of the State Treaty was celebrated as the casting off of foreign domination, expressed symbolically in the refashioning of the familiar eagle, now clutching broken chains to represent Austria's liberation.[12] In different ways, both 1945 and 1955 were evoked as moments of liberation, first by the Allies and then from them, which, as Margarete Lamb-Faffelberger has noted, underscores the ambiguity of Austria's relationship to its past.[13] There is no dearth of evidence for this ambiguity. For example, one could look to the staging of Beethoven's *Fidelio* as the performance chosen to celebrate the reopening of the State Opera in 1955 as a celebration of freedom, while the simultaneous unwillingness to de-Nazify the opera and philharmonic and the failure to encourage Jewish musicians who had lost their positions in the orchestra to return after the war conveyed quite a different message. Hella Pick has pointed to the irony of the choice of conductor for this 1955 gala: Karl Böhm, director of the philharmonic during the final years of the war. In a performance cast as a celebration of Austrian independence, "one of the people who had embraced the cultural *Anschluss* with Hitler's Reich was acting the role of master of ceremonies."[14]

A particular strand of the claim to victimhood that also fostered a sense of national community was the instrumentalization of the suffering of the Austrian populace during the final years of the war. This strategy, which was inscribed in the

Rot-Weiss-Rot-Buch by the political elite, made every Austrian a victim, amounting to a leveling of the suffering of those persecuted under National Socialism. In order to bolster the sense of an Austrian community bonded together through common suffering a taboo was erected against the discussion of any particular forms of suffering that might compete with a focus on the deprivations and losses suffered by the general population.

The interpretation of events from 1938 to 1945, on which the new Austrian national identity rested, required the construction and enforcement of a number of taboo topics. Unacceptable subjects included the approval of Austria's annexation by Nazi Germany among a wide segment of the Austrian populace; the espousal of National Socialism by Austrian citizens; the extent of the identification by Austrian soldiers with the German *Wehrmacht;* crimes against Jews, other minorities, and political opponents of the Nazis; and participation by Austrians in war crimes.[15] As Ruth Beckermann has noted, whereas West Germany undertook an extensive examination of the Nazi years and the Holocaust as an integral part of its postwar development, the rule in Austria was "*Hände weg von dem heißen Eisen*" (Hands off this hot potato).[16]

In the name of stabilization, reconciliation, and healing from the trauma of war, the Second Republic availed itself of this catalog of taboos and denial that set the tone for postwar Austrian politics, society, and culture. Anton Pelinka has written, "Taboos and other self-deceptions have an ambivalent protective function. They cover painful wounds and make healing possible though a ritualized banning of contact, especially a banning of discussion. However, this function of taboos is ... effective only for a limited time. There is a point when the healing process must be completed."[17] The leadership of the Second Republic was to prove remarkably adept at drawing out this "healing process," and it would largely be the work of the next generation to break these taboos and undertake a critical examination of a chapter that had been effectively bracketed from the national history.

The protracted nature of the ban on discussion of Austria's immediate past was due in part to the development of a political culture that supported such taboos and narrow framing of history. With the focus on stabilization and reconstruction, the Second Republic ushered in an era of consensus politics during which the two major parties shared power and tacitly agreed not to ruffle each other's feathers. Under the system of proportional governance—the *Proporz* system—the SPÖ and ÖVP divvied up public offices both large and small to the effect that, as Pelinka has suggested, the postwar period was dominated not by a political market, but by a permanent monopoly of power.[18] In this era of consociational democracy, with a mutually sustaining consensus among the political elites, the two major established parties collaborated to rehabilitate former Nazis, respect each other's reigning taboos, and refrain from challenging each other on politically sensitive issues.

The effect of the taboos and denials, the silence and cultivation of forgetting, and the myth-making and historical revisionism was a process Ruth Beckermann has described as *"die Irrealisierung des Nazismus"* (rendering Nazism unreal).[19] This process is not identical with forgetting or denial but rather is a means by which to justify past behavior in a manner that makes it possible to get over the past (*fertig werden*) without ever truly coming to terms with it (*auseinandersetzen*): "This rendering unreal means to justify immoral modes of conduct by the exceptional situation of the war and thus—as though it had never it had never taken place—to deny the necessity of the consequences."[20] This is the mechanism that made it possible for an Austrian who had denounced a neighbor as a Jew to greet him upon his return as though nothing had ever happened, Beckermann explains: "He lives in such a distorted reality, that he cannot even imagine that the Jew remembers it all indeed and quite precisely."[21]

All of these tendencies, inscribed as they were into the framing documents of the Second Republic and mobilized in the name of a homogeneous national community, persisted far beyond the initial postwar period of recovery and reconstruction. The highly acclaimed Kreisky era of the Second Republic—the period from 1970 to 1983 during which the Social Democrat Bruno Kreisky served as chancellor—witnessed the continued exploitation of the victim myth in the service of increasing Austria's status in the international community. In the domestic arena, Kreisky continued to focus on nation-building and national reconciliation. Robert Wistrich describes the Kreisky era as synonymous with prosperity, full employment, a liberal cultural climate, and a progressive approach to social problems—all positive developments that fostered a deeper sense of Austrian patriotism and national identity.[22] Kreisky had little interest in threatening this domestic sense of well-being or the rise of Austria's star in the international arena by staging a difficult confrontation with Austria's past. A number of scholars have suggested that Kreisky's Jewish background paradoxically fostered his avoidance of an examination of the past. Hella Pick writes of Kreisky, "As a Jew who was never comfortable in that identity, he was willing to compromise to great lengths in order to prove to himself, as much as to others, that his first and only public loyalty was to Austria."[23] Certainly the chancellor's Jewish identity served to shield the Austrians from the compulsion to take up this onerous task.

Robert Wistrich characterizes Kreisky's background as one of the paradoxes of his career.[24] Raised in a cosmopolitan, bourgeois Jewish milieu, Kreisky viewed himself as highly assimilated and without a religious affiliation. His view of Judaism and Jewishness seem to have been shaped by his political involvement with the Left. He espoused a view of Judaism common within the Left, which viewed it as a relic of the past; according to this view, the Jews were an ethno-religious group that no longer shared any significant characteristics and were bound together merely by the negative force of anti-Semitism. Although anti-Semitism found many forms of powerful expression during Kreisky's youth and rise to political prominence, he did not view himself as having suffered personally from anti-Semitic discrimination or hostility. Kreisky always characterized the forced emigration of his family in 1938 as stemming from their Socialist activism, not their Jewish background. Wistrich suggests that Kreisky's absence from Austria during the years of Nazi rule may have made it easier for him to personally repress memory of the persecution of Austrian Jews, even though he lost members of his family in the Holocaust.[25] In any event, because of his passionate focus on advancing Austrian legitimacy, Kreisky steered clear of the events from 1938 to 1945, all of which were, according to Wistrich, "wholly antithetical and counterproductive to his own life strategy."[26] Kreisky's unwillingness to confront the past undoubtedly delayed Austria's day of reckoning, which ultimately came only as the result of international pressure in response to Kurt Waldheim's election as president. In large measure, Kreisky's views were a reflection of the society he governed.

Austrian Jews and the Second Republic

Having mapped out the trajectory of and the factors that determined Austria's relationship to the recent past, it remains to reconstruct what this meant for Austria's treatment of those Jews who survived the war and returned to Austria. The central issue that shaped Austria's dealing with returning Jewish émigrés was the myth of Austria's victimhood. In a culture in which the general Austrian population sought to cast itself as a victim of an unwanted military takeover by the National Socialist Germans, the presence of Jews represented a problem in the rival claim to victimhood they could legitimately assert. As outlined above, Austrian authorities unsurprisingly did little to encourage exiled Austrian Jews to return. As Austria looked to establish a self-image as the antithesis of an imported Nazi state supported by an ideology of racial hierarchy, the presence of Jews with a keen memory of the experience of the *Anschluss* was awkward. With the claim that the annexation of Austria by Germany was an act of foreign aggression undesired by the populace, it was difficult to explain not only the cheering crowds that greeted the arrival of the German troops, but the spontaneous pogroms against Jews undertaken by the indigenous population in 1938.[27]

Various means were adopted to create an inhospitable climate for Jews considering return to Austria. Citizenship was not automatically restored but instead required Jews to renounce any other citizenship they may have acquired in the interim. This was often a psychological obstacle as well as a bureaucratic one, as Jewish exiles had often made considerable progress in integrating themselves into their new nations and felt loyalty to the states that had taken them in. The return to a prewar professional or social status was often very difficult. And, significantly, no high-ranking government official ever issued a single call for the remigration of surviving Jews. As Robert Knight has noted, "The methods adopted for keeping the Jews away were no less effective for being informal."[28]

Yet it would have run counter to Austria's attempt to reinsert itself into the community of "civilized nations" had they appeared to be discriminating against Jews overtly. Accordingly, the discrimination aimed at returning Jews was couched in the language of equality.[29] Jews were denied any special concessions because, it was said, this would entail the privileging of one race over another. In effect, the Jews seeking compensation and official assistance in reestablishing themselves within Austrian society were equated with their Nazi persecutors as perpetuating race-based distinctions that were not desired in the new Austria. Chancellor Leopold Figl's address to the Palestine Committee may be understood in this light:

> It is … clear that in restricting rights no distinctions can be made on the grounds of belief or race among citizens of the state. All Austrians have to be reinstated to their former rights without distinction. We wish only to be Austrians, irrespective of what religion we belong to. We have all suffered. I agreed that the solidarity of the nation [Volk] should apply even-handedly for everyone who returns from the camps and prisons. They are Austrians like all of us. The Jews, too, of course. If the Jews who emigrated return, they will be just as welcome as all other Austrians. They have the same right to be reinstated to their former right s as all the others.[30]

The Jews were thus free to return as Austrians, but not as Jews. The principle of equal rights for all was in this way refashioned into a tool to impose conditions on Jewish return, to prevent returning Jewish émigrés from making claims to restitution by framing those claims in terms of special Jewish privilege. As Knight succinctly states, the principle of equality before the law was in practice transformed into a tactical weapon.[31]

In light of this inhospitable climate, it is not surprising that the number of survivors who opted to return was small and that the experience of return was challenging and painful. The return to Austria entailed difficult encounters with authorities as well as the mainstream population. It frequently unfolded as a heartbreaking process by which exiled Jews came to recognize that return was not even the operative concept, for the Austria to which they returned was fundamentally changed, familiar yet profoundly alienating.

The motivations of those who took this path were of course mixed and often difficult to pinpoint. Jewish returnees may have been principally motivated by either political or personal concerns. In the case of the generation of those who were children during the war or were born in exile, the decision to return was made by the parents. The first to return were those who were politically motivated, Social Democrats and Communists seeking to take part in the rebuilding of the Austrian nation. This remigration began as early as 1945 and was essentially complete by 1947. By contrast, those who returned primarily for personal reasons tended to return in the late 1940s and early 1950s.[32]

The experience of exile was a key factor in the decision to return, as those who struggled the most to reestablish themselves in the country of exile were more likely to contemplate going back to Austria. The ability to integrate into the host country depended to a great extent on where and under what conditions exile occurred. Additionally, certain preconditions played a significant role, including the professional background of the exile, language ability, gender, and the existence of a social network.[33]

Homesickness was experienced in various ways by Austrian Jewish exiles. When most pronounced, homesickness contributed to an inability to develop a feeling of belonging and make connections to the culture and mentality of the new nation. Homesickness tended to express a longing that was more cultural than national, and for many Austrian Jews, the object of longing was specifically the cultural milieu of Vienna. The exiled writer Jean Améry coined the term *"Entborgenheit"* (the absence of a sense of security) to describe the homesickness of exiles. Améry powerfully expressed the way the exile's loss of *Heimat* encompassed a severing of connections to the Austrian community and suggested that this alienation from one's native surroundings and compatriots brought about a profound self-alienation in the exiled individual. He wrote, "I was a person who could no longer say 'we' and who therefore said 'I' merely out of habit, but not with the feeling of full possession of my self."[34] For Améry this self-alienation was irreversible, the loss of *Heimat* irreparable. The lesson of the Holocaust was of the impossibility of return. Améry perceived the loss of *Heimat* as total, in that the exile not only experienced an unbridgeable gulf separating him from the homeland, but even the memory of the past ceased to belong to him. He referred to the painful realization that the Jew's relationship to Austria and its people was illusory. He described what he called the *Lebensmißverständnis* (existential misunderstanding) of Austrian Jews: "We, however, had not lost our country, but had to realize that it had never been ours. For us, whatever was linked with this land and its people was an existential misunderstanding."[35]

The confrontation with the cruel insight that all assimilatory hopes were in vain and that any perceived sense of belonging rested on a fundamental misreading of the relations between Jews and non-Jews in Austria had a tragic outcome for Améry, who committed suicide in Salzburg, in 1978.[36] His sense of the inextricability of *Heimat* from a concept of selfhood was, however, widely shared by Austrian Jews who did seek to return, who wanted to reconnect to *Heimat* and reformulate a sense of identity. Unfortunately, as Jacqueline Vansant has demonstrated in her work on the memoirs of returnees, many would also come to their own experience of Améry's "existential misunderstanding," as their hopes for reconnecting to *Heimat* and to a prewar identity were frustrated.

The Austrian populace supported the exclusionary stance of the government and helped to create a discriminatory culture through the adoption of radically different discourses to refer to returning Jews and to former Nazis, prisoners of war, and their families. Many returning refugees spoke of a "gulf of sensibility" separating them from non-Jewish Austrian society.[37] Hilde Spiel wrote of her return: "However much I grow into the Austrian milieu later in life, this starting position after the lost-won war creates a gulf between me and the other citizens that is never to close."[38] Egon Schwarz described how Jews returning from exile were at times greeted with the attitude that they had been the lucky ones, living in the safety of New York while the Viennese suffered bombing attacks and the deprivations of war.[39] Vansant has detailed how the attempt to rejoin Austrian society, to reintegrate oneself into a nation that had once been home, could bring about a renewed loss of *Heimat* rather than its recovery.[40] For these returning Jews alienation was not solely located in the past—in their experiences of the Nazi years—but also surfaced sometimes as a response to the challenges of adjusting to an Austria very different from the one they had left and one that was inhospitable in unexpected ways.

There were several ways in which to relate to this changed Austria. Returnees could be ambivalent in their relationship to the nation and Austrian society; they could have a primarily positive relationship, as did the writer and critic Hans Weigel, or a predominantly negative one. Christoph Reinprecht has characterized these possibilities as a sliding scale of "*Wieder-Heimischwerden-Könnens*" (the ability to make oneself at home again).[41] The most prevalent reaction was ambivalence, a simultaneous feeling of familiarity, even belonging, alongside a feeling of isolation stemming from a perceived distance between Jews and non-Jews in postwar Austria's daily life. The experience of return was in large measure determined by expectations. The hope that the return to Austria would bring about a resumption of "normal life" was frequently dashed, and the related expectation that a returning Austrian Jew could reconnect to a prewar concept of identity proved very difficult to realize. The new reality of the Second Republic scarcely permitted this. Moreover, the effects of 1938 to 1945 on Jewish identity could not be erased.

Jewish Identity after 1945

As I have discussed, the rise of the Nazis within Austria and the escalation of anti-Semitism during the 1930s created a climate in which the range of possibilities for identity creation by Austrian Jews was gradually constricted to the point of a single, one-dimensional, and externally imposed identification as Jew. Under the Nazis all of the constituent elements of identity, such as gender, age, class, professional background, and political orientation, were stripped away, reducing identity for Jews to the sole, overdetermined category of ethnic identity. The experiences of terror, torture, loss, and exile intensified this condensation of identity imposed by the Nazis. A collective Jewish identity was forged from the experience of suffering and loss so that after Auschwitz, identification as a Jew was not a choice freely undertaken but an ethical imperative. The disappearance of a prewar identity necessitated the adoption of a new one, but not surprisingly, the conditions of war and the Nazi terror, as well as the traumatic experiences of exile, were not favorable to making much headway in this regard. The experience of return also demanded a fundamental reorientation. Austrian Jewish returnees were forced to undertake this work of rebuilding an identity under very challenging conditions. Returning Jews were stigmatized as Jews by mainstream Austrian society, and this stigmatized Jewish identity created a distance between Jews and non-Jews that was inherited by successive generations.

One factor that distinguishes this period from the other eras considered in this study is the isolation experienced by Jewish returnees. In returning to Vienna, Jews were not returning to a Viennese Jewish community, because that community had been destroyed. The cultural conditions that had given shape to Jewish life before the war were gone, and the reconstitution of a visible, vital Jewish community would require decades. As Chancellor Figl's remarks made clear, Jews who wished to return were expected to do so as Austrians, not as Jews. There was no arena for Jews to associate as a group in the postwar period, and thus the conflicts described here were experienced on an individual basis. According to Reinprecht, the returnees "came back as isolated, scattered individuals and had to orient themselves anew as isolated individuals."[42]

Returning Austrian Jewish writers experienced this sense of alienation and isolation both personally and professionally. Their texts and memoirs express again and again the sense of being a stranger on familiar ground. This alienation from mainstream Austrian society was, however, not only acutely painful but also productive. These estranged positions informed the work of postwar Jewish writers and helped them to give voice to a critique of the conditions that created it. As we shall see, Austrian society took a long time to arrive at a position at which it was ready to engage with this criticism. The work of these writers was nevertheless critical in breaking through the reigning taboos of the postwar period, and they established a basis upon which a subsequent, more extensive critique of the mechanisms of denial, repression, and exclusion would be founded.

Ilse Aichinger

Each experience of return considered in this study is unique. Every writer discussed here approached the decision differently, and the timing of the return, as well as the writers' ongoing relationships to the countries that had taken them in, all had a significant impact on their reentry into Austrian society. The way each writer chose to write about their recent past also shaped their ability to reinsert themselves into the Austrian literary scene. Ilse Aichinger's case is marked by an exceptionally late departure and return. Aichinger actually stayed in Vienna during the war, surviving as a *"Mischling."* She began her writing career in the city at the end of the war, but moved abroad in the early 1950s—not long after Friedrich Torberg, for example, had returned to Vienna from exile in the United States—and she stayed outside Austria for decades. Aichinger returned to Vienna only in 1988. While her personal experience does not entail the dynamic of exile and return, Aichinger's writing, in early as well as later texts, shares the perspective of alienation and isolation that runs as a common thread in the writing of Austrian Jewish writers during and after exile. In many ways Aichinger was an outsider within the postwar Austrian literary scene. Her writing style differed sharply from her contemporaries, and she began to thematize the persecution of Jews by Austrians and Germans in her writing as early as 1945. Throughout her career, Aichinger's work always seemed to stem from the margins, which for her clearly represented a productive place from which to work.

Ilse Aichinger was born in Vienna, along with a twin sister, Helga, in 1921. Her mother, Bertha Kremer Aichinger, was a physician from a Jewish background. Her father, Ludwig Aichinger, was a non-Jewish teacher. Aichinger was raised Catholic, living first in Linz and then Vienna. Her father divorced her mother and left the family to avoid having his career hampered by his wife's Jewish heritage. After this, Ilse moved with her mother and sister to Vienna, where she lived with her grandmother and attended a number of boarding schools. After the *Anschluss,* Aichinger's mother could no longer practice medicine, but she was not interred because she was the guardian of her children, who were considered by the Nazis *"Michlinge 1. Grades."* Ilse was able to complete her secondary education, attaining the *Matura* in 1939; however, she was barred from university study, and both she and her mother were conscripted into forced labor. Her sister Helga fled to England in 1939, with one of the last *Kindertransporte,* but the rest of the family was unable to follow. Bertha Aichinger survived the war in Vienna, but her mother and younger siblings were killed in concentration camps.

After the war, Aichinger enrolled in medical school at the University of Vienna. She broke off her studies after five semesters, however, in order to pursue a literary career. Her first publication, *Das vierte Tor (The Fourth Gate),* which appeared in September 1945, was the first Austrian text to depict the concentration camps. Aichinger's novel *Die größere Hoffnung (Herod's Children,* 1948) met with a mixed reception, as it dealt with the persecution of the Jews, a subject the Austrians were little inclined to examine in the immediate postwar years. The novel did, however, establish Aichinger as a major figure in the post-1945 literary scene.

From 1949–50 Aichinger worked as an editor for the Viennese publishing house Bermann-Fischer. She traveled to England to visit her sister, Helga Michie, who had become an English-language writer. Aichinger went to Ulm to work with Inge Scholl on the establishment of a design school and also held a position as an editor for the Fischer publishing house. In 1951, she was invited to appear with the *Gruppe 47*, where she read her short story "Der Gefesselte" ("The Bound Man"). The following year she received that group's prize for *Spiegelgeschichte* (*Mirror Story*), as well as the Austrian State Prize for the Encouragement of Literature. Throughout her career she received a number of significant literary honors, including the Trakl Prize, the Franz Kafka Prize, and the Nelly Sachs Prize. In her work of the 1960s Aichinger would turn to a depiction of the preoccupations of the immediate postwar years, examining the enduring effects of the war on Austrian society.[43] Aichinger married the poet Günter Eich in 1953. The couple traveled widely and lived with their two children in a number of southern German towns until Eich's death in 1972. In 1988 Aichinger moved to Vienna. Her writing career was interspersed with several substantial pauses. At the end of the 1990s she resumed writing, and in 2000, after a fourteen-year pause, her autobiographical work *Film und Verhängnis* (*Film and Catastrophe*) appeared.

In many respects Aichinger's early fiction thematizing the war, the persecution of Jews in daily life during the Nazi period, and the extermination in the death camps was presented to an Austrian public ill prepared and little inclined to receive it. The impact of *Die größere Hoffnung* would chiefly be felt many years after its initial publication. The year of its appearance, 1948, was highly significant in that a number of significant texts dealing with the Holocaust appeared in Vienna: alongside Aichinger's novel there was also Celan's poem "Todesfuge" ("Death Fugue"), which appeared in the volume *Der Sand aus den Urnen* (*The Sand from the Urns*), as well as Friedrich Torberg's *Hier bin ich, mein Vater* (*Here I Am, My Father*), written in American exile. Neither Torberg's traditional narrative nor Aichinger's more experimental text initially found an echo among the critics or a popular audience. These texts, however, were vitally important with regard to future developments in post-1945 Austrian literature. Ready or not, Austrian readers were confronted with literature depicting Austria's treatment of its Jewish population. Once launched with these initial works, this topos secured a place within Austrian literature that would persist over decades and grow in significance. Writers were among the first in the nation to call attention to and begin to dismantle the prohibition on dealing with the Austrian experience under Nazism. As Bernhard Fetz has noted, "It was Austrian literature that catalyzed, provoked, even forced a confrontation with the past when politics and society had failed or were reluctant to do so."[44] This development would take a generation to coalesce, but the subsequent writers that pushed it forward made frequent reference to the writings of this survivor generation. Peter Härtling has referred to Aichinger's novel as "a book that waits patiently for us."[45] A generation later, the text found a readership that was not large, but significant.

If Aichinger was a forerunner of subsequent generations of post-Holocaust writers, she was an outsider in the early postwar period, not only with respect to mainstream Austrian society, but even among other writers. In light of the different experience of war in Austria and Germany, Austrian postwar literature exhibited a set of characteristics that differed from the literary developments of either of the two Germanies. Austrian literature tended to reflect the trauma of the final years of the war, the common feeling of having suffered disproportionately the hardships and deprivations of war. Aichinger, of course, had direct personal experience with National Socialist persecution. Yet her early work reflects a surprising degree of optimism, giving her a critical, yet hopeful, stance that set her apart from other Austrian writers. Her approach to language separates her from the general tendencies of German postwar writing as well, as she favored a richly expressive figurative language rather than the sparing linguistic minimalism of writers like Heinrich Böll and Wolfgang Borchert. As Dagmar Lorenz has explained, Aichinger's political engagement differed from such writers as well, as she rejected participation in any particular political movement and expressed her political concerns only obliquely in her writing. Lorenz sees in her work a "positive anarchy" aimed at unrestricted freedom for the individual, unconditional tolerance toward others, and a sweeping universal change that could not be channeled into any particular reforms.[46]

Aichinger's novel *Die größere Hoffnung* relates an experience of war that is not far removed from that of the author and centers on a protagonist who shares her background and gender. Nonetheless, as Lorenz insists on the first page of her Aichinger study, the work is not strictly autobiographical. While the text sometimes relates closely to experiences of Aichinger's life, the events related in the novel serve as points of departure into broader inquiries with which the author is concerned rather than as the primary focus of the narrative. She is neither concerned with presenting a full account of her own past nor with the kind of documentary-style rendering of objective events of recent history that characterizes other postwar writing. Even though she depicts the persecution of the Jews, memorialization is not the operative motivation underlying her work. This first novel is not an admonition to "never forget" but is an examination of individual and collective consciousness.

Through her young protagonist, Ellen, a young girl of eleven or twelve from a mixed Jewish and Catholic background like her own, Aichinger explores Jewish identity as the product of a process imposed from without. As the offspring of a Jewish mother and non-Jewish father, Ellen finds herself situated between the two traditions. In her own imagination the two traditions coexist and at times merge without any problems, but no such harmonious synthesis is permitted in Nazi-occupied Austria. Ellen arrives at one of the first substantive experiences of her own Jewish identity by being labeled a Jew by non-Jewish children and being excluded from their company. She then seeks to join a group of Jewish children who at first also view her with suspicion. She persists until she is accepted by this group, choosing to identify with the persecuted as a more palatable choice than aligning herself with the persecutors.[47] Ellen's initial experience of Jewishness is thus crucially bound up with a personal experience of anti-Semitism.

The novel does not seek to provide a photographic rendering of the past. There is vivid detail of certain aspects of daily life under National Socialism, but the events, people, and places of the past are transformed through the consciousness of a child. The setting of the story, for example, is most likely Vienna, but the narrative is not grounded in the concrete space of the city. At the level of the plot, Ellen and her friends are depicted as alternately evading and clashing with the oppressive forces of Nazi rule. As we experience Ellen's thoughts, dreams, and fantasies alongside the children's spontaneous interactions through their play, the inner processes come to light through which Ellen is able to transcend an unbearable reality. Tanja Hetzer has described the "intrusion of the catastrophe" as a recurring leitmotif in narratives told from the perspective of the victim.[48] While this often refers to a singular, life-changing event in the life of a fictional character or memoir writer, such as the rise of Hitler, the *Anschluss*, emigration, or deportation, in Aichinger's novel the catastrophe looms as a more obtuse, ever-present threat from which there are moments of respite but always expectations of recurrence and intensification of danger.

Die größere Hoffnung moves between the imaginative world of the children's play and the frequent, sudden intrusion of reality and the threats it carries for them. When Ellen chooses to don the yellow star that as a "*Mischling*" she is not obligated to wear, she does so playfully, viewing the star as a kind of ornament all the more alluring because she is not its intended wearer. This transformation of the star's symbolic meaning cannot be sustained, of course, once she steps out into the social world, where in a local bakery she encounters the full force of the prejudice and discrimination the star unleashes in the majority population. The outside world again intrudes into the children's existence as a literal threat when an adult man they know, one who had promised to warn them of any serious developments, joins them in their staging of a Nativity play, secretly attempting to detain the children in their play until the arrival of the transport for their deportation. Klaus Kastberger emphasizes the way in which this play functions as a means of flouting reality for the children, seeing in the depiction of the children's play a "firm ludic self-presence," or a foregrounding of the children's awareness of play alongside the knowledge that things could become deadly serious at any time.[49] The children understand that just as they create their own games to make their lives bearable, they are also pawns in a game that is beyond their control:

"Keep playing!"
"What play do you mean?"
"The one we're playing or the one that's being played with us?"[50]

The realization of the fragility of their autonomous space of play is difficult. The children resolutely play on, even as they sense the encroachment of the larger game upon their own.

But what's being played with us is only transformed through pain into what we are playing. They found themselves in the middle of the transformation, clearly sensed the fumes of the rags on their bodies and even more strongly the glass of the Christmas tree garlands concealed around their hips and necks. The two plays began already to flow into each other and wove themselves inextricably into a new one.[51]

The world the children create through their play is not a means of escape from reality but an alternative with which they continually confront reality in act of resistance and refusal.

Aichinger's novel presents a variety of Jewish fates stemming from the wartime persecution of Jews. Given Aichinger's portrayal of the arbitrariness of the system that oppresses the Jews, it is fitting that none of the few paths open to Jews in these grave circumstances is really privileged over the others. On one hand, the grandmother's suicide results from a false assumption—we learn that the footsteps in the corridor were not those of the soldiers coming to carry her off to the camps but instead belonged to a deserted soldier—yet her decision is freely chosen, an assertion of her own will against a fate determined by her oppressors. Dagmar Lorenz describes the characters of Julia and Anna as representing two divergent fates, emigration and deportation to the extermination camps. While Julia's refusal to wear the yellow star forces her withdrawal from society, first by never leaving her room and then by fleeing the country, Anna is presented as choosing not to deny her Jewish identity, as she determinedly polishes her star until it gleams.

The Jewish children wait in vain in the first chapter for a miracle to redeem them in the eyes of the dominant society, and they have little power over the incursion of the adult world into their own, yet their play represents a powerful tool for survival. In Ellen we see the power of this play to open up an internal world that liberates her from the real world of persecution, suffering, and loss. Her death by an exploding grenade near the end of the war does not negate the transcendence Ellen has realized through her own imaginative response to the world around her. Aichinger's novel performs what Ellen also accomplishes, the transformation of historic, quotidian, lived reality into a poetic one.

In the chapter that introduces us to Ellen, Aichinger employs the cipher of the visa to indicate the means by which she must face the obstacles to her freedom. The consul cannot give her the visa she seeks but instead offers an evasive answer that nonetheless contains a simple truth: "Whoever doesn't grant himself the visa can travel around the whole world and yet never cross over. Whoever doesn't grant himself the visa remains trapped forever. Only those who give themselves a visa become free."[52] Ellen creates and signs her own visa, authorizing herself to claim her own freedom.

It appears incongruous that the author who posits the possibility of transcendence in a novel of surprising optimism would, within the space of a few years, issue a general summons to the citizens of the postwar world to a mistrust of the self in the important text "Aufruf zum Misstrauen" ("A Summons to Mistrust"). Perhaps the key to the discrepancy between the admonition given to Ellen to forge her own way and claim her own freedom and this subsequent call to mistrust our intentions, our thoughts, our articulations of self, lies in the youth of the fictional character. In an adult world fully corrupted by ideology, prejudice, and violence, Ellen and the Jewish children of the text offer up their own reality in an act of resistance. In the latter essay Aichinger rails against any complacent assumption that the corrupted world belongs only to the past. She evokes the horrors of the war in the opening sentences of the essay in order to underscore the jarring, radical nature of what she is suggesting: "Is it not the explosive charge that blows the bridges between nations up into the air, this terrible mistrust, is it not the cruel hand that scatters the good of this world into the ocean, that overshadows mankind's gaze and, encroaching on it, obscures it?"[53] Was a lack of trust not the source of the catastrophic events of recent years? Here Aichinger makes clear that we must radically redirect our mistrust, that the appropriate object of our mistrust must be our own selves. She protests, "Barely have we learned to say a stammering 'I' when we have already begun once again to emphasize it. Barely have we dared to once again say 'you' when we have already misused it."[54] Aichinger's text is a protest against the self-assured, unreflective quality of postwar efforts aimed at reconstruction and reconciliation that would justify selective memory of the past. She denies the possibility of a nostalgic turn to a "simpler time":

> Didn't you say that you would have preferred living in the past century? It was a very elegant and rational century. Whoever had a full stomach and a white shirt had trust in himself. One praised its reason, its kindness, its humanity. And one put up a thousand safety measures to protect oneself against those who were dirty, ragged, and starved.[55]

In this elegant and presentable past, we ignored the dangers we were cultivating, she suggests, and we could all too easily repeat this mistake.

This essay stems from a perspective that set Aichinger at odds with postwar Austrian society. In the volume *Kurzschlüsse* (*Short Circuits*), Aichinger describes the distanced perspective she has attained as a result of living through the Nazi terror, referring to her "*Sicht der Entfremdung*" (view of alienation).[56] Throughout her literary career Aichinger embraced this alienated perspective and increasingly sought an approach to language commensurate with this experience of alienation. The rich figurative language of *Die Größere Hoffnung* gave way over time to a literal and negative use of language as she aimed at achieving a correspondence between her use of language and her perception of reality. She chose not to rely on familiar literary devices and distanced herself from models that might have appealed to her.

In the text "Meine Sprache und Ich" ("My Language and I"), first published in 1968, Aichinger formulates her relationship to language. She writes, "My language is one that tends towards foreign words. I look for them, I fetch them from far away. But it is a small language. It doesn't reach very far. Around and around, around me and so on. We move ahead, against our will."[57] For Sigrid Schmid-Bortenschlager this is a deterritorialized view of language in line with Deleuze and Guattari's conception of minor literature.[58] Aichinger denies the conventional meanings of words, creating her own nonreferential language. As Schmid-Bortenschlager makes clear, Aichinger's transformation of language is subtle: "Departing from clear banal statements, her texts lead imperceptibly into a completely different linguistic world, in which the everyday certainties that are the basis of our lives are no longer a given, in which even sharks can give comfort, as [we see] already in *Die grössere Hoffnung.*"[59]

Aichinger's alienated perspective, born of the traumatic experiences of the war and the Holocaust, gives rise to an alienated language, evoked in her reference to her preference for "foreign" words. All words become "foreign" as she strips away the customary set of meanings and associations, rejecting common language as a social construct in order to convey something else. This something else, as suggested by her imagery of a language closely encircling her, is intensely personal. As Hans Wolfschütz has suggested, Aichinger "withdraws her language from public commerce and retires into the distance of a remote sphere all her own."[60] While critics have placed Aichinger within an Austrian tradition of *Sprachkritik,* her encounter with the limits of language seems to be idiosyncratic in nature and not necessarily heavily indebted to Wittgenstein or Hofmannsthal. Certainly Wittgenstein's conclusion that "What we cannot speak about we must pass over in silence" was antithetical to a writer such as Aichinger, who conceived of "*Poetik des Schweigens*" (poetics of silence) as a positive alternative to silence.

Even as she questions the validity of all attempts to express oneself or to express reality in language, Aichinger envisioned in her transformation of language the capacity for its revitalization. In a 1975 interview that appeared in *Die Presse,* Aichinger commented, "Maybe I see my task as an author in freeing language from its communicative nature and restoring it to itself in such a way that it can communicate again."[61] Within the Austrian tradition of *Sprachkritik,* Aichinger may in fact be closest to Elfriede Jelinek, who similarly undertakes to remove language from the sphere of everyday social conversations—and in Jelinek's case, commercial exchanges—in order to endow it with new meaning. Wolfschütz's characterization of Aichinger's withdrawal of language from a public to a private realm would apply equally to Jelinek. Certainly the two writers are quite similar in placing extraordinary demands on the reader to first abandon the usual processes of making meaning and only then attempt to follow them as they seek to communicate a new meaning to the reader. Both supply few clues to the reader who attempts to negotiate their strategies of withholding and withdrawal to arrive at the communication their works ultimately strive for. Where they differ perhaps is not only in terms of tone, but also motivation. While they both undertake a Kraussian campaign against what they view as debased language, Jelinek's impulse is a radical one of postmodern linguistic play and experimentation; she has spoken of her desire to "smash language, to strip it to the bone, to tear the last bits of truth out of it, to rip open its chest."[62] Aichinger's approach to language, by contrast, is ultimately redemptive, smashing only in order to rebuild.

Aichinger's alienated perspective is also evident in her relationship to postwar Vienna. She often eschews the concrete setting of Vienna for her works, but even in those texts in which she clearly depicts a particular, identifiable area of the urban Viennese environment, the city of her writing is more imagined than observed, described, or remembered. The concrete space of the Judengasse or the Renngasse is transformed into an imagined space that is not immediately accessible to the reader. As Joanna Ratych has noted of Aichinger's work, "So-called realities are subjected to an estrangement process which makes them part and parcel of that other reality, the highly personalized world view of Ilse Aichinger."[63] In the avoidance of referential language, Aichinger's treatment of Vienna is like other thematic aspects of her writing. The title of Aichinger's 1987 work *Kleist, Moos, Fasane* (*Kleist, Moss, Pheasants*) exemplifies the contradictory nature of texts that are firmly grounded in a specific concrete space and yet resist such a clear reading. Kleist, Moos, and Fasane are three streets in Vienna's third district, in close proximity to her grandmother's home, whose kitchen is the central focus of the work. The streets connect the kitchen to the cityscape and to Aichinger's autobiography, but, significantly, Aichinger performed a distancing move. The three streets are not successive, as Aichinger has omitted the Bahngasse. Moreover, a map of the third district reveals no Moosgasse, only a Mohsstrasse.[64] Any reader seeking to gain a foothold is perplexed—is this an identifiable Viennese neighborhood or a creation of the author? Are these street names referential or no longer so?

This tendency to defamilarize the familiar and to foreground an alienated perspective is common both to Aichinger's later work and her writing of the early postwar years. In the text "Wo ich wohne" ("Where I Live"), part of the collection *Der Gefesselte,* written between 1948 and 1952, this alienated perspective is brought to bear on the most intimate and personal space, the private apartment. Even this space reveals itself to be untrustworthy; while the narrator is out for the evening, her apartment slips from the fourth to the third floor. This slippage continues until she finds herself living in the basement, while the other tenants of the building carry on as though nothing unusual has occurred. The narrator appears not to be surprised that her neighbors fail to comment on or ask about the situation; no enlightenment is expected from those around her, and, indeed, the narrator anticipates hostility in keeping with her diminished status as one who now resides in the basement. When she imagines conversations with the custodian or with fellow neighbors, their exchanges reflect only misunderstanding and miscommunication.

The narrator identifies thoroughly with her sinking dwelling, as both she and her apartment have come down in the world. She begins to fear she will sink all the way down into the canal beneath the city streets: "I ask myself what it will be like when I will live in the canal. Because I am gradually getting used to this thought."[65] Her fears quickly give way to a resigned acceptance of this fate: "It would be pointless to be afraid of the vapors of the canal, since then I would have to start to be afraid of the fires within the earth—there is too much I would have to be afraid of." The text reflects a position of extreme alienation and isolation, as the narrator imagines her own disappearance and diminishment, a gradual slide into oblivion that provokes no reaction whatsoever from those around her.

"Plätze und Strassen" ("Squares and Streets"), written in 1954, is less intimate in its scope and setting, but the distanced perspective is similar. Even when an "*ich*" or "*wir*" is posited, the narrative voice speaks from a position of detachment, seemingly removed from the immediate surroundings even while observing them. Aichinger's *Sicht der Entfremdung* (alienated perspective) is evident in the particular focus of the observations rendered: on the *Rennweg*, the narrator is drawn to the driver of a hearse; the presence of death is evident elsewhere as well, as when the narrator looks at the *Servitenkirche* and is reminded of the occasions when the dead are carried out from there, or in her terse description of three sisters who return from a ball to find their father dead. The narrative turns to the *Judengasse*, but this site is not so much observed as apprehended symbolically, calling forth a reflection on Jewish Diaspora life. Aichinger writes, "Our pride has gotten entangled. There is no Red Sea whooshing there. Only our laundry still drying in an easterly wind."[66] The existence of Jewish life at Vienna's *Judengasse* is cast as an historical accident, a byproduct of westward migration: "It happened because we didn't wait out the night. As the sun went down, we trailed behind it. And this is the spot where we grew tired, here we built houses. Here the sun went down, here we buckled without yielding."[67]

The narrative voice is written into this experience as a part of the "*wir*" of the Jewish people. Even as Aichinger's treatment of the private and public spaces of the city expresses a position of isolation and alienation, she nonetheless frequently asserts a connection between the narrative voice and the places described. Just as the fate of the narrator of "Wo ich wohne" is tied to her sinking apartment, Aichinger repeatedly creates an intimate relationship between subject and place, as this subject observes, remembers, or imagines each place. Person and place open up to each other, as in a passage from "Plätze und Strassen" in which she writes, "The places that we saw look back at us."[68] This is not a simple process by which memory entails the recall of the familiar, but a dynamic process in which both place and subject may be transformed. In *Kleist, Moos, Fasane,* Aichinger wrote, "By giving myself over to place and time completely, I am set apart. I become like an intersection to myself."[69] Experiencing Viennese reality as alien and sometimes threatening, Aichinger transforms her environment through her writing, stripping this reality of expected and customary meanings by replacing them with abstractions and highly personal references that rarely produce instant recognition in the reader or a singular, definitive line of interpretation.

Ilse Aichinger's poetic language underwent substantial changes throughout her long career. From her earliest publications, however, she established herself as an avant-garde writer who would for decades remain profoundly—yet highly productively—out of step with the times.

Friedrich Torberg

Friedrich Torberg became one of the most influential of the Viennese Jewish writers who had been forced into exile at the time of the *Anschluss* and later chose to return to Austria. In many respects Torberg was also representative of the reémigré Austrian Jewish writers. He was thirty years old at the time of the *Anschluss*, in clear possession of a relatively straightforward, positive Jewish identity. As many other Austrian Jews, Torberg experienced the shattering of this identity after 1938, as the world of Central European Jewry was destroyed. In exile and upon his return, he would face the task of reestablishing an identity as an Austrian and Jew. Torberg was more successful than others in reconnecting to his prewar Jewish identity, but this process was not without complications and contradictions. In his postwar literary career he became a highly influential critic, successful translator, and widely read author, thus achieving what other returning Jewish authors were unable to accomplish: finding a receptive audience within the Austrian cultural arena. However, while he did not refrain from writing on Jewish topics, Torberg's work of the 1950s was not as bold as his work written in exile, which dealt directly with the Holocaust; nor did he remain the vocal critic of the persistence of anti-Semitism or of the Austrian nation's collective amnesia regarding the war years as he had from his vantage point in American exile. According to the Austrian Jewish filmmaker and essayist Ruth Beckermann, Torberg viewed himself as a *"Jud vom Dienst"* ("token Jew") in postwar Austria, as a writer who received attention only because he was Jewish and only if he presented that Jewishness in certain acceptable forms.[70] In this section I will examine Torberg's negotiation as a Jewish writer of the postwar cultural arena, assessing his experience of return and his recreation of a lost world of Austrian Jewry in *Tante Jolesch*.

Torberg was born Friedrich Kantor-Berg in Vienna, in 1908. His parents were Prague Jews who made the move to Vienna in order for his father, Alfred Kantor, to fill a post representing a leading Prague schnapps manufacturer in Vienna. The family moved into Alsergrund, the ninth district, where Friedrich was born. There he attended *Gymnasium* in the Wasagasse. As an adolescent, Torberg played water polo for the Jewish sports club Hakoah. The family was called back to Prague in 1921 by his father's firm, and Friedrich attained Czechoslovakian citizenship, which he maintained until 1945. In 1927 he began to write for the *Prager Tagblatt* as a theater critic and sportswriter. At this time he began friendships with Egon Erwin Kisch, Joseph Roth, and Alfred Polgar. Back in Vienna, Torberg had been a regular guest at the literary Café Herrenhof. In 1928, Torberg began legal studies at the University of Prague; he broke off his studies, however, after three semesters.

In 1930, with the help of Max Brod, Torberg published his first novel, *Der Schüler Gerber hat absolviert* (*The Schoolboy Gerber Has Graduated*), with the Zsolnay Verlag publishing house. At this point he took on the pseudonym of Torberg, a composite of the last syllable of his last name, Kantor, and his mother's maiden name, Berg. This first novel was a great success, which not only set Torberg on firm financial footing but also propelled him into Prague's literary scene. The timing of this career launch, however, was unfortunate, and his success was short lived. Torberg's books were banned in Germany after 1933, and he was only able to support himself through film work produced under another pseudonym, masking his Jewishness.

At the time of the *Anschluss,* Torberg was in Prague. He left for Zurich several months later and remained there for the rest of the year, until the extension of his visa was denied by Swiss authorities. He went to France and then to Spain, where as one of the PEN Club's ten "Oustanding German Anti-Nazi Writers" he secured a visa for the United States. After a brief stay in New York, Torberg joined the German community of exiles in Hollywood. He went to work for Warner Brothers and socialized with the émigré community that included Alfred Polgar, Franz Werfel and Alma Mahler Werfel, Thomas and Heinrich Mann, Lion Feuchtwanger, and Bertolt Brecht. In 1944 he left Hollywood for New York and attained U.S. citizenship shortly thereafter. In American exile Torberg produced some of his most significant works. He wrote the novella *Mein ist die Rache* (*Revenge Is Mine*) in 1943, the novel *Hier bin ich, mein Vater* (*Here I am, Father*) between 1943 and 1946, and the text *Auch das war Wien* (*This Too Was Vienna*), his treatment of Vienna at the time of the *Anschluss*. (This appeared posthumously in 1984.)[71] Torberg wrote of the war and the Holocaust from exile with a boldness that eluded him upon returning to Vienna.[72] After returning from exile, his prose style changes considerably.

In 1951 Torberg returned to Vienna. Here he wrote for a number of newspapers and, in 1954, founded his own cultural journal. This journal, *Forum,* which Torberg edited for twenty years, was funded by the Congress for Cultural Freedom, an organization that had ties to the CIA. In keeping with this support, the journal was firmly anti-Communist, a stance with which Torberg thoroughly identified. The journal was also in step with the conservative climate of Austria of the fifties and sixties. While Torberg was outspoken elsewhere, his editorial policy for the journal seemed to rest on not rocking the boat. In light of Torberg's beliefs, experiences, and the criticism he expressed elsewhere, one might have expected the journal to take Austrian society to task for its cultivation of a culture of forgetting. Yet Sigurd Paul Scheichl has examined the full run of the journal under Torberg's leadership and concluded that the journal participated in the avoidance of the past that characterized the Second Republic.[73] Scheichl concludes, "[*Forum*] should have written about the Austrian roots of Hitler's thought, about Austria's guilt, about the attempt to forget about its involvement in National Socialism and about the general tolerance for the remnants of Nazi ideology."[74]

It is, of course, difficult to write about statements that were never made or texts that were never written. Still, whatever conclusions one might reach about the critical role the journal might have played, its pages contain scarcely any mention of the Nazi era. According to Scheichl, the journal's anti-Communist agenda was of paramount importance to Torberg, and he would have been loath to identify himself in any way with the Left, from which the principal voices emerged to denounce the remnants of the Nazi past. He reads these omissions as Torberg's "concessions both to the Austrian style of shunning conflicts and [as] a conscious act of self-censorship in order to advance his anti-Communist agenda."[75] Torberg may well have perceived Communism as a greater threat than the lingering effects of Nazism. After the war he was contemptuous of Jews who had embraced Communism in order to escape from Nazism, remarking, "Stalin has nothing against the Jews, therefore I'm for him. With this, Buchenwald becomes the standard for our claims and the Nuremberg Laws the barometer of our rights."[76]

Torberg would certainly have met with resistance had he adopted a more strident tone or substantive critique on issues in which his views were not reflective of prevailing attitudes. The robust intellectual climate of the Vienna of 1900 or 1920 had vanished. A conservative literary culture was cultivated to express the mood of unreflective tranquility. To echo Ruth Beckermann, "*Hände weg vom heissen Eisen*" ("*Hands off this hot potato!*") was the order of the day. Given that these tendencies were evident by the time of Torberg's return in 1951, one may wonder what drew him back to Vienna and to Austria. Did he seek to resume his prior life? Was he looking to reestablish a Jewish presence within Austrian culture in spite of the challenges this would entail? Was he perhaps not sufficiently aware of the nature of those challenges?

With Torberg, as with other Jewish returnees, it is not possible to identify a single motivating factor that prompted his return to Austria. By examining Torberg's correspondence from exile, however, one can be fairly clear that he was not operating under any illusions about what he would encounter upon return. It is also evident that he had reservations about the decision. According to Beckermann, "In his letters, he viewed the problem from all sides, entertained no false hopes of retrieving *his* Vienna, and saw with unsparing clarity how sad and provincial the city had become since the expulsion of the Jews. With loden coats and Styrian hats, the Austrians, who had again arrived at their own state, showed just how much they would differentiate themselves from the Germans."[77] With this image of the Austrian populace sporting loden coats and Styrian hats, Beckermann evokes the thoroughly provincial Vienna of Hugo Bettauer's *Stadt ohne Juden*. In her reading of Torberg's assessment of postwar Vienna, the city had become a cultural wasteland in the absence of Jews.

The best insight into Torberg's view of postwar Austria prior to his return is afforded by his correspondence with a fellow Viennese Jew, Hans Weigel. Like Torberg, Weigel was born in 1908. His family belonged to Vienna's assimilated Jewish upper bourgeoisie. His father was the director of a glass manufacturing company. After his father died, Weigel withdrew from the IKG, calling himself a non-Jew. Weigel began writing for the cabaret during the 1930s and left for Switzerland just after the *Anschluss*. He rejected a visa to the United States in order to remain in Europe, characterizing his exile experience as "just a way station on the journey from Vienna to Vienna."[78] Weigel returned quickly after the war, in the fall of 1945.

The following year Weigel and Torberg corresponded regarding the challenges of return and the situation in Vienna. Weigel was unequivocally positive in his depiction of highly favorable conditions for return. He wrote:

> What is great is that one doesn't feel a foreigner for a moment, that one has no inhibitions regarding the people, that one belongs. … Great miracles occurred in Vienna. In the first moment one is of course touched and moved. But from the second moment on, or at the latest from the third, even that ceases. One moves about here so naturally, geographically as well as humanly, as though one had just returned from vacation or from a year-long engagement abroad. The gulf you are afraid of and I used to be afraid of, does not exist.[79]

It is stunning that Weigel could compare the return from exile with arriving home from a vacation, but throughout these remarks he is unrestrained in his efforts to portray an unproblematic climate for returning Jews. In the letter he further emphasizes a continued Jewish presence in Vienna that simply did not conform to reality. In a newsletter to friends in April 1946, Weigel denied the existence of anti-Semitism and downplayed the reintegration of former Nazis into Austrian society.[80]

For his part, Torberg appears to have been unmoved. He was prepared to return to Austria, but he well understood that this return was contingent upon his acceptance of certain conditions and that doing so would put him in a position in which ever more conditions might be imposed. On the proposition of considering the score to be settled between Austrian Gentiles and Jews, Torberg was dubious. He writes of the unspoken terms under which non-Jewish Austrians would welcome Austrian Jews back from exile:

Or he says: "yes, okay, we're even"—but of course you have not returned as a Jew, but as an Austrian. In short: he sets conditions. He sets conditions! ... And if I don't want to meet them, he will make very plain to me that he was not the one who had called me. I find, however—and hopefully I don't have to guard against any sort of verbal misunderstanding—I find, however: he ought to call me. If he does not do this, then he gives his belated approval to my forced departure in those days (which was ostensibly forced upon him just as on me), and as far as he is concerned I can go right ahead and stay where I am. If I choose nonetheless to come back, that's my concern, and he sees it as a concession that he doesn't hinder me in doing so. And that is not at all what I consider a settled score."[81]

Torberg tempered this oppositional stance with the conciliatory gesture of returning in 1951 despite of his keen awareness of the conditions set by mainstream Austrian society. The best way to understand this move, I would suggest, is to think of the returning Torberg as an Austrian as well as a Jew, and, crucially, as a writer. Torberg viewed himself as the last in the line of Jewish writers considered up to this point in this study. And whereas other Jewish writers had considerable difficulties establishing a footing in the literary culture of postwar Austria, Torberg quickly claimed an important position in cultural life. Torberg and Weigel both were highly influential during the 1940s and 1950s. While Torberg seems to have taken some pleasure in playing along with his assigned role as representative Jew and cultural icon, Weigel sought vehemently to distance himself from any identification as a Jew. In fact, in a series of articles in the journal *Heute* bearing the title "Es gibt keine Juden" ("There Are No Jews"), Weigel not only declined this identification for himself, but for all Jews. Jews as Jews ceased to exist as a result of the Nazi persecution, he felt, and to persist in even the use of the word Jew was for Weigel tantamount to perpetuating Nazi racial policy. The racial classification "Jew" belonged to the Nazis alongside *"Nichtarier,"* (*"Non-Aryan"*) and it seemed there was no other way of understanding Jewishness; a cultural identification, for example, was ruled out. There are no Jewish writers, he argued, only Austrian and German ones. Torberg was incensed and wrote a letter to the editor in which he took Weigel to task:

> As I gather from the latest edition of *Heute,* Hans Weigel is having a go at doing away with the Jews; he's thus steering towards a final solution that already occurred to the Führer.[82]

Torberg then reminds the journal's readers that proudly self-conscious Jews in fact continue to exist. Hans Weigel's assimilationism was perhaps even more extreme than Karl Kraus's had been. Weigel was an enthusiastic participant in the denial of anti-Semitism, the exculpation of the Austrian people for the crimes of National Socialism, and the cultivation of a culture of forgetting. Unlike Torberg, Weigel had no trouble accepting the reigning conditions for return. In 1945

Weigel wrote in the *Wiener Kurier,* "We have nothing for which to reproach each other. No one can bring the other's dead back to life—among you many are dead and among us—we survivors are even. We are not thinking terribly much about yesterday."[83]

Weigel undoubtedly adopted a highly accomodationist stance vis-à-vis the mainstream Austrian public and the official line taken by the government. By participating in the culture of denial, he played a role in excluding Jewish voices from the Second Republic. As Weigel rose to prominence he helped to replicate the practices of denial and avoidance of conflict from the political arena within the cultural sphere. Unlike in postwar Germany, Austrian literature was not underscored by political activism by its leading practitioners. Instead, a conservative literary establishment was erected that emphasized continuity with the prewar past. Donald Daviau refers to the "tendency of Austria to gather strength from its cultural heritage."[84] The *Stefansdom,* the opera, and the *Burgtheater* were restored and reopened almost immediately following the war, positive developments to be sure, but also perhaps symbolic of a culture oriented toward the past rather than the future. In the oppressive cultural climate of the postwar period, the voices of Jewish returnees were isolated and largely ignored, and theirs were among the very few that were critical of the social and political climate. It was not until the late 1950s that the emergence of the *Wiener Gruppe* brought new critical impulses into Austrian culture. Nonetheless it must be remembered that while Weigel in many respects reflected and promoted a conservative cultural orientation, he also played an important role in fostering young writers. As editor of the series *Stimmen der Gegenwart (Voices of the Present)* and *Junge österreichische Autoren (Young Austrian Writers)* in the early 1950s, Weigel championed such writers as Gerhard Fritsch and Ingeborg Bachmann. The traditionalism of his own work and his personal convictions were thus not applied in the mentoring of young talent.

Torberg's role in postwar Vienna was very different. He channeled his political as well as cultural engagement into the publication of the journal *Forum* for two decades. He became a highly influential critic and successful translator. While his literary work was long put aside in favor of this other agenda, Torberg never ceased to regard himself as a Jewish writer; rather, he viewed his Jewishness as a central tenet of his literature. He later returned to Jewish topics, publishing *Süßkind von Trimberg (Susskind of Trimberg)* in 1972 and his satirical cultural history *Die Tante Jolesch oder der Untergang des Abendlandes in Anekdoten (Tante Jolesch or the Decline of the West in Anecdotes),* in 1975. These are not the provocative texts of the exile years, however. The *Süßkind* novel is temporally and spatially removed from postwar Austria, and *Tante Jolesch,* as Matti Bunzl has suggested, is transhistorical in its depiction of Austrian Jewry and therefore nonthreatening.[85] With this work Torberg conformed to the Austrian version of mastery of the past through the construction of a nostalgically recalled, lost world of Central European Jewry in harmonious coexistence with non-Jewish citizens of the monarchy and the Austrian First Republic. In creating this work as a monument to this lost world, Torberg relegated the Jews to the past and effectively established himself—in keeping with his self-image—as the last of Austria's Jewish writers.

In the introduction to *Tante Jolesch,* Torberg explicitly claims this position. Reflecting on his personal experience of Habsburg Austria and its Jewish bourgeoisie, he notes, "I am probably one of the last who not only know of that particular fountain of memory, but still remember those served by it out of personal experience."[86] Throughout the work the authorial voice is clearly established as Torberg's own, as frequent reference is made to his personal experience—as in his proud involvement with the Hakoah sports club—memories of the world-changing historical events he experienced directly—such as the night of the *Anschluss* (which he witnessed from Prague), his exile experience, and his writing career.

Torberg further underscores the importance of his role as chronicler by emphasizing that his own life occurred at a remarkable time in history, affording him a unique vantage point. Born in 1908, he cannot place himself in the whirlwind of cultural activity that characterized *fin de siècle* Vienna, but, surprisingly, he suggests that he knows that world all the better for having experienced its echoes after it was gone. He came of age, he writes, "in an age of euphoria and of the last glowing flares of a lifestyle that preserved and maintained itself out of Austria's collapse until it fell victim to a greater and more final collapse."[87] Here Torberg extends what is generally seen as a rather long turn of the century, even beyond its usual scope. The interwar years figure not only as an extension of the *fin de siècle,* but as its zenith. Torberg's recasting of the limits of historical periods is deliberate, serving his view that the world he depicts in *Tante Jolesch* came to an end not in 1918, but in 1938. He ignores the fall of the monarchy and dissolution of the empire in order to assert that this world persisted via many meaningful continuities until the *Anschluss.* Although he came of age in the First Republic, Torberg posits his own roots in the Habsburg era: "Then in answer to the question, 'what is left of the double eagle?' I could reply with a certain authority: 'Me, for example.'"[88]

Torberg similarly overlooks the significance of 1918 in his characterization of the world of his youth as borderless. The world of Tante Jolesch stretched across the Austrian Empire just as the Jewish families from which this figure came, an amalgamation of formidable and witty Jewish matriarchs, formed networks that spanned the major cities of the empire. Torberg's narrative spills between Vienna, Prague, Budapest, and a handful of other Eastern European cities. When, for example, he describes a charitable organization for Jewish students, he explains, "The club under discussion happened to be located in Vienna, but could just as easily have been in Prague or Cracow or Czernowitz."[89] Elsewhere he discusses food, eliding regional differences or specialties in favor of a unified Central European culinary umbrella, referring to "the customary pleasures of Austrian-Hungarian-Czech-Jewish cuisine."[90]

Torberg describes a Central European, principally Jewish, world of fluid borders and casts himself as a cosmopolitan border-crosser within it. He refers to the years in which he commuted between Prague and Vienna, staying in his mother's apartment in Prague and living like a student in Vienna in a room rented from a widow. Torberg is at home in both cities and indeed all over this world. He establishes himself as a particular authority on the culture and society of Prague, acting as a guide to the reader he presumes to be less informed. He explains, for instance, that when one speaks of Prague's German society, in fact the German-Jewish minority is meant, as the non-Jewish Germans in Prague are topographically and ideologically distant from this group. He repeatedly explains what he terms the "*Prager Terminologie*" and coaches the reader on the Prague dialect until he assumes the lesson has been sufficiently absorbed: "Of course she said '*griess*' [for *gross*], but I gradually have to assume that the reader supplies the correct pronunciation himself."[91] Throughout the narrative, Torberg is concerned with imparting to the reader of *Tante Jolesch* the nuances of a multinational existence that once represented an Austrian way of life.

While Torberg insists in the preface of *Tante Jolesch* that he has not written a work of nostalgia, this protestation cannot hide the underlying sentimentality of the work. The anecdotes of the book produce an image of Jewish life prior to the Nazi takeover as harmonious and thoroughly integrated into mainstream Austrian society. Torberg's emphasis on 1938 as the locus of the loss of this life, while justified with respect to the devastating consequences of the rise of fascism and the *Anschluss,* creates a utopian past channeling collective memory into palatable visions of a past golden age.

Torberg does not comment extensively on life in Vienna at the time of the publication of *Tante Jolesch.* He does recount Alfred Polgar's acerbic observation on returning to Vienna from Zurich, where he remained after the war. Torberg wrote, "'I have to pronounce a devastating judgment on this city,' Polgar said. 'Vienna remains Vienna.'"[92] Torberg may have enjoyed this quip, but his own characterization of the city decades after the end of the war places the emphasis squarely on the gulf that separates prewar from postwar Austria. Torberg's tale centers on the loss of a way of life and the loss of the people that were its leading practitioners. At the end of the narrative he suggests his concentration on stories involving Jews might be a justification for the theory "that a part of the West ceased to exist along with the part of European Jewry that perished."[93] The loss he identifies within the Western world is also reflected in Vienna. Not only are the Viennese Jews he describes in the narrative gone, the places they inhabited have been transformed by their absence. Torberg writes, "They all used to exist and now none of them do, neither them nor the realms and settings in which they moved about. Not the coffeehouses or editorial offices, not the family tables or the summer resorts, nothing."[94]

What remains is, of course, Torberg himself. His view of himself as standing with one foot in this vanished world of the past is evident throughout the narrative, and indeed, decades before he wrote *Tante Jolesch,* Torberg wrote to his friend Max Brod, "I am a German-Jewish writer, that is, a Jew writing in the German language; I have known from the first that I am one, and this knowledge has since then at the most been increased to include the likelihood that I will be the last."[95]

As an Austrian Jewish writer, Torberg sees himself as occupying an outsider position in Austrian society, a position he addresses with the kind of coffeehouse wit that characterizes the whole collection of anecdotes. Torberg departs from a comment made by Egon Erwin Kisch shortly before the outbreak of the war: "You know, nothing can really happen to me. I am a German. I am a Czech. I am a Jew. I am from a good family. I am a Communist. *Something* in there helps me every time."[96] To describe his own situation in postwar Austria, he revises Kisch's remark: "I am a Jew. I live in Austria. I emigrated. I have something against Brecht. *Something* in there hurts me every time."[97] Torberg readily assumes the outsider status implied in this statement. His postwar writings reflect his view of the role this status afforded him. He was not a watchdog of postwar Austrian society on the lookout for signs of the persistence of fascist elements within it, nor was he an outspoken critic of anti-democratic developments within Austrian politics. He saw himself in his literary work as fulfilling a significant role simply by writing from a self-consciously Jewish perspective. As a writer he performed the role of an initiate of Jewish Austria, and given that few others remained to share this role, he saw little cause to take on a different, more critical one. In 1955 Torberg wrote Max Brod, "If I still have a Jewish function at all, then it is strictly this—that I shape my public activity such that as many non-Jews as possible experience the death of the last German-Jewish writer as a loss. Whether they are mourning or breathing a sigh of relief I don't care; they should just notice that something has come to an end for which they have no replacement …"[98]

Friedrich Torberg played a crucial role in reinserting a Jewish presence into Austrian literature during the Second Republic. His negotiation of the obstacles that stood in the way of that undertaking, ranging from outspoken criticism to the adoption of accomodationist positions, reveals much about the status of returning Jewish writers, their place in the cultural arena, and their relations with mainstream Austrian society.

Hilde Spiel

Unlike Torberg, Hilde Spiel never considered herself a Jewish writer. Though both sides of her family had Jewish origins, they were highly assimilated and ultimately converted to Catholicism. Prior to the war Spiel seems to have given little thought to her Jewish origins, even as the rise of fascism began to put pressure on families like hers, who considered their Jewishness a remnant of the past. After the war Spiel bristled at being viewed as a Jew, neither conceiving of herself in a tradition of Jewish writing nor identifying personally with the victims or survivors of the Holocaust.

So why include Spiel in this study? Hilde Spiel is representative of those highly assimilated Jews whose identity was fractured by the coming of fascism. If for assimilated or converted Jews, Jewishness was no longer considered a relevant category of identification, the Nazis reversed this course. The other strands of identity that had been determinant for these people—in terms of profession, social class, political affiliation, gender, generation, or neighborhood—were wiped away after 1933 by the single, overdetermined category of race. After the war Spiel protested bitterly at being forced to take on an identity that did not feel authentic to her. She wrote, "What torment to be rudely nailed to an affiliation, to a solidarity that only existed in the fictions of the Nuremberg Race Laws!"[99] Spiel's protest at the one-dimensional identity imposed on her by the National Socialists is justified, and I certainly do not want to employ the Nuremberg Laws as the standard for inclusion in this study. Yet it is precisely this protest that makes her important in this work, for it is representative of what for Spiel amounted to decades of struggle to define herself in her own terms and to locate a space of belonging. Spiel's ambivalence about her Jewish origins is evident. The contours of a self-defined, non-Jewish identity are, however, far less clear. Spiel has often been characterized as living between two cultures, those of Austria and Britain. The dynamic of emigration and return unfolded in Spiel's life in an unusually protracted, cyclical pattern. Much of her life was devoted to the pursuit of an answer to the question with which she titled the second volume of her memoirs: *Welche Welt ist meine Welt?* (*Which World Is My World?*). Hilde Spiel stands as a case in point that identity is not constructed in a linear fashion but must be continually refashioned in a process that is always provisional and always ongoing.

Hilde Spiel was born in Vienna in 1911, into a prosperous assimilated Jewish family. Hilde's paternal grandfather had already attained a level of prominence in Vienna, making his living as a salesman with an address in the central first district. Her father, Hugo Spiel, was an engineer and served during the First World War as an officer in the Habsburg army. Hilde spent her early years of childhood in Heiligenstadt, the nineteenth district (another prominent address), where her mother's family had lived for a number of generations. Hilde had no siblings and was reportedly a nervous child. Biographer Sandra Wiesinger-Stock writes that as a young girl, Spiel developed a "*Schluckhysterie*" (difficulty in swallowing) for which she was treated for a number of months without success.[100]

Spiel attended the important school for girls run by Eugenie Schwarzwald, one of the few institutions at the time in which girls could attain the *Matura*.

Like a number of students and teachers at the school, Spiel frequented the literary Café Herrenhof, which she viewed an extension of her education, "a kind of academy."[101] Spiel completed the *Matura* in 1929 and entered the University of Vienna in 1930. She explored several disciplines before settling on philosophy and psychology. Her first novel stems from this period. In 1933, when Spiel was just twenty-one, the Zsolnay Verlag published her debut novel, *Kati auf der Brücke* (*Kati on the Bridge*). At the university Spiel worked at the Wirtschaftspsychologische Forschungsstelle (Behavioral Economics Research Institute) run by Ludwig Wagner and Paul Lazarsfeld, where she also became involved with the Socialist movement. She joined the Social Democratic Party in 1933 and was active during the civil war of 1934. Spiel established ties to the British Labor Party and facilitated their aid to Socialists in need through an underground network. In her memoirs Spiel recalls that she narrowly escaped arrest more than once. In later years Spiel abstained from any political involvement and never joined another political party.

In the wake of the civil war Spiel began to contemplate leaving Austria. Spiel's path to exile was markedly different from that of many of her contemporaries. She did not leave the country when the Social Democratic Party was outlawed in May of 1934, when the party leadership was forced into exile. She did not seem to fear persecution as a result of her political involvement, for she made the pragmatic decision to remain in Vienna until she had completed her studies. Nor did she choose exile in anticipation of persecution as a Jew. Spiel did not identify as a Jew, and those around her apparently were unaware of her Jewish origins.[102] Reflecting on this time in her memoirs, she stresses her family's complete integration into Viennese society. Unlike the Canettis, for example, who were forced to flee the country, Spiel was—at least in 1936—in a position to freely choose emigration. While the choice was certainly undertaken as an act of opposition to the authoritarian *Ständestaat* under Schuschnigg, Spiel did not see herself leaving as a Socialist or a Jew, but rather as the result of a deliberate decision of conscience. (Even decades later, in her memoirs, Spiel assigned little importance to the social, political, and economic pressures that factored into her decision to leave Austria.) When Spiel's mentor at the university, philosophy professor Moritz Schlick, was murdered by a former student, this eruption of violence into her own social world was the last straw, and she accelerated her preparations to leave. For Hilde Spiel, political developments had become intolerable and life in Vienna unbearable.

Spiel was invited to follow the writer Peter de Mendelssohn to England, and in October 1936, she did so, marrying him shortly after her arrival. The couple lived in straitened circumstances, a condition they shared with other German and Austrian exiles. Their situation improved in 1939, when Mendelssohn began working in the Ministry of Information, which not only ensured a steady income but also provided a measure of protection against internment by the British authorities. This was a pressing concern after the outbreak of the war, when the status of Austrian and German refugees from National Socialism shifted to "alien enemies" overnight. Over a hundred tribunals were established across England in the first months of the war, charged by the Home Office with classifying the "alien enemies" according to the level of risk they represented. Hilde Spiel was placed in the intermediate category because she had left Austria early enough not to be considered an exile; shortly thereafter, however, her classification was upgraded to the group whose loyalty was not in doubt, thanks to her husband's job in the Ministry of Information. Spiel worked very hard through her many English and American contacts to bring her parents to England, which did not occur until the summer of 1938. Although they were officially recognized as "Refugees from Nazi Oppression," this classification did not preclude their arrest. It is not clear what happened to Spiel's mother and aunt during the war, but her father was placed in an internment camp on the Isle of Man.[103] While Spiel's father was able to briefly reenter his profession as a chemist after the war, the couple did not live long enough to build a new postwar existence in England or back in Austria. Spiel's father died suddenly in the summer of 1945, and her mother died three years later. Spiel and Mendelssohn had two children, both born in London during the war.

As writers, both Spiel and Mendelssohn differed from the majority of exiled writers, as from the start they sought to establish a new readership by writing in the English language. Their orientation toward their host country is also reflected in their acquisition of British citizenship in 1941 and the fact that they spoke only English with their young children. Spiel's memoirs foreground the couple's desire to integrate into English society as quickly and thoroughly as possible, and she suggests that consequently they socialized chiefly with English writers. In fact, their social circle consisted of a mix of writers and intellectuals, both natives and exiles. While Spiel did maintain friendships with a number of Austrian and German writers in exile, her assertion that she eschewed exile circles likely had less to do with any individuals than with a certainly mentality she rejected, which sought to import the culture of the homeland wholesale into the new environment. In an interview published in 1992 she commented, "We did not aspire to this flocking together, this self-colonialization on an island within English society."[104] Spiel and her husband were intent on integration, and they worked quickly to reorient their writing careers toward England. Spiel was active in the London PEN Club (whereas she never formally joined the German PEN), she worked for the BBC, published a number of stories in English, and began to write for the *New Statesman* in 1944, embarking on a journalistic career she would continue alongside her literary work for many years.

Spiel and Mendelssohn suffered through the war and the London Blitz shoulder to shoulder with the English, and there were certainly times during the war that they felt at one with the British populace, united by suffering and a common cause. It was at the war's end that the couple came to a painful realization of the limits of their integration. The couple was shocked and deeply hurt by the common assumption by their British friends and neighbors that they would return to Austria once the war was over. It was only in retrospect that Spiel reflected in her writing that their integration was never more than partial and provisional. I will return to Spiel's treatment of these feelings of dislocation and isolation when I examine the role occupied by the theme of exile in two of her significant later works.

In the early months just after the end of the war, Peter de Mendelssohn was sent by the Allies to Berlin, where he was to help rebuild the German press corps. Spiel was not yet prepared for a confrontation with those who had supported the regime, and she chose to stay in England with the children. Quite soon, however, her own curiosity about Austria began to stir, and by the end of the year, she had proposed to the *New Statesman* that she return to Vienna to serve as a correspondent for the paper. In January and February 1946, still classified as a war correspondent and wearing the khaki uniform of the British army, Spiel reported on political developments in occupied Vienna. Her more personal reflections on this early return appeared in German, decades after the experience. In 1968 Spiel published *Rückkehr nach Wien* (*Return to Vienna*), an extended essay based on her journals from the time. In addition, there is the brief essay "Die Wiederkehr" ("The Return"), which is dated 13 February 1946, but which appeared in the collection *Städte und Menschen* (*Cities and People*) in 1970. It is possible that this text was reworked in the intervening years, but it does appear to convey the author's initial impressions of her reencounter with Vienna.

In the short essay "Die Wiederkehr" Spiel's temporal focus is on the first moments of the return and even before, as she relates the many variations of her dream of returning to Vienna, dreams that she had in the half-sleep between air raid sirens during the bombing of London. Some of these dreams are visions of a harmonious reunion, but the majority revolve around alienation, as either the familiar streets have turned threatening or the dreaming subject herself is defamiliarized, "a stranger on the streets of childhood."[105] Spiel's recollection of the first contact with Austrian soil reflects this tension between the foreign and the familiar: "Now we touch the ground—once native but now tainted with the slightly frightening impulse of the unfamiliar—and we drive along the muddy and bumpy streets towards the city."[106] The perspective is thus a combination of distance and familiarity in which explicit attempt is made to take the measure of what has remained and what has vanished from Vienna. The narrative voice emphasizes its own emotional connection to the city, reflecting, "Everything here is a reminder of the past, everything touches the heart."[107] In spite of the widespread destruction of the city, the narrator insists that the city's essential character has endured. She writes, "Everything that memory had latched on to remains. Much is destroyed, but the contours, colors, and tones remain the same; the soul of the city lives, even if her body has been badly mistreated."[108]

Spiel does report significant changes, chiefly in terms of the provincialization of the once-great city. She laments, "It gradually becomes clear how the Austrian countryside has overtaken Vienna, how the urban is flooded over with the rural in clothing, language, and lifestyle."[109] Spiel's description of the loden-clad populace having penetrated the cultural institutions that were once the reserve of a worldly elite could have been taken directly from Bettauer's *Stadt ohne Juden:* "Women in headscarves are sitting at Demel, there is a Styrian hat hanging in the cloakroom of the opera, people attend the symphony in loden coats."[110] The cosmopolitanism that had formerly characterized the city and with which the author had formerly identified had now vanished. She does, however, see continuity in the intimate relationship of the Viennese to art and music.

Spiel's more extensive treatment of this experience of return appears in *Rückkehr nach Wien* (*Return to Vienna*), a volume composed of a layering of journal entries and commentary written in retrospect. Peter Pabisch emphasizes the memoir character of the work, noting, "What wants to be a diary is actually much more a contemplative reminiscence of a clever person who is doing her utmost to intelligently come to terms with her fate."[111] The spatial and temporal distance of the author to the events related is decisive, placing this text in line with Canetti's memoirs. For Pabisch, this slim genre of *Rückkehrliteratur* (the literature of return) is a special variant of exile literature.

The sense of being confronted with one's own foreignness in familiar surroundings is even more in evidence here than in "Die Wiederkehr." Spiel experiences this alienation in spatial terms, in a painful recognition of her lack of connectedness to the very place she had missed the most in exile, the *Pfarrplatz* in Heiligenstadt. Standing there, where her mother's family had been at home for generations, she contemplates the role it had come to occupy in her memories and fantasies of an imagined *Heimat:* "In the dim light I stand at the *Pfarrplatz.* Here my soul is buried. Whenever I was homesick during the ten years of my absence, it was for this place. Whenever I heard certain passages from Beethoven or Schubert, it appeared before my eyes. A small village square: to the left there is a farmhouse in which *Eroica* was written; and in the middle the little church of St. Jacob."[112] Yet these experiences, however important to Spiel personally, belong to the past. The meaning she ascribes to this place is part of her personal history; in Spiel's remembered and imagined Vienna, she fixes her origins at the *Pfarrplatz.* Returning to this place, she is made aware that she lacks any connection to it in the present.

Hilde Spiel's early return to Vienna in 1946 drew her back into an irretrievable past just as it confronted her with painful new realities of the present. The experience could hardly have resolved any questions of identity and belonging. Rather it opened the way for the realization that these questions would remain open. She reflects, "It's not a matter of loyalty: I owe that to my rescuers. It's about the inner position [*Standort*] that has been unsettled. Now that no compulsion expels me from here and keeps me over there, I am caught in a pendulum. ... Again and again I will have to put to the test where I am really at home."[113]

This question became a central preoccupation in Spiel's writing. Its centrality becomes clear when we consider that there are texts in English or in German from every decade of her postwar life in which the question of belonging figures as a central concern. After two months in Vienna in 1946, Spiel followed her husband to Berlin, where they lived for two years in a rented villa in Grünewald. She returned to England at the end of 1948 and remained there, living principally apart from her husband for the next fifteen years. Spiel would later make the distinction that England offered her asylum but never represented home.[114]

In 1963 Spiel was offered a position as cultural correspondent in Austria for the *Frankfurter Allgemeine Zeitung*. She accepted, returned to Vienna, and began what would become twenty years of highly influential cultural reporting for the paper. Spiel and Mendelssohn divorced before this return. Spiel was at that time involved in a relationship with Hans Flesch-Brunningen, who also returned to Austria; the two married in 1971.

In the works written after her return to Austria, Spiel devoted significant attention to the theme of exile, one part of her sustained exploration of questions of identity and belonging. In the volume *Kleine Schritte* (*Small Steps*), published in 1976, she described the painful experiences constitutive of exile, all of which together she referred to as "*Krankheit Exil*" (the illness of exile): "homesickness, the feeling of being an outcast, of not being understood, of the unbridgeable barriers of language, tradition, upbringing, habits, familial relations that separate the emigrant from those among whom he has found asylum."[115] Here exile represents a permanent condition of alienation and isolation that cannot be overcome.

The condition of exile, in which the individual has been uprooted, separated from familiar surroundings—from family, language, nation, and from personal history—requires a fundamentally new orientation under conditions that make such an undertaking nearly impossible. Elisabeth Bronfen has described three possibilities of identification for those in exile: one can identify with the exile condition itself, with the danger of fetishizing the loss one has experienced and creating obstacles to integration into the new culture; one can identify with the country that offered refuge; or one may continue to identify with the land of origin, running the risk of falling into nostalgia.[116] In her 1965 novel *Lisas Zimmer* (*Lisa's Room*), Spiel contrasts two central characters who opt for the first two of these possibilities. The protagonist, Lisa Leitner, is an Austrian émigré living in New York, an eccentric cosmopolitan with roots in the Habsburg Empire. Lisa remains deeply attached to Vienna and, indeed, her fundamental orientation toward Europe and toward the vanished Habsburg past prevents her from gaining a hold in her new existence. Instead, she chooses to live among the "*ewigen Emigranten*" (eternal emigrants), reflecting the colonializing mentality Spiel rejected for herself. Lisa's world is a no-man's land, suspended between cultures; she is not a part of New York but lives withdrawn in her own room, which is full of relics of the past. Lisa's demise—she dies of a morphine overdose—signals the failure of her assimilation.

The narrator, Lele, by contrast, is a young Latvian woman who successfully integrates into America. Lele views her new orientation as a kind of religious conversion; her integration into Californian life figures as an imagined return to paradise.[117] Yet Spiel does not unambiguously portray Lele and Lisa in terms of success and failure, as Lele is an unreliable narrator inclined to overlook Lisa's positive characteristics and to fashion a narrative that serves to legitimate her own choices. However idiosyncratic, Lisa is rational and tolerant, while Lele, in spite of having been imprisoned in a concentration camp, maintains unreflected fascist views, which she simply translates into the new American context.[118] Both characters are ultimately denied a new beginning; the paths of assimilation and to resistance against assimilation both prove to be dead ends.

Spiel also reflected on the exile experience in the drama *Anna & Anna*, which was published and also performed in the Vestibule Theater of the *Burgtheater* in 1988, fifty years after the *Anschluss*. Spiel also adapted the work into a film script, in which she included the text of the Moscow Declaration. When the play was produced at the *Burgtheater*, Spiel had the document read in its entirety. While the Moscow Declaration asserts Austria's victim status, Spiel emphasized in a television interview at the time that her interest lay primarily in the declaration's last paragraph. She noted, "Austria is reminded, however, that she has a responsibility which she cannot evade for participation in the war on the side of Hitlerite Germany and that in the final settlement, account will inevitably be taken of her own contribution to her liberation."[119]

Anna & Anna employs a doppelgänger motif in order to explore the choice between emigration and remaining in Austria on the eve of the Nazi takeover. Splitting the character of Anna allows Spiel to leave Anna I in Vienna, while Anna II emigrates to England. Anna opposes the regime, but like Spiel herself, she does not appear to be immediately threatened in a personal way by its policies; rather, she contemplates exile as a political decision. Facing doubts about whether to stay or go, Anna's characterization of herself places her in a distinctly grey area: "I am neither Jew nor Red. Or maybe a little of both."[120] Anna has a Jewish background, alluded to by her employer, but she does not identify as a Jew and seems to be only dimly aware of the implications of Jewish origins in the new political climate.

Through Anna I, who remains in Vienna, Spiel examines the complex negotiation of life under a hostile regime. All around her, colleagues, friends, and acquaintances are continually making concessions to the Nazis while Anna struggles not to. Thomas, a man to whom she has clearly given her heart, has long since left Austria, and Anna questions whether she should do the same. She has since begun a relationship with Stefan, who embodies the accomodationist behavior of their fellow Viennese. Stefan is the feuilleton editor of a Viennese newspaper, where he maintains positive relations with the Nazi sympathizers on staff. After the Jewish journalists are removed from their posts, Stefan is drawn into political reporting, where he is required to report enthusiastically on the advances of Hitler's army. He justifies each concession he makes with the excuse that if his responsibilities rested with a true sympathizer, things would be far worse: "Somebody has to stay here. Otherwise everything goes to the dogs."[121] Stefan's willingness to take any action in the interest of self-preservation, expressed most dramatically in his search for a doctor who will put a cast on his leg so that he can avoid military service, eventually estranges him from Anna, who had foreseen this trajectory all too clearly. Anna II, preparing to leave, ends her relationship in a letter to Stefan in which she expresses the fear both Annas share: "We comply, we resign ourselves, we make one concession after another, and in the end we are a part of them, even end up in the party."[122]

While Anna II leaves so as not to have to witness these developments, Anna I remains, her own behavior a mixture of small-but-dangerous acts of resistance—taking a Jewish actress from Berlin into her apartment for the night and supplying a friend with paper to print oppositional materials—and trying to live under National Socialism without lending the regime her support. In the end, Anna learns that shortly before the war's finish, her friend in the resistance has been arrested, and she wonders about her own complicity: "Hardly anyone gets off completely without guilt."[123]

Anna II's life in England during the war does not present the same moral dilemmas faced by Anna I. She survives the war, finds work, and establishes relationships, yet she seems adrift in her exile existence. Anna II has an affair with the married Englishman in whose home she works as a domestic servant, but there is no future with this man, and in any event, her heart is with Thomas, now serving as a war correspondent in the Middle East. She has some contact with the Austrian émigré community, but she refrains from fully joining it. She elects not to adopt any clear political stance, explaining, "I really always just wanted to be a respectable person."[124]

What Spiel's depiction of Anna II's wartime experiences makes clear is the gendered aspect of the life of an exile. Anna's experiences are those of a female refugee and émigré. She works as a domestic and waitress before being helped into a position at the BBC, reflecting a common experience of women exiles who frequently took low-status positions irrespective of their education or past professional development in their home countries. She is perceived differently from her male counterparts by the British population, which is evident not only in her relationship with a British man but also in her avoidance of internment after the outbreak of the war.[125] Being a woman does not help Anna to integrate into British society, however. She remains an isolated outsider and returns to Vienna as a war correspondent just at the end of the war. The Anna II story reads like a chapter in a larger narrative that has to be finished in Vienna.

Spiel's drama ends abruptly, and we are given few clues as to how Anna—both Annas have now merged once again into one—will negotiate the challenges of life in the aftermath of the devastating war. She is alone at the end of the play. She has experienced the loss of community. The polarization of her own identity may be only outwardly reconciled. Anna will have to reconstitute her fragmented self in an environment of destruction and deprivation. She has gained an awareness of two cultures, which may well play a significant role in sustaining her, but she must also recognize that the act of returning will not be restorative. The space of exile and the space of origin both contain a mixture of the familiar and the alien, a condition that will shape her environment wherever she chooses to live.

Spiel was quite familiar with this dual condition in her own life, after her return to Austria in 1963. Undoubtedly, however, she played a leading role in Austrian culture from the time of her return, as a writer, cultural critic, and journalist. Through her journalism, as well as her writing in English, she was perhaps even more influential as an ambassador and interpreter of Austrian culture abroad. During the seventies and eighties Spiel published a number of essay collections, bridging the two cultures in which she had lived. These included *Städte und Menschen* (1972), *Kleine Schritte* (1976), *In meinem Garten schlendernd* (*Strolling in My Garden*, 1981), *Englische Ansichten* (*English Perspectives*, 1984), and *Dämonie der Gemütlichkeit* (*The Demonic Nature of Coziness*, 1991). In 1987 she published *Vienna's Golden Autumn*, an English-language cultural history of Vienna until the *Anschluss*. Near the end of her life, Spiel published two volumes of memoirs: *Die hellen und die finsteren Zeiten* (*Bright and Dark Times*, 1989) and *Welche Welt ist meine Welt?* (*Which World is my World?*, 1990).

Spiel was a celebrated author during these years, receiving a number of significant prizes in both Austria and Germany. Nonetheless Spiel's relations with the official state were frequently tense, and her later life was punctuated with episodes that caused her to question her decision to live in Austria, in spite of the success and acclaim she enjoyed.

One such episode involved the Austrian PEN club, which Spiel joined upon her return. She served the organization as general secretary for five years during the late 1960s, before becoming its vice president. She was a candidate for its president in 1972, at a time when generational conflicts had created substantial rifts within the membership. Spiel aligned herself with the younger writers, seeking to wrest control of the organization from the old guard. Her platform included support for extending membership to the avant-garde group of writers in Graz. Spiel narrowly lost the election and took her defeat very hard. She complained in the media that the club had become an old-boys' network intent on keeping her out of power, and she publicly accused Friedrich Torberg of carrying out a defamatory campaign against her. Spiel referred to Torberg as her *Freundfeind* ("*Frenemy*"); theirs was always a tense relationship based on ideological differences. Spiel's electoral loss made her feel the entire literary establishment was hostile to her, and she later commented that the episode shook her confidence in her decision to return.[126]

Spiel's relationship to her Jewish origins was highly ambivalent. While she never identified as a Jewish writer, she exhibited keen interest in Jewish topics in her writing from exile. In 1962 she published a biography of Fanny von Arnstein, a Jewish socialite credited with importing the intellectual salon—as well as the Christmas tree—from Berlin to the Vienna of Joseph II (*Fanny von Arnstein oder Die Emanzipation*). During the early years of exile, she also wrote a novel about an assimilated Jewish family. Spiel wrote the novel in English, translated it into German, and was first able to find a German publisher for the work, *Früchte des Wohlstands* (*Fruits of Prosperity*), in 1981.

This interest in Jewish culture was perhaps more intellectual than personal. In the postwar era, Spiel made a number of comments distancing herself from the Jewish victims and survivors of the Holocaust that are jarring in their apparent lack of empathy. In spite of decades of living in postwar Austria, and although her grandmother perished at Theresienstadt, Spiel noted dismissively in a 1989 *Profil* interview, "I have more in common with my grocer than with the Jews who live in Vienna today."[127] Spiel opposed Kurt Waldheim's election as president, declining to deliver the opening address of the Salzburg Festival so as not to share a stage with him. Yet during the Waldheim affair she was not among those who pushed for Austria to critically examine its role in the war and the Holocaust. She noted then, "Certain dark impulses in the collective unconscious should be left in peace and not awakened. I do not believe that dragging something to light removes it from the world. ... because a collective analysis does not exist."[128] During this time Spiel found herself on the same side of a generational divide as many far more conservative fellow Austrians. While in the early years of her return to Austria, Spiel was openly critical of the limited de-Nazification process in Austria and the ease with which former Nazis could resume prominent positions, the latent anti-Semitism inscribed into postwar life in Austria was never the specific target of her public criticism.

The ambivalence of Spiel's comments on Jews and anti-Semitism make it clear that a positive relationship to her own Jewish origins never provided an answer to her many years of probing for a space of belonging and identification. While her essays, fiction, and autobiographical writing all reveal her sense of the importance of writing for identity construction, one can search these writings in vain for clear outcomes of this process. This, however, should not surprise. Spiel's biography is riddled with ruptures—1936, 1938, 1946, 1963—each of which was sufficiently traumatic as to necessitate a fundamentally new orientation. The shock of exile and the shock of return recurred often in Spiel's life, precluding the establishment of this new orientation and rendering the process of questioning and stock-taking always open.

Conclusion

This chapter is necessarily the shortest in this study, as its focus is narrow: Within the relatively small group of Austrian Jewish writers who survived the Holocaust, I examine here solely the very few who chose to return to Vienna after the war to attempt to rebuild a life and literary career in the city. One can hardly speak of these writers as a group, not only as they were so few in number, but because the process of return and struggle for reintegration was an intensely isolating undertaking. Aichinger, Spiel, and Torberg did not return to any established Jewish community, nor were they encouraged to create one. Their experiences of return were separated by years, as well as by the unique set of circumstances surrounding both their exile experiences and their reentries into Austrian life. Returning Jews were not welcomed back as Jews, and thus these writers did not forge ties to each other stemming from shared experiences of suffering and loss. In the case of Spiel and Torberg, there was a relationship between the two, but it took the form of a complex rivalry—in Spiel's terms, a *Freundfeindschaft*—the significance of which is difficult to gauge. In these three writers we have three isolated individuals who faced similar situations and challenges, but individually rather than collectively.

These writers were isolated in the social worlds they occupied upon return to Vienna, experiencing a gulf dividing them from their fellow Viennese and Austrians. In a literary sense, however, they forged connections that were vital. To write after the Holocaust from a self-consciously Jewish position, as Aichinger and Torberg did, meant that the great rupture of the Holocaust did not bring about the end of the tradition of Jewish writing in Vienna. Torberg's self-conception was closely related to this sense of acting as a torchbearer of Austrian Jewish literature. While he imagined himself as the last in this line, the torch was ultimately passed to writers of the second and third generations. We cannot fully understand Ruth Beckermann, Doron Rabinovici, or Eva Menasse (who we will look at in the following chapter) without considering their parents' experiences of survival, as well as of return and reintegration, and the role these experiences played in the lives of their children.

The literary works of Spiel, Torberg, and Aichinger differ significantly. They differ in their responses to the pressures placed on Jewish identity during and after the war, as even the notion that the Holocaust forged a collective Jewish identity is challenged by Spiel. The three responded in very different ways to the challenges of becoming Austrian—and Austrian *writers*—again. They did share common experiences of alienation, and for each of them, in some way, the return to Austria meant a renewal of the loss of *Heimat*. The common thread to be found in their writing is simply a deep note of ambivalence vis-à-vis the prospects of reestablishing themselves in the postwar context.

Notes

1. Cited in Heidemarie Uhl, "The Politics of Memory: Austria's Perception of the Second World War and the National Socialist Period," in *Austrian Historical Memory and National Identity*, Contemporary Austrian Studies, Vol. 5, eds. Günter Bischof and Anton Pelinka, (New Brunswick, NJ: Transaction publishers, 1997), 65.
2. *Rot-Weiss-Rot-Buch* (1946), 94 ff., cited in Uhl, "The Politics of Memory," 68.
3. Ernst Bruckmüller, *The Austrian Nation: Cultural Consciousness and Socio-Political Processes* (Riverside, CA: Ariadne Press, 2003), 354.
4. Uhl, "The Politics of Memory," 71–72.
5. Robert Knight, "'Neutrality' Not Sympathy: Jews in Postwar Austria," in *Austrians and Jews in the Twentieth Century: from Franz Joseph to Waldheim*, ed. Robert S. Wistrich (New York: St. Martin's Press, 1992), 226.
6. Brigitte Bailer, "They Were All Victims: The Selective Treatment of the Consequences of National Socialism," in Bischof and Pelinka, *Austrian Historical Memory and National Identity*, 113.
7. Robert Knight reports that 8,038 Jews were registered with the IKG at the end of 1948 (See Knight, 220), whereas Bruce Pauley puts the estimate at just over 11,000. See Pauley, "Austria," in *The World Reacts to the Holocaust*, ed. David S. Wyman (Baltimore: Johns Hopkins University Press, 1996), 492.
8. Robert Menasse, *Das Land ohne Eigenschaften*, 3rd ed. (Vienna: Sonderzahl, 1993), 15.
9. Egon Schwarz, "Mass Emigration and Intellectual Exile from National Socialism: The Austrian Case," in *From World War to Waldheim: Culture and Politics in Austria and the United States*, eds. David F. Good and Ruth Wodak, Austrian History, Culture, and Society (New York: Berghahn Books, 1999), 104.
10. See Anton Pelinka, "Taboos and Self-Deception: The Second Republic's Reconstruction of History," in Bischof and Pelinka, *Austrian Historical Memory and National Identity*, 96–97.
11. Franz Mathis, "1,000 Years of Austria and Austria Identity: Founding Myths," in Bischof and Pelinka, *Austrian Historical Memory and National Identity*, 21.
12. Uhl, "The Politics of Memory," 66.
13. Margarete Lamb-Faffelberger, "Beyond 'The Sound of Music': The Quest for Cultural Identity in Modern Austria," *The German Quarterly*, 76:3 (Summer 2003): 293.
14. Hella Pick, *Guilty Victim: Austria from the Holocaust to Haider* (London: I.B. Tauris Publishers, 2000), 96.
15. Uhl, "The Politics of Memory," 69, 73.
16. Ruth Beckermann, *Unzugehörig. Österreicher und Juden Nach 1945* (Vienna: Löcker Verlag, 1989), 23.
17. Pelinka, "Taboos and Self-Deception," 100.
18. Ibid.
19. Beckermann, *Unzugehörig*, 29.
20. Ibid., 28.
21. Ibid., 29.
22. Robert S. Wistrich, "The Kreisky Phenomenon: A Reassessment," in Wistrich, *Austrians and Jews in the Twentieth Century*, 234.
23. Pick, *Guilty Victim*, 65.
24. See Wistrich, "The Kreisky Phenomenon: A Reassessment," 235 ff.
25. Ibid., 236.
26. Ibid.
27. Knight, "Jews in Postwar Austria," 222.
28. Ibid.

29. Ibid., 222–23.
30. Ibid., 223.
31. Ibid.
32. Christoph Reinprecht, *Zurückgekehrt. Identität und Bruch in der Biographie österreichischer Juden* (Vienna: Braumüller, 1992), 40.
33. Ibid.
34. Jean Améry, "Wieviel Heimat braucht der Mensch?" (1966), cited and translated in Jacqueline Vansant, *Reclaiming Heimat: Trauma and Mourning in Memoirs by Jewish Austrian Réemigrées* (Detroit: Wayne State University Press, 2001), 37.
35. Améry, cited and translated in Vansant, *Reclaiming Heimat*, 39.
36. For more on Améry, see Vansant, *Reclaiming Heimat*, especially 35–41; Reinprecht, *Zurückgekehrt*, 44ff.; as well as Karen Remmler, "Sheltering Battered Bodies in Language: Imprisonment Once More?" in *Displacements: Cultural Identities in Question*, ed. Angelika Bammer (Bloomington: Indiana University Press), 216–32.
37. Knight, "Jews in Postwar Austria," 226.
38. Hilde Spiel, *Die hellen und finsteren Zeiten*, 224, cited in Vansant, *Reclaiming Heimat*, 54.
39. Schwarz, "Mass Emigration and Intellectual Exile from National Socialism," 105.
40. Vansant, *Reclaiming Heimat*.
41. Reinprecht, *Zurückgekehrt*, 83.
42. Ibid., 96.
43. See, for example, Ilse Aichinger, "Mein Vater aus Stroh" (1962) and "Alte Liebe" (1964). In *Ilse Aichinger: Dialoge, Erzählungen, Gedichte*, ed. Heinz F. Shafroth (Stuttgart: Reclam, 1971).
44. Bernhard Fetz, "Representing the Holocaust: On Paul Celan, Ilse Aichinger, Albert Drach and Heimrad Backer, With an Appeal for Critical Reflection on the Cultural and Political Field in which Holocaust Literature Is Inscribed," *New German Critique*, no. 93 (Autumn 2004): 58.
45. Cited in Heinz F. Schafroth, "Ilse Aichinger," in *Metzler Autoren Lexikon*, ed. Bernd Lutz and Benedikt Jeßing (Stuttgart: Verlag J. B. Metzler, 1994), 6.
46. Dagmar C. G. Lorenz, *Ilse Aichinger* (Königstein/Ts.: Athenäum Verlag, 1981), 7.
47. Lorenz, *Ilse Aichinger*, 14.
48. Tanja Hetzer, *Kinderblick auf die Shoah. Formen der Erinnerung bei Ilse Aichinger, Hubert Fichte und Danilo Kis* (Würzburg: Königshausen und Neumann, 1999), 21.
49. Klaus Kastberger, "Survival: Child's Play. Ilse Aichinger's *Die Groessere Hoffnung*," *New German Critique*, no. 93 (Autumn 2004): 74.
50. Ilse Aichinger, *Die größere Hoffnung* (Frankfurt: Fischer Taschenbuch, 1991), 146.
51. Ibid.
52. Ibid., 20.
53. Ilse Aichinger, "A Summons to Mistrust," in *Contemporary Jewish Writing in Austria: An Anthology*, ed. Dagmar C. G. Lorenz (Lincoln: University of Nebraska Press, 1999), 159.
54. Ibid., 160.
55. Ibid.
56. Ilse Aichinger, "Die Sicht der Entfremdung. Über Berichte und Geschichten von Ernst Schnabel," in *Frankfurter Hefte* 9 (1954): 56–60.
57. Cited in Sigrid Schmid-Bortenschlager, "Der Ort der Sprache. Zu Ilse Aichinger," in *Das Schreiben der Frauen in Oesterreich seit 1950* (Vienna: Böhlau, 1991), 93.
58. Schmid-Bortenschlager, "Der Ort der Sprache. Zu Ilse Aichinger," 92–94.
59. Ibid., 87.
60. Hans Wolfschütz, "Ilse Aichinger: The Skeptical Narrator," in *Modern Austrian Writing: Literature and Society after 1945*, eds. Alan Best and Hans Wolfschütz (London: Oswald Wolff, 1980), 172.

61. Interview with Ilse Aichinger, *Die Presse,* 14/15.6.1975. Cited in Wolfschütz, "Ilse Aichinger: The Sceptical Narrator," 159.
62. Cited in Steve Dowden, "Ethical Style: Susan Sontag in Sarajevo, Elfriede Jelinek in Vienna," *Gegenwartsliteratur* 5 (2006): 126.
63. Joanna M. Ratych, "Ilse Aichinger," in *Major Figures of Contemporary Austrian Literature,* ed. Donald G. Daviau (New York: Peter Lang, 1987), 40.
64. For further interpretation of this text, see Patrick Greaney, "Estranging Memory in Ilse Aichinger," *The German Quarterly,* 80.1 (Winter 2007): 42–58, and Schmid-Bortenschlager, "Der Ort der Sprache. Zu Ilse Aichinger."
65. Ilse Aichinger, "Wo ich wohne," in *Der Gefesselte. Erzählungen I (1948–52)* (Frankfurt: Fischer Taschenbuch, 1991), 96.
66. Ilse Aichinger, "Plätze und Strassen," *Jahresring 54. Ein Schnitt durch Literatur und Kunst der Gegenwart* (Stuttgart: Deutsche Verlagsanstalt, 1954), 19–24.
67. Ibid.
68. Ibid.
69. Ilse Aichinger, *Kleist, Moos, Fasane,* 63, cited in Greaney, "Estranging Memory in Ilse Aichinger," 49.
70. Ruth Beckermann, "1938, During the Austrian Anschluss to the Third Reich, Friedrich Torberg escapes from Prague, first to Zurich, and then to Paris," translated by Hillary Herzog and Todd Herzog, in Gilman and Zipes, *Yale Companion to Jewish Writing and Thought in German Culture,* 552.
71. Jörg Thunecke considers this to be among Torberg's most significant writing in his article, "Man *wird* nicht Jude, man *ist* es: Zur Funktion der jüdischen Moral in Friedrich Trobergs Novelle *Mein ist die Rache,*" *Modern Austrian Literature,* 27:3/4 (1994): 19–36.
72. For more on Torberg's *Mein ist die Rache* and *Hier bin ich, mein Vater,* see the following: Felix Tweraser, "Heimweh as Creative Impetus: Friedrich Torberg's Literary Work in American Exile," *Trans: Internet-Zeitschrift für Kulturwissenschaften* (15), 2003. (Electronic publication.); Cornelius Schnauber, "Werk und Leben Friedrich Torbergs im amerikanischen Exil," *Literatur und Kritik,* Feb.–March, 181/182 (1984): 60–67; Erna Moore, "Friedrich Torberg's *Mein ist die Rache* as a Literary Work of Art," in *Protest—Form—Tradition: Essays on German Exile Literature,* eds. Joseph P. Strelka, Robert F. Bell, and Eugene Dobson (Tuscaloosa, AL: University of Alabama Press, 1979), 111–21; and Joseph P. Strelka, "Friedrich Torberg," in *Deutsche Exilliteratur seit 1933: Band I, Kalifornien,* ed. Joseph Strelka, John M. Spalek, and Sandra H. Hawrylchak (Bern: Francke, 1976), 616–32.
73. Sigurd Paul Scheichl, "Why and How Friedrich Torberg's Forum Did Not Confront the Past," *New German Critique* 93 (Fall 2004): 87–102.
74. Ibid., 89.
75. Ibid., 101–2.
76. Friedrich Torberg, *In diesem Sinne...Briefe an Freunde und Zeitgenossen* (Frankfurt: Ullstein, 1988), 56. Cited and translated in Beckermann, "Friedrich Torberg escapes from Prague," 554.
77. Beckermann, "Friedrich Torberg escapes from Prague," 556.
78. Hans Weigel, cited in Evelyn Adunka, "Friedrich Torberg und Hans Weigel—Zwei Jüdische Schriftsteller im Nachkriegsösterreich," in *Modern Austrian Literature* 27:3/4 (1994): 214.
79. Hans Weigel, letter to Friedrich Torberg, 28 February 1946, cited in Adunka, "Friedrich Torberg und Hans Weigel," 214.
80. Hans Weigel, "Liebe Freunde, Ende April 1946," cited in Adunka, "Friedrich Torberg und Hans Weigel," 216.
81. Torberg, *In diesem Sinne,* 411–12, cited and translated in Beckermann, "Friedrich Torberg escapes from Prague," 556.

82. Friedrich Torberg, letter to the editor, *Heute*, cited in Franz Krahberger, "Die umfassenden Tätigkeiten des Genossen Hans Weigel," e-journal *Literatur primaer*, http://ejournal.thing.at/Essay/weigel.html.
83. Hans Weigel, *Wiener Kurier*, cited in Krahberger, "Die umfassenden Tätigkeiten des Genossen Hans Weigel."
84. Donald G. Daviau, ed., *Major Figures of Contemporary Austrian Literature* (New York: Peter Lang, 1987), 5.
85. Matti Bunzl, "Political Inscription, Artistic Reflection: A Recontextualization of Contemporary Viennese-Jewish Literature," *The German Quarterly*, 73: 2 (Spring, 2000): 164.
86. Friedrich Torberg, *Die Tante Jolesch oder Der Untergang des Abendlandes in Anekdoten* (Munich: dtv, 2002), 10.
87. Ibid., 11.
88. Ibid., 219.
89. Ibid., 34.
90. Ibid., 54.
91. Ibid., 91.
92. Ibid., 196.
93. Ibid., 213.
94. Ibid., 12.
95. Friedrich Torberg correspondence to Max Brod, cited in Beckermann, "Friedrich Torberg escapes from Prague," 552.
96. Torberg, *Die Tante Jolesch*, 189–90.
97. Ibid., 190.
98. Torberg to Max Brod, 1955, cited in Adunka, "Friedrich Torberg und Hans Weigel," 234.
99. Hilde Spiel, preface to *Anna & Anna* (Vienna: Kremayr & Scheriau, 1989), 7.
100. Sandra Wiesinger-Stock, *Hilde Spiel. Ein Leben ohne Heimat?* (Vienna: Verlag für Gesellschaftskritik, 1996), 31.
101. Hilde Spiel, cited in Wiesinger-Stock, *Hilde Spiel*, 33.
102. Wiesinger-Stock, *Hilde Spiel*, 51.
103. Ibid., 80.
104. Ingo Hermann, ed., *Hilde Spiel. Die Grande Dame, Gespräch mit Anne Linsel in der Reihe 'Zeugen des Jahrhunderts'* (Göttingen: Lamuv, 1992), 44. Cited in Wiesinger-Stock, *Hilde Spiel*, 71.
105. Hilde Spiel, *Kleine Schritte. Berichte und Geschichten* (Munich: Edition Spangenberg, 1976), 14–15.
106. Ibid., 14.
107. Ibid., 15.
108. Ibid.
109. Ibid., 16.
110. Ibid., 17.
111. Peter Pabisch, "Hilde Spiels *Rückkehr nach Wien*—eine besondere Thematik der Exilliteratur," in *Exil: Wirkung und Wertung*, eds. Donald G. Daviau and Ludwig M. Fischer (Columbia, SC: Camden House, 1985), 182.
112. Hilde Spiel, *Rückkehr nach Wien* (Munich: Nymphenburger, 1991), 54–55.
113. Ibid., 151–52.
114. Wiesinger-Stock, *Hilde Spiel*, 105.
115. Hilde Spiel, *Kleine Schritte*, 31.
116. Elisabeth Bronfen, "Entortung und Identität: Ein Thema der modernen Exilliteratur," *The Germanic Review* 69:2 (1994): 71.
117. See Bronfen, "Entortung und Identität," 73–77.

118. For more on the novel, see Dagmar C. G. Lorenz, "Hilde Spiel: *Lisas Zimmer.* Frau, Jüdin, Verfolgte," *Modern Austrian Literature* 25:2 (1992): 79–95, and Dagmar C. G. Lorenz, *Keepers of the Motherland: German Texts by Jewish Women Writers* (Lincoln, NE: University of Nebraska Press, 1997), 175–82.
119. Hilde Spiel, interview with Anne Linsel for *Zeugen des Jahrhunderts,* August 1988. Cited in Andrea Hammel, "Hilde Spiel and the Possibility of a Multicultural Society: *Die Früchte des Wohlstands* and *Mirko und Franca,*" in *'Other' Austrians: Post-1945 Austrian Women's Writing,* ed. Allyson Fiddler (Bern: Peter Lang, 1998), 131.
120. Spiel, *Anna & Anna,* 39–40.
121. Ibid., 54.
122. Ibid., 44.
123. Ibid., 169.
124. Ibid., 69.
125. For more on the gendered nature of the lives of women exiles, see Marion Berghahn, "Women Emigres in England," in *Between Sorrow and Strength: Women Refugees of the Nazi Period,* ed. Sibylle Quack (Cambridge: Cambridge University Press, 1995).
126. Wiesinger-Stock, *Hilde Spiel,* 50ff.
127. *Profil,* 23.10.1989, 11.
128. Hilde Spiel, cited in Wiesinger-Stock, *Hilde Spiel,* 180.

Chapter 4

VIENNESE JEWS FROM WALDHEIM TO HAIDER AND BEYOND

Two events in Austria's recent history have had a decisive impact on Vienna's Jewish community and, in a dramatically different fashion, on the nation as a whole: the 1986 election of Kurt Waldheim to president just after the disclosure of his Nazi past and the entrance of Jörg Haider's *Freiheitliche Partei Österreichs* (Austrian Freedom Party) into the federal government in 2000. The Waldheim affair drew Austria reluctantly into the international limelight as the World Jewish Congress and the international press brought to light the wartime activities that Waldheim had long suppressed and, after Waldheim was elected in spite of these revelations, aimed intense criticism not only at Waldheim, but also at the nation that elected him. This unwanted international attention raised the ire of broad segments of the Austrian electorate but was welcomed by a smaller chorus of critical voices within Austria, including the Jewish writers considered here, as a powerful signal that Austria could no longer truck such efforts to cover up unsavory elements of the past, but at last had to acknowledge its role in the crimes of the Nazis. The Waldheim affair thus had contradictory implications: On the one hand, it laid bare deep divisions within the Austrian populace, allowing anti-Jewish prejudice that had been just barely submerged to come to the surface. On the other hand, Austria was forced to come to terms with its Nazi past, and a public dialogue was finally opened, with the Jewish writers I will examine in this chapter playing an active part.

The outcome of the 2000 elections was no more amenable to these writers than Waldheim's election had been. Haider's right-wing Freedom Party had climbed to national prominence not least because of its success in mobilizing xenophobic and anti-Semitic rhetoric to garner votes. Some feared that the mainstream Austrian population would readily embrace right-wing populism with clear ties to a fascist legacy. Haider's electoral success was undoubtedly a disturbing indicator that perhaps the lessons of the past had not yet been learned. Yet writers like Ruth Beckermann, Doron Rabinovici, Elfriede Jelinek, and Robert Menasse were unwilling to let Austria off the hook. Instead they raised their voices in essays, literary texts, and films, viewing Haider's success as a challenge to Austrian democracy that they would rise to meet. Both challenges revealed the depth of the civic commitment these writers share, their stubborn determination to dispel the myth of Austria's victimhood, to confront the nation with its suppressed past, and to emerge as a highly visible presence in Austrian culture.

In this chapter I will examine this reemergence of a self-consciously Jewish literature in Vienna. Particular attention will be devoted to the relationship of this writing to the traditions of Viennese Jewish writing discussed in previous chapters. I will elaborate the way a number of prominent writers of the contemporary scene, including Jelinek and Robert Schindel, articulate their self-definitions as writers by referencing a number of important Jewish literary antecedents. I also focus on identity, not only in terms of the Jewish identities articulated by these writers, but on their concern with uncovering the complexities of identity-formation more broadly. Jelinek, Menasse, Beckermann, and Rabinovici have all engaged in a critique of an Austrian national identity constructed on the suppression of the past and thus have come to the forefront as some of the most important critical voices in contemporary Austrian society.

The Waldheim Affair

As the highly acclaimed Kreisky era came to an end in 1983, a rather complacent Austrian society was in for a series of shake-ups. The Austrian PR machine was, as ever, working away promoting the clichés associated with Austria around the world. However, a number of scandals were about to unfold that would tarnish the nation's reputation abroad in spite of these efforts to keep the focus on *The Sound of Music* and the *Mozartkugel*. In the winter of 1985 Austrian defense minister Frischenschläger gave a warm, personal welcome home to convicted war criminal and former SS major Walter Reder at an out-of-the-way airfield near Graz. Apologies were quickly made, but this handshake incident damaged the credibility of the government and invited the view that Austria was unreflective and unrepentant regarding its past. Looking back on the incident, Hella Pick, a British journalist originally from Austria, sees far-reaching repercussions, viewing it as "the prelude to, and the trigger for, Austria's fall from grace during the Waldheim era."[1]

Later that year, traces of glycol alcohol, an ingredient in antifreeze, were found in the Grüner Veltliner wines of the Burgenland, slipped in by unscrupulous wholesalers to sweeten the wines. The untainted wines soon became no more sellable than the contaminated bottles, and the reputation of Austria's wine industry was destroyed. In any other year, the scandal might well have flamed out more quickly, but Pick suggests that following the Reder incident, this looked like another Austrian effort to gloss over its weaknesses and present an unblemished image to the world.² As if that weren't enough, it had recently been revealed that millions of shillings in tax revenue had been lost in ill-advised oil speculation by a nationalized trading firm.³

While these scandals tarnished Austria's carefully cultivated image in the eyes of the international community, they were mere bumps in the road in comparison with the fallout over the Waldheim scandal. This episode dealt a very serious blow to Austria's reputation abroad and simply could not be glossed over with clever public relations. As historian Richard Mitten has noted, "Basking in the reflected glory of *fin-de-siècle* artistic brilliance could not obscure the less coeval features of Austria's political past."⁴

Although rumors about Waldheim's war service had already begun circulating in the preceding months, the scandal broke on 3 March 1986, when the first article appeared exposing aspects of the hidden past of the former UN secretary general. The following day similar reports appeared in the *New York Times* and were released by the World Jewish Congress. Waldheim supporters quickly seized on the notion of an international Jewish conspiracy and railed against Jewish influence in the American press. The reports revealed that Waldheim had been a member of two National Socialist youth organizations and had served as a Wehrmacht intelligence officer in the Balkans, attached to units that carried out brutal reprisals against Yugoslav partisans and that executed civilians. The allegations pointed to—but did not directly suggest—Waldheim's possible complicity in the commission of war crimes and explicitly accused Waldheim of dishonesty regarding his past.

Waldheim denied all accusations and dismissed them as malicious lies. He maintained that he had served as an interpreter during the time in question. He claimed as well to have had no knowledge of the atrocities carried out in the areas in which he served. Later, however, he did admit to having been aware of the crimes, though he continued to deny any personal involvement, and stressed that throughout the war he had merely carried out his duty. Over the course of the election Waldheim rather deftly deflected the issue of his having covered up his past, reducing the question to the central issue of his potential guilt for war crimes, which he denied.

The response by Waldheim's supporters is perhaps more interesting, as it was grounded, as I noted above, in a Jewish conspiracy theory. The Waldheim camp made use of negative stereotypes of Jews, which Mitten views as having contributed to the construction of a new anti-Semitic *Feindbild* in Austrian politics, a refurbished image of the Jew as enemy inserted into the political discourse. The particular contours of this negative image never fully emerged, but vagueness has never impinged on the efficacy of negative stereotyping, and that did not occur here either. The charges by the World Jewish Congress (WJC) were cast as slander against Waldheim as a person and as an affront to the Austrian people. Distinctions were blurred between the WJC, the international Jewish community, and "*das Ausland*" (those outside of Austria), all cast as representing a "threat" to Austria.[5]

A factor in the indignant reaction by Waldheim supporters was that after Waldheim's election to the presidency in the second round of voting, the focus of international criticism shifted from Waldheim to Austria. When the disclosure of Waldheim's suppressed past did not sink his election hopes but rather seemed to have possibly improved his chances, the election assumed a symbolic significance as a referendum on Waldheim's and Austria's relationships to the past. Writing in the *New York Times,* William Safire condemned Waldheim's candidacy as "an outrage to Western values and a sickening referendum on nostalgia for Nazism."[6] Historian Gordon Craig published an article in the *New York Review of Books* focusing squarely on the implications of the election for Austria. Here he stated that the 1943 Moscow Declaration, which absolved Austria of any responsibility for the war, enabled the nation to leave only Germany to come to terms with the past. Now these disclosures would put an end to this escapist tendency. Craig also expresses his concern over the xenophobia and anti-Semitism he identified in the campaign, as well as the defiant attitude of the Austrians in the face of international pressure.[7]

When Waldheim took office he was treated as a pariah by world leaders. He received no official invitations from any country in Western Europe. In 1987 the U.S. Department of Justice placed Waldheim on the Watch List, which barred him from entering the United States. This diplomatic isolation was broken by the Pope, who received Waldheim in June 1987. A meeting with German president Richard von Weizsäcker and Czechoslovakian president Vaclav Havel followed at the Salzburg Festival, in 1990. Within Austria, one might also speak of a gradual thaw in relations toward Waldheim. While some (including the writers in this study) remained constant in their view of Waldheim as an embarrassment and affront to liberal values, acceptance seemingly grew within the mainstream population as Waldheim's presidency wore on.

Austria's reputation had been badly damaged by the affair, but it also had the effect of ending the escapism to which Craig referred regarding the Austrian past. International pressure was strong enough that a confrontation with the past could no longer be put off. As Pick writes, "The compromises on which Austria's postwar identity was constructed became unsustainable."[8] The new chancellor, Franz Vranitzky, likewise elected in 1986 and the first member of the postwar generation to hold that office, was also the first to acknowledge Austrian responsibility for the crimes of Austrians during the Nazi era. The post-Waldheim–election challenges he faced were considerable: repairing Austria's damaged reputation, addressing the deep rifts that were evident in Austrian society for the first time since the end of the war, and playing a role in a national dialogue about Austria's identity and its relationship to the past.

In his extensive treatment of the Waldheim election, Richard Mitten distinguishes between the Waldheim affair, the controversy surrounding his election as president, and a "Waldheim phenomenon," the legacy of the affair. The phenomenon relates to the shift that occurred as a result of the affair in the role of anti-Semitism in Austrian politics. Mitten explains:

> What I have termed the Waldheim phenomenon in Austria is the persistence among broad sections of the population of anti-Jewish beliefs, coupled with an actual willingness on the part of some politicians to tap it, encoded in an appropriate post-Auschwitz idiom, for political ends short of discrimination.[9]

The resonance among broad segments of the population of the Jewish conspiracy theory as an explanatory model that could bring about a shift between victim and perpetrator was evidence of this resurfacing of anti-Semitism during the affair. There were also unrestrained anti-Semitic outbursts in the public sphere both during and after the election. A very large anti-Waldheim demonstration in Vienna in 1988 led to clashes between demonstrators and Waldheim supporters, who verbally, and sometimes physically, attacked them as Jews.[10] (This demonstration figures in the works of both Rabinovici and Beckermann and will be discussed later in this chapter.) These open conflicts would of course subside, but Mitten has been proven correct in his argument that the Waldheim phenomenon persists after Waldheim. The politics of anti-Semitic prejudice are a continued presence and have been effectively mobilized at other junctures during the subsequent two decades. The rise of the Austrian Right is a related development, as Haider's Freedom Party drew successfully on anti-Semitic and xenophobic rhetoric to garner support. And just as the Waldheim phenomenon continued after Waldheim, Haider's legacy is still affecting the political landscape now that Haider is gone.

The Waldheim affair mobilized Viennese Jewish writers as both activists and artists. Assimilation no longer seemed a permissible option, and silence in the face of open expressions of anti-Semitism was equally distasteful. In their works they have given literary (and filmic) expression to the Waldheim controversy, the social divisions it exposed, and the emotions and beliefs that spurred both camps into action. In their political activism and essay writing they played a role in spurring the national discussion on identity and the past that it had so long delayed to confront. In dealing with the individual writers of this group I will examine a number of texts in which these episodes in the history of the Second Republic are foregrounded. Their effects on the political views and convictions of these writers concerning the way they perceive their roles in the public sphere will, I hope, also become clearer.

Jewish Writers and Vienna after Waldheim

The events that followed the Waldheim affair in Austria kept the national discussion that had begun with respect to Austria's past alive, advancing it by degrees. There were significant efforts to repair Austria's damaged reputation in the international community, some at the level of public relations but many that were substantive as well. One event that occurred while the Waldheim controversy still raged was the U.S. opening of the exhibit "Vienna 1900—Art, Architecture and Design," in 1986. The mayor of Vienna, Helmut Zilk, was invited to New York to officially open the exhibit, and he used the occasion to announce plans for a new Jewish museum in Vienna. The museum was officially founded in 1988. (It moved into the renovated Palais Eskeles in the Dorotheergasse in 1996.) Shortly thereafter, the city's main synagogue, the *Stadttempel* of the Seitenstettengasse, was rededicated. These events were early manifestations of an emerging and increasingly visible Jewish community in Vienna during the eighties and nineties.

As Austria entered the 1990s, optimism reigned. Waldheim remained in office, but the role of the presidency had been reduced, and he was marginalized both domestically and abroad. The Cold War was over, and Austria was able to establish itself as an important player in international diplomacy by carving out a role as facilitator of an East-West dialogue. In 1995 Austria joined the European Union, another landmark in the nation's post-Waldheim rehabilitation. In 1998 the Wehrmacht exhibit came to Austria, creating significant controversies, but also spurring discussions of an aspect of Austria's history in the Nazi era that had numbered among the taboo subjects in the postwar era.[11] Ruth Beckermann's 1998 film, *Jenseits des Krieges* (*East of War*), documents the shape of these intergenerational discussions in Austria.

New debates would dominate political discourse with Jörg Haider's rise to national prominence. In 1986 Haider became the leader of the Freedom Party (FPÖ), a dwindling party when he took it over but one that he would personally transform into a major political force. In the 1999 federal election the party received 27 percent of the vote, up from just 5 percent before he took the helm.[12] By 2000, the FPÖ was the second largest party in the country. In the 1999 elections Haider's party garnered many protest votes of those disillusioned with the major parties, the Social Democrats (People's Party) and the Österreichische Volkspartei (ÖVP). The right-wing populist party also played on hostility toward foreigners with the motto "*Stopp der Überfremdung*" (a halt to infiltration by foreigners).

After this election the FPÖ entered the federal government in a coalition with the ÖVP, a move received with great trepidation outside Austria. The United States and the European Union were deeply uneasy about the rise of right-wing extremism across Europe and were dismayed to see this kind of coalition being formed. Haider stepped down as party leader, but his influence did not diminish as he withdrew to Carinthia. His party, however, soon began to experience internal strife. There were significant losses in the 2002 federal elections, with the party's share of the vote reduced to 10 percent; the Freedom Party was still a partner in a coalition government in 2003, however. The following years saw continued losses in local and regional elections. In 2005 Haider led a faction of the party leadership to withdraw from the party and create a second party, the Bündnis Zukunft Österreich (Alliance for the Future of Austria). In 2006 this new party received 4 percent of the vote, narrowly maintaining its seven seats in parliament.

The entrance of the Freedom Party into national politics was not hailed by all Austrians; rather, Haider and the party met with substantial opposition in the form of civic activism. In February 2000 the so-called *Donnerstagsdemonstrationen* (Thursday demonstrations) began. These were public protests against the FPÖ-ÖVP coalition, but they also rallied against racism, anti-Semitism, and *Ausländerfeindlichkeit* (*xenophobia*) exhibited by the Right and the stance of the ÖVP regarding abortion and homosexuals. On February 2, twenty thousand demonstrators took part in a *Demokratische Offensive* in Vienna; on February 4, ten thousand demonstrators gathered at the Hofburg. February saw further protests on a daily basis. At its peak, estimates place the number of demonstrators anywhere from one hundred fifty thousand people to twice that number. Weekly protests continued through the year and into 2001. The number of participants gradually diminished, but the anniversary of the first demonstrations continues to draw supporters of the movement into the streets of Vienna.[13] This long-running campaign is unprecedented in Austrian history.

The events described here were of considerable interest to the generation of Jewish writers at work in Vienna today. This group of writers shares a political commitment (if not a single unifying ideology), and these events figure prominently in their works. In fact, an interesting form of intertextuality emerges when the same seminal events surface as shared topoi in the short stories, dramas, and films produced by this group. Dagmar Lorenz refers to political developments as the building blocks of this politically engaged literature.[14] Viennese Jewish writers place at the center of their work certain socio-political issues rooted in their own experiences as the children of survivors living in Austria—issues of marginalization, identity, visibility, and invisibility. In what follows, I will thus return to a number of events discussed above.

Contemporary Viennese Jewish Writing

Before turning to individual treatments of these writers, I would like to establish what I see as common concerns shared by this heterogeneous group. My foremost concern here is to articulate my view of the relationship between this contemporary Viennese writing and the Viennese Jewish literary tradition that preceded it. My focus, therefore, is first, what unites these divergent contemporary works, and, second, how these texts relate to earlier texts by Viennese Jews and how their authors conceive of that relationship.

Living and working as Jewish writers in Vienna, these writers are of course keenly aware of the legacy of *fin de siècle* Jewish Vienna. Having grown up in postwar Vienna mainly in the company of other Jews, as described by Ruth Beckermann in her essay *Unzugehörig: Österreicher und Juden nach 1945* (*Not Belonging: Austrians and Jews after 1945*), they are also well acquainted with the Jewish writers of the postwar era. But there is more than familiarity that defines this relationship to the Viennese Jewish writers that preceded them. In a 1998 interview with Andrea Reiter, Beckermann said of Schnitzler, "I will never in my life understand another literature the way I understand Schnitzler. That is very clear."[15] The majority of these writers position themselves and their own work within a Viennese Jewish tradition, identifying particular Jewish writers of the past as literary antecedents that inform their self-conceptions as writers, provide the discursive practices from which they draw in their own writing, and inform their thinking about what it means to be an Austrian Jew. Beckermann draws on the Jewish cultural legacy of the *fin de siècle*. What she seeks there, however, is not an uncritical or nostalgic re-creation; rather, she makes use of the critical models provided in the literature of the turn of the century. She makes numerous references to Schnitzler in the essay, borrowing the title "*Jugend in Wien*" for her concluding chapter and invoking characters from the novel *Der Weg ins Freie*. Just as Beckermann expresses her affection for and debt to Schnitzler, nearly all of the other writers have also been explicit in identifying the influences on their work from within this tradition, not only via the intertextuality that is a hallmark of this writing, but in their attempts to explain their self-conceptions as writers and, significantly, as Jews. Beckermann has also expressed an affinity for the writing of Jean Améry, along with being influenced by Schnitzler. Elfriede Jelinek sees herself as indebted to Kraus and Canetti, and indeed, for her, this connection shapes not only her view of herself as a writer, but also her identification as a Jew. Similarly, Robert Schindel places himself within the tradition of Jewish coffeehouse literature.

Referring to the tradition of Jewish satire, Dagmar Lorenz has written, "Writing as an outsider who is intimately familiar with the mainstream point of view had long been a characteristic of Jewish writing of the interwar period, the Jewish cabaret, and the works of Jewish journalists."[16] This tension between familiarity and detachment is a crucial element in satire, but the insider-outsider position she describes could equally be applied to Viennese Jewish writers from Schnitzler to Jelinek. Occupying a unique vantage point that is simultaneously at the center and at the margins of Austrian culture, these writers expose the hypocrisies and the hidden anxieties of the society in which they live; they offer critique, at times they point toward alternatives, and they alternately satirize and elegize their environment, all the while producing literature that is itself an organic part of that environment. In spite of the great rupture brought about by the Holocaust, there are powerful continuities between this writing and the Viennese Jewish writing of the past, because of the self-conscious engagement of contemporary writers with this tradition.

If we examine a bit more of the quote by Ruth Beckermann, it becomes clear how this relationship to the Jewish literary tradition forms the basis for her experience of Vienna. Beckermann stated, "I love Vienna, and I will never in my life understand another literature the way I understand Schnitzler. That is very clear."[17] Declaring her love for Vienna and keen understanding of Schnitzler, she conflates the two, or rather she evokes Schnitzler as a vital presence, an integral part of her emotional attachment to the city. I see Beckermann as expressing a sentiment common to the other writers in this group. Vienna is in large measure a literary space for them, one they experienced through the Jewish writing of the past they know so well and one they construct and reconstruct in their own writing. The relationship is defined primarily in cultural terms. Lorenz contends, "All of them use the concept of Vienna and the corresponding associations of a complex Central European urban culture and a rich Jewish past as a communicative device and an arsenal of images, names, characters, topoi, attitudes, and, of course, language."[18] The Jewish past is richly present in the Vienna they create.

I return one last time to Reiter's interview with Beckermann to let the artist complete her thought. Her response actually begins, "The pleasant thing, when you don't live here, is that you can take with you what you like, the literature, the music."[19] At the time of the interview, Beckermann was living principally in Paris, though she maintained an apartment in Vienna. Several other contemporary Jewish writers in Vienna also have strong ties to another place: Schindel and Rabinovici to Israel, Robert Menasse to Brazil, Eva Menasse to Berlin. Most of them have at one time or another maintained heavy travel schedules. In order to continue to write and be productive, it seems these writers need to be in Vienna and, at times, to be distinctly elsewhere. They all write from a perspective that is at the same time cosmopolitan and very much rooted in Vienna. The themes they explore in their work seem to require this dynamic of exploration and return.

For these writers, Vienna serves as a more powerful referent than Austria. Indeed, their approaches to the difficult task of negotiating an identity as an Austrian Jew are rooted in a primary identification with Vienna. However important Austria is in their self-conceptions, there is nonetheless a highly complex relationship between these Jewish writers and the city in which they live and work, and in which they create in their literature. As they seek to create new narratives of the Jewish experience of the past and present, they are continually confronted with a city that exists at once as a lived experience in the present but is, at the same time, located in the past—a space of both personal and collective Jewish history.

Beckermann has used the term *"unheimlich heimisch"* (*"uncannily at home"*) to convey her sense of being simultaneously at home and without a home in Vienna, describing the insider-outsider position marked by the contradictory positions of familiarity and distance, as well as belonging and alienation. This feeling is constitutive of these artists' experience of living in Vienna, and it provides them a unique point of access to the culture about which they write. For me, an image from Beckermann's 1987 film *Die Papierene Brücke* (*The Paper Bridge*) captures the uneasy-yet-familiar position these writers occupy. Near the end of the film, there is a scene shot in a Viennese café in which Beckermann and these other writers spend a great deal of time together. Of all of the cafés in the city, this group of Jewish writers, the children of survivors, chooses to be regular patrons of the Café Prückl, located on *Karl Lueger Platz*. The windows of the café look out at a statue of Lueger, still accorded a place of honor in the city's representative first district. Rather than avoid the square valorizing the city's most famous anti-Semite, these Austrian Jewish writers have carved a place for themselves alongside it, where it stands as a reminder they seem to welcome. Their relationship to Vienna is in many respects a difficult one, but as we shall see—once again—the challenges of Jewish life in Vienna somehow give rise to creative tensions that produce remarkable work.

Ruth Beckermann

Ruth Beckermann was born in Vienna in 1952, the daughter of Holocaust survivors who returned to Vienna after the war. Beckermann grew up in Vienna and went on to study art history and journalism there, as well as in Tel Aviv and New York. She earned a doctorate from the University of Vienna in 1977. During her studies Beckermann worked as an editor for *Trend* and *Die Weltwoche*. Beckermann was seventeen when the watershed year of 1968 occurred, and from this time she was drawn into a long involvement with the Left. Her first documentary film (*Arena besetzt*, 1977) was devoted to the 1976 occupation of a former slaughterhouse in the third district that had been slated for demolition. The three-month occupation was ultimately resolved through a compromise with the city that allowed the buildings to be transformed into an alternative cultural center. The arena film project was the work of the Videogruppe Arena, in which Beckermann worked alongside Josef Aichholzer and Franz Grafl, with whom she then founded the film distribution company Filmladen in 1977.

For a time Beckermann's leftist activism dominated her intellectual engagement. Gradually, however, the anti-Zionism of the New Left led Beckermann to the recognition of what she would later characterize as latent anti-Semitism embedded within the movement. Her confrontation with the hostility of the Left toward Jewish matters prompted her to reevaluate not only the accepted political positions of the Austrian Left, but her own relationship to her Jewish background, as well.

Beckermann's works in film and in prose reflect this process of coming to a Jewish consciousness. Since 1984, when Beckermann published the historical essay *Die Mazzesinsel* (*Isle of Matzo*) on Jewish life in Vienna's Leopoldstadt, she has been engaged in explorations of the experience of European Jews since the Holocaust. Beckermann's style of documentary filmmaking is rooted in an approach similar to that of *Die Mazzesinsel,* as she favors the film essay, a genre that allows her to blend historical concerns—chiefly the depiction of Jewish experience in Austria's Second Republic—with more subjective and personal interests, including reflections on Jewish identity and on her own family's position within this broader history. Beckermann inserts herself into her films as a consciously subjective presence, posing question after question evoked in the travel, historical research, and interviews she undertakes for the films. Three of Beckermann's films, *Wien Retour* (*Return to Vienna,* 1983), *Die papierene Brücke* (1987), and *Nach Jerusalem* (*Toward Jerusalem,* 1990), form a trilogy of travelogues in which she layers a personal identity quest as a Jewish woman artist and intellectual from Vienna over a broader consideration of Diaspora Jewish life after the Holocaust.

In this endeavor Beckermann departs from the very personal question of why her parents and others of their generation chose to return to Vienna after the war, a city that was hardly welcoming of Jewish returnees. Her reflections on the Jewish Diaspora begin in the streets of Vienna. *Die Mazzesinsel* chronicles Jewish life in the second district up until 1938. An early scene in the film *Die papierene Brücke* unfolds with the filmmaker riding a tram around the *Ringstrasse* as she poses rhetorical questions as to whether the questions about personal and family history she is pursuing can be answered in Vienna. Her film of 2000, *homemad(e),* presents a slice of the lives of Jews who settled in the street in which Beckermann lives, while her most recent work, *Zorros Bar Mitzwa* (2006) brings to light the diversity of Vienna's Jewish community by documenting a wide range of bar and bat mitzvah celebrations being staged within it. Throughout Beckermann's work Vienna is at the center of a process of exploration marked by a dynamic of departure and return, distance and proximity, and the fluid movement between the past and present. Focusing on Vienna, Beckermann's works invite reflection on its place in European Jewish history and memory. What sorts of stories can be told in this city? How does Beckermann see the link between Jewish experience in the present and the legacy of Jewish Vienna? What kind of climate does the city offer an artist who wishes to examine topics previously taboo or underexamined? The city is a constant and significant presence in Beckermann's work, and she requires both access to and distance from Vienna in creating her narratives of Jewish history and memory.

In the essay *Unzugehörig*, Beckermann reflects on the complexity of the generational conflicts between survivors of the Holocaust and their children, describing her generation's struggle to come to terms with their parents' decision to return to Vienna, a city that clearly did not welcome their return and seemed merely to tolerate it. She writes, "To remain in Vienna the Jews had to let themselves in for conditions that dictated: repressing their own history. Considering the score settled. Starting from scratch. Acting as though that were possible."[20] Beckermann characterizes the postwar atmosphere as one in which the presence of Jews was an unwelcome reminder of a past that the dominant culture was eager to forget and that therefore required this presence remain undetectable. Those who wished to return were to do so as Austrians, and not as Jews.

Beckermann's critique is directed not only against the culture that established this strict set of conditions and constraints upon Jewish life in postwar Austria; she also discusses the negative effects of Jewish compliance with these imposed conditions. She characterizes the silence of her parents' generation on the Nazi era as contributing to the erasure of Jewish history and further suggests that living in Vienna under such conditions has produced a selective relationship to the past, corresponding to the official version of Austrian history of the Second Republic.

> The Viennese Jews staked everything on keeping the peace through inconspicuousness and silence on *sensitive issues*—and every issue that has to do with Jews can become sensitive. They mythologize their own history, cling to the great musicians and poets that Jewish Vienna brought forth, and forget the dark sides of emancipation and assimilation. They fantasize themselves back into a sugarcoated day-before-yesterday [*das geschönte Vorgestern*] without making clear to themselves realizing that it was this day-before-yesterday that lead to the yesterday of National Socialist persecution.[21]

This mythologization of history depends on the elision of the First Republic, the *Anschluss*, and the Second World War in order to reconnect to a nostalgic and sanitized image of Vienna.

> It seems to be no accident that for the Jews who remained in Vienna after the liberation, precisely those places became popular meeting points that corresponded to their view of the former monarchy, like the Meierei in the *Stadtpark*, Cobenzl, and Semmering.[22]

When Beckermann suggests that her parents' generation has clung to the great Jewish musicians and poets of a hundred years ago and developed a deep attachment to the scenery of Habsburg Vienna, she sees them as projecting a harmonious and productive Austrian-Jewish symbiosis onto the *fin de siècle*. The creation of an idealized image of Vienna in 1900 offers them the psychological means for coping with Vienna in the present. Turning to the Vienna of Freud and Schnitzler, of Mahler and Schoenberg, they effectively create bridges to the past, establishing a connection between nostalgic memories and present reality that obscure the experience of the war and the Holocaust.

For Beckermann's parents' generation, the cherished spaces of the city are the representational spaces that evoke the Habsburg monarchy. While it was important that these Jewish survivors of the Holocaust laid claim to such spaces upon their return to Vienna, they never aimed at establishing themselves as a visible Jewish presence. Beckermann's films at times revisit these central Viennese sites, consciously reclaiming them by placing them in the context of her explorations of Jewish history. When she films the tram circling the first district or takes her camera to *Stephansplatz* to film a demonstration during the Waldheim affair, these moments work to reverse the invisibility of the prior generation of Viennese Jews. However, as revealed by the film's *Stephansplatz* sequence in which Beckermann and her father are attacked by Waldheim supporters, the moment a visible Jewish presence is established, these central spaces can quickly be contested.

The major thrust of Beckermann's filmic treatment of Vienna does not revolve around these representational spaces, however. Christina Guenther has characterized Beckermann as a kind of cartographer, charting the lost spaces of Jewish memory and experience to reclaim them for the present. Beckermann's films and writings frequently draw us to the margins, to spaces at the periphery in the dominant narratives of Vienna's history but of great significance for its Jewish past and present—Leopoldstadt, the Prater, and *Marc Aurel Strasse,* for example. Guenther writes, "Thus, she engages in a subjective historiography of what Vienna might signify, using coordinates of both time and space to chart Jewish experience in Vienna in order to restore Jewish personal and collective presence to Austrian history."[23]

The film *Die papierene Brücke* explores these margins as points of intersection of the past and present. The boundaries between history and memory, between the personal and the collective, are fluid in this film, as in a number of her other works. In a voice-over at the beginning of the film, Beckermann explains her motivations for making the film. Having spent the summer reflecting on her family history, looking at old photographs and asking questions of her living relatives, she then left Vienna in the early winter, heading east, to trace in reverse the path that brought her family to Austria. It is evident that she approaches this personal history in the context of a broader concern with Central European Jewish history, as she notes that she was perplexed to just read that the fate of the Jews would only become the focus of study for scholars once there were no longer any living survivors. Beckermann comments later in the film that her own fear of forgetting this story that needed to be further explored is bound up with a fear of her parents' death. She seems compelled to document a history that is at once both personal and collective. She states, "It is a strange feeling when the events that shape your life become history. When you become an object of scientific inquiry."[24]

But just what does Beckermann seek as she leaves Vienna, traveling to Romania and into Yugoslavia, ultimately pushing on to the Russian border? As she describes her reasons for undertaking this film project, both the spoken and the visual narratives of the film underscore the impossibility of telling the story she wishes to tell from within the city of Vienna. Dismissing months of intensive study and reflection on her family history, Beckermann concludes, "I no longer understood anything during this summer." As we hear these words, the camera captures an unfolding street scene, filmed from inside a tram traveling along the *Ringstrasse*. The street is immediately recognizable, and even before Beckermann declares that her intellectual engagement with the Central European Jewish experience often makes her head spin, we can clearly see that she is, quite literally, going in circles.

Ceasing this circular motion and breaking out of the bounded space of Vienna, Beckermann travels east in pursuit of the stories her relatives had told her during her childhood. Her film suggests that the telling of and listening to the stories in Vienna is somehow inadequate to understanding her relatives' experiences. Her attempts to remember, record, and understand are insufficient and require a different approach. In Vienna these stories could not be fully explored. As the tram moves around the Ring, Beckermann tells the story of her grandmother Rosa, who survived the war in Vienna in hiding. Oma Rosa was able to escape detection not by disappearing, but by remaining in full view, erasing only her voice. Pretending to be mute, she was not recognized as a Jew. In a sense, Beckermann's film seeks to fill the void created by her grandmother's silence, seeking out the stories her grandmother did not tell her.

Beckermann addresses the spectator directly in a voice-over early in the film, asking, "The story of Hagazussa. Do you know it?" She then relates the story of an outsider named Hagazussa, who had little contact with the villagers among whom she lived. Gradually, Hagazussa became nearly invisible and was able to move unseen through the attics and cellars of the homes in the village. Thus moving freely, Hagazussa learned many stories, such as the tale of the paper bridge that gives the film its title. In many of her films, Beckermann makes use of this freedom of movement to trace the narratives she wishes to depict, moving among various sites of memory to produce a coherent narrative.

The film has two parts: the travel narrative of the trip to Romania and, upon Beckermann's return, an exploration of Jewish life in Vienna. The first part is a documentary of the Jewish communities encountered in the East. The Vienna portion of the film includes her parents' accounts of their experiences of the war and postwar return to Vienna, as well as a fascinating record of an American production of a Holocaust film being shot in Vienna.

Underlying the trip to Eastern Europe is the notion that those Jewish stories that remain unfinished or unsatisfying in Vienna will be completed. More specifically, the Jews Beckermann seeks out in Eastern European are those whose recent history is not marked by assimilation, accommodation, and silence, but are pockets of surviving Jews whose identity as Jews appears to be self-evident. In Radautz, Romania, she visits a community composed of ten Jewish men, all advanced in years, who meet daily in a small synagogue. Beckermann is candid in describing her impressions. She notes, "Like photos—that's how they appeared to me." The filmmaker's desire to integrate the scenes and images she encounters into a stream of memory and fantasy are foregrounded in the film, playing as important a role as the scenes and images themselves. In another village, she attends the synagogue on Hanukkah, finding the community very welcoming and happy to include "the visitors from abroad who want to take a quick look at where they come from, where their parents come from, their grandparents, and stories."

Yet Beckermann is also aware that this apparent simplicity and clarity is largely the projection of her own desires. In this last village, where the synagogue is full and lively and young people study Hebrew, all is not as it first appears. The community is challenged in its attempts to preserve itself and its traditions by the continual drain of emigration. There are only two young students in the Hebrew class. Adults both young and old are all asking themselves whether they should make a new start in Israel. As she travels further, Beckermann reflects, "The landscape drew me into it. I traveled as far as the Russian border. But the closer I came to the destination, the less accessible it became." While the film's interviews and scenes like the one in the temple suggest the continued presence of small Jewish communities in Eastern Europe, these are gradually overshadowed by a focus on empty spaces visually depicting the loss of community.

The pursuit of history and memory becomes more personal as Beckermann returns to Vienna to film interviews with her parents recounting what brought them to Vienna. Her father had come to Vienna after World War One from Czernowitz, eventually opening a clothing store and becoming a successful and respected businessman. Beckermann films her father in his clothing shop, neatly refolding his merchandise as he describes his experiences. The interview contains a number of comments on his relationship to his chosen city and to Austria. He tells her that there is a picture of the Emperor Franz Joseph hanging in his office, a lingering symbol of a once enthusiastic and unreserved identification by Jews with the Habsburg monarchy. His relationship to Vienna and the nation in the present is less clear; a sentence in which he begins to describe his relationship to Vienna after living there for so many years breaks off without conclusion.

When asked how he dealt with anti-Semitism after the Holocaust, Beckermann's father shrugs and states that he has always known how to defend himself, with words and, when necessary, with force. Although Beckermann's father downplays these experiences, the film seems to appraise them differently. The interview with Beckermann's father is interspersed with footage of the anti-Waldheim demonstration mentioned above. Beckermann films the arrest of an anti-Waldheim protestor, while the protestor shouts to the police officers, the crowd, and the camera, proclaiming his right to a peaceful demonstration. Beckermann's father appears, arguing with Waldheim supporters, who unleash a stream of anti-Semitic comments, each one more brazen than the last. In a voice-over, Beckermann asks ironically, "Who says the Viennese don't recognize Jews anymore? They exposed my father as a Jew right away."

Beckermann's mother's story is not explored as extensively in the film as that of her father. The film does contain an interview, however, in which she tells of her own return to Vienna after the war. She sees her own fate as having been determined by meeting and falling in love with Beckermann's father. She settled in Vienna with him because he was determined to make a new life there. Although born in Vienna, Beckermann's mother did not feel at home upon her return and would gladly have left. Yet she never felt she had the right to force her husband to leave. She reflects that because she had children, she was never able to justify to herself living among the perpetrators. Even after so many years, she says, she feels at home in Israel, and not in Austria.

In Vienna, as in Romania, the film takes up the experiences of other Jews outside of Beckermann's family. While she films her parents at home, at work, and in the street, Beckermann captures other Jews in a most unusual situation, far removed from everyday life in Vienna. Forty Viennese Jews assemble on the set of an American movie production (the filming of Herman Wouk's *War and Remembrance*) to serve as extras for a fictional Theresienstadt Ghetto created at the outskirts of the city.[25] As they shuffle past a sign announcing the ghetto marked with the proclamation "*Stehenbleiben verboten*" (No Stopping), the film visually establishes a contrast between the impossibility of remaining still and the surreal quality of their movements—a visual commentary on the Diaspora experience. In spite of the blunt prohibition, these Jews are rooted in Vienna, while at the same time their experience is one of movement.

Warming themselves in a tent on the set, some are reluctant to speak to Beckermann of their experiences, objecting to talking about it in that particular place, while others feel compelled to speak about the difficult memories evoked by the set. Beckermann notes that she finds herself thinking nostalgically of Romania, "where everything seems so simple." For these Jews, things are clearly not simple. Unable to tell their own stories in a city that long made these stories taboo, they end up as extras in an American version of their story—a narrative only possible because of the spatial and temporal distance that Americans have to the Holocaust, a distance that is impossible for Austrian Jews. The unreal space of the film set, bringing the past eerily into the present, becomes a site of memory, a site at which, for some, new narratives are possible. Beckermann films for a long time, commenting that she can't get enough of their stories of survival.

Beckermann's pursuit of stories of both loss and survival continually draws her in and out of Vienna. Dagmar Lorenz has noted the centrality of this travel motif in Beckermann's works. Lorenz sees the filmmaker as a traveler occupying a position as a deterritorialized outsider, an appropriate vantage point from which to explore the Central European Jewish experience.²⁶ A key aspect of Beckermann's film essays has been the pursuit of her own Jewish identity. This quest led her in *Die papierene Brücke* from Vienna to the far reaches of Eastern Europe, and back. Neither the Bukovina nor Vienna provided the answers sought by the filmmaker, who resolutely leaves the central questions of the film open. For Christina Guenther, the dynamic of departure and return may in itself offer the best approach to identity questions: "Beckermann's visual and aural trek in search of her paternal roots ends with the realization that locating Jewish identity in terms of rootedness within a fixed, geographically definable space, such as Vienna, is impossible; charting identity signifies a never-ending nomadic enterprise, a continuous routing or wayfinding without a specific destination."²⁷ The continued importance of travel and movement in her films of the eighties and nineties supports this claim, and Beckermann's shift to films shot solely in Vienna after 2000 may well signal that she has turned to new sets of questions.

While these earlier films continually shift between the past and present, Beckermann's 2000 film *homemad(e)* is more firmly rooted in the present. The film captures a pivotal moment in contemporary Austrian life, as the FPÖ coalition is assuming power. In this film Beckermann moves not only into the present, but back to the street where she grew up and still lives. A voice-over at the beginning of the film foregrounds the film's homemade quality reflected in its production and subject matter: "Having returned from a big trip with a big camera, I take along a small camera on small trips, no further than my own front door in the middle of Vienna."²⁸ The smaller camera limits the distancing effect between the photographer and subject. Similarly, a more limited use in this film of voice-over narrative distinct from the visual track keeps the viewer focused on the film's subject, the people who live and work in the *Marc Aurel Strasse*, while also shifting Beckermann's position from a detached perspective outside of the filmic images to sometimes being captured within, or partly within, the frame. Beckermann herself is thus nearly as much a visual as an aural presence in *homemad(e)*. This film shares with her other documentary work a highly personal quality, but here the filmmaker is a part of the film in a new way. In filming her neighbors and acquaintances, she engages in dialogues with the subjects of her interviews. They joke with her, ask her questions, draw her into a conversation. No longer the deterritorialized solo traveler, Beckermann is clearly a part of this community. But is she really at home? The *(e)* of the film's title, creating the unsteady adjective "home-mad," suggests that there is no simple answer to this question. For Lorenz, this film is a continuation of Beckermann's "search for the appropriate cultural and geographical space."²⁹

Like her next film, *Zorros Bar Mitzwa, homemad(e)* is an affirmation of Jewish life in contemporary Vienna. The film depicts vital, interesting people who form a community anchored by the sidewalks of the *Marc Aurel Strasse* and the Café Salzgries. Beckermann's identification and personal engagement with this world is underscored by the intimacy of her portraits of the street's inhabitants. Her interviews are conversations on intimate matters. She asks the interviewees about how they live, where they get together with their friends, how they get ready to go out, why they frequent the café and what it means to them.

While the familiarity between Beckermann and the people she films shows the filmmaker to be a part of the community she depicts in the film, when the discussion shifts from the intimate and personal to the public and political, it is no longer clear to what extent Beckermann or her subjects feel at home. The sense of belonging and community is attached to the street, and with Jörg Haider's rise to political prominence at the national level at this time, it is not integrated into a greater sense of municipal or national community. Is it possible to feel a part of this broader community when, as Beckermann's voice-over states, every third Austrian and every fourth Viennese voted for Haider? As the regular customers at the Café Salzgries relate their opinions about the election results, one man laments the artificial simplicity and clarity that Haider's party projects and wonders whether he can identify with this image of Austrian life. Another posits that the Café Salzgries will remain the same no matter who is in power but concludes on a more pessimistic note, looking ahead to the new century with a sense of foreboding. An unchanging Café Salzgries may continue to provide a respite for the people of the *Marc Aurel Strasse*. One of the film's subjects describes the role of this street in the life of the city, likening it to a village created within the city in order to be able to bear the stresses of city life. Still, the street does not shield its inhabitants from a confrontation with the nation of which they are a part. A number of the interviewees are involved in political resistance against Haider and thus play an active, if oppositional, role in civic life beyond the street. Beckermann, too, is committed to life in Vienna. This is the space where the stories she wishes to tell, usually rooted in the past, unfold. And her storytelling is, in an important sense, a Jewish endeavor, representing Beckermann's response to the compromises of her parents' generation of Jews when they returned to Vienna, an answer to the silence imposed on postwar Jewish life.

Robert Schindel

With numerous essays as well as poems on Austria's relationship to its recent past and on the relations between Jews and non-Jews in Austria, Schindel has much in common with Viennese Jewish writers of the second generation. They are his friends and partners in dialogue. But Schindel's biography sets him apart from these writers with whom he shares so much. He was born in 1944. His parents were active in the Communist resistance and were arrested and deported that same year. Schindel survived the war by being successfully hidden in, of all places, a Viennese children's home that was part of the National Socialist welfare program. Schindel has commented that this unlikely start in life places him in a position between two generations:

> I see myself in between, because the first year of my life belongs to Herr Hitler. And that first year is a very important year, as one knows from child psychology and psychoanalysis. And I spent this first year with my mother and then, after her arrest by the Nazis—that was a radical separation from one hour to the next—in the dark rooms of a nursery, moving from one childhood illness to another under the constant bombing attacks on Vienna. I can't remember anything, to be sure, as I was born in April 1944 and in April 1945 the war was over. But of course it impressed itself on me like an engram, marked my dreams, above all my childhood dreams and my suit of nerves. In that respect I am a survivor. One would have killed me if I had been found. But I can't be a remembering survivor in the literal sense ... [30]

Ironically, this National Socialist nursery was located in Leopoldstadt. It was here that Schindel's mother, one of only two of Schindel's extended family to survive the war, was able to find her son at war's end. Schindel spent his childhood in Vienna, growing up in a Communist milieu, in a city intent on reconstruction and moving on. Schindel described the atmosphere of the Vienna of his childhood in the 1950s as follows: "There were of course no writers, no artists, no scientists, no reliable newspapers, but who needed something like that? One was rooted to the soil, just us, average, but arrogant. Under these conditions the reconstruction of my city succeeded excellently."[31]

Schindel describes being derided as a Jew by children and adults alike. From a very early age he took refuge in language. He writes, "I ran screaming from the past, I still recall, I ran into the German language as though it were an eagle's nest. So I, the stranger, had to learn by listening to the smallest linguistic inflections and learn the unnamed languages, to translate the gestures."[32] Language came to serve the young Schindel not only as a refuge but as a defensive weapon as well. "With language came power and separated me from the past. Who spoke both High German and the broadest *Wienerisch*? We all threw stones at each other back then, yet I tried to construct an arsenal of words as extra protection and more and more came to replace the stone with the word, when possible more quickly, more tightly packed, more accurately than my classmates."[33]

Schindel characterizes the postwar atmosphere much like Beckermann does in *Unzugehörig*, as one in which the presence of Jews was an unwelcome reminder of a past that the dominant culture was eager to forget and which therefore required that this presence remain undetectable. He states simply, "After the catastrophe the silence was notorious."[34] In Austria, this silence prevailed for decades.

By age twenty, Schindel had decided that this silence was not for him. His first poem appeared at this time. At twenty-six he cofounded the literary journal *Hundsblume* and was well under way to launching a literary career as a poet, essayist, and novelist. Schindel has published six volumes of poetry with Suhrkamp.

His 1992 novel *Gebürtig* (*Born-Where*) won him a broad audience in Austria and Germany, and when the novel was made into a film in 2001, Schindel's audience broadened further. Now in his midsixties, Schindel is a cultural luminary in the German-speaking world, with a busy calendar. He has received several prestigious literary prizes and is frequently called upon to present such awards; he makes numerous appearances, giving talks and public readings, and often appears on German television as a writer and cultural critic.

Yet Schindel's prominence does not correspond to his self-image and self-understanding as a writer. As a Jew, Schindel would have a difficult time assuming the mantle of any kind of star status in Austria, and as a Jewish writer he occupies a complex position that is both part of—and removed from—mainstream Austrian culture. Schindel has raised the question of this insider-outsider status: "And yet are people like me Austrian writers of Jewish origin, or Jewish authors, Austrian-Jewish authors, or have I extracted my linguistic reference from the unterritorial clouds?"[35] The ambiguity of this position, the notion of hovering near the margin, is important to Schindel's perspective as a writer.

Schindel's sixtieth year was celebrated with the publication of a volume of poetry containing nearly forty years of poems: *Fremd bei mir Selbst* (*A Stranger to Myself,* 2004), and a volume of collected essays and recent lectures, *Mein liebster Feind* (*My Dearest Enemy,* 2004). In the latter title, the author refers to himself. With his choice of titles, Schindel surprises: do these works not contain the insights and reminiscences of a man experiencing his seventh decade? Still, we should certainly not look to this writer for a polished and self-congratulatory memoir. His nod towards self-alienation with these chosen titles is part of a decades-long process of reflecting on his writer's identity and his self-conception as a Jew. In his afterword to the poetry volume, Marcel Reich-Ranicki characterizes Schindel as an obsessed man whom you either accept as he is or turn your back on. Schindel, he notes, does not make it easy for his readers and critics, but above all, he never makes it easy for himself.[36]

Schindel's work is marked by a fluid movement between personal narrative and historical account, between Austrian and Jewish perspectives and positions, between past and present. His essays on a variety of topics occasion reflections on his particular perspective and thus draw him again and again to his own biography. This is the case in the essays collected in *Mein liebster Feind,* in which Schindel considers his own identity, Vienna and Austria, and his vocation as a writer.

One essay is devoted to prevailing attitudes regarding Austria's relationship to its National Socialist past prior to the Waldheim affair. He depicts a strictly superficial treatment of the past: "Besides Hitler there was as good as nobody to blame. More and more films were devoted to the topic; the U.S. film *Holocaust* let the Germans cry out of sympathy. We went from *Jud Süß* [Jew Sweet] to *der süße Jud* [the sweet Jew]."[37] Schindel asks pointedly, "Was that a dialogue? The survivors were as a rule silent, if for other reasons than the non-Jews of the same age. Yet in the second generation our discussion was too short term."[38] Schindel describes how the student movement turned its attention all too quickly from internal matters to foreign policy under the sway of what he terms the "infection of ideology."[39] Focus shifted, he claimed: "The dialogue about all that had passed and how this influenced the present became a monologue about world revolution."[40] In Schindel's view, as the Left—including the Jews of the Left—began to identify with many oppressed peoples of the world, the ongoing discussion was diverted; more specifically, as feelings for the Palestinians rose, sympathy for Holocaust survivors and their offspring sank.

Gradually, however, Austrian Jews became more self-conscious, coalescing into groups, becoming vocal critics of all forms of anti-Semitism. According to Schindel, the model was no longer one of accommodation and assimilation: "These were certainly self-confident people, who wouldn't think of having to accommodate themselves to non-Jews. We knew perfectly well that assimilation failed. And we know that the German-Jewish symbiosis never existed."[41]

Under pressure from the Jewish community, discussions of the war and the Holocaust continued. Schindel writes, "We talked and talked. Everyone else talked as well. A flood of films, events, symposia. ... The perpetrator countries are covered with a notorious babble about Auschwitz. From Bitburg to Börneplatz, the Fassbinder debate, to Goldhagen and the Walser-Bubis debate, we are constantly shouting, one against the other. It goes so far that people seriously take the debate on the memorial for the memorial itself."[42] Schindel admonishes that the victims of the Holocaust are being buried under these heaps of words and that the effect of these discussions is to make the Holocaust appear more and more unreal.

What then are the prospects for understanding between Jews and non-Jews in Austria and Germany? For Schindel, normalcy is an impossibility that must be accepted as such. Only then can a dialogue beyond what he calls "the soup of babble" be possible. In the face of this rather grim prognosis, Schindel has been asked to comment on the tense situation of living as a Jew in the land of the perpetrators. In an interview in the online journal *Trans,* Schindel commented:

> Vienna generates itself for me as a home in the Viennese language and not necessarily in the Viennese people, as they give me to understand from time to time that I don't actually belong. To exaggerate: no Jew can be a real Viennese. ... I can only feel at home where my belonging is self-evident and not where according to political circumstances I sometimes belong and sometimes don't. Seen this way Vienna/Austria can't really be my home.

Schindel goes on to explain the way that he has nevertheless managed to create a home for himself in Vienna:

> But Vienna and Austria is represented for me in the typical Viennese, Austrian, and German language. And there I found my home, there I can build houses through

sentences, raise walls, produce people I am friends with. In this way I can produce a home for myself through language.⁴³

Just as Schindel has consciously examined his relationship to Vienna and to Austria in order to understand the world in which he lives and his place in it, he has similarly considered his relationship to Jewishness. Schindel's essays contain reflections on how he came to see himself as a Jew, what role this plays in his self-understanding, and how this affects his writing. He explains that in many ways he came late to an identification as a Jew, as an adult. Having lost nearly his entire family, Schindel's childhood was not steeped in Jewish culture. He is quick to point out, however, that because his physiognomy was stereotypically Jewish, he never saw much point in resisting such an identification. Schindel describes his first conscious positive identification as a Jew as an experience at the instinctual level: As an adult, while walking through Vienna's textile district, a traditionally Jewish neighborhood (the subject of Beckermann's *homemad(e)*), Schindel felt an unanticipated connection to the people he saw and realized "those are my people." Does being Jewish make him a Jewish writer, he wonders. "Is there in me that cultural-historical memory and could this be a river in the process of word formation, through which the syllables swim, stemming against the river of forgetting, a memory?" he asks.⁴⁴

Schindel answers his own question by returning to the notion that an author's home is the language in which he lives. If his triple identifications as Viennese, Austrian, and Jew inform his relationship to language, then Schindel is certainly in good company. He has been more explicit than other Austrian Jewish writers in situating himself along a trajectory extending back to the *fin de siècle*. Schindel pointedly and consciously locates himself within the tradition of the *Kaffeehaus Literaten* (coffeehouse writers), linking himself to the past, and specifically to the Jewish past of 1900, through his writing: "especially in Viennese Jewish literature I somehow find a home: In Vienna I feel strongly that I am a Jew and see myself in a certain tradition with Kuh, Polgar, and Schnitzler," he writes.⁴⁵

In situating himself in relation to the legacy of Jewish Vienna of 1900, Schindel has thus found a productive position from which to write. Interestingly, to a large extent his relationship to language retains the defensive character that shaped it in his childhood. This, too, may well be a characteristic he shares with the literary forebears he cites. When asked whether the process of writing his novel *Gebürtig* had a therapeutic effect, Schindel noted, "It was clearly a little bit of *Kaddisch* for my family, who with the exception of two people all perished. I didn't really write something from the soul, rather I would more likely call it a casting out of fear. In the moment in which I put the fear into words, it goes away."⁴⁶ Through living and writing in Austria, he explains, he continues to find in language and the writing process both a place of refuge and a weapon. Schindel has remarked, "There I had to cast out the net of fear, catch words and hotly cry them into a linguistic suit of armor and chill it with iciness, so that it would harden me, yet itself remain supple."[47]

The Jewish characters in *Gebürtig* exhibit a variety of ways of relating to their Jewish background, but they seem to share the author's sense of a compulsion to write. The narrative structure of the text reflects both the importance and problematic nature of writing, as the narration shifts back and forth between Alexander Demant (who is also referred to as Sascha Graffito) and his twin brother, Danny, who together occupy the twin roles of actor and observer. It is never firmly established whether Alexander, the main narrator of the novel, actually exists as a character; his is a paper, note-taking existence that does not yield a coherent narrative but merely shields him from the need to participate actively in life. At the same time, his other half, Danny, is able to live problem free by avoiding the obsessive writing that consumes Alexander. Nearly every other important character in the novel is somehow engaged in the process of writing. Emanuel Katz, the son of survivors, takes up a number of writing projects and "empties his soul by filling up manuscript pages."[48] The Jewish playwright Hermann Gebirtig, a survivor whose parents died at Auschwitz, pointedly writes comedies from his New York home and avoids the subject of the war, as well as the German language and the German publishing industry.

While many of the characters in the novel engage in writing as identity-formation, it is striking that only the non-Jewish Konrad Sachs seems to have a problem-free relationship to writing. Indeed, Sachs "comes out" as the son of the former Nazi governor general of Poland by writing his memoirs, freeing himself of the guilt unleashed by the return of repressed memories from his childhood. His book—while not universally well received—is the only one that has any evidence of reaching the public in this novel. It seems that the "trauma" of the perpetrators lends itself to narration in a way that the trauma of the survivors and the children of survivors does not.

In Schindel's novel, writing and language are the means by which identity is established and expressed, but such projects are continually fraught with problems. Whether one tries to write one's story as an Austrian Jew or to write oneself out of such an identity, the task appears to be impossible. The latter attempt is represented in the novel by the Austrian Jewish poet Paul Hirschfeld, who refuses to emphasize his Jewish identity (taking a position reminiscent of Hilde Spiel)—"And besides, I don't let Hitler dictate who I am"[49]—and fears disappearing into a "ghetto" of Jewish writers.[50] The editor Danny Demant tells him, however, that his "relationship to language has something Jewish to it."[51] When he protests, pointing out that he writes "impeccable German," Demant responds that it is precisely this endless attempt to prove that he can write as an Austrian and not a Jew that sets him apart from non-Jewish writers.[52] There is thus no way out of the double bind, a need to tell one's story and an inability to tell that story effectively.

For Schindel, the key to overcoming this challenge lies in the past. By locating his writing within the tradition of Viennese Jewish writing extending back to the *fin de siècle,* Schindel has created a linguistic home that enables him to write. Taking his place alongside Polgar, Kuh, and Schnitzler, he writes himself into a tradition in a way that both maintains the vitality of that tradition and fuels his own creativity.

Doron Rabinovici

Doron Rabinovici first emerged in the political arena in the wake of Waldheim's election. In the debates surrounding the election and the disclosure of Waldheim's wartime activities, Rabinovici came forward as a representative of the Jewish students' organization from the University of Vienna, joining a chorus of critical voices that at last came to challenge that founding myth of the Second Republic—the notion of Austria as the first victim of fascism. Rabinovici's literary work is marked by his political engagement, and he has also continued to be a presence in the public arena, contributing essays and public addresses on current political and cultural issues in Austria.

Rabinovici was born in 1961, in Tel Aviv, where his parents had sought refuge from the Nazis, fleeing from Romania and Lithuania. At the age of three, he moved to Vienna with his family and has maintained both Israeli and Austrian citizenship throughout his lifetime. Rabinovici studied history, ethnology, medicine, and psychology at the University of Vienna, earning a Ph.D. in history in 2000, with a dissertation on the activities of the *Judenrat* (Jewish Council) during the Holocaust. This work appeared with Suhrkamp in 2000 as *Instanzen der Ohnmacht: Wien 1938–1945. Der Weg zum Judenrat (Authorities of Powerlessness: Vienna 1938–1945. The Path to the Judenrat).* Rabinovici has published a collection of stories, *Papirnik* (1994), a volume of essays, *Credo und Credit* (2001), and the novels *Suche nach M. (The Search for M,* 1997) and *Ohnehin* (2005). In 2008 Rabinovici published *Der ewige Widerstand: Über einen strittigen Begriff (Eternal Resistance: On a Controversial Term).* Like Robert, Elizabeth, and Eva Menasse, Rabinovici has also written for children. His book *Das Jooloomooloo,* a children's story with an ecological message, also appeared in 2008.

For Rabinovici, the Austrian and Israeli poles of his existence combine to constitute his identity, albeit as a rather unstable construct. The various components of his self-identification—as Austrian, Israeli, writer, and Jew—do not always share a harmonious relationship. On 18 October 1999, in the wake of the startling success of Haider's Freedom Party in the federal elections, Rabinovici published an essay in the newspaper *Der Standard.* In the essay, which ran under the title, "Der nationale Doppler" ("The National Doubler"), Rabinovici portrays himself as a cultural hybrid, split into two halves, Israeli and Austrian. The two identities, however, appear irreconcilable, with each side pitted against the other in a heated debate:

> A few days ago Doron R., born in Tel Aviv, threatened to reconsider his relationship to D. Rabinovici, who lives in Vienna. Ever since my inner life has been in turmoil. The two of them cannot leave each other alone, they fight and pronounce harsh judgments on the media, but just over that of the other country respectively.[53]

Rabinovici constructs a dialogue in which his Israeli self threatens to cut off relations with his Austrian self, which in turn bristles at international pressures being brought to bear on the internal matter of national elections. The conflict deepens: "So I go around as a national double, as a high-percentage cocktail, through the streets in which flames of hatred against foreigners were just fanned, flame-yellow, and I feel so much at home and totally alien."[54]

In Rabinovici's fantasy, the Israeli self, to which he refers in the essay as *"mein innerer Orientale"* (my inner Oriental), gains the upper hand, exerting a sense of moral superiority over his Austrian self: "You Diaspora Jews celebrate the Israeli Independence Day, you take it easy because you know that you can find sanctuary with us at any time. What are you even still doing here in Vienna, you *Überfremdling [excess alien]*?"[55] The two halves of the term "Austrian-Jewish" seem irreconcilably split by the hyphen that is supposed to join them.

Evoking the term *Überfremdung*, which was resurrected from the Nazi era in the Freedom Party's 1999 campaign, Rabinovici signals the extent of the divide between his two selves. Employing this loaded term, the Israeli in him calls upon his Austrian counterpart to be mindful of the historical parallels between the present and Austria's repressed past; implicit is the notion that recalling this history renders life in Austria untenable for Jews. The debate continues, although the dialogue breaks down before reaching any sort of resolution, as each side merely stakes out its own position. Rabinovici's Austrian self argues that a global, multicultural Diaspora life is a universal feature of the modern world. Yet this position is undermined as he suggests that while common issues and concerns may exist in different parts of the world, the responses are always contingent and divergent. He illustrates the extent of the culture gap on such issues by highlighting the limits of language. What constitutes a neo-Nazi, for example, is very different in Austria than in Israel. Given the very different valence of language in these two contexts, even a discussion of problems of racism within Haider's populist politics is difficult.

Rabinovici's two selves seem to speak to each other across an unbridgeable divide; his identity is fractured. He writes:

> My two agree only that they live in a schizoid situation. In a world that celebrates populist successes with the unambiguousness of ethnic belonging, a Babel of different identities buzzes within me. And I listen to what is said in multiple soundscapes. I hear spatially and live in the echo of many cultures.[56]

The space that Rabinovici occupies as a Jewish writer living in Vienna is thus a conflicted one. The fragmentation of his identity is not overcome at the close of the essay. Yet, ultimately, this position is depicted in positive terms. Exposed to the "*Stimmengewirr verschiedener Identitäten*" (babble of different identities), Rabinovici is open to multiple voices and cultures. In his writing he gives voice to both parts of his identity. As historian and essayist Rabinovici has continued to play a prominent role commenting on Austrian politics, as well as participating in social and cultural debates. He has also been a political activist since his student days, speaking out against racism and anti-Semitism as a member of the Republican Club New Austria, a group that formed during the Waldheim election campaign. He belongs to the Demokratische Offensive, an anti-Haider movement. Along with Robert Misik, Rabinovici coedited the volume *Republik der Courage: Wider die Verhaiderung* (2000), denouncing the "Haiderization" of Austria and spurring the nation's civil society to action. Well aware that this phenomenon lives on after the death of the populist leader in October 2008, Rabinovici continues his activism and role as commentator on Austria's past and present.

In his literary work, past and present are interwoven in the pursuit of questions of identity and memory. In Rabinovici's 1997 novel, *Suche nach M. (Search for M.),* Austria's repression of the past inhibits his characters' capacity for expression. Like Schindel's *Gebürtig, Suche nach M.* can be seen as something of a ghost story in which the post-Shoah generation is haunted by the victims of the Shoah and the unresolved questions of guilt and responsibility that they pose.[57] Though Rabinovici's novel does not deal explicitly with the process of writing in the way that Schindel's novel does, it does seem to connect the trauma experienced by the main characters—Arieh Arthur Bein and Dani Morgenthau—to their parents' unwillingness and inability to tell their own stories. Arieh's father has continually changed his name and identity throughout his life, re-creating himself and his life story several times, and he seems to bequeath this instability of identity to his son, who has the talent of being able to profile criminals by putting himself in their place. Dani Morgenthau demands from his parents "a proper story,"[58] yet again and again they give him only the repeated and aborted opening line: "There was once a small boy and his name was Dani."[59] The attempts at a continuation of the story repeatedly confuse Dani with victims of the Holocaust, leading to Dani's curse/talent of experiencing the guilt of those around him. Neither Rabinovici's nor Schindel's novel ends on a particularly hopeful note, concluding that a satisfying story might never be able to be told. In fact, *Gebürtig* ends with a highly ironic scene of the Viennese Jewish characters in the novel serving as extras on a location shoot of an American film about the Holocaust set in a concentration camp (Schindel's treatment of the scene filmed by Beckermann). Unable to tell their own stories, they end up as characters in an American version of their story.

In 1995, Rabinovici was asked in an interview whether he would leave Austria if Haider were elected chancellor. The question subsequently became an occasion for him to reflect on the political climate at the time and his relationship to it as a Jew. For Rabinovici the question may have been motivated by sensitivity to the problematic relationship of Jews to Austria, particularly when broad segments of the non-Jewish Austrian population were embracing Haider's politics, but the question was ultimately based on a fundamental misunderstanding: "The inquiry into Jewish thoughts of exile implies that Jews, by virtue of an inherited impotence, are incessant victims. Traumatized, a frightened flock that has been sitting on packed suitcases since 1945. Utterly the 'wandering Jew.'"[60] Rabinovici rejected such identification as a victim, insisting instead on his rights as a citizen of the Austrian Republic. While he resisted being read strictly as a Jewish writer, he also openly proclaimed his Jewish identity and suggested that it plays an important role in defining his critique. Reflecting on the interview, he noted, "Seen in this way maybe my texts are, when I really think about it, also a Jewish articulation against the reality of this republic, but on the other hand, an insistence on autonomy."[61] This assessment allows for the possibility of recognizing in his works the ways in which his Jewish identity informs his perspective. As a writer who embraces the often dissenting and contradictory elements of his own identity, Rabinovici's texts underscore the instability of cultural identity and serve to illuminate and critique the harmonizing tendency of Austrian culture that seeks to exclude difference and dissent.

Rabinovici's 2004 novel *Ohnehin*, like his other fictional work, has a contemporary focus. The novel unfolds in Vienna in the fall of 1995. Rabinovici concretizes the temporal setting by referencing the election campaign that would result in significant gains for Haider's Freedom Party. He also refers to the brutal murder of four Roma men the same year. While Rabinovici is clearly capturing a contemporary moment in Viennese life, there are multiple temporal frames at work in the novel. Even as he reflects on his own time in his writing, Rabinovici's novel resembles others considered here in its evocation of the past in the present. In various ways, many characters of the novel experience an aspect of the past as a palpable and significant part of their current lives. The whole city seems to be groaning under the weight of its past, as the protagonist, the neurologist Stefan Sandtner, encounters the refrain "*Einmal muss Schluss sein*" (At some point, there has to be an end to it) everywhere he goes. No one experiences the simultaneity of past and present more dramatically than Sandtner's former neighbor Herbert Kerber, who becomes his patient. Kerber suffers from the neurological disorder Korsakoff syndrome, which diminishes his ability to make new memories and collapses the present into the past, leaving him convinced that he is living in 1945. The former SS man believes he is experiencing the end of the war and is waiting to be reunited with his wife, who has sought refuge in the provinces. Kerber is frozen in this other time, wholly unaware of the present, and complains of his suffering during the war. Kerber's assessment of his wartime activities is reminiscent of Waldheim, and, when pressed, he intones that he was merely doing his duty, becoming another source of the ubiquitous *"Einmal muss Schluss sein."*

Kerber's inability to distinguish between past and present is acute, a brain disorder that sets him apart from the other characters of the novel. Rabinovici peppers the narrative, however, with other characters for whom the unresolved past is a burden. Kerber's daughter, Bärbl, long unaware of her father's Nazi past, becomes obsessed with forcing her father to acknowledge his wartime crimes. She stages a farcical interrogation of her father over a number of days in which she seemingly loses all awareness of her father's physical state—an elderly man in need of medical care. Kerber's Jewish neighbor, Paul Guttmann, has a healthier approach to the past. His decision to live in Vienna after the war represents a choice of a conscious, a continual confrontation with the past: "For Guttmann, to live at this place meant to stay on the lookout, to affirm every day the defeat of the murderers and his own survival."[62] Guttmann's family, however, does not share his taste for a daily confrontation with the recent past as a reminder of the triumph of his survival. Guttmann was Romanian, but his wife was Viennese, and for her, the return to her hometown meant only a confrontation with the losses she had suffered. She returned only for his sake. Their son, Mischa, who goes to live in Tel Aviv as soon as he had completed his medical training, has never understood his father's decision, never grasped "what he ever came here for."[63]

Sandtner has other patients with memory issues related to their wartime experiences. Kerber's is not the only case in which memory and forgetting are not two opposite poles, but are entities that are intricately bound together. Another man was brought to consult Sandtner because he had begun to talk incessantly of the war in the form of nostalgic reminiscences that he had never articulated before. The unpleasant aspects of the war have receded from his memory, leaving more room for other memories. "Forgetting was the prerequisite of his remembering," Sandtner concludes."[64] This view is not limited to a diagnosis of patients with memory disturbances but is posited in the novel as an expression of the intimate connection between remembering and forgetting. While en route to the town of Bärnberg to represent Vienna's official Jewish community at a memorial for the town's murdered Jews, Sandtner's friend Lew Feininger shares his view on the kind of monuments he was about to dedicate: "Monuments are really more landmarks of forgetting."[65] He continues, "Maybe every commemoration, all rituals and memorials, are always instruments of both representation and forgetting at once."[66] Just as the present is not clearly separated from the past, remembering and forgetting are shown to be closely related and the act of memorialization, a matter of simultaneously retaining and dispensing with the past.

Sandtner's own experience of the present is not overly saturated with the past, but only because he is engaged in a temporary suspension of time. He has taken a sabbatical from his job after breaking up with his girlfriend, Sonja, who is also his colleague at the psychiatric clinic. The breakup sends him into a professional crisis in which he begins to question the value of his work. He begins a new relationship with Flora, a filmmaker from the former Yugoslavia, in which he resolutely pursues a path of living strictly in the moment as a strategy to avoid both the past (his breakup with Sonja) and the future (his professional path, his relationship with Flora). He focuses all of his attention on their evenings together—what and where they might eat together, how they might best enjoy themselves—never inquiring about her experiences in Kosovo or even her legal status in Austria. Flora is forced to leave the country when her visa expires.

Rabinovici's novel dissolves the boundaries between past, present, and future, positing the past and the future as challenging but integral elements of present experience that not all of his characters are equipped to deal with effectively. The necessity of being mindful of the past, present, and future is experienced as a burden, and, frequently enough, the failure to give the past or future sufficient attention leads to some form of breakdown. Sandtner's friend Lew Feininger may have the best approach to living with these multiple times. When Bärbl Kerber turns to him seeking to forge a connection, to posit a *"wir"* composed of the children of victims and perpetrators, Feininger declines. He refuses to play the role of offering her absolution for her father's sins, he refuses the victim role for himself, and he ultimately refuses the identification as a child of survivors. He insists, "I don't want to be a child anymore. I am an adult. You, too. It's about time."[67] *"Es ist an der Zeit"* may well be the antidote to the novel's leitmotif, *"Einmal muss Schluss sein."* While both positions seek to circumscribe the role of the past in the present, the latter phrase is always uttered in the desire to put to rest a past that has clearly not been sufficiently worked through. The same cannot be said of Feininger's position, however. Involved with the city's efforts at memorialization, he has engaged with the past represented by the war and the Holocaust sufficiently to be able to reject taking on a role that would allow it to overshadow the present.

Like Paul Guttman, Feininger may be in favor of a confrontation with the past in a measured dose, just a little history in order to live consciously in the present. As with Guttman's decision to live in Vienna, this approach has a spatial dimension for Feininger. The chosen *Stammcafé* of Feininger, Sandtner, and their friends is the Café Prückl, located at *Luegerplatz,* (also the chosen café of Rabinovici, Beckermann, and other Jewish writers). As Rabinovici explicitly links Karl Lueger to Hitler, we understand that Sandtner and friends do not trivialize Lueger's anti-Semitic legacy, as do many of their fellow Viennese, but consciously take in—rather than overlook—the statue as they routinely enter the café. An engagement with the city's anti-Semitic past is part of their critical engagement with Vienna in the present.

The friends' other favored site in Vienna is clearly the *Naschmarkt.* The open-air market occupies a very prominent space within the novel, and it functions symbolically very much the way the Prater did in a number of texts of the turn of the last century. Like the Prater, the *Naschmarkt* is cast as a world apart: "The place was its own world, an island in the middle of the metropolis."[68] And as in Felix Salten's Prater, social interactions across ethnicities and social classes are possible only in the park and would not take place otherwise. The fact that such interactions are at their core business transactions does not diminish the unique role of the *Naschmarkt* in bringing the Viennese together, particularly because, like the Prater of 1900, the market has its own social hierarchy:

> The *Naschmarkt* was a wedge that pushed from the suburbs into the city, forcing itself in between the districts. Whoever went shopping along the *Wienzeile*, whether a bourgeois lady or a petty bourgeois retiree, jostled their way through the throng of the crowd and first had to make themselves heard. The transaction seemed to be an intimate relationship in the public eye. ... It was the simple tradespeople who stood up higher here, up on the platform of their wares, and whoever wanted to hand them money had to bend over the fruit stand, on the verge of losing their balance, of flopping head over heels, while the business people waited nonchalantly and with a single movement extended the paper bag and collected the cash.[69]

Although Sandtner lives very nearby, the *Naschmarkt* is a new experience for him—his friends greet him with "Stefan, *you* at the *Naschmarkt*?"—and he must first learn to negotiate it. His first experience of the space in the novel is involuntary, instinctual, as the market draws him in against his will: "He wanted to hurry past to go find the patient, to rush through the *Naschmarkt,* but Stefan submerged into the crush of the crowd. ... Stefan sank into the dance of voices and no longer heard the noise of the cars. The tradespeople sang out their wares, lured him in. He dove down into the mixture of pungent aromas and sweet fragrances."[70] The *Naschmarkt* was a space of Sandtner's childhood, and he remembers his experiences there—holding the hand of his mother, an experienced practitioner of the whole market, and going from the elegant, more expensive stands adjacent to the city center to the more modest stands at the outskirts. Stefan possesses none of these skills and has to be schooled in the ways of the market, and he becomes the willing student of the Greek proprietor of a number of *Naschmarkt* stands, Georgios Alexandrus, a grand old man of the market. Rabinovici underscores the diversity and cosmopolitanism of the market, its unique position within the city as a multicultural space that brings people together and offers a sense of belonging to all. It had been the *Naschmarkt* that provided the young Paul Guttmann the opportunity to make a living and gain a foothold in his new surroundings, giving him access to the city: "This place helped him to feel at home in Vienna, even if he wasn't from here." (*Dieser Platz half ihm, sich in Wien zu Hause zu fühlen, wenn er hier auch nicht daheim war*).[71]

The *Naschmarkt* continues to function as a space of possibility in the Vienna of 1995 depicted in the novel. Multiculturalism reigns, and Haider's xenophobic populism has not penetrated the oasis of the market. Here a Turkish-Greek love affair is possible, and when it results in a pregnancy out of wedlock, powerful traditional tropes of family honor, national pride, and historical grievances are put aside in a new union of the two families. Rabinovici's *Naschmarkt* may be idealized in the way that Salten's Prater was idealized as a space of integration and the suspension of prejudice, but both imagined spaces constitute an important gesture of reimagining the city based on the recognition of real potential. Like Joseph Roth's image of Austria as a house of many rooms, Rabinovici's *Naschmarkt* represents an alternative Vienna rooted in inclusion and tolerance.

Robert Menasse

Robert Menasse differs somewhat from the other writers of this chapter in that the position he occupies as a writer is not a self-consciously Jewish one. Like Beckermann, Rabinovici, and the others, he views himself as an outsider in Viennese and Austrian society; however, this outsider position is determined by his role as a writer and not because of his Jewish heritage. He chooses a position of detachment from which to view and critique Austrian society.[72] Menasse rarely addresses Jewish themes in his writing, although his 2001 novel *Die Vertreibung aus der Hölle* (*Expulsion from Hell*) is an important exception, as it addresses his own history and Jewish roots. What he does share with the other writers, however, is a strong critical impulse in his writing—his essays comprise a compelling critique of the Second Republic, as well as a concern with the past and its relationship to the present. Critics have compared Robert Menasse with Karl Kraus, not least because each of them downplays their Jewishness in the name of intellectual independence.[73]

Menasse was born in Vienna in 1952. He studied philosophy, political science, and *Germanistik* in Vienna, Salzburg, and Messina, earning a doctorate in 1980. The following year he took a visiting position teaching literature at the University of São Paulo, in Brazil, where he remained for seven years. He returned to Vienna in 1988, the year his first novel, *Sinnliche Gewissheit* (*Sensuous Certainty*), appeared with Suhrkamp. Along with this work, Menasse's next two novels, *Selige Zeiten, brüchige Welt* (1991, translated into English as *Wings of Stone*), and *Schubumkehr* (*Thrust Reversal*, 1995) comprise his *"Trilogie der Entgeisterung"* (*"Trilogy of Spiritual Breakdown"*), Menasse has since written two additional novels, *Die Vertreibung aus der Hölle* (*Expulsion from Hell,* 2001) and *Don Juan de la Mancha* (2007), also published with Suhrkamp. Menasse has not only established himself as a major German-language novelist, but he is widely published and respected essayist, with numerous volumes of cultural, social, and political criticism. Menasse's essay collections include *Die sozialpartnerschaftliche Ästhetik* (*The Aesthetics of Social Partnership,* 1990), *Das Land ohne Eigenschaften* (*The Land*

Without Qualities, 1992), *Dummheit ist machbar* (*Stupidity Is Doable,* 1999), *Erklär mir Österreich* (*Explain Austria to Me,* 2000), and *Das war Österreich* (*That Was Austria,* 2005). He has received many significant prizes for both his literary work and essays. The writer resides chiefly in Vienna but has also lived in Berlin and Amsterdam.

As an essayist, Menasse comments on Austria's past and present from a perspective that is marked by both distance and familiarity. In an early essay, he foregrounds his detachment and isolation by describing the physical space in which he writes—a rented writers' studio in a house that was formerly a bordello, the first building in Vienna constructed explicitly for that purpose, he explains. The building sports a nondescript façade, which gives way to a far more striking interior—a grand, winding staircase snakes up the walls with landings opening onto many tiny rooms, providing numerous vantage points from which to survey the entire scene. The building is mainly inhabited by writers, since each of the tiny rooms, designed after all for brief encounters between two people, are unsuitable as living spaces. Menasse describes the theatrical quality of the building, immediately apparent to visitors seeing the space for the first time. Most visitors conclude that the building must have formerly housed a theater, but noting the lack of space for a stage, the second line of speculation often suggests a prison. For Menasse, the bordello is, in a sense, both of these things: "Theater or prison and repressed or forgotten history. An attractive appearance, unclear essence [*Schöner Schein, unklares Sein*]."[74]

In this house, built with conscious concern for outward appearances, Menasse sees a reflection of the city of Vienna. Just as the plain and respectable exterior of the building conceals the original purpose of the structure, Vienna is deeply marked by a discrepancy between its appearance and its deeper reality, he notes:

> Vienna is not the city it was constructed to be. The imperial no longer belongs to any empire, the Baroque to any Phaeaceans, the Biedermeier to any gentle idylls, the modern to any modernizers. Just as no desire strolls through the galleries of this house of pleasure."[75]

Menasse's analogy suggests a questioning of reality in a city of appearances. What does it mean for the artist to live and work in an environment that is all "*Schöner Schein, unklares Sein*"? Menasse seems at first to imply the impossibility of a productive existence in this unreal space. "Vienna is a city of backdrops. One cannot look behind them all, but in front of nearly all of them one can or must think: something was here. What is behind it? Nothing. In front is the appearance without essence, behind the essence without appearance [*Vorne ist der Schein ohne Sein, dahinter das Sein ohne Schein*]."[76] Here the vitality of the city is located squarely in the past—in the *gewesene*. Vienna, he suggests, is like a cell—too small and isolated, cut off from life. Yet Menasse's image does not ultimately suggest an empty or dead space. The vitality of the city is not extinguished, it is merely different from that which it projects. Tucked away in the former bordello with the misleading exterior is a colony of artists at work. Menasse closes the essay with a reference to his writing, indicating that his Vienna, in all of its complexity, is in fact a productive environment:

> Then I keep writing away on my novel in this cell in which one feels shut away from life the way it appears. And yet in these few square meters one can feel a part of the world the way it is, at least in this strange city, in Vienna."[77]

If here Menasse has considered Vienna as a cultural space for the production of literature, in the penetrating essay "Das Land ohne Eigenschaften" he focuses not on Vienna but on Austria, again considering the relationship between present and past. In this essay Menasse reflects at length on the problematic concept of Austrian identity. He laments Austria's stubborn reluctance to engage in serious self-evaluation: "No country of the world has fundamentally reflected on itself or its problems in public as little as the Second Austrian Republic."[78] In Menasse's view Austrians long ignored the question of national identity just as they suspended the difficult work of coming to terms with recent history. Menasse suggests that self-reflection has only occurred as a response to challenges from without, as in the Waldheim affair. He characterizes this process as forced and superficial and sees Austria's relationship to history as highly selective, based on a model of forgetting rather than remembering. The Austrian model of relating to the past is not, he suggests, the Freudian therapeutic model of "remember, repeat, work through." The Austrian approach, he suggests, is: "forget, repeat, explain abroad."[79] Menasse's writing challenges this readiness to forget the past both in the potent cultural criticism of his essays and in the creation of new narratives of the past and present in his fictional work.

In Menasse's novel *Selige Zeiten, brüchige Welt,* the character Judith reflects, "The exile of the parents also means exile for the next generation, and it is in exile no matter where it is. Here or there, that doesn't matter at all. The question is: can something arise out of exile? And the answer has already been given many times over."[80] Judith has grown up in Brazil, the site of her parents' exile from Vienna. When she goes to Vienna to study and experience the place of her parents' past, she does not feel at home but accepts this position of foreignness and unfamiliarity as the inevitable condition of her existence. The important issue for her is simply whether this position can be productive. As is the case with Schindel and Rabinovici, Menasse personally fares considerably better in overcoming the challenges that stand in the way of finding that productive space from which to work (to write) than his characters manage to.

In his 2001 novel *Die Vertreibung aus der Hölle,* Menasse turns his attention to Jewish culture. While much of the work depicts the persecution of seventeenth-century Sephardic Jews during the Spanish Inquisition, Menasse did not produce a straightforward historical novel, and indeed the author has repeatedly objected to this descriptor. Rather, the novel inhabits multiple genres. It is constructed via two major strands, dual biographies separated by three centuries that intertwine in important ways. Part biography and part Bildungsroman, the novel focuses on the development of the characters Rabbi Samuel Manasseh and Viktor Abravanel. The novel is a historical novel and contemporary novel at once, presenting a narrative of the events that led to the expulsion of Jews from the Iberian Peninsula and the establishment of a Jewish community in Amsterdam, as well as a nuanced portrait of the Second Austrian Republic. For Irmela von der Lühe, this work's pursuit of a dual narrative and experimentation with parallels and blending shows Menasse engaging in a postmodern play with the laws of genre.[81]

What is most important in Menasse's drawing on multiple genres is, first, the relationship between the two strands of the story and, second, his approach to history. The two characters Viktor and Mane are similar in background and personality, and they share a surprising number of experiences in spite of the temporal distance that separates them. Both are the children of survivors and both are unaware of their Jewish origins as young children. Mane's family is Portuguese Marrano, cryptic Jews practicing their faith in secret after the forced conversion of all Portuguese Jews. In order to protect the family's secret, the parents withhold from Mane his background and the meaning of the rituals that shape their lives. Viktor is born in postwar Austria—on the day of the signing of the Austrian State Treaty marking the end of the Allied occupation. Viktor's parents and grandparents take pains to avoid any discussion of the war and tolerate no questions on the subject. Although he is unclear on his family's history, Viktor's childhood is shaped by the attempt to assimilate, to go unnoticed and avoid trouble. Through many years Viktor wonders, "How long could one live without ever breathing deeply?"[82] Even as an adult, Viktor has trouble answering his former classmate when she asks if he is Jewish.

Both Mane and Viktor remain outsiders despite their significant efforts to fit in. They both experiment with humiliating other children but far more often suffer humiliation themselves, as when each of them is cast as Maria as their schools stage the Nativity. Mane and Viktor even share family ties, and near the end of the novel we learn that Viktor, now an historian of the Early Modern period, is slated to present a paper on Rabbi Samuel Manasseh at a conference in Amsterdam. Von der Lühe views the relationship between the two stories as a careful interweaving of two independent strands: "The concept and the approach to historical material are determined by mirroring and not parallelization, narrative reflection and not causal connections."[83]

The clear parallels between the two individual biographies invite the reader, as Margy Garber has argued, to draw further connections between the two historical eras in which the dual protagonists lived.[84] By placing the Spanish Inquisition and the persecution and murder of Sephardic Jews alongside the Austrian experience of National Socialism and the Holocaust, Menasse invites the reader to reflect on fanaticism, racism, persecution, and the lasting effects of historical trauma. While the biographies reflect each other and intersect in interesting ways, the broader experiences of seventeenth- and twentieth-century Jews are treated quite differently. Menasse's novel includes depictions of the forced conversions of Spanish and Portuguese Jews, the terror of the tribunals of the Inquisition, the auto-da-fé of Lisbon Jews, the expulsion and flight of the Jews from Spain and Portugal, and the establishment of a Sephardic community in the ethnically diverse city of Amsterdam. There is no similarly direct treatment of World War II or the Holocaust, however. Menasse's concern is with a depiction of the Second Republic, in which those events loom large as part of the nation's recent-but-unreflected past. Whereas Menasse needs to present the experiences of the Sephardic community in order to illuminate Rabbi Samuel Manasseh's life, the notion of the Holocaust as a submerged subtext to Viktor Abravanel's life is well understood by contemporary readers.

The simultaneous pursuit of two historical frames and the clear presence of the past in Viktor's life reflect Menasse's approach to history not as a closed-off, completed past, but as a thoroughly present-oriented concern.[85] Beginning with his response in the early trilogy of novels to a Hegelian philosophy of history, Menasse has variously expressed his view of history in different contexts. In this novel a powerful relationship between the past and present is posited. Menasse has written, "History is like a mirror that we bought at the flea market that is so and so many years old. But the image does not show how it was back when the mirror was produced, but how we look as we peer into it."[86]

The mirror of history reveals critical differences in terms of Jewish culture of the two eras. After surviving the flight from Portugal, Manasseh joins the Jewish community of Amsterdam, a diverse city of multiple languages, ethnicities, and religions in which the exiled Jews are soon able to establish a flourishing new Sephardic community. While the community prospers, this is no utopia, and Manasseh's life is far from ideal. The dark side of the community's prosperity is revealed when the Mahamad, Amsterdam's Jewish court, expels Uriel da Costa for challenging the dogmatism that has taken hold of the community. Thus the rabbis of Amsterdam, once persecuted by the Inquisition, become the oppressors themselves. Manasseh would like to emerge as the leader of the community, but his limitations are laid bare by his passivity in face of the court's treatment of Costa. While he fails in the attempt to bring about a second rebirth of the community, the novel includes a harbinger of a better future in the figure of the young Spinoza.[87]

In depicting Viktor Abravanel's life in Vienna, the Jewish community is not a presence at all. During the years in which Viktor comes of age the city had no visible Jewish community, and the presence of Jews was submerged under a far-reaching cloak of silence. Viktor's family may have gone further than others to suppress their Jewish identity, but the weight of stories untold and topics left undiscussed, so commonly felt in this era by Jewish and Gentile families alike, cannot be ignored. Viktor is not integrated into Jewish culture but exists at its margins. Suffering as a result of his own unresolved origins, Viktor would like to become the conscience of Austrian society, to admonish the nation to confront its past. Yet his denunciation of his former *Gymnasium* teachers for their alleged National Socialist past is a sham—his denunciation is based on fabricated evidence and is motivated by an inchoate desire for revenge. Viktor, now a historian, would like to be the moral conscience of his society, insisting on a confrontation with the past, but ironically he emerges as a case study of the profound alienation that stems from insufficient historical knowledge.

The dual strands of Menasse's novel allow him to explore two Jewish communities that faced the brink of extinction. Through the juxtaposition he reflects on visibility and invisibility within these communities and on the effects of the experience of persecution and trauma including, strikingly, the possibility for identification with the oppressor and for assuming that role oneself. Menasse's innovative experimentation with dual life stories, with individual and collective history, with two historical frames, and play with genre creates a new narrative of the past and the present. Like the other writers considered here, his evocation of the past in the present provides an illuminating lens from which to consider contemporary Austria.

Eva Menasse

Eva Menasse was born in Vienna in 1970. She is the half-sister of Robert Menasse. Theirs is a family of mixed background that Eva Menasse views as quintessentially Viennese. In a 2005 interview she described Vienna as a kind of melting pot and her family as one of its typical products: "For example, I have a Polish grandmother, an Austrian grandfather, an Austrian-Jewish grandfather, and a Moravian grandmother. That is a typical Viennese existence."[88]

After completing her studies in history and *Germanistik,* Eva Menasse entered the field of journalism, working as an editor at the news magazine *Profil,* in Vienna. She then took a position as feuilleton editor at the *Frankfurter Allgemeine Zeitung.* Menasse became widely known as the result of her coverage of the London trial of Holocaust denier David Irving. A volume of her reporting on the trial, *Der Holocaust vor Gericht* (*The Holocaust on Trial,* 2000), appeared with the Siedler Verlag, in Berlin. She subsequently did further journalistic work as a cultural correspondent in Prague and Vienna.

Menasse's debut novel, *Vienna,* appeared in 2005. The novel was critically well received in Germany, netted mixed reviews in Austria, and spent a number of months on the best-seller lists in both countries. Menasse received the Rolf Heyne Debütpreis for the novel in the year of its publication. Since 2003, Menasse has been living as a freelance writer in Berlin. She is married to the German writer Michael Kumpfmüller. Her latest work, a volume of stories titled *Lässliche Todsünden* (*Forgivable Deadly Sins*), appeared in August 2009 with Kiepenheuer & Witsch. Menasse has written a number of pieces on Austrian politics for the German press, including a commentary on the elections in Carinthia five months after Jörg Haider's death, for *Die Zeit*. Menasse's novel was better received in Germany than in Austria, which she attributes to the differences between how the two countries deal with their pasts. In her view, German readers appreciated her subdued critique of the persistence of latent anti-Semitism in Austrian society, whereas Austrian readers expected more outrage: "To be taken seriously in Austria, you have to go around with the moral cudgel and constantly scream 'Murderers and fascists!' like the generation of writers before me did."[89] Menasse insists on leaving the reader to draw his or her own conclusions.

Mona Körte characterizes Menasse's *Vienna* as a family novel, an important genre for writers belonging to the second and third generations of Jews since the Holocaust.[90] With an extended family at the center of the narrative, the contemporary Jewish family novel adheres to the tradition of the *Großstadtroman* (*urban novel*), depicting a particular Viennese social milieu and relations among Jews and Gentiles within it, in the vein of Schnitzler's *Der Weg ins Freie* or Adolf Dessauer's *Großstadtjuden*. Like Schnitzler and Dessauer, contemporary writers also highlight the different relationships to a Jewish identity characteristic of successive generations within a single family. While the novels of the turn of the twentieth century reveal the generational conflicts that stemmed from the pressures of assimilationism, new forms of anti-Semitism, and the political alternatives represented by Zionism and Socialism, the Holocaust stands as a looming silent presence in the center of the families of contemporary texts, an experiential divide determining the relations across generations.

Eva Menasse's novel reads like an extended familial dialogue; the exchange of stories across generations is the principal means for family members to relate to the world. Within the fairly closed social world of the family, lived experience takes a clear backseat to the relating of the experience. Menasse refers early in the novel to the family's *Anekdotenschatz,* a shared trove of the stories that comprise family history, in which each story is gradually divorced from its original teller and transformed into common property, hotly debated and differently inflected through each retelling. The real treasures among these family stories, it is clear, are those of the parents and grandparents. Both the cherished anecdotes of life in prewar Vienna and the largely untold stories of survival dominate not only the narrative, but the lives of the children and grandchildren of the survivors.

The narrator in *Vienna* is a young woman of the third generation. She remains nameless and largely undeveloped throughout the novel, representing more a point of reference—*mein Vater, meine Großmutter* (*my father, my grandmother*)—than a clear narrative perspective. Körte has investigated the prevalence of similar, nearly invisible third generation narrators as they struggle to find a voice and gain mastery over the family narratives that threaten to overwhelm them. She writes, "In the literature of the so-called second and third generations, the children and grandchildren of survivors, the overwhelming story of the parents and grandparents obscures one's own place. One's own small biography reveals itself even before its own discovery to be overlaid with the single, very large, but intangible story of the parents and grandparents."[91]

Körte has termed such narratives *"Literatur des kleinen Ichs,"* in which the author brings to light the narrator's attempts to develop strategies of self-empowerment through the act of narration.[92] In Menasse's novel, however, Körte rightly points out that these attempts yield only limited results. While by the end of the novel the narrator has successfully related decades of family history via a myriad anecdotes chiefly involving other members of the family, she is a faithful steward of the *Anekdotenschatz* without truly making it her own. The narrator reveals little of herself over the course of the novel, though we gain some insight into her relationships with her father and siblings. She views her role within the family as an observer, and even in the presentation of so much family lore, she emerges more as an archivist than a storyteller. In leaving us with this curiously undefined narrative voice, Menasse raises doubts as to the potential success of storytelling as a path to identity.

The stories favored by the family are polished anecdotes, well crafted and finely tuned after years of being told and retold at every family gathering. Indeed, any of the stories could be taken straight from Torberg's *Tante Jolesch*. The fact that the stories are well known to both teller and listeners only enhances their appeal within the family—many of the tales end with a quip by the Jewish grandfather or another relative of his generation, and the line is delivered in unison by everyone present. The grandfather, for example, was fond of dismissing any suggestion of outdoor activity with the oft-repeated line, "A Jew belongs in the coffeehouse...Am I a deer?" (*A Jud geheert ins Kaffeehaus...bin I a Reh?*).[93] Another highly quotable family member was Dolly Königsbee, the Christian bank-director husband of the grandfather's sister, Tante Gustl. Königsbee was beloved "because there was hardly a figure of speech and hardly a foreign word that he didn't twist and deform."[94] These slips and malapropisms were not only frequently repeated but also imitated, as successive generations tried to craft their own misbegotten phrases in the manner of Königsbee.

Within the storytelling tradition of the narrator's family, form is privileged over content. There are, however, a number of central events from the family's past that are related again and again. The story of her father's birth is one such tale: he was born in the family's apartment rather than a hospital, because despite the onset of labor, the grandmother was unwilling to interrupt her bridge party; the inconvenience of the birth is further underscored in family lore in that the grandmother never fully forgave her son for spoiling her best fur coat with his birth. The telling of this story reveals much about the grandparents' relationship, their lifestyle, family dynamics, and the development of the father's personality. While some tales such as this one revolve around births and deaths and the more significant developments of the lives of family members, most are anecdotal in content as well as form. Even the aforementioned story is as much a story of a bridge party as of the birth of a child. Weightier matters are generally avoided, along the lines Ruth Beckermann described for her own family as she was growing up in the postwar era: "silence on sensitive issues."

Chief among the family's taboo topics are the war and the Holocaust. We learn little about family members' wartime experiences, although the narrator gradually pieces together an account, even as she explains that these experiences were never discussed. We learn that the Jewish grandfather survived the war in Vienna because he was married to a Catholic woman, that he practiced strategies of *"untertauchen,"* or hiding in plain sight, by carrying no identification papers with him and, as long as he could, neglecting to wear the yellow star he termed the *"reichsdeutsche Hundemarke"* (German dog tag).[95] His two sons were sent to England with the *Kindertransporte*. When they returned to Vienna after the war, the narrator's uncle was a decorated British soldier and her father had forgotten how to speak German. The narrator describes the relationship between her father and his parents as distanced; they were apart for too many significant years to know and understand each other well, and the silence imposed about those years made it impossible to bridge the gap. The fate of the father's sister is another forbidden topic; she married and moved to Canada during the war, but she contracted tuberculosis and died in a Canadian hospital before the war ended.

Within the family there is little interest in telling or even hearing the stories of the war. Only the narrator's brother expresses interest in the past and pushes for discussion of these closed subjects. Finding no willingness within the family to discuss the past or their mixed heritage, the brother later joins a support group called *"Mischlinge* 2000." Here he learns that his family's silence is not the only response to the Holocaust. He comments, "The children of Holocaust survivors that he knew mostly suffered under that fact that they grew up with all of the dead, who were perpetually seated alongside them at the table."[96] In his own family, the dead were differently present, as a result of never being mentioned: "One lost relatives in the war and then covered it over with silence."[97]

The brother's interest not only makes him an anomaly within the family, it also marks him as an outsider within Austrian society. The brother becomes an historian focused on contemporary history, launching his career with a dissertation on the National Socialist past of Felix Popelnik, president of the Austrian National Ski Association, a beloved national hero dubbed the "sports pope." This provocative research is equally unwelcome at the university and among the broader public, and the brother's pariah status only deepens when Popelnik dies unexpectedly while working out at home. The episode is cast as a prelude to the Waldheim election, laying bare deep divisions within Austrian society that permeate even familial relations. The father, whose life's ambition was to be regarded as typical, as an *"echter Österreicher"* (*"true Austrian"*), cannot understand his son's motivations for exposing the man's involvement in the SS. As a former soccer star, the father's attempts at "passing" as a typical Austrian have proved to be fairly successful; he spends most of his life ignoring his Jewish heritage and begins to question his identity only in the 1980s. The father's social world revolves around the tennis club SC Schneuzl, a microcosm of bourgeois Vienna. While other family members sought the company of other Jews or seemed to be singularly focused on the family, the father belonged to mainstream Viennese culture: "Only my father was—willingly, but what difference does that make?—immersed in a world of car dealers and fashion retailers, builders, gas-station owners and other people of more average education."[98] The father shared the social and political views of the Gentile club members, voting for Waldheim and seeing no point in stirring up difficult aspects of the recent past.

The amnesiac climate of these pre-Waldheim years is represented via a contrast between the owner of a local bar and one of his patrons: when the Jewish survivor Heinrich H. has too much to drink and begins to tell stories of Dachau, people around him react with, "Come on, don't be such an idiot" (*Geh, sei net so deppert*). The bar owner Vickerl Weisskopf, on the other hand, is highly regarded as a "*klassischer Bursch*" (great guy), chiefly for not making too much of his own wartime experiences.[99] Menasse describes the climate as hostile to any attempt to draw attention to Austria's role in the war: "The majority of Austrians at this time had forgotten that there had ever been a war, let alone any crimes. A couple of historians had in fact tried in numerous essays to invalidate the myth of Austria as 'the first victims of Hitler,' but they were contemptuously called 'leftists' and punished with disrespect."[100] The narrator's brother received a similar treatment; he was widely attacked for his first work and largely ignored in subsequent efforts. He later withdrew from contemporary history to focus his studies on Sephardic Jews.

While this family closely resembles Menasse's own, which she views as typically Viennese, she presents the family not as rooted in the city but as constituting their own private world within it. The stories of the prior generations are the only ones that are anchored in concrete spaces of the city. The great-grandfather was an immigrant bookkeeper who settled in the *Mazzesinsel,* near the Augarten, "in these gray streets, where it was cool and damp in the summer, too, and the staircases smell like mustiness and cabbage."[101] The grandfather achieved a bit more success and consequently left Leopoldstadt for Döbling, "the district of doctors and lawyers, notaries and opera singers, landlords and silk manufacturers."[102] The grandfather hadn't fully arrived in this elevated social world, however; he could only afford an apartment at the edge of the district. Menasse's portrayal of Vienna suggests a city sharply demarcated along lines separating the social classes. Even the city's cafés reflect this geographic and social hierarchy. After Tante Gustl marries a bank director, she will no longer play bridge at the Bauernfeind or Zögernitz, frequented by the narrator's grandparents, but only at the cafés of the *Ringstrasse* in the company of "wives of court counselors and widows of manufacturers and impoverished baronesses."[103]

The lives of the narrator's immediate family are not similarly described as playing out in any particular district or neighborhood. Certain bars are important, as well as the tennis club, but these institutions represent essentially closed social worlds that function much like the family dinner table, the privileged site of social interaction within the family. As at the table, social exchanges at the bar and club revolve around the telling of well-known anecdotes, and while differences of opinion exist, the bar patrons and club members seem to be acting out prescribed roles recognized and sanctioned by all. The ritualized character of these exchanges determines that real intimacy is neither possible nor, it would seem, desired. More important is the maintenance of a certain atmosphere, a lively discourse and sufficient activity. The tennis club, for example, is the place where the father's unhappy second marriage appears to function well. The family's proclivity for keeping up appearances can be traced back to the grandparents, whose marriage the narrator is unable to pronounce happy or unhappy and who lived according to the axiom "Keep up appearances and keep still."[104]

The family's preference for exchanging well-rehearsed stories over free and open discussion leaves them ill equipped to deal with conflicts when they occasionally arise. It also leaves family members essentially on their own to address the questions of identity that present themselves to this half-Jewish, half-Catholic family.[105] Körte has rightly pointed out how the family's focus on anecdotes and euphemisms regulates what may be said and frames the family's reality in a certain acceptable way.[106] The narrator is conscious of their practice of "manic mythologizing." The existence of unresolved identity questions is clear enough, indicated by the nameless narrator and, ironically, by the brother's participation in the *Mischlinge* 2000 support group. Yet the characters find few answers. Only the father seems to arrive at the clear answer he seeks when he visits the Viennese Jewish *Gemeinde* and sees the registration of his birth in their records. The father's unreflective nature enables him to accept this evidence as a stamp of approval by the Jewish community. The brother, by contrast, engages most extensively in both family history and European Jewish history. His Jewish background is perfunctorily dismissed, however, by a Jewish Canadian historian, who pronounces him merely a quarter-Jew. Menasse eschews in this novel a single, straightforward concept of identity, leaving these questions resolutely unresolved and highlighting instead the obstacles to a clear identity, especially those obstacles we create ourselves.

Elfriede Jelinek

Elfriede Jelinek shares a position with Robert Menasse that seems to straddle an identification with the other Viennese Jewish writers of this chapter. Jelinek is a Jewish-identified writer not generally included in scholarly works addressing contemporary Austrian Jewish writing. It seems entirely appropriate to point out that Jelinek is no easy fit alongside these other writers given the highly complex character of her self-positioning within Austria's cultural sphere. In her own *Selbstinszenierung* (the way she presents herself to the public), she is a high-profile, highly acclaimed author who shuns the limelight. By choosing to deliver her 2004 Nobel Prize essay in absentia, Jelinek was able to accommodate her social phobia by avoiding the large crowds of the awards ceremony. But far from escaping the public eye, which she abhors, in her videotaped delivery of the address, Jelinek ironically renders this occasion subject to endless repetition, as both the text and video are continually available on the Nobel Prize website. This contradictory moment is entirely typical of a writer who is at once a public persona, provocateur, and intensely private. Fatima Naqvi has assessed Jelinek's contradictory stance vis-à-vis the authorial persona in her writing and statements about the theater, as Jelinek simultaneously downplays and deifies the author and aggressively maintains a stance of the author as victim.[107] The process by which Jelinek has negotiated and performed an identity as a writer is directly tied to her ambivalent stance vis-à-vis an identification as an Austrian Jew.

In interviews of the 1990s Jelinek frequently evoked Jewish writers of the past as her most important literary antecedents, situating her work within the tradition of Jewish satire and underscoring the influence of Elias Canetti and Karl Kraus. Alongside this literary heritage, Jelinek casts her relationship to Jewishness in terms of family history, describing her paternal Jewish ancestry. Asked in a 1994 interview whether she considered Austria her home, Jelinek gave a qualified positive response: "Yes it is [home], but only in its great ethnic and cultural diversity. Especially Eastern Austria. I'd say Vienna is home, this Eastern Slavic-Jewish culture I come from, my family comes from."[108]

Yet Jelinek is surely not to be viewed in the same light as the other writers considered here, for whom Jewishness is a constitutive feature of their identity. Schindel, Menasse, Rabinovici, Beckermann have been concerned with producing work which has laid bare and challenged the mechanisms by which Jews have been systematically marginalized and excluded from the Austrian body politic. Their works foreground the Austrian Jewish experience, collectively positing an affirmative, post-Waldheim Jewish identity.

Taken alongside these writers, Jelinek seems to be driven by a rather different critical impulse or, at least, to have reached different conclusions as the result of her critical perspectives. She is, to be sure, something of an awkward fit within this group of contemporary Viennese Jewish writers. Matthias Konzett has suggested that the very concept of an ethnically defined contemporary Austrian Jewish literature is complicated as a result of the rupture in Austrian Jewish history represented by the Shoah and in light of the diversity of the present Jewish community in Vienna,[109] and this complexity is surely intensified by throwing Jelinek into the mix. Yet Jelinek's identity politics place her firmly within this context. Her identification as an Austrian is expressed in strictly cultural terms. The cultural tradition with which she principally identifies is the Viennese Jewish literary tradition of early twentieth-century satire. She foregrounds this tradition when characterizing her work and her identity as a writer. There is a complex layering of identities here at the core of which is a defining relationship to the Viennese Jewish literature of the past. Jelinek shares a common cultural arena with the other writers discussed in this chapter, and they are also united by common experiences, the most significant of which are a relationship to the historical phenomenon of Jewish assimilation; a common fate of persecution and loss (rendering them members of a kind of *Schicksalsgemeinschaft*, a community brought together by fate); a share in the simultaneous experiences of belonging and exclusion—Beckermann's sense of feeling "*unheimlich heimisch*" in Vienna and Austria; and a shared sense of the inherent instability of categories of identity.

Elfriede Jelinek is a writer who has been deeply affected by these experiences, and it thus bears asking how she views her Jewish heritage and what it means to her as a writer. And, if her writing does bear the stamp of this heritage in important ways, what then is the nature of her particular contribution to Austrian Jewish literature? I see Jelinek as staking out an alternative position within the Jewish tradition, differing from the affirmative, post-Waldheim identity claims of the other contemporary Jewish writers. To assess Jelinek's particular negotiation of Jewish identity, my analysis will have two strands, focusing on the author's relationship to Karl Kraus and the tradition of Jewish satire and her commitment to the creation of a textual memory space for the victims of the Holocaust.

Kraus figures prominently in Jelinek's view of her relationship to literary tradition. She frequently underscores the importance of his influence and situates her writing in the tradition of Jewish modernism. She has noted, for example, "My early prose is clearly experimental. Otherwise I stand in the tradition of dissection, in the Jewish tradition of Karl Kraus and Elias Canetti that was destroyed by the Nazis or that is just now dying out."[110] Here and in similar comments she not only identifies her cultural roots, but she establishes herself as the only remaining living link to a culture that is dead and gone. Referring again to the tradition represented by Kraus and Canetti, as well as Joseph Roth, she has stated, "That is really a dying culture. … In 1938 a whole culture was foreclosed and destroyed. I am most likely anyway the last poet of this tendency. I come from this Eastern space, have this irony, this humor, and this sensuousness. All of that has been destroyed."[111] Claudia Liebrand has commented on the way Jelinek repeatedly stylizes herself in relation to something that is dead, as a kind of zombie of this literary tradition, a revenant of classical Jewish modernism.[112]

If we press Jelinek on this stated connection and seek to identify the Krausian elements of her writing, her debt to what she has called Kraus's *Spracharbeit* does indeed emerge as significant. In stylistic terms, Jelinek's use of hyperbole, intertextuality, deliberate catachresis, and, above all, her practice of citation all find echoes in Kraus's satire. The two differ, of course, in the particular ways in which they employ these devices, as each was keenly aware of the requirements of their respective audiences. Whereas Kraus could appropriate extensive quotations by the politicians, the economic elites, and, above all, the journalists who were the objects of his satire in order to lay bare the ideologies submerged within their language, Jelinek cannot necessarily assume that hidden meanings in her work will come to the surface through citation, considering the barrage of information in which's readers revolve. To decrease the likelihood her readers will miss the point—altogether possible given the difficulty her work poses—she frequently makes use of parody and hyperbole to intensify her satirical barbs.[113]

More significantly, there seems to be a difference of intent behind their respective satirical discourses. Underlying Kraus's critique of journalistic language was a sense of outrage at the debasement of language performed routinely in the press and also a deep desire to restore linguistic purity, a rescuing telos identified by that avid reader of *Die Fackel*, Walter Benjamin. As John Pizer has argued, "Regardless of its vitriol, Kraus's satire was composed in the spirit of a striving after redemption, aesthetic harmony, and social cohesion reflective both of early twentieth century Jewish thought in Central Europe and the modernist period in general."[114] In Jelinek's work we can detect no such redemptive impulse, no corresponding view of art as a site of transcendence; indeed, as Pizer has suggested, Jelinek would be deeply skeptical of such an undertaking. In an interview in 1994, Jelinek stated her desire to "smash language, to strip it to the bone, to tear the last bits of truth out of it, to rip open its chest."[115] Notably, there is no reference to building it back up again or closing the wound.

In spite of her affinity to Jewish modernism, Jelinek of course is grounded in a distinctly different cultural reality, and Kraus's redemptive modernist impulses seem to have given way to postmodernist skepticism, irony, and playfulness. Through Jelinek's wordplay—the repetition, the multiple allusions built into a single metaphor, and the very brazenness of linguistic play—the writer engages in a postmodern experiment with the performative aspect of language. Her aggressive staging of the author-reader relationship, including her manipulation of the reader, her frustration of any attempt at conventional identification with her characters, and the unyielding demand for active involvement in the text by the reader, is reflective of a postmodern sensibility in which nothing is sacred and no one is spared.

In Jelinek's magnum opus, the novel *Die Kinder der Toten* (*The Children of the Dead,* 1995), this playfulness is evident, the difficult subject matter notwithstanding. In this work Jelinek takes up a number of themes of her previous work and develops them further. Her primary focus is on the persistence of fascist influences in present-day Austria and, more specifically, on the repression of the memory of Jewish victims of the Holocaust enacted in postwar Austria. For Regina Kecht, *Die Kinder der Toten* is a literary intervention on behalf of the forgotten Jewish dead.[116] Jelinek draws the past radically and grotesquely into the present in a confrontation between Austria's living, dead, and undead. She has commented on how the work brings to light "how Austrian society is indeed a society of the undead. History is dead and buried and at the same time it is the most lively thing. We are not freed of it, the more it is supposed to be buried."[117]

This text reads as many texts in one, both as a result of the wide range of stylistic devices employed and the mix of genres with which Jelinek plays—the gothic novel, a parody of the gothic novel, and parable. Into this heteroglossia Jelinek further inserts numerous other texts, alternately journalistic, medical, musical, political, even meteorological.[118] The many shifts, collisions, distortions, and sudden turns of the text are not the sole means by which Jelinek challenges the reader. Kecht characterizes this work as a kind of staged oratory demanding the most exacting analysis and interpretation. She writes, "Jelinek's text is a speech-act in which every word, every sentence, and every paragraph is double-voiced or even heteroglot, that is intentionally dialogical or polyphonic, giving voice simultaneously to several intentions or viewpoints."[119] If readers were momentarily tempted to let their guard down—though there is little in the text to invite any relaxation—they are prevented from doing so, as Jelinek forecloses this possibility by implicating the reader in the text in a number of different, unsettling ways. Parallels are drawn between the reader and the Jewish victims, only to be undermined by linkages to the Nazis, as well as to the undead, implicating the reader in the suppression of the memory of the Jewish dead. No critical distance vis-à-vis the Austrian past can be maintained nor can the reader opt for an empathetic identification with the victims, as her depiction of the Jewish dead, like those of most of Jelinek's victims, is far from sympathetic. She does not resurrect the dead so that some easy emotional connection might be forged that could ease our collective conscience. Rather, we are violently called to remember.

Die Kinder der Toten is marked by an inherent instability that unquestionably makes for tough going for the reader. In its radically destabilized narrative, this text is markedly different from the more conventional narratives of Jewish life in postwar Austria put forward by other contemporary Viennese Jewish writers. Jelinek does take part, however, in a common critique of postwar Austrian society, laying bare the myths on which the Second Republic was founded. Whereas the focus in the writing of Schindel, Rabinovici, Beckermann, and Robert and

Eva Menasse has been on the mechanisms of exclusion and marginalization of Austria's Jewish community since the Holocaust, Jelinek writes not of the living, but of the dead. In her texts she has established a relationship to Austria's dead and forgotten Jews, stemming against the tendency to forget and, more powerfully, exposing the way in which forgetting has been constitutive of postwar Austrian identity. Jelinek's strategies of destabilization are ultimately aimed at the very core of Austrian self-conceptions.

Regina Kecht thus describes the way in which *Die Kinder der Toten* takes aim at notions of Austrianness. She writes, "The idea of a single collective (Austrian) identity that might guarantee a secure sense of 'we,' of *Heimat,* is radically, unsettlingly dissolved."[120] Not only is identity a problematic issue for Austrian Jews since the Holocaust, Jelinek sees to it that it is similarly destabilized for all Austrians. As she takes aim at postwar Austrian identity politics, she reveals the constructed nature of Austrian identity, indicating that not only minority identities must be negotiated. Matti Bunzl has posited a recontextualization of this Viennese Jewish literature, citing the aesthetic heterogeneity of this body of writing as evidence of a shift to postmodernity.[121] Reading Jelinek alongside these other writers we gain greater insight into the multivalent quality of this writing and the divergent ways of representing the negotiation of identity in post-Waldheim Austria.

Conclusion

The political debates of the 1980s and 1990s exposed deep divisions within Austrian society that had previously been somewhat obscured by studious avoidance of controversial issues. At the same time, the election of Kurt Waldheim and the rise of the Right sparked national discussions that were long overdue and reawakened Austria's civic life. As the Freedom Party entered the national political scene, tens of thousands rallied in opposition. The last two decades of the twentieth century also witnessed the reemergence of a robust and prominent Jewish community in Vienna, producing a vital and visible Jewish culture. A substantial body of literature emerged in Vienna that was not only written by Viennese Jews, but portrayed contemporary Jewish life in the city and presented Jewish perspectives, chiefly in terms of challenging Austria's amnesiac relationship to its past.

This literature is closely linked to the Austrian Jewish literature of prior eras. Contemporary Jewish writers in Vienna have repeatedly expressed a debt to prior generations of Viennese Jewish writers both as being their literary forebears and in terms of molding their self-understanding as Austrian Jews. In thinking about Jewish identity, these writers turn again and again to the prominent Jewish writers of the long turn of the twentieth century. The texts covered in the previous chapters of this book, in which Jewish writers have reflected creatively on what it means to be Jewish in modern Austria and have responded in many different ways to the twentieth-century challenges posed to an Austrian Jewish existence, seem to serve as the primary lens through which contemporary writers have framed their own Jewish identities.

The writers discussed in this chapter share an interesting perspective on Viennese and Austrian society. They are simultaneously insiders and outsiders. They doubtless belong to the cultural elite of the nation, but like the Jewish writers that preceded them, they have at times been confronted with attitudes from mainstream society that seek to relegate them to the margins. Ruth Beckermann's apt phrase *unheimlich heimisch* describes this contradictory position of intimacy and alienation. The texts discussed here reveal the richness of the insights such a perspective affords.

Vienna is both a place and a concept for these writers. The city is both a setting for and, in important ways, an object of their intellectual engagement. As they write the city, they in effect create a new Vienna, or many new Viennas, by shifting focus to sites that are important in Jewish life of the past and present and also by transforming the symbolic meaning attached to other spaces that play a more central role in the culture of the city and the nation. Here, too, in their intense engagement with the city, they continually inscribe themselves into the Austrian Jewish tradition.

Notes

1. Pick, *Guilty Victim*, 155.
2. Ibid., 158.
3. Richard Mitten, *The Politics of Antisemitic Prejudice: The Waldheim Phenomenon in Austria* (Boulder, CO: Westview Press, 1992), 1.
4. Ibid., 2.
5. Ibid., 202.
6. William Safire, "Waldheim's Secret Life," *New York Times*, 21 April 1986, cited in Mitten, *The Politics of Antisemitic Prejudice*, 177.
7. Pick, *Guilty Victim*, 165.
8. Ibid., 150.
9. Mitten, *The Politics of Antisemitic Prejudice*, 257.
10. These were not the first violent attacks against Jews and Jewish property in Vienna's recent past. The city's main synagogue, the *Stadttempel*, was bombed during services by a Palestinian terrorist group in 1981. Two people were killed and more than twenty were injured during the attack. Additionally, the Schöps department store was bombed in 1982.
11. On the Wehrmacht exhibition in Austria see, for example, Walter Manoschek, "Die Wehrmachtsaustellung in Österreich," *Mittelweg* 36 (1996): 25–32.
12. Pick, *Guilty Victim*, 182.
13. For more on the *Donnerstagdemos*, see Frederick Baker and Elisabeth Boyer, *Wiener Wandertage* (Vienna: Wieser, 2002) and Robert Foltin, *Und wir bewegen uns doch. Soziale Be-*

wegungen in Österreich (Vienna: Edition Grundrisse, 2004). I am also grateful to Susanne Hochreiter for her insightful talk on the demonstrations at the 2008 MALCA conference at the University of Washington.
14. Dagmar C. G. Lorenz, "Disruption and Continuity: The Situation of Jewish Writing in Contemporary Austria," introduction to *Contemporary Jewish Writing in Austria: An Anthology*, ed. C.G. Lorenz (Lincoln: University of Nebraska Press, 1999), xxix.
15. Andrea Reiter, "Ruth Beckermann und die jüdische Nachkriegsgeneration in Österreich," in Fiddler, *Austrian Women's Writing*, 162.
16. Lorenz, "Disruption and Continuity," xx–xxi.
17. Reiter, "Ruth Beckermann und die jüdische Nachkriegsgeneration in Österreich," 162.
18. Lorenz, "Disruption and Continuity," xiv.
19. Reiter, "Ruth Beckermann und die jüdische Nachkriegsgeneration in Österreich," 162.
20. Beckermann, *Unzugehörig*, 111.
21. Ibid., 109.
22. Ibid., 102.
23. Christina Guenther, "The Politics of Location in Ruth Beckermann's 'Vienna Films,'" *Modern Austrian Literature* 37:3/4 (2004): 3.
24. *Die Papierene Brücke*, Ruth Beckermann: Ruth Beckermann-Filmproduktion, 1987.
25. This is one of the real events that surfaces in the works of several writers. Robert Schindel appears as an extra in the film. He is featured briefly in Beckermann's film and also depicts the experience in his novel *Gebürtig* (Frankfurt: Suhrkamp, 1994).
26. *Die Papierene Brücke*, 164.
27. Guenther, "The Politics of Location in Ruth Beckermann's 'Vienna Films,'" 13.
28. *Homemad(e)*, Ruth Beckermann: Ruth Beckermann-Filmproduktion, 2000.
29. Lorenz, "Disruption and Continuity," 170.
30. "Gedächtnis und Erinnern: Robert Schindel im Gespräch mit Motoi Hatsumi, Naomi Ikeya, Minoru Iwasaki und Karin-Ruprechter-Prenn," *Trans*, no. 7 (May 2001).
31. Robert Schindel, "Mein Wien," in *Mein liebster Feind: Essays, Reden, Miniaturen* (Frankfurt: Suhrkamp, 2004), 28.
32. Robert Schindel, "Zeitpumpen: Rede zum Mörike-Preis 2000," in Schindel, *Mein liebster Feind*, 67.
33. Ibid., 67.
34. Robert Schindel, "Schweigend ins Gespräch vertieft: Anmerkungen zu Geschichte und Gegenwart des jüdisch-nichtjüdischen Verhältnisses in den Täterländern," in Schindel, *Mein liebster Feind*, 19.
35. Robert Schindel, "Was man versitzt, kann man nicht verstehen: Randbemerkungen zum Nationalen in der Literatur," in *Mein liebster Feind*, 42.
36. Marcel Reich-Ranicki, "Nachwort," in Robert Schindel, *Fremd bei mir selbst* (Frankfurt: Suhrkamp, 2004), 460.
37. Schindel, "Schweigend ins Gespräch vertieft," 20.
38. Ibid.
39. Schindel, "Zeitpumpen," 69..
40. Schindel, "Schweigend ins Gespräch vertieft," 20–21.
41. Ibid., 21.
42. Ibid., 21–22.
43. "Gedächtnis und Erinnern."
44. Schindel, "Was man versitzt, kann man nicht verstehen," 39.
45. "Gedächtnis und Erinnern."
46. "Ich war kein schlechter Ping-Pong Spieler": Interview with Robert Schindel, *wortlaut.de*, http://www.hainholz.de/wortlaut/schindel.htm.

47. Schindel, "Zeitpumpen," 70.
48. Schindel, *Gebürtig*, 162.
49. Ibid., 264.
50. Ibid., 275.
51. Ibid.
52. Ibid.
53. Doron Rabinovici, "Der nationale Doppler," *Der Standard* (18 October 1999).
54. Ibid.
55. Ibid.
56. Ibid.
57. Michael Roloff refers to *Gebürtig* as a ghost story in the afterword to his English translation of the novel. See Robert Schindel, *Born-Where*, trans. Michael Roloff (Riverside, CA: Ariadne Press, 1995), 287–94.
58. Doron Rabinovici, *Suche nach M.* (Frankfurt: Suhrkamp, 1997), 27.
59. Ibid.
60. Doron Rabinovici, "Literatur und Republik oder Ganz Baden Liest Die Krone," in *"Was wird das Ausland dazu sagen?": Literatur und Republik in Österreich nach 1945*, ed. Gerald Leitner (Vienna: Pincus Verlag, 1995), 129.
61. Ibid., 138.
62. Doron Rabinovici, *Ohnehin* (Frankfurt: Suhrkamp Taschenbuchverlag, 2005), 48.
63. Ibid., 36.
64. Ibid., 66.
65. Ibid., 92
66. Ibid.
67. Ibid., 118–19.
68. Ibid., 18.
69. Ibid., 42.
70. Ibid., 16.
71. Ibid., 39.
72. Geoffrey C. Howes, "Karl Kraus and Robert Menasse," in *Literature in Vienna at the Turn of the Centuries: Continuities and Discontinuities around 1900 and 2000*, eds. Ernst Grabovszki and James Hardin (Rochester, NY: Camden House, 2003), 144.
73. Ibid.
74. Robert Menasse, *Dummheit ist machbar* (Vienna: Sonderzahl, 1999), 85.
75. Ibid., 89.
76. Ibid.
77. Ibid.
78. Menasse, *Das Land ohne Eigenschaften*, 12.
79. Ibid., 71.
80. Robert Menasse, *Selige Zeiten, brüchige Welt* (Salzburg: Residenz, 1991), 140.
81. Irmela von der Lühe, "Geschichte als Lehrmeisterin? Robert Menasses Roman *Die Vertreibung aus der Hölle*," in *Akten des XI. Internationalen Germanistenkongresses Paris 2005, Band 12: Europadiskurse in der deutschen Literatur und Literaturwissenschaft—Deutschjüdische Kulturdialoge/-konflikte* (Bern: Peter Lang, 2007), 251.
82. Robert Menasse, *Die Vertreibung aus der Hölle* (Frankfurt: Suhrkamp Taschenbuch Verlag, 2003), 95.
83. Von der Lühe, "Geschichte als Lehrmeisterin? Robert Menasses Roman *Die Vertreibung aus der Hölle*," 253.
84. Margy Garber, "'What once was, will always be possible': The Echoes of History in Robert Menasse's *Die Vertreibung aus der Hölle*," in *Rebirth of a Culture: Jewish Identity and Jewish*

Writing in Germany and Austria Today, eds. Hillary Hope Herzog, Todd Herzog, and Benjamin Lapp (New York: Berghahn Books, 2008), 91.
85. Von der Lühe, "Geschichte als Lehrmeisterin? Robert Menasses Roman *Die Vertreibung aus der Hölle*," 256.
86. Robert Menasse, cited in Von der Lühe, "Geschichte als Lehrmeisterin? Robert Menasses Roman *Die Vertreibung aus der Hölle*," 256. The statement originally appeared in *Freitag* 46, 8 Nov. 2002.
87. Garber, "'What once was, will always be possible,'" 93.
88. Eva Menasse in an interview with Stefanie Graf, Christoph Hassenzahl, and Turid Weingartz, 4 July 2005, web.fu-berlin.de.
89. Ibid.
90. Mona Körte, "Die Toten am Tisch. 'Familienromane' nach dem Holocaust," *Zeitschrift für deutsche Philologie* 4 (2008): 573–94.
91. Ibid., 573.
92. Ibid., 577.
93. Eva Menasse, *Vienna*, 135.
94. Ibid., 32.
95. Ibid., 86.
96. Ibid., 322.
97. Ibid., 323.
98. Ibid., 302.
99. Ibid., 38–39.
100. Ibid., 298–99.
101. Ibid., 13.
102. Ibid., 14.
103. Ibid.
104. Ibid., 86.
105. I am grateful to Martina Hamidouche of the University of Illinois at Urbana-Champaign for an interesting paper presented on this topic, "The Quest for Identity in Eva Menasse's *Vienna*," presented at the MALCA conference in Atlanta in 2009.
106. Körte, "Die Toten am Tisch," 585.
107. Fatima Naqvi, "Elfriede Jelinek's Post-Dramatic Stress Disorder: Analysis of a Programmatic Aggression," *Gegenwartsliteratur* 5 (2006): 88–92.
108. Elfriede Jelinek, "This German Language…," *theater* 25 (1994): 22, cited in Matthias Konzett, "The Politics of Recognition in Contemporary Austrian Jewish Literature," *Monatshefte* 90/1 (Spring 1998): 78.
109. Matthias Konzett, "The Politics of Recognition in Contemporary Austrian Jewish Literature," 78.
110. Elfriede Jelinek, cited in John Pizer, "Modern vs. Postmodern Satire: Karl Kraus and Elfriede Jelinek," *Monatshefte* 86:4 (1994): 500.
111. Claudia Liebrand, "Traditionsbezuege: Canetti, Kafka und Elfriede Jelineks Roman *Die Klavierspielerin*," *Gegenwartsliteratur* 5 (2006): 25–26.
112. Liebrand, "Traditionsbezuege," 45, see note 4.
113. See Pizer, "Modern vs. Postmodern Satire," 500–513, especially 509.
114. Ibid., 501.
115. Cited in Dowden, "Ethical Style," 126.
116. See Maria-Regina Kecht, "The Polyphony of Remembrance: Reading *Die Kinder der Toten*," in *Elfriede Jelinek: Writing Woman, Nation, and Identity. A Critical Anthology*, ed. Matthias Konzett and Margarete Lamb-Faffelberger (Madison, NJ: Fairleigh Dickinson University Press, 2007), 189–217.

117. Elfriede Jelinek, "Im Gespräch," *Der Standard*, 9–10 Oct. 2004, cited in Kecht, "The Polyphony of Remembrance," 189.
118. Kecht, "The Polyphony of Remembrance," 191, 206.
119. Ibid., 194.
120. Ibid., 210.
121. See Bunzl, "Political Inscription, Artistic Reflection," 163–70.

Conclusion

My approach to each writer included in this study has taken the form of an investigation of certain central, recurring questions: In what way is this author a Jewish writer? Is there a Jewish element to this writing, and, if so, what form does it take? How does one writer's work relate, if at all, to the works of other Austrian Jewish writers? The same set of questions, reframed in terms of the writer's relationship not to Jewishness but to Vienna, also shaped my inquiry. The investigations produced a variety of answers. Taken as a whole, the broader inquiry into these writers as a group has not yielded a unifying theory of what constitutes Austrian Jewish literature, however. The diversity of these texts defies that kind of comprehensive definition. Rather, this investigation has led to a different conclusion, namely that the concept of Austrian Jewish literature makes sense. One can speak of Austrian Jewish literature across the whole of the twentieth century and into the first decade of the twenty-first century as a cohesive literary tradition. This apparently modest claim is actually remarkable. Despite the breaks, dislocations, and disruptions experienced by authors over the course of a century, including the unbridgeable gap represented by the Holocaust, this literature does indeed constitute a unified tradition.

What unites these writers, from Schnitzler to Jelinek? One answer to this question lies in the fact that writers such as Jelinek at this contemporary end of the trajectory are keenly aware of the many Jewish writers that preceded them. It is an important distinguishing feature of Austrian Jewish writing that it explicitly references itself, that is, that the writers of the turn of the century and the interwar years serve as models in terms of style and tone, approach to social criticism, political engagement, even views of Jewishness and Austrianness for those who came later. Contemporary German Jewish writing, by contrast, tends to look abroad for literary influences and is more likely to reference Jewish American literature than Heine or Feuchtwanger. The authors' awareness of a particular Austrian Jewish tradition is significantly reflected in their writing in terms of intertextuality, preference for certain genres, and stylistic affinities. It also seems to be of personal significance for the writers of the last chapter who, when asked to reflect on their own Jewish identities, tend to frame their response in terms of their affection for one or more great Viennese Jewish writers of the past. Viewing themselves as part of this tradition, then, both informs their writing and is a constitutive element of their experience of what it means to be Jewish.

This Austrian Jewish literature also coheres in that the approaches of these writers to Jewish issues reflect the specificity of the Austrian Jewish experience. The writers I have examined here have largely focused their attention on depicting the world in which they lived. Their focus has often been on Jewish life in Vienna under the particular set of historical circumstances that governed each era. All too frequently the dramatic events of the twentieth century necessitated a fundamental reordering of Jewish existence in the Austrian capital. Writing was a vital part of this process.

To a striking degree these writers assign to the city of Vienna a very prominent place within their literary work. The city is no mere backdrop to the stories they choose to tell. Rather, their writing reflects an intense critical engagement with the city, and the imagined Vienna they posit in their works is as fully developed as any of the characters they create to inhabit it. Across the century, these writers have often been drawn to the same spaces or types of spaces within the city. While they haven't always eschewed the representational spaces of the city center—the *Ringstrasse*, the *Hofburg, Stephansplatz*, etc.—they have pointedly drawn attention to the periphery, in keeping with a particular topography of Jewish experience. Three privileged sites on this redrawn literary map of Vienna are the Prater, the *Mazzesinsel*, and the *Naschmarkt*. The texts that revolve around the second district, Leopoldstadt, frequently present a slice of life of newly arrived Jewish immigrants from the provinces or more settled working-class Jews. They thus feature *"das andere Wien"* (*"the other Vienna"*) far removed from the grandiosity of the first district or the lavish elegance of other fashionable districts. A contemporary text set in this district invariably seeks to evoke the vibrant Jewish community of Vienna early in the century.

The Prater and *Naschmarkt* share a symbolic function in this literature as a self-enclosed world apart, representing an alternative to the larger city. The Prater has appeared in texts from the turn of the twentieth century to the present as a free, open world apart, in which legal codes as well as social mores appear to be suspended. Sometimes it becomes a space of sinister possibilities, but far more often the Prater stands as a space in which social interaction that would not be possible under normal circumstances unfolds unfettered, dissolving barriers related to gender, social class, and ethnicity. For contemporary writer Doron Rabinovici, the *Naschmarkt* carries that same potential as a space of tolerance and integration. These gestures by Jewish writers involve more than mere setting; this is a redrawing of the map, presenting an alternative Vienna that accommodates a broad range of Jewish experience.

The perspective of these writers on Viennese society is marked by both intimacy and alienation. Jewish writers in the city have always occupied the center and the margins at once, and this duality has been constitutive of their critical engagement with it. It is misleading to speak of a Jewish contribution to Viennese culture, because, of course, Jews have been an integral part of that culture and not extraneous to it. Yet the marginalization of Jews in Austria has a longer history than the scope of the present study and undeniably persists in the present. This experience has significantly shaped the work these writers have produced. The unique insider-outsider position of Viennese Jewish writers appears to be as much a phenomenon of the present as the past, and one can only imagine, along with these writers, what kind of climate the city might offer the next generation of Jewish writers.

The position of belonging to both the margins and the center, a theme common to this writing, does not produce a single approach to identity. Rather, this is a literary tradition that for more than a hundred years has worked to deconstruct notions of a unified identity. This work of deconstruction has been carried out in numerous ways, via a myriad of aesthetic choices and textual strategies. While a fragmented identity may appear to be an inheritance of Viennese modernism or a response to the experience of the Holocaust, only the skepticism regarding the possibility of a stable identity is shared. All articulations of identity by the writers in this study are unique, creative undertakings that reflect individual, conscious choices. This may be the principal reason that Jewish identity is so hard to define in these works and may also help to explain the challenge of characterizing Jewish literature, yet it is also at the very core of its richness.

BIBLIOGRAPHY

Adunka, Evelyn. "Friedrich Torberg und Hans Weigel—Zwei Jüdische Schriftsteller im Nachkreigsösterreich." *Modern Austrian Literature* 27:3/4 (1994): 213–37.
Aichinger, Ilse. "A Summons to Mistrust." In *Contemporary Jewish Writing in Austria: An Anthology,* ed. Dagmar C. G. Lorenz, 159–60. Lincoln: University of Nebraska Press, 1999.
———. *Der Gefesselte. Erzählungen I (1948–52).* Frankfurt: Fischer Taschenbuch, 1991.
———. *Die größere Hoffnung.* Frankfurt: Fischer Taschenbuch, 1991.
———. "Die Sicht der Entfremdung. Über Berichte und Geschichten von Ernst Schnabel." *Frankfurter Hefte* 9 (1954): 56–60.
———. "Plätze und Strassen." In *Jahresring 54. Ein Schnitt durch Literatur und Kunst der Gegenwart.* Stuttgart: Deutsche Verlagsanstalt, 1954.
Anderson, Mark. *Kafka's Clothes: Ornament and Aestheticism in the Habsburg Fin de Siècle.* New York: Oxford University Press, 1992.
Bailey, Sarah. "Cultural Translation and the Problem of Language: Yiddish in Joseph Roth's Juden auf Wanderschaft." *Transit* 1:1 (2005): 1–10.
Bartsch, Kurt, and Gerhard Melzer, eds. *Elias Canetti.* Graz: Literaturverlag Droschl, 2005.
Beckermann, Ruth. "1938, During the Austrian Anschluss to the Third Reich, Friedrich Torberg escapes from Prague, first to Zurich, and then to Paris," trans. Hillary Herzog and Todd Herzog. In *Yale Companion to Jewish Writing and Thought in German Culture, 1096–1996,* eds. Sander L. Gilman and Jack Zipes, 551–57. New Haven: Yale University Press, 1997.
———. *Die Mazzesinsel. Juden in der Wiener Leopoldstadt 1918–1938.* Vienna: Löcker, 1984.
———. *Unzugehörig. Österreicher und Juden Nach 1945.* Vienna: Löcker Verlag, 1989.
Beer-Hofmann, Richard. *Der Tod Georgs. Gesammelte Werke.* Frankurt: Fischer, 1963.
———. "Schlaflied für Mirjam." In *Richard Beer-Hofmann und die Wiener Moderne.* Stefan Scherer. Conditio judaica 6. Tübingen: Max Niemeyer Verlag, 1993.
Beller, Steven. *Herzl.* London: Peter Halban, 1991.

———, ed. *Rethinking Vienna 1900*. New York: Berghahn Books, 2001.
———. *Vienna and the Jews: 1867–1938, A Cultural History*. Cambridge: Cambridge University Press, 1989.
Berghahn, Marion. "Women Emigres in England." In *Between Sorrow and Strength: Women Refugees of the Nazi Period*, ed. Sibylle Quack. Cambridge: Cambridge University Press, 1995.
Berkley, George E. *Vienna and Its Jews: The Tragedy of Success, 1880s–1980s*. Cambridge, MA: Abt Books, 1988.
Berlin, Jeffrey B., Jorun B. Johns, and Richard H. Lawson, eds. *Turn-of- the-Century Vienna and its Legacy: Essays in Honor of Donald G. Daviau*. Vienna: Edition Atelier, 1993.
Best, Alan, and Hans Wolfschütz, eds. *Modern Austrian Writing: Literature and Society after 1945*. London: Oswald Wolff, 1980.
Bettauer, Hugo. *Die Stadt ohne Juden. Ein Roman von Übermorgen*. Vienna: R. Löwit, 1926.
Billroth, Theodor. *Ueber das Lehren und Lernen der medizinischen Wissenschaften an die Universitäten der deutschen Nation nebst allgemeine Bemerkungen über Universitäten: Eine culturhistorische Studie*. Vienna: Carl Gerolds Sohn, 1876.
Birk, Matjaz. *"Vielleicht führen wir zwei verschiedene Sprachen… ": Zum Briefwechsel zwischen Joseph Roth und Stefan Zweig*. Münster: Lit Verlag, 1997.
Botz, Gerhard, Ivan Oxaal, and Michael Pollak, eds. *Eine Zerstörte Kultur. Jüdisches Leben und Antisemitismus in Wien seit dem 19. Jahrhundert*. Vienna: Czernin Verlag, 1990.
Boyarin, Daniel. *Unheroic Conduct: The Rise of Heterosexuality and the Invention of the Jewish Man*. Berkeley: University of California Press, 1997.
———, and Jonathan Boyarin, "Diaspora: Generation and the Ground of Jewish Identity." In *Identities*, eds. Kwame Anthony Appiah and Henry Louis Gates, Jr., 305–337. Chicago: University of Chicago Press, 1995.
Boyer, John. *Political Radicalism in Late Imperial Vienna: Origins of the Christian Social Movement, 1848–1897*. Chicago: University of Chicago Press, 1981.
Brix, Emil, and Allan Janik, eds. *Kreatives Milieu, Wien um 1900. Ergebnisse eines Forschungsgespräches der Arbeitsgemeinschaft Wien um 1900*. Vienna: Verlag für Geschichte und Politik, 1993.
Bronfen, Elisabeth. "Entortung und Identität: Ein Thema der modernen Exilliteratur." *The Germanic Review*. 69:2 (1994): 70–78.
Bronsen, David. *Joseph Roth. Eine Biographie*. Cologne: Kiepenheuer & Witsch, 1974.
Bruckmüller, Ernst. *The Austrian Nation: Cultural Consciousness and Socio-Political Processes*. Riverside, CA: Ariadne Press, 2003.
Bunzl, Matti. "Political Inscription, Artistic Reflection: A Recontextualization of Contemporary Viennese-Jewish Literature." *The German Quarterly*. 73:2 (Spring 2000): 163–70.
———. "The Poetics of Politics and the Politics of Poetics: Richard Beer-Hofmann and Theodor Herzl Reconsidered." *The German Quarterly*. 69:3 (Summer 1996): 277–304.
Canetti, Elias. *Aufzeichnungen 1942–1985. Die Provinz des Menschen. Das Geheimherz der Uhr*. Munich: Hanser Verlag, 1993.
———. *Aufzeichnungen 1954–1993. Die Fliegenpein. Nachträge aus Hampstead. Posthum veröffentlichte Aufzeichnungen*. Munich: Hanser Verlag, 2004.

———. *Die Blendung*. Frankfurt: Fischer Taschenbuch Verlag, 1997.
———. *Die Fackel im Ohr. Lebensgeschichte 1921–1931*. Frankfurt: Fischer Taschenbuch Verlag, 2002.
———. *Die gerettete Zunge. Geschichte einer Jugend*. Frankfurt: Fischer Taschenbuch Verlag, 1997.
Canetti, Veza. *Geduld bringt Rosen*. Munich: dtv, 1992.
———. *Die Schildkröten*. Munich: dtv, 1999.
Daviau, Donald G. *Austrian Writers and the Anschluss: Understanding the Past—Overcoming the Past*. Riverside, CA: Ariadne Press, 1991.
———, ed. *Major Figures of Contemporary Austrian Literature*. New York: Peter Lang, 1987.
Deák, István. *Beyond Nationalism: A Social and Political History of the Habsburg Officer Corps, 1848–1918*. Oxford: Oxford University Press, 1990.
Dessauer, Adolf. *Großstadtjuden*. Vienna: Braumüller, 1910.
Dickel, Manfred. *"Ein Dilettant des Lebens will ich nicht sein": Felix Salten zwischen Zionismus und Jungwiener Moderne*. Heidelberg: Universitätsverlag Winter, 2007.
Die Papierene Brücke, Dir. Ruth Beckermann. Ruth Beckermann-Filmproduktion, 1987.
Donahue, William Collins. *The End of Modernism: Elias Canetti's Auto-da-Fé*. Chapel Hill: University of North Carolina Press, 2001.
Dowden, Steve. "Ethical Style: Susan Sontag in Sarajevo, Elfriede Jelinek in Vienna." In *Gegenwartsliteratur* 5 (2006): 124–41.
Efron, John. *Medicine and the German Jews: A History*. New Haven: Yale University Press, 2001.
Ehneß, Jürgen. *Felix Saltens erzählerisches Werk. Beschreibung und Dichtung*. Frankfurt: Peter Lang, 2002.
Eichner, Hans. "City Without Jews: Hugo Bettauer's Vienna." In *Hinter dem schwarzen Vorhang: Die Katastrophe und die epische Tradition. Festschrift für Anthony W. Riley*, eds. Anthony W. Riley, Friedrich Gaede, Patrick O'Neill, and Ulrich Scheck. Tübingen: Francke, 1994.
Fetz, Bernhard. "Representing the Holocaust: On Paul Celan, Ilse Aichinger, Albert Drach and Heimrad Backer, with an Appeal for Critical Reflection on the Cultural and Political Field in which Holocaust Literature Is Inscribed." In *New German Critique* 93 (Autumn 2004): 55–86.
Foell, Kristie A. "July 15, 1927, The Vienna Palace of Justice is burned in a mass uprising of Viennese workers, a central experience in the life and work of Elias Canetti." In *Yale Companion to Jewish Writing and Thought in German Culture, 1096–1996*, eds. Sander L. Gilman and Jack Zipes, 464–70. New Haven: Yale University Press, 1997.
———. *Blind Reflections: Gender in Elias Canetti's 'Die Blendung.'* Riverside, CA: Ariadne Press, 1994.
Fraenkel, Josef, ed. *The Jews of Austria: Essays on Their Life, History and Destruction*. London: Vallentine, Mitchell & Co., 1967.
Fraiman, Sarah. "Das Tragende Symbol: Ambivalenz Jüdischer Identität in Stefan Zweigs Werk." *German Life and Letters* 55:3 (July 2002): 248–65.
Fraiman-Morris, Sarah. "Naturgefühl und Religiosität in den Werken österreichisch-jüdischer Schriftsteller: Franz Werfel, Stefan Zweig, Joseph Roth, Richard Beer-Hofmann." *Modern Austrian Literature* 38:1/2 (2005): 29–49.

Freidenreich, Harriet Pass. *Jewish Politics in Vienna, 1918–1938*. Bloomington: Indiana University Press, 1991.
Garloff, Katja. "Femininity and Assimilatory Desire in Joseph Roth." In *Modern Fiction Studies* 51:2 (Summer 2005): 354–73.
Gay, Peter. *Schnitzler's Century: The Making of Middle-Class Culture, 1815–1914*. New York: Norton, 2001.
Gelber, Mark, ed. *Stefan Zweig Heute*. New York: Peter Lang, 1987.
———. *Stefan Zweig Reconsidered: New Perspectives on his Literary and Biographical Writings*. Conditio Judaica 62. Tübingen: Niemeyer, 2007.
Gilman, Sander L. *Difference and Pathology: Stereotypes of Sexuality, Race, and Madness*. Ithaca: Cornell University Press, 1985.
———. *Jewish Self-Hatred: Anti-Semitism and the Hidden Language of the Jews*. Baltimore: The Johns Hopkins University Press, 1986.
———. *The Jew's Body*. New York: Routledge, 1991.
Grabovszki, Ernst, and James Hardin, eds. *Literature in Vienna at the Turn of the Centuries: Continuities and Discontinuities around 1900 and 2000*. Rochester, NY: Camden House, 2003.
Greaney, Patrick. "Estranging Memory in Ilse Aichinger." *The German Quarterly* 80.1 (Winter 2007): 42–58.
Grimm, Gunter E., and Hans-Peter Bayerdörfer. *Im Zeichen Hiobs. Jüdische Schriftsteller und deutsche Literatur im 20. Jahrhundert*. Frankfurt: Athenäum, 1986.
Guenther, Christina. "The Politics of Location in Ruth Beckermann's 'Vienna Films.'" *Modern Austrian Literature* 37: 3/4 (2004): 33–46.
Hall, Murray. *Der Fall Bettauer*. Vienna: Löcker, 1978.
Hammel, Andrea. *Everyday Life as Alternative Space in Exile Writing: The Novels of Anna Gmeyner, Selma Kahn, Hilde Spiel, Martina Wied und Hermynia Zur Mühlen*. New York: Peter Lang, 2008.
———. "Hilde Spiel and the Possibility of a Multicultural Society: *Die Früchte des Wohlstands* and *Mirko und Franca*." In *'Other' Austrians: Post-1945 Austrian Women's Writing*, ed. Allyson Fiddler, 129–39. Bern: Peter Lang, 1998.
Hanuschek, Sven, ed. *Der Zukunftsfette. Neue Beiträge zum Werk Elias Canettis*. Dresden: Neisse Verlag, 2007.
Harrowitz, Nancy A., and Barbara Hyam, eds. *Jews and Gender: Responses to Otto Weininger*. Philadelphia: Temple University Press, 1995.
Hermann, Ingo, ed. *Hilde Spiel. Die Grande Dame, Gespräch mit Anne Linsel in der Reihe 'Zeugen des Jahrhunderts.'* Göttingen: Lamuv, 1992.
Herzl, Theodor. *Altneuland, Old-New Land*. Trans. Paula Arnold. Haifa: Haifa Publishing Company, 1961.
———. *Das neue Ghetto, Gesammelte Zionistische Werke*. V. Band. Berlin: Jüdischer Verlag, 1935. II:1, 46–47.
———. *Ein echter Wiener. Feuilletons, kommentiert von André Heller*. Vienna: Edition Wien, 1986.
———. *The Jews' State, Theodor Herzl: A Critical English Translation*. Translated by Henk Overberg. Northvale, NJ: Jason Aronson Inc., 1997.
———. *Zionistisches Tagebuch, 1895–1899, Briefe und Tagebücher*, vol. II. Eds. Johannes Wachen, et al. Berlin: Propyläen, 1983.

Herzog, Andreas. "Die Mischehe zur Lösung der Judenfrage: Adolf Dessauers Roman Großstadtjuden im soziokulturellen Kontext der Wiener Jahrhundertwende." http://www.kakanien.ac.at/beitr/fallstudie/AHerzog3.pdf.

Herzog, Hillary Hope, Todd Herzog, and Benjamin Lapp, eds. *Rebirth of a Culture: Jewish Identity and Jewish Writing in Germany and Austria Today*. New York: Berghahn Books, 2008.

Hetzer, Tanja. *Kinderblick auf die Shoah. Formen der Erinnerung bei Ilse Aichinger, Hubert Fichte und Danilo Kis*. Würzburg: Königshausen und Neumann, 1999.

Hödl, Klaus. *Wiener Juden—jüdische Wiener: Identität, Gedächtnis und Performanz im 19. Jahrhundert*. Vienna: Studienverlag, 2006.

Hofmannsthal, Hugo von. *Hugo von Hofmannsthal—Arthur Schnitzler, Briefwechsel*. Eds. Therese Nickl and Heinrich Schnitzler. Frankfurt: Fischer Taschenbuch, 1983.

Homemad(e). Dir. Ruth Beckermann. Ruth Beckermann-Filmproduktion, 2000.

Horrocks, David. "The Construction of Eastern Jewry in Joseph Roth's *Juden auf Wanderschaft*." In *Ghetto Writing: Traditional and Eastern Jewry in German-Jewish Literature from Heine to Hilsenrath*, eds. Anne Fuchs and Florian Krobb, 126–39. Columbia, SC: Camden House, 1999.

———. "The Representation of Jews and of Anti-Semitism in Joseph Roth's Early Journalism." *German Life and Letters* 58:2 (April 2005): 141–54.

Huml, Ariane, and Monika Fludernik, eds. *Fin de Siècle*. Trier: Wissenschaftlicher Verlag, 2002.

Iser, Wolfgang. "German Jewish Writers during the Decline of the Habsburg Monarchy: Assessing the Assessment of Gershon Shaked." In *Ideology and Jewish Identity in Israeli and American Literature*, ed. Emily Miller Budick. Albany: SUNY Press, 2001.

Janz, Rolf-Peter, and Klaus Laermann. *Zur Diagnose des Wiener Bürgertums im Fin de Siècle*. Stuttgart: Metzler, 1977.

Jelavich, Barbara. *Modern Austria: Empire and Republic, 1800–1986*. Cambridge: Cambridge University Press, 1987.

Jelinek, Elfriede. *Kinder der Toten*. Reinbek bei Hamburg: Rowohlt, 1995.

John, Michael. "We Do Not Even Possess Ourselves: On Identity and Ethnicity in Austria, 1880–1937." *Austrian History Yearbook*. 30 (1999): 17–64.

Kaplan, Marion A. *The Making of the Jewish Middle Class: Women, Family and Identity in Imperial Germany*. New York: Oxford University Press, 1991.

Kastberger, Klaus. "Survival: Child's Play. Ilse Aichinger's *Die Groessere Hoffnung*." *New German Critique* 93 (Autumn 2004): 72–77.

Kecht, Maria-Regina. "The Polyphony of Remembrance: Reading *Die Kinder der Toten*." In *Elfriede Jelinek: Writing Woman, Nation, and Identity. A Critical Anthology*, eds. Matthias Konzett and Margarete Lamb-Faffelberger, 189–217. Madison, NJ: Fairleigh Dickinson University Press, 2007.

Kessler, Michael, and Fritz Hackert, eds. *Joseph Roth: Interpretation—Kritik—Rezeption*. Tübingen: Stauffenburg Verlag, 1990.

Konzett, Matthias. "The Politics of Recognition in Contemporary Austrian Jewish Literature." In *Monatshefte* 90/1 (Spring 1998): 71–88.

Körte, Mona. "Die Toten am Tisch. 'Familienromane' nach dem Holocaust." In *Zeitschrift für deutsche Philologie*. 4 (2008): 573–94.

Krahberger, Franz. "Die umfassenden Tätigkeiten des Genossen Hans Weigel." In e-journal *Literatur primaer.* http://ejournal.thing.at/Essay/weigel.html.

Kraus, Karl. "Die demolirte Literatur." In *Fruhe Schriften I, 1892–96*. Munich: Kosel Verlag, 1979. 269–89.

———. *Die Fackel.* 23.1. 1899.

———. *Die Fackel.* 386.15. 1913.

———. "Eine Krone für Zion." In *Fruhe Schriften II, 1897–1900*. Munich: Kosel Verlag, 1979. 298–314.

Krobb, Florian. "Gefühlszionismus und Zionsgefühle: Zum Palästina-Diskurs bei Schnitzler, Herzl, Salten und Lasker-Schüler." In *Sentiment, Gefühle, Empfindungen. Zur Geschichte und Literatur des Affektiven von 1770 bis heute*. Ann Fuchs and Sabine Strümper-Krobb, eds, 149–164. Würzburg: Königshausen und Neumann, 2003

Kucher, Primus-Heinz. *Literatur und Kultur im Österreich der Zwanziger Jahre*. Bielefeld: Aisthesis Verlag, 2007.

Lamb-Faffelberger, Margarete. "Beyond 'The Sound of Music': The Quest for Cultural Identity in Modern Austria." *The German Quarterly* 76:3 (Summer 2003): 289–99.

Lawson, Richard H. *Understanding Elias Canetti*. Columbia: University of South Carolina Press, 1991.

Le Rider, Jacques. *Modernity and Crises of Identity. Culture and Society in Fin-de-Siècle Vienna*. Translated by Rosemary Morris. New York: Continuum, 1993.

Lichtblau, Albert, ed. *Als hätten wir dazugehört. Österreichisch-jüdische Lebensgeschichten aus der Habsburgermonarchie*. Vienna: Böhlau, 1999.

Liebrand, Claudia. "Traditionsbezuege: Canetti, Kafka und Elfriede Jelineks Roman *Die Klavierspielerin*." *Gegenwartsliteratur* 5 (2006): 25–47.

Lorenz, Dagmar C. G., ed. *A Companion to the Works of Arthur Schnitzler*. Rochester, NY: Camden House, 2003.

———, ed. *A Companion to the Works of Elias Canetti*. Rochester, NY: Camden House, 2004.

———, ed. *Contemporary Jewish Writing in Austria: An Anthology*. Lincoln: University of Nebraska Press, 1999.

———. "Hilde Spiel: *Lisas Zimmer*. Frau, Jüdin, Verfolgte." *Modern Austrian Literature* 25:2 (1992): 79–95.

———. *Ilse Aichinger*. Königstein/Ts.: Athenäum Verlag, 1981.

———. *Keepers of the Motherland: German Texts by Jewish Women Writers*. Lincoln: University of Nebraska Press, 1997.

———. "Mass Culture and the City in the Works of German-Jewish Novelists: Claire Goll, Veza Canetti, Else Lasker-Schüler, and Gertrud Kolmar." In *Gender and Judaism: The Transformation of Tradition*, ed. T. M. Rudavsky. New York: New York University Press, 1995.

Mattl, Siegfried, Klaus Müller-Richter, and Werner Michael Schwarz. *Felix Salten: Wurselprater. Ein Schlüsseltext zur Wiener Moderne*. Vienna: Promedia, 2004.

———. and Werner Michael Schwarz. *Felix Salten, Schriftsteller—Journalist—Exilant*. Vienna: Holzhausen, 2006.

Menasse, Eva. *Vienna*. Cologne: Kiepenheuer & Witsch, 2005.

Menasse, Robert. *Das Land ohne Eigenschaften*. 3rd ed. Vienna: Sonderzahl, 1993.

———. *Die Vertreibung aus der Hölle.* Frankfurt: Suhrkamp Taschenbuch Verlag, 2003.
———. *Dummheit ist machbar.* Vienna: Sonderzahl, 1999.
———. *Selige Zeiten, brüchige Welt.* Salzburg: Residenz, 1991.
Mitten, Richard. *The Politics of Antisemitic Prejudice: The Waldheim Phenomenon in Austria.* Boulder, CO: Westview Press, 1992.
Moore, Erna. "Friedrich Torberg's *Mein ist die Rache* as a Literary Work of Art," in *Protest —Form—Tradition: Essays on German Exile Literature.* Joseph P. Strelka, Robert F. Bell, and Eugene Dobson, eds, 111–21. Tuscaloosa, AL: University of Alabama Press, 1979
Nach Jerusalem. Dir. Ruth Beckermann. Ruth Beckermann-Filmproduktion, 1990.
Naqvi, Fatima. "Elfriede Jelinek's Post-Dramatic Stress Disorder: Analysis of a Programmatic Aggression." *Gegenwartsliteratur* 5 (2006): 88–92.
Oxaal, Ivaar, Michael Pollak, and Gerhard Botz, eds. *Jews, Antisemitism and Culture in Vienna.* New York: Routledge, 1987.
Pabisch, Peter. "Hilde Spiels *Rückkehr nach Wien*—eine besondere Thematik der Exilliteratur." In *Exil: Wirkung und Wertung,* eds. Donald G. Daviau and Ludwig M. Fischer. Columbia, SC: Camden House, 1985.
Pazi, Margarita. "Stefan Zweig, Europäer und Jude." *Modern Austrian Literature* 14: 3/4 (1981): 291–311.
Pfeiffer, Peter C. "1893, Hugo von Hofmannsthal worries about his Jewish mixed ancestry." In *Yale Companion to Jewish Writing and Thought in German Culture, 1096–1996,* eds. Sander L. Gilman and Jack Zipes, 212–18. New Haven: Yale University Press, 1997.
Pick, Hella. *Guilty Victim: Austria from the Holocaust to Haider.* London: I.B. Tauris Publishers, 2000.
Pizer, John. "'Last Austrians' in 'Turn of the Century' Works by Franz Grillparzer, Joseph Roth, and Alfred Kolleritsch." *The German Quarterly* 74:1 (Winter 2001): 8–21.
———. "Modern vs. Postmodern Satire: Karl Kraus and Elfriede Jelinek." *Monatshefte* 86:4 (1994): 500–13.
Preece, Julian. *The Rediscovered Writings of Veza Canetti: Out of the Shadows of a Husband.* Rochester, NY: Camden House, 207.
Pulzer, Peter. *The Rise of Political Anti-Semitism in Germany and Austria.* Cambridge: Harvard University Press, 1988.
Rabinovici, Doron. "Der nationale Doppler." In *Der Standard.* 18 October 1999.
———. *Instanzen der Ohnmacht. Wien 1938–1945. Der Weg zum Judenrat.* Frankfurt: Jüdischer Verlag, 2000.
———. "Literatur und Republik oder Ganz Baden liest die Krone." In *"Was wird das Ausland dazu sagen": Literatur und Republik in Österreich nach 1945.* Gerald Leitner, ed. Vienna: Picus Verlag, 1995.
———. *Ohnehin.* Frankfurt: Suhrkamp Taschenbuchverlag, 2005.
———. *Suche nach M.* Frankfurt: Suhrkamp, 1997.
Ratych, Joanna M. "Ilse Aichinger." In *Major Figures of Contemporary Austrian Literature,* ed. Donald G. Daviau. New York: Peter Lang, 1987.
Reinharz, Jehuda, and Walter Schatzberg, eds. *The Jewish Response to German Culture: From the Enlightenment to the Second World War.* Hanover, NH: University Press of New England for Clark University, 1985.

Reinprecht, Christoph. *Zurückgekehrt. Identität und Bruch in der Biographie österreichischer Juden.* Vienna: Braumüller, 1992.
Reiter, Andrea. "Ruth Beckermann und die jüdische Nachkriegsgeneration in Österreich." In *'Other' Austrians: Post-1945 Austrian Women's Writing,* ed. Allyson Fiddler. Bern: Peter Lang, 1998.
Reitter, Paul. "Karl Kraus and the Jewish Self-Hatred Question." *Jewish Social Studies* 10.1. (2003): 78–116.
Remmler, Karen. "Sheltering Battered Bodies in Language: Imprisonment Once More?" In *Displacements: Cultural Identities in Question,* ed. Angelika Bammer, 216–32. Bloomington: Indiana University Press, 1994.
Rieckmann, Jens. "Zwischen Bewusstsein und Verdrängung: Hofmannsthals jüdisches Erbe." In *Deutsche Vierteljahrsschrift für Literaturwissenschaft und Geistesgeschichte* 67:3 (September 1993): 466–83.
Robertson, Ritchie. *The Jewish Question in German Literature, 1749–1939: Emancipation and Its Discontents.* Oxford: Oxford University Press, 1999.
———. "The Problem of 'Jewish Self-Hatred' in Herzl, Kraus and Kafka." In *Oxford German Studies* 16 (1985): 81–108.
Roth, Joseph. *Juden auf Wanderschaft.* Munich: dtv, 2006.
Rozenblit, Marsha. *The Jews of Vienna, 1867–1914: Assimilation and Identity.* Albany: SUNY Press, 1983.
———. *Reconstructing a National Identity: The Jews of Habsburg Austria During World War I.* Oxford: Oxford University Press, 2001.
Sabler, Wolfgang. "Theodor Herzl, *Das neue Ghetto.* Antisemitismus und Dramaturgie." In *Aspekte des politischen Theaters und Dramas von Calderón bis Georg Seidel; deutschfranzösische Perspektiven,* Horst Turk and Jean-Marie Valentin, eds., 229–54. New York: Peter Lang, 1996.
Salten, Felix. *Bambi. Eine Lebensgeschichte aus dem Wald.* Vienna: Zsolnay Verlag, 1923.
———. *Das österreichische Antlitz.* Berlin: Fischer, nd.
———. *Neue Menschen auf alter Erde. Eine Palästinafahrt.* Königstein/Ts.: Athenäum, 1986.
Schafroth, Heinz F. "Ilse Aichinger." In *Metzler Autoren Lexikon.* Bernd Lutz and Benedikt Jeßing, eds, 6. Stuttgart: Verlag J. B. Metzler, 1994.
Scheichl, Sigurd Paul. "Why and How Friedrich Torberg's Forum Did Not Confront the Past." *New German Critique* 93 (Fall 2004): 87–102.
Scherer, Stefan. *Richard Beer-Hofmann und die Wiener Moderne.* Conditio judaica 6. Tübingen: Max Niemeyer Verlag, 1993.
Schindel, Robert. *Fremd bei mir selbst.* Frankfurt: Suhrkamp, 2004.
———. *Gebürtig.* Frankfurt: Suhrkamp, 1994.
———. *Mein liebster Feind: Essays, Reden, Miniaturen.* Frankfurt: Suhrkamp, 2004.
Schmid-Bortenschlager, Sigrid. "Der Ort der Sprache. Zu Ilse Aichinger." In *Das Schreiben der Frauen in Oesterreich seit 1950.* Walter Buchebner Gesellschaft, ed, 86–94. Vienna: Böhlau, 1991.
Schnauber, Cornelius. "Werk und Leben Friedrich Torbergs im amerikanischen Exil." In *Literatur und Kritik* 181/182 (Feb.– March 1984): 60–67.
Schnitzler, Arthur. *Der Weg ins Freie.* Berlin: S. Fischer Verlag, 1922.

———. *Jugend in Wien.* Frankfurt: Fischer Taschenbuchverlag, 1981.
———. *Professor Bernhardi, Das Weite Land: Dramen, 1909–1912.* Frankfurt: Fischer, 1993.
Schorske, Carl. *Fin de Siècle Vienna: Politics and Culture.* New York: Vintage Books, 1980.
Schwarz, Egon. "Mass Emigration and Intellectual Exile from National Socialism: The Austrian Case." In *From World War to Waldheim: Culture and Politics in Austria and the United States,* eds. David F. Good and Ruth Wodak, 87–108. New York: Berghahn Books, 1999.
———. "1921: The staging of Arthur Schnitzler's play *Reigen* in Vienna creates a public uproar that draws involvement by the press, the police, the Viennese city administration, and Austrian parliament." In *Yale Companion to Jewish Writing and Thought in German Culture, 1096–1996,* eds. Sander L. Gilman and Jack Zipes, 412–19. New Haven: Yale University Press, 1997.
Segar, Kenneth, and John Warren, eds. *Austria in the Thirties: Culture and Politics.* Riverside, CA: Ariadne Press, 1991.
Seibert, Ernst, and Susanne Blumesberger, eds. *Felix Salten—der unbekannte Bekannte.* Vienna: Praesens, 2006.
Shaked, Gershon. "Wie jüdisch ist ein deutsch-jüdischer Roman? Über Joseph Roths *Hiob, Roman eines einfachen Mannes.*" In *Juden in der deutschen Literatur. Ein deutsch-israelisches Symposion,* eds. Stéphane Moses and Albrecht Schöne. Frankfurt: Suhrkamp, 1986.
Silverman, Lisa. "Jewish Intellectual Women and the Public Sphere in Inter-War Vienna." In *Women in Europe Between the Wars: Politics, Culture and Society,* eds. Angela Kershaw and Angela Kimyongür, 155–70. Hampshire, England: Ashgate Publishing Ltd, 2007.
———. "Zwischenzeit und Zwischenort: Veza Canetti, Else Feldmann, and Jewish Writing in Interwar Vienna." *Prooftexts* 26 (2006): 40.
Sokel, Walter H. "Narzissmus und Judentum. Zu Richard Beer-Hofmanns 'Der Tod Georgs.'" In *Literatur und Kritik.* (Feb., March 1988): 221–222.
Sonnenfeld, Marion. *Stefan Zweig: The World of Yesterday's Humanist Today, Proceedings of the Stefan Zweig Symposium.* Albany: SUNY Press, 1983.
Spiel, Hilde. *Anna & Anna.* Vienna: Kremayr & Scheriau, 1989.
———. *Kleine Schritte. Berichte und Geschichten.* Munich: Edition Spangenberg, 1976.
———. *Rückkehr nach Wien.* Munich: Nymphenburger, 1991.
Spörk, Ingrid, and Alexandra Strohmaier. *Veza Canetti.* Graz: Literatur Verlag Droschl, 2005.
Strelka, Joseph P. "Friedrich Torberg." In *Deutsche Exilliteratur seit 1933: Band I, Kalifornien,* eds. Joseph P. Strelka, John M. Spalek, and Sandra H. Hawrylchak, 616–32. Bern: Francke, 1976.
———. *Stefan Zweig: Freier Geist der Menschlichkeit.* Vienna: Österreichischer Bundesverlag, 1981.
Thompson, Bruce. *Schnitzler's Vienna: Image of a Society.* New York: Routledge, 1990.
Thunecke, Jörg. "'Dynamite' or 'Affront'? The Jewish Question in Herzl's Play *Das neue Ghetto.*" In *Theodor Herzl and the Origins of Zionism,* eds. Ritchie Robertson and Edward Timms, 62–73. Austrian Studies VIII. Edinburgh: Edinburgh University Press, 1997.

———. "Man *wird* nicht Jude, man *ist* es: Zur Funktion der jüdischen Moral in Friedrich Torbergs Novelle *Mein ist die Rache.*" *Modern Austrian Literature* 27:3/4 (1994): 19–36.
Timms, Edward. *Karl Kraus, Apocalyptic Satirist: Culture and Catastrophe in Habsburg Vienna.* New Haven: Yale University Press, 1986.
———. *Karl Kraus, Apocalyptic Satirist: The Post-War Crisis and the Rise of the Swastika.* New Haven: Yale University Press, 2005.
Torberg, Friedrich. *In diesem Sinne…Briefe an Freunde und Zeitgenossen.* Frankfurt: Ullstein, 1988.
———. *Die Tante Jolesch oder Der Untergang des Abendlandes in Anekdoten.* Munich: dtv, 2002.
Turner, David. *Moral Values and the Human Zoo: The Novellen of Stefan Zweig.* Hull, England: Hull University Press, 1988.
Tweraser, Felix. "Heimweh as Creative Impetus: Friedrich Torberg's Literary Work in American Exile." *Trans: Internet-Zeitschrift für Kulturwissenschaften* 15 (2003). Electronic publication.
Uhl, Heidemarie. "The Politics of Memory: Austria's Perception of the Second World War and the National Socialist Period." In *Austrian Historical Memory and National Identity,* eds. Günter Bischof and Anton Pelinka, 64–94. Contemporary Austrian Studies 5. New Brunswick, NJ: Transaction Publishers, 1997.
Vansant, Jacqueline. *Reclaiming Heimat: Trauma and Mourning in Memoirs by Jewish Austrian Réemigrées.* Detroit: Wayne State University Press, 2001.
Vassiliev, Guennadi. "Richard Beer-Hofmanns 'Der Tod Georgs'. Zum Problem Ästhetizismus und Judentum." *Österreich in Geschichte und Literatur* 46:2 (2002): 120–33.
Vital, David. *The Origins of Zionism.* Oxford: Oxford University Press, 1975.
Völpel, Annegret. "1928, The first issue of the Jewish Children's Calendar, edited by Emil Bernhard Cohn, is published in cooperation with the Commission on Literary Works for Youth of the Grand Lodge for Germany of the Independent Order of B'Nai B'rith." In *Yale Companion to Jewish Writing and Thought in German Culture, 1096–1996,* eds. Sander L. Gilman and Jack Zipes, 485–91. New Haven: Yale University Press, 1997.
Von der Lühe, Irmela. "Geschichte als Lehrmeisterin? Robert Menasses Roman *Die Vertreibung aus der Hölle.*" In *Akten des XI. Internationalen Germanistenkongresses Paris 2005, Bd. 12: Europadiskurse in der deutschen Literatur und Literaturwissenschaft—Deutsch-jüdische Kulturdialoge/-konflikte.* Jean-Marie Valentin, ed. Bern: Peter Lang, 2007. 251–56.
Wien Retour. Dir. Ruth Beckermann. Ruth Beckermann-Filmproduktion, 1983.
Wiesinger-Stock, Sandra. *Hilde Spiel. Ein Leben ohne Heimat?* Vienna: Verlag für Gesellschaftskritik, 1996.
Wistrich, Robert S., ed. *Austrians and Jews in the Twentieth Century: From Franz Joseph to Waldheim.* New York: St. Martin's Press, 1992.
———. *The Jews of Vienna in the Age of Franz Joseph.* Oxford: Oxford University Press, 1989.
———. *Laboratory for World Destruction: German and Jews in Central Europe.* Lincoln: University of Nebraska Press for the Vidal Sassoon International Center for the Study of Antisemitism, The Hebrew University of Jerusalem, 2007.

Worbs, Michael. *Nervenkunst: Literatur und Psychoanalyse im Wien der Jahrhunderwende.* Frankfurt: Europäische Verlagsanstalt, 1983.
Wyman, David S., ed. *The World Reacts to the Holocaust.* Baltimore: Johns Hopkins University Press, 1996.
Yerushalmi, Yosef Hayim. *Freud's Moses: Judaism Terminable and Interminable.* New Haven: Yale University Press, 1991.
Zohn, Harry. "1897. Herzl draws international attention to Zionism, and the Young Vienna circle flourishes." In *Yale Companion to Jewish Writing and Thought in German Culture, 1096–1996,* eds. Sander L. Gilman and Jack Zipes. New Haven: Yale University Press, 1997. 232–39.
Zorro's Bar Mitzvah. Dir. Ruth Beckermann. Ruth Beckermann-Filmproduktion, 2006.
Zweig, Stefan. *Die Welt von Gestern.* Frankfurt: Fischer, 1970.
———. *Jeremias.* Leipzig: Insel Verlag, 1920.
———. *Phantastische Nacht: Erzählungen.* Frankfurt: Fischer, 1982.

INDEX

A
Abeles, Otto, 117
Adler, Viktor, 22, 100–101
aestheticism, 78–80
Aichinger, Ilse, 6, 185–95, 214
  "Aufruf zum Misstrauen," 191
  Das vierte Tor, 186
  "Der Gefesselte," 187, 193
  Die größere Hoffnung, 186–92
  Film und Verhängnis, 187
  Kleist, Moos, Fasane, 193–94
  Kurzschlüsse, 191
  "Meine Sprache und Ich," 191–92
  Spiegelgeschichte, 187
Altenberg, Peter, 45, 48, 58
Améry, Jean, 183, 217
Anschluss, 6, 44, 93, 99, 103, 105–6, 109, 157, 165–67, 171, 174–75, 178, 181, 186, 189, 195–96, 198, 201–202, 210, 212, 217, 231
Anti-Semitism, 5–6, 11, 16–22, 25–32, 24–35, 38–39, 42, 48, 55, 58–63, 65, 67–68, 70–73, 84, 86, 89, 98, 101–108, 110–117, 120–21, 127–29, 134–36, 143–47, 151, 154–55, 158, 160, 163, 165–66, 169, 180, 184, 188, 195, 198–99, 213, 223–26, 230, 234, 240, 245, 256
  and nationalism, 16
  Jewish responses to, 19–20, 22–25
  in politics, 17–18
Austrian Freedom Party (FPÖ), 220, 224–26, 236, 243–46, 265
Austro-fascism, 93, 109, 121, 141

Austro-Hungarian Empire, 5, 10–13, 20–24 58, 93–99, 106–108, 127–32, 174

B
Bahr, Hermann, 17, 24, 65
Bauer, Otto, 101
Beckermann, Ruth, 2, 5, 179–80, 195–98, 214, 221, 224–25, 227–28, 229–37, 238, 241, 245, 248, 250, 258, 261, 262, 264, 266
  Die Mazzesinsel, 230
  Die papierene Brücke, 229–30, 232
  homemad(e), 230, 236, 241
  Jenseits des Krieges, 225
  Nach Jerusalem, 230
  Unzugehörig, 227, 231, 238
  Wien Retour, 230
  Zorros Bar Mitzwa, 230, 236
Beer-Hofmann, Richard, 24, 25, 56, 77–82, 108, 114–16, 122, 165
  Der Tod Georgs, 79–82
  "Schlaflied für Mirjam," 79
Berlin, 50, 110, 129, 135–36, 139, 142, 148, 151, 207, 209, 211, 213, 228, 251, 255–56
Bettauer, Hugo, 6, 8–9, 108, 111, 142–47, 198, 208
  Er und Sie, 143
  Die Stadt ohne Juden, 142–46
Billroth, Theodor, 17
Bloch, Joseph, 21–22
Böhm, Karl, 178
Brazil, 50, 228, 250, 252
Brigittenau, 129, 161

Bulgaria, 147–50, 171n175
Burgtheater, 44, 46, 115, 151, 200, 210

C

Café Griensteidl, 24, 43
Café Herrenhof, 196, 205
Café Prückl, 229, 248
Café Salzgries, 236–37
Canetti, Elias, 6, 78, 104, 109, 140, 147–155, 156, 157, 159, 160, 172n200, 205, 208, 227, 261, 262
    Das Augenspiel, 149
    Die Blendung, 148–49, 152–55, 160
    Die Fackel im Ohr, 149
    Die gerettete Zunge, 149
    Die Komödie der Eitelkeit, 149
    Hochzeit, 149
    Masse und Macht, 149, 152, 155, 160
    Party im Blitz, 149
Canetti, Veza, 6, 109, 149, 156–64, 205
    "Der Sieger," 162
    "Der Verbrecher," 162
    Die Gelbe Strasse, 158, 160–61
    Die Schildkröten, 159, 163–64
    "Drei Helden und eine Frau," 162
    Geduld bringt Rosen, 158, 162
Catholicism, 13, 16–18, 22–23, 107, 143, 186, 188, 258
conversion of Jews to, 54, 59, 139, 204
children's literature, 116, 243

D

de-Nazification, 176–77
Der Standard, 243
Dessauer, Adlof, 38–43
    Großstadtujden, 38–42
Dollfuss, Engelbert, 104, 141, 158

E

education, 3–4, 13–17, 21–22, 25, 84n17, 84n19, 101, 128, 148, 157, 205, 211, 259
    and anti-Semitism, 16–17, 102
    Jewish involvement in, 4, 13–14, 43–44
emancipation of Jews, 11–16, 69–72, 231
exile, 6–7, 174, 177, 181–85, 214, 246, 252, 254
    and Elias and Veza Canetti, 147–151, 159, 163
    and Felix Salten, 44
    and Friedrich Torberg, 195–98, 200–201
    and Hilde Spiel, 205–13
    and Ilse Aichinger, 186–87
    and Joseph Roth, 128–131
    and Stefan Zweig, 50–51, 113, 127–28

F

First Republic, 103–106, 175, 201, 231
Forum, 196–97, 200
Franz Joseph, 1, 16, 59, 96, 98, 129, 142, 234
Freud, Sigmund, 1, 17, 22–25, 32–34, 50, 115, 157, 232, 252

G

Galicia, 11, 51, 76, 94, 97–98, 100, 108, 122, 128–29, 132, 150
generational relations, 32–33, 43, 126
geography and identity, 38
Grinzing, 149, 157, 163
Grüner Veltliner, 222
Gruppe 47, 187

H

Haider, Jörg, 220–21, 224–26, 237, 244–46, 249, 256
Heiligenstadt, 204, 208
Heimat, 147, 150–51, 164, 183–84, 208, 214, 265
Herzl, Theodor, 17, 20, 24–25, 33–34, 42, 44, 50, 51, 58, 63–77, 81, 82
    Altneuland, 74–77, 118
    Das neue Ghetto, 68–71, 126, 146
    "Frühling im Elend," 66
    on Vienna, 66–68
Heuriger, 45, 47
historical novel, 252–53
Hofmannsthal, Hugo von, 24, 45, 54–57, 78, 80, 107, 115, 192
    Chandos-Brief, 24, 80
    Das Salzburger grosse Welttheater, 139
    on Beer-Hofmann, 56
    Jewish ancestry of, 54–57
    on Schnitzler, 56
Hungary, 11, 95, 99, 102, 104, 111, 131

I

Immigration
    and anti-Semitism, 102
    of Jews to Vienna 5, 10–15
Israelitische Kultusgemeinde, 94, 101, 104, 106, 167n48, 198, 215n7

J

Jelinek, Elfriede, 6, 9, 192–93, 221, 227–28, 261–65, 271
Die Kinder der Toten, 264–65
Judenrat, 243
Jungjüdische Bewegung, 81
Jung Wien, 24, 32, 43–44, 51, 55–58, 60–61, 67, 78, 81

K

Karl Lueger Platz, 229, 248
Keun, Irmgard, 130
Kisch, Egon Erwin, 129, 196, 203
Kraus, Karl, 9, 22, 44–45, 57–63, 78, 82, 107–108, 117, 120, 139–42, 148, 151, 157, 193, 199, 227, 250, 261–63
    and anti-Semitism 61–62
    "Der Hort der Republik," 140
    "Die demolirte Literatur" 44, 48, 60, 78
    Die Fackel, 45, 57–63, 140–42, 149, 263
    Die letzen Tage der Menschheit, 140
    Dritte Walpurgisnacht, 141
    Eine Krone für Zion, 58–59, 140
    "Er ist doch ä Jud," 61
    "Man frage nicht," 141
    on Zionism, 59–60
Kreisky, Bruno, 180–81, 221

L

Leopoldstadt, 11, 14–15, 39, 41, 105, 128, 135–36, 148, 156–61, 230–32, 258–59, 272
Lessing, G.E., 16
Lessing, Theodor, 62, 107, 155
    Der jüdische Selbsthaß, 62, 107, 155
Liberal Party
    Jewish ties to, 15–16, 18
Linz Program, 18
London, 117, 150, 159, 206–207
Lueger, Karl, 18–19, 45, 47, 68, 70, 120, 229, 248

M

Mazzesinsel. See Leopoldstadt
Menasse, Eva, 6, 214, 228, 243, 255–60, 265
    Der Holocaust vor Gericht, 255
    Lässliche Todsünden, 256
    Vienna, 255, 256–60
Menasse, Robert, 2, 6, 177, 214, 221, 228, 250–55, 261
    Das Land ohne Eigenschaften, 250–51
    Das sozialpartnerschaftliche Ästhetik, 250
    Die Vertreibung aus der Hölle, 250, 252–53
    Das war Österreich, 251
    Don Juan de la Mancha, 250
    Dummheit ist machbar, 251
    Erklär mir Österreich, 251
    Selige Zeiten, bruchige Welt, 2, 250, 252
    Sinnliche Gewissheit, 250
    Schubumkehr, 250
Mendelssohn, Moses, 16
Mendelssohn, Peter de, 205–207, 209
modernism, 2, 5, 24–25, 88n142, 262–63, 273
Moscow Declaration, 175–77, 210, 223
Mozartkugel 221

N

Naschmarkt, 248–250, 272
Nationalism, 16–18, 48, 65, 108, 118, 125–27, 131
    and anti-Semitism, 16, 134
    and Diaspora, 106–107
    Jewish, 16, 21, 94, 101, 165
    and Zionism, 119
National Socialism, 141, 165, 177, 179, 189, 197, 199, 206, 211, 253
Neue Freie Presse, 21, 44–45, 50, 58, 65, 115–16, 120, 143
Nordau, Max, 33–34
Nuremberg Laws, 105, 197, 204

O

Österreichisch-israelitische Union (Austrian Israelite Union), 94

P

Palace of Justice
    Fire, 103–104, 120, 140–41, 152, 167n41

Pabst, G.W., 143
  Die freudlose Gasse, 143
Paris, 68, 70, 90n184, 130, 136, 138, 145–46, 148–49, 159, 228
Prater, 48–49, 52–53, 65–67, 87n115, 113, 135–36, 161–62, 232, 249–50, 272

R

Rabinovici, Doron, 2, 5, 6, 214, 221, 224, 228, 243–250, 252, 261, 264, 272
  Credo und Credit, 243
  Das Jooloomooloo, 243
  Der ewige Widerstand 243
  "Der nationale Doppler," 243–44
  Instanzen der Ohnmacht, 243
  Ohnehin, 243, 246–50
  Papirnik, 243
  Republik der Courage, 245
  Suche nach M., 243, 245
Red Vienna 101, 158
Reigen-Affair 110–11, 143, 167n57
Renner, Karl, 175–76
Ringstrasse, 230, 233, 260, 272
Rot-Weiss-Rot Buch, 175–76, 179
Roth, Joseph, 6, 108–109, 128–39, 150, 158, 165, 196, 250, 262
  Das falsche Gewicht, 132
  Der Leviathan, 132
  Die Büste des Kaisers, 131, 132
  Die Kapuzinergruft, 132
  Hiob, 108, 132, 137, 138
  Juden auf Wanderschaft, 108, 131, 132–38
  Radetzkymarsch, 132
  Tarabas, 132

S

Salten, Felix 24, 31, 32, 40, 42–49, 50, 42, 53, 54, 55, 64, 65, 70, 107, 114–21, 128, 135, 165, 249, 250
  Bambi, 45, 115–21
  Bambis Kinder, 120
  "Beim Brady," 47
  Das österreichische Antlitz, 45
  Der Hund von Florenz, 115
  "Die Wiener Straße," 46
  "Frühjahrsparade," 46
  Fünfzehn Hasen, 120
  Heimfahrt, 45
  Josefine Mutzenbacher, 44
  Neue Menschen auf alter Erde, 116–17
  relationship to language, 45
  "Spaziergang in der Vorstadt," 47
  "Wurstelprater," 48–49, 53
Salzburg, 107, 113, 128, 139, 183, 250
Salzburg Festival, 113, 213, 223
Schindel, Robert, 6, 221, 227, 228, 237–43, 245, 252, 261, 264
  Fremd bei mir selbst, 239
  Gebürtig, 239, 241–42, 245
  Mein liebster Feind, 239
Schnitzler, Arthur, 1, 2, 3, 5, 8, 13, 17, 19, 23, 24, 25–38, 39, 41, 43, 44, 45, 50, 52, 54, 56, 61, 70, 78, 82, 96, 108, 109–114, 115, 116, 117, 119, 126, 143, 227–28, 241, 243, 256, 271
  as chronicler of bourgeois society, 26
  Der Weg ins Freie, 26–31, 36, 38, 56, 111, 117, 126, 227, 256
  on Felix Salten, 45
  Fräulein Else, 109, 110
  on Jewish masculinity, 31–32, 37–38
  Jugend in Wien, 8, 17, 19, 32, 110, 111–12, 227
  Professor Bernhardi, 31–38, 56, 70, 111, 113
  Reigen, 110, 143, 167n57
  on the relationship between geography and identity, 38
  relationship with his father, 32–33
  Traumnovelle, 109, 110
  Therese, 109, 110
Schnitzler, Johann, 13, 23, 32–37
Schoenberg, Arnold, 22, 58, 232
Schönbrunn, 80
Schönerer, Georg Ritter von, 17–18, 65, 68
Schuschnigg, Kurt von, 104, 205
Second Republic, 174–84, 197, 200, 203, 225, 230–31, 243, 250, 254, 264
Social Democratic Party, 100, 104, 158, 175, 205
  Jewish involvement with, 20
Socialism, 20, 100, 165, 256
  Jewish involvement with, 22–23, 106, 158
Spiel, Hilde, 9, 158, 184, 203–14, 242
  Anna & Anna, 210–12
  "Die Wiederkehr," 207
  Kati auf der Brücke, 205
  Kleine Schritte, 209, 212

Rückkehr nach Wien, 207, 208
Welche Welt ist meine Welt?, 204, 212
Strauss, Johann, 1

T
Tel Aviv, 229, 243–44, 247
The Sound of Music, 221
Torberg, Friedrich, 6, 8, 186, 187, 212, 214, 195–203, 257
    Auch das war Wien, 196
    Der Schüler Gerber hat absolviert, 196
    Die Tante Jolesch, 195, 200–203, 257
    Hier bin ich, mein Vater, 187, 196
    Mein ist die Rache, 196
    Süßkind von Trimberg, 200

U
Uganda Crisis, 77
University of Vienna, 13, 17, 50, 58, 64–65, 78, 148, 205, 229, 243

V
Vienna
    fin de siècle 2–3, 6–7, 10–25, 31, 37, 50, 77, 201, 222, 227, 231, 241, 243
    first district of, 14, 27, 30, 46, 175, 229, 232, 272
    public spaces of 52, 152, 161, 194
    Theodor Herzl's views on, 66–68
    tourism in, 1
Volkspartei (ÖVP), 18, 225
Vranitzky, Franz, 224

Währing, 43, 47, 66

Waldheim, Kurt, 6, 181, 213 220–25, 232, 234–35, 243, 245, 247, 252, 259, 261, 262, 265
Walt Disney, 45, 116
Weininger, Otto, 22, 54, 62, 63, 154
    Geschlecht und Charakter, 54, 154
Wilde, Oscar, 58
World Jewish Congress, 220–23
World War I, 6, 20, 44, 50–51, 59, 78, 83n9, 93–96, 100–103, 106, 108–9, 114–15, 121–22, 125–26, 128–29, 131, 137, 139–40, 143, 147, 148, 157, 164–65, 204
World War II, 174–76, 178, 231, 254

Y
Yiddish, 39, 120, 133, 136–37

Z
Zionism, 20–21, 23, 27–28, 33, 39, 45, 51, 58–64, 68–77, 81–82, 90n184, 94, 101, 107, 112, 116–21, 126, 165, 230, 256
Zweig, Stefan, 3, 7, 23, 40, 42, 45, 50–54, 67, 96, 108, 109, 113, 121–28, 130–31, 165
    Brennendes Geheimnis, 50
    Buchmendel, 125–26
    Die Liebe der Erika Ewald, 50
    Die Welt von Gestern, 7, 40, 50–54, 67, 121, 127, 128
    Jeremias, 122–125, 127
    Phantastische Nacht, 52–53
    Silberne Saiten, 50
    Untergang eines Herzens, 126
Zsolnay Publishing House, 115, 117, 205
Zurich, 149, 150, 196, 202

www.ingramcontent.com/pod-product-compliance
Lightning Source LLC
Chambersburg PA
CBHW072146100526
44589CB00015B/2117